THE ORAL HISTORY OF
Captain Ernest L. Schwab
U.S. Navy (Retired)

INTERVIEWED BY
Paul Stillwell

U.S. Naval Institute • Annapolis, Maryland

Copyright © 2015

Preface

This oral memoir resulted from a suggestion by Captain Ernest Schwab's son Donald, with whom I served in the Naval Reserve in the mid-1980s. He said that his father had a career worthy of recording for the benefit of history. His dad went from the Naval Academy in 1939 to the U.S. Fleet flagship, the battleship *Pennsylvania*, and from there to Submarine School. The senior Schwab then made a number of successful war patrols in the *Guardfish* and *Darter*. The last patrol of the *Darter* was spectacular in that she played an important role in the 1944 Battle of Leyte Gulf before running hard aground. Schwab was the exec and navigator and explains in this memoir the dramatic circumstances through which the submarine was lost.

After leaving the *Darter*, he was executive officer of the *Capitaine* for a while and was on the verge of getting his own submarine command when World War II came to an end in the summer of 1945. Command of his own boat came later in the *Toro*, part of Submarine Development Group Two. In that billet and a later one in the Bureau of Ships, Schwab was involved in early research and development work on SOSUS, the underwater sound system that remains a key to submarine detection to this day.

As a more senior officer, Schwab commanded the destroyer *Wedderburn* in the Pacific and then was tapped to do postgraduate work at the Fletcher School of Law and Diplomacy, part of Tufts University. It was an interesting change of direction for an officer who had up to then been in war-fighting and technical development. Now he became a politico-military specialist as well—a vivid demonstration of the versatility expected of naval officers. He served in the appropriate OpNav branch for his specialty and later returned to sea as chief of staff to Commander Carrier Division 20 and as commanding officer of a deep-draft ship, the *Mount McKinley*, an amphibious group commander's flagship. Later he was involved in more politico-military work, first in the Office of the Secretary of Defense and later at the headquarters of the North Atlantic Treaty Organization in Europe.

After the interviews were transcribed, Captain Schwab edited the text of the first interview and part of the second. Then the project went into an unfortunate limbo for an extended period. Earlier this year the captain's son Don came to the rescue and offered to edit the remainder of the transcript on behalf of his dad. The editorial contributions from both of them have been incorporated in the version that follows. I have done some additional editing and inserted footnotes to provide background information. In a few cases I have rearranged the sequence of the transcript to enhance the chronological flow for the benefit of the readers. Don Schwab also tracked down useful biographical information that appears at the beginning of the volume, and in several cases he was able to fill in names in the text. Don's help has been invaluable in completing the oral history.

Thanks go to Ms. Janis Jorgensen of the Naval Institute staff, who urged the completion of this volume. In finishing this volume, the Naval Institute expresses its gratitude to the Tawani Foundation and the Pritzker Military Museum & Library of Chicago for their generous financial support of the oral history program that produced this memoir.

Paul Stillwell
June 2015

CAPTAIN ERNEST LOUIS SCHWAB JR.
UNITED STATES NAVY (RETIRED)

Ernest Louis Schwab Jr. was born in Brooklyn, New York, on 27 January 1917. He was the son of Ernest L. Schwab Sr. and Elizabeth Schaeffer Schwab. He attended Brooklyn Technical High School before entering the U.S. Naval Academy, Annapolis, Maryland, in 1935. He was graduated and was commissioned ensign on 1 June 1939 and subsequently advanced in rank to captain, to date from 1 January 1958.

After graduation from the Naval Academy, he reported on board the battleship *Pennsylvania* (BB-38) and served in that vessel until detached in 1941. He was then a student at Submarine School, New London, Connecticut, from July to September. During the period from 1941 to 1946 he served successively in four diesel submarines: *Marlin* (SS-205), 27 September 1941 to 27 April 1942; *Guardfish* (SS-217), 8 May 1942 to 2 April 1943; *Darter* (SS-227), 7 September 1943 to 23 October 1944; and *Capitaine* (SS-336), 19 January 1945 to 28 July 1945. He was executive officer of the latter two boats. From 1946 to 1948 he served ashore at the New London Submarine Base as communication officer, officer in charge of the radio station, and first lieutenant. In 1948-49 he spent a year of study in the senior logistics course at the Naval War College, Newport, Rhode Island. From June 1949 to July 1951 he commanded the diesel submarine *Toro* (SS-422) during the boat's service as part of Submarine Development Group Two.

Commander Schwab served ashore from 1951 to 1954 in the Bureau of Ships, Washington, D.C., as head of the Underwater Sound Branch and development plans staff. From August 1954 to August 1956 he commanded the destroyer *Wedderburn* (DD-684) in the Pacific Fleet. He did postgraduate work from 1956 to 1958 at the Fletcher School of Law and Diplomacy, Tufts University, Medford, Massachusetts, where he earned a master of arts in 1957 and a master of arts in law and diplomacy in 1958. That led to a tour from July 1958 to September 1960 in OP-611, on the OpNav staff in Washington. He was assistant branch head of the political-military policy division.

As a captain, Schwab returned to sea for a tour from September 1960 to December 1961 as chief of staff to Commander Carrier Division 20 and from January 1962 to March 1963 commanded the amphibious force flagship *Mount McKinley* (AGC-7). In 1963-64 Captain Schwab served in the Office of the Assistant Secretary of Defense (International Security Affairs) in Washington. In 1964-65, while still on active naval service, he was a member of the U.S. mission to the North Atlantic Treaty Organization (NATO). He retired from active duty on 1 August 1965. At that point he became a Foreign Service Reserve Officer and remained part of the mission to NATO as director of the defense planning division and later as special assistant to the ambassador. He stayed as part of the mission to NATO until August 1970, when he retired from government service. Subsequently he worked as a research analyst with the Research Analysis Corporation, the RAND Corporation, and the Institute for Defense Analyses.

On 22 April 1943 Schwab married Betty Ruth Sandgren. They had three children: Donald Ernest Schwab, born 1 March 1944; Holly Elizabeth Schwab, born 15 December 1946; and Trudi Sandgren Schwab, born 21 April 1948. Mrs. Schwab died 20 September 2002, and Captain Schwab died on 23 October 2007. Holly died 27 June 2014. Captain Schwab's awards included the Silver Star Medal, the Bronze Star Medal, the Presidential Unit Citation, the Navy Unit Commendation, and the Joint Service Commendation Medal.

In 1991 Crescent Books published Captain Schwab's *Undersea Warriors: Submarines of the World*, which reviewed the history of the development of submarines as naval vessels, covered the submarine fleets of all nations that employed them as of the time of publication, and discussed coming future developments in submarines.

Deed of Gift

The U.S. Naval Institute is hereby authorized to make available to individuals, libraries, and other repositories of its choosing the tapes and/or transcripts of a series of oral history interviews concerning the life and naval career of the undersigned. The Naval Institute may also, at its discretion, use the material in electronic/digital format, including posting on the Internet. The interviews were recorded in 1987 in collaboration with Paul Stillwell for the U.S. Naval Institute.

The undersigned does hereby release and assign to the U.S. Naval Institute the rights and title to these interviews, with the exception that the undersigned and his heirs have the right to use the material as they see fit. The copyright in both the oral and transcribed versions shall be the sole property of the U.S. Naval Institute. The tape recordings of the interviews are and will remain the property of the U.S. Naval Institute.

Signed and sealed this 20th day of December 2003.

Ernest L. Schwab
Captain, U.S. Navy (Retired)

Interview Number 1 with Captain Ernest L. Schwab, U.S. Navy (Retired)
Place: Captain Schwab's home in Potomac, Maryland
Date: Wednesday, 28 January 1987

Paul Stillwell: Captain Schwab, it's a pleasure to see you on this snowy morning. The appropriate place to begin a life story is at the beginning, so perhaps you could start by telling me something about your parents and your early childhood.

Captain Schwab: I was born in Brooklyn, New York, in January 27, 1917, so yesterday I was 70 years old. My father was a New York City fireman, and my mother was a registered nurse, but she was no longer active at nursing. When I was about seven years old, we moved out to Queens County on Long Island.

My father, as an officer in the fire department, had a good friend in the same company that he was in; his last name was Ryan. He had a son, Al Ryan, in the Naval Academy class of 1933.* My interest in the Naval Academy probably started at that time, about 1930. When I was in high school, Brooklyn Technical High School, my father and I drove down to Annapolis to talk to Al Ryan, to see whether or not the Naval Academy would be a good place for me to go. It looked great, because those were the Depression years.† My family wasn't suffering, however, since my father was a New York civil servant. But it was a nice way to get an education with minimum expense. That was in 1932 or '33 when we drove down, so I had some time to think about it and secure an appointment. I entered the Naval Academy in June 1935 and graduated in June 1939.

Paul Stillwell: Could you please cover your growing-up years before you get into that—your childhood, early educational experiences.

---

* Midshipman Albert F. Ryan Jr., USN.
† Following the crash of the New York Stock Exchange in late October 1929, the United States was plunged into the Great Depression, from which it did not recover until the nation geared up for World War II at the beginning of the 1940s. The Depression was marked by high unemployment and many business failures.

Captain Schwab: Well, all my schooling was at the New York City public schools, in Brooklyn and in Queens. It was just a normal childhood life. I had a sister who was born seven years after I was, so there were two children in the family.

Paul Stillwell: Did you have any extracurricular activities in school that you particularly took part in?

Captain Schwab: Oh, yes. Well, of course, in grammar school you don't do that much, but when I was in high school I became the editor of the school paper. I started writing the very first year in Brooklyn Technical High School. Brooklyn Tech, incidentally, was one of the few high schools in the city at that time which took students from the whole New York City area, and you had to take an entrance exam to get in there. In fact, that entrance exam was harder than the entrance exams I took to get in the Naval Academy. Let's see, I think they admitted around 1,000, and only 250 graduated. In my Naval Academy class 900 went in and 500 graduated, so the attrition was greater.[*]

Paul Stillwell: Was it a very competitive atmosphere in the school in New York?

Captain Schwab: Yes, very competitive, because it was not a manual training school or anything of that sort. Let's say 90% of the courses were college preparatory, with technical emphasis and also some manual shop work in metal working, wood working, and so on. For one of the years there, you went to school from 8:00 o'clock in the morning to almost 5:00 o'clock at night, because that was the one year of the four in which they added manual classes. You were taught how to run different kinds of shop equipment and everything connected with woodworking, metal work, and foundry work. It was all in the school. Henry Ford, I believe, had a lot to do with founding that school, and I think there was one in Chicago called Cass Technical Institute along the same line.[†]

---

[*] The Naval Academy class of 1939 comprised 581 graduates and 220 non-graduates.
[†] Before and during World War II, automaker Henry Ford (1863-1947) operated a metalsmith school at Dearborn, Michigan, for the benefit of the Navy. It was an adjunct to the Ford Motor Company. The Naval Institute oral history of Vice Admiral Joe Williams Jr., USN (Ret.), also describes this machinist's mate school run by Ford, as does the USNI oral history of Mr. Elda E. Logue.

Paul Stillwell: Did you read a lot as a boy?

Captain Schwab: Yes, I was reading constantly. We always had a large library of good fiction and non-fiction.

Paul Stillwell: What were some of the things that you were interested in?

Captain Schwab: Well, I read a lot of books about naval matters, even before knowing about Al Ryan. I read just about everything on Nelson, John Paul Jones, and Decatur—things of that sort.* On the fictional things side, I read sea stories like those by Marryatt, for example, *Masterman Ready* and *Midshipman Easy*.†

Paul Stillwell: Might that have been what sparked your interest in the Navy?

Captain Schwab: Well, it's really hard to say what sparked my interest in the Navy, except that every year they'd have a Navy game or an Army game. I guess I went to one or two of those and liked the look of the midshipmen, better than I did the cadets. West Point seemed sort of a dull place—I'd seen that—compared to the Naval Academy.

Paul Stillwell: Well, and there was a Navy yard in Brooklyn, too. Did you visit there?

Captain Schwab: Well, yes, I forgot about that. Brooklyn Tech, before it went to a new building in the last year I was there, was only a short distance from the Navy Yard. Some friends and I used to go over there, get permission, and look around. You'd pass the yard

---

* Lord Horatio Viscount Nelson (1758-1805), British naval hero of the Battle of Cape St. Vincent, 1797, Battle of the Nile, 1798, Trafalgar, 1805.
John Paul Jones (1747-1792) was the young country's first great naval officer and a hero of the Revolutionary War. He is credited with the following statement, though he probably did not express it in precisely these words: "It is by no means enough that an officer of the Navy should be a capable mariner. He must be that of course, but also a great deal more. He should be as well a gentleman of liberal education, refined manners, punctilious courtesy, and the nicest sense of personal honor."
Stephen Decatur (1779-1820) was a noted American naval officer of the early 19th century. He fought against the Barbary Pirates in the Mediterranean. He burned the American frigate *Philadelphia* near Tripoli in 1803 to keep the pirates from seizing her.
† Frederick Marryatt (1792-1848) was a British naval officer and novelist. Among his works were *Mr. Midshipman Easy* (1836) and *Masterman Ready, or the Wreck of the Pacific* (1841)

on the way to school. And then whenever the ships would come to the yard or anchor in the Hudson River, we'd go there and look at the ships. One memory was going out to the *Saratoga*. We had just two carriers at that time, the *Saratoga* and the *Lexington*, and they were tremendous ships.* We went all through them—very impressive. You couldn't do anything like that with Army, and there wasn't any Air Force as such.

Paul Stillwell: And the sorts of things that the Army has are necessarily a lot less impressive than something like the *Saratoga*.

What hobbies did you have as a boy?

Captain Schwab: Well, when I was still in high school, I managed to buy my own printing press. I had a small Chandler and Price press and many type fonts. I used to print things such as flyers, not on a union basis, for the churches and small stores. I earned enough money to pay for my own clothing and lunches and things of that sort. Other hobbies—well, I used to ride a bicycle and swim a lot. One of my uncles had a beach place in New Jersey, and every summer we'd all go there and do the normal things: swimming, playing baseball, eating, just lying around the beach. Finally I took up photography as a hobby; I did my own developing and printing. I still do darkroom work, but enlarging only.

Paul Stillwell: Were you an athlete in school?

---

* USS *Langley* (CV-1) was originally commissioned as the collier *Jupiter* (AC-3) in 1913 with Commander Joseph M. Reeves, USN, in command. She was later converted to the U.S. Navy's first aircraft carrier. She was commissioned as the *Langley* in 1922 with Commander Kenneth Whiting, USN, in command. She was sunk early in World War II.

USS *Lexington* CV-2) was commissioned 14 December 1927. She had a standard displacement of 33,000 tons, was 888 feet long, 106 feet in the beam, an extreme width of 130 feet on the flight deck, and had a draft of 24 feet. She had a top speed of 33.5 knots and could accommodate approximately 60-70 aircraft. She was originally armed with eight 8-inch guns that were later removed in World War II. USS *Lexington* (CV-2) was sunk 8 May 1942 during the Battle of the Coral Sea.

USS *Saratoga* (CV-3), a *Lexington*-class aircraft carrier, was commissioned 16 November 1927. She had a standard displacement of 33,000 tons, was 888 feet long, 106 feet in the beam, an extreme width of 130 feet on the flight deck, and had a draft of 24 feet. She had a top speed of 33.5 knots and could accommodate approximately 60-70 aircraft. She was originally armed with eight 8-inch guns that were later removed in World War II. She was sunk in 1946 postwar atomic bomb tests in the Pacific.

Captain Schwab: No. Well, I did try out for the soccer team, and I wound up with quite a few dents in my shins, but nothing spectacular. I was never that kind of an athlete. And I ran a little bit, but I didn't do very well at any of that. The long commute to my high school also was a problem in extracurricular activities.

Paul Stillwell: How much of an interest did you have in current events and world affairs?

Captain Schwab: Well, I used to read everything in the newspaper. I read constantly, especially newspaper articles. My family always had a lot of books in the house and subscribed to current events magazines, such as one now out of print, *The Literary Digest*, and others of that sort. *Time* didn't exist until later.* I used to go to the library a lot. The libraries in New York are very good, and they were always open on Saturdays and Sundays. The librarians were very helpful to kids. They'd lead you to books of interest—ask you what you were interested in and show you around.

Paul Stillwell: Did your parents foster this interest in learning and education?

Captain Schwab: Oh, yes. They didn't force you to read anything, but we always had books around. There was a good book on the Panama Canal that I read over and over again. A man by the name of Ruskin wrote that. You can see I have books of every kind here.

Paul Stillwell: Did you have an interest in technical/engineering type things? Did that grow out of your high school experience?

Captain Schwab: Well, at Brooklyn Tech I got to know a lot about industrial processes. In fact, that was the name of one of the courses. I won a citywide contest for high school children who maintained special notebooks, illustrated notebooks. Mine was on industrial processes. I don't think any other schools had an industrial process course, but

---

* *Time* magazine has published continuously since 1923.

Brooklyn Tech did. I remember my father took me over to City Hall for the award. I got a certificate and a $5.00 prize.

Paul Stillwell: With such a large area as New York, I would think that the competition for Naval Academy appointments would be rather intense. How did you manage that?

Captain Schwab: Well, my father, although a New York City fireman in the civil service, was always active in local Democratic political party things, especially with a Democratic Club in Brooklyn, where we lived originally. I was born on Bainbridge Street in Flatbush, Brooklyn, near where the Brooklyn Dodgers used to be.* But then we moved near a Democratic Club in Greenpoint. A politician by the name of Pete McGuinness was the head of it. He was a real character. He was an old-fashioned political ward boss, you might say, and took care of all the old people. And the poor people got turkeys at the appropriate times—things of that sort.

My father kept up a membership in that club and helped make sure all our relatives would vote for the right party. McGuinness used to call Greenpoint—which is sort of run-down now; it wasn't so hot then—the "Garden spot of the Univoise." Through the club, when it came time to get a Naval Academy appointment, the local congressman in that area was asked to help. By that time we were living in Queens, but I was commuting to Brooklyn Tech, which was in downtown Brooklyn, near the Manhattan Bridge.

The only appointment that was possible was through a congressman by the name of Lindsay.† Another one of his constituents, who had died, had been either a postman or an assistant postmaster in one of the local post offices. But before the postman died, Lindsay had promised he'd give his son the appointment to the Naval Academy. So the son got a principal appointment in 1934.‡ I was also trying to get one in 1934. I had

---

* From 1913 to 1957 the Brooklyn Dodgers played in Ebbets Field. Following the 1957 season the team moved to Los Angeles and remains there to this day.
† George Washington Lindsay, a Democrat from New York, served in the House of Representatives from 4 March 1923 to 3 January 1935.
‡ The "principal" referred to here was the individual who received the congressman's principal appointment for a particular opening at the Naval Academy. Someone with an alternate appointment would get in only if the person with the principal appointment was found to be unqualified or if he decided not to accept the appointment.

enough credits to graduate from high school, even though I hadn't formally graduated. However, the postman's son got the principal, and there were no alternates left. They didn't have many competitive exams in those days. This young fellow went to Annapolis for his physical exam. Apparently he was worried about his eyes, so he and another friend went to a local drugstore and got some drops the night before the physical. This effectively ruined their eyes the next day. So they didn't get in.

So my father went right back to the congressman and said, well, now I should have the principal. Congressman Lindsay said no. He'd promised the postman's son he'd let him have two shots, that his eye exam failure wasn't really his fault. But he wanted to interview me anyhow to see if I should have the first alternate. So we went around to see Congressman Lindsay, who was in his bedroom, in his bed, and very weak looking. He talked to me for a while and asked for a report on a preliminary physical exam. He then said I could have the first alternate. Right after all the paperwork was signed and sealed, Mr. Lindsay died. So, in a way, I was appointed by a dead congressman.* I then took all five entrance exams in the spring of 1935.

Paul Stillwell: What had happened to the second chance for the principal appointment?

Captain Schwab: Well, Mr. Lindsay gave it to the postman's son again, but he never showed up for his physical exam. So I guess he had a private eye exam and decided against it. So on June 24, 1935, I went down to Annapolis, passed the physical, and went into the Naval Academy and a naval career.

Paul Stillwell: The Brooklyn Tech education had been very beneficial preparation.

Captain Schwab: Oh, yes, entirely. Quite a few boys from Brooklyn Tech, which was an all-boys school, had gone to the Naval Academy, and no one had ever bilged out. In fact, I starred the whole first year at the academy.† I didn't have to study very much; I'd had

---

* Actually, Lindsay was defeated, rather than dead, at that point. He was an unsuccessful candidate for renomination in 1934 and left the House of Representatives on 3 January 1935. He died 15 March 1938.
† To "star" in this context means to rank high in the academic standings.

almost everything already. It was really a pretty good background for going into the Naval Academy.

Paul Stillwell: What do you recall about the plebe summer indoctrination?[*]

Captain Schwab: That wasn't too bad, because they were pretty tough on you at Brooklyn Technical High School. I mean, if you got out of line—you were talking or something—the teachers had no objection to picking up an eraser or chalk and whacking you, or throwing it across the room and hitting you. They did some pretty rough things. But if you live in New York, you're used to almost anything.

Having talked to Al Ryan, and then other friends when they'd come to New York, I'd gathered it was going to be pretty rough and just take it, and say "Yes, sir" and "No, sir" at the proper time. And "I'll find out"—never say "I don't know." They told me all that ahead of time. But it wasn't bad. We were lucky in a way, because the class of '37 was a very nice class and ran plebe summer. The class of '36 were our first classmen. We got away with it to a certain extent, because it was a very small class. I think it had 200 in it and we had 900.[†] So every first classman, in those days—I don't know if they still do the same thing—had several plebes. I had a very nice one. His name was Hank Schwaner, and he was a baseball player—a very nice person, helped a lot.[‡] I had no problems there. You got your normal amount of running, sitting on the edges of chairs and getting whacked once in a while, but nothing sadistic. You read about all these things; I never ran into any of that.

Paul Stillwell: It may just depend on the individual that you run into.

Captain Schwab: That's possible. I don't really remember too many people having problems. There were a couple who could have been, but actually your first classman

---

[*] A midshipman in his or her first year is called a plebe; second year, youngster or third classman; third year, second classman; fourth year, first classman.
[†] The class of 1937 comprised 323 graduates.
[‡] Midshipman Henry C. Schwaner Jr., USN.

and your friendly second classman sort of let you know to stay away from those people. They protected you, so it was not bad at all.

Paul Stillwell: Were there any of your classmates whom you were particularly close to while you were at the Academy?

Captain Schwab: Well, my roommate, Bill Hogaboom.* It was unusual, I gather, for people to room together for four years. And of course, you're always thrown in with a lot of people with the same last initial—on cruises and so on. One who was a very good friend just died here a few months ago, Ernie Schreiter.† I gave a little talk at his funeral services, but he was a good friend. I had a lot of them; all the people who were in your own battalion you got to know very well.

Before I took the Naval Academy exam, because of the appointment lapse of a year, my father said I should go to a special prep school. I had good marks at Brooklyn Technical High School, and I could have taken what they called a substantiating examination, which was just English and mathematics. There was a lot of mythology in those days connected with getting into the Naval Academy. For example, my father heard from Mr. Ryan and his son that it was a good idea to take what they called a regular exam, which was five subjects—one of them being ancient history, which I had never studied in my whole life.

To prepare me for that exam, when I found out I had the alternate appointment, I went to the William Lawrence Leonard Preparatory School, which was a small school that had about 10 or 15 boys. All we did was work out on previous Naval Academy and West Point entrance exams, a real cram course. It was in a private dwelling on West End Avenue in Manhattan, right across the street from the Schwab estate—Charles M. Schwab; he was still alive then.‡ He had a whole city block with a high fence around it. So I went to the prep school from about September of 1934 until I took the entrance

---

* Midshipman William F. Hogaboom, USN. Hogaboom died on 19 December 1944 while serving in the Philippines as a Marine Corps first lieutenant.
† Midshipman Ernest F. Schreiter, USN.
‡ Charles M. Schwab (1862-1939) was the head of Bethlehem Steel Company for many years.

exam, whenever that was—April 1935. Then I went back and took a couple more courses in high school and finished editing the paper, which was called *The Survey*.

In that prep class with me there were a couple of other good friends of mine. There was one, Tom Rudden, who just died here last year as an admiral.* And Chuck Nace—I think he's still alive—made admiral.† Nace was in submarines with me, and we maintained a friendship that way. Rudden went into surface ships. I didn't get to see Nace or Rudden too much after the academy, but at the academy I knew them well. I don't know if you know—the class of '39 has quite a history of staying together. For years they had the largest attendance at the Naval Academy Alumni Association things the third Wednesday of every month at Fort Myer.‡ In fact, this last one, when Admiral Crowe was supposed to speak, the class of '51 for some reason was the largest.§ I don't know if that's Crowe's class or not.

Paul Stillwell: No, it isn't.**

Captain Schwab: They had the largest number, and we were number two. Normally we're number one. We had a lot of people there, though. But Crowe didn't show up, because he was testifying in front of the Senate.

Paul Stillwell: I guess Lou Roddis was almost a legend in that class.

Captain Schwab: Yes, Lou Roddis and also Ned Beach.†† Lou Roddis was in my battalion; he and Beach were always fighting it out for number one in class standing. Beach wound up number two and Roddis, number one.

Paul Stillwell: Yes. There's the famous story about the Martian invasion in 1938.

---

* Rear Admiral Thomas F. Rudden Jr., USN (Ret.).
† Rear Admiral Charles D. Nace, USN (Ret.).
‡ Fort Myer, an Army post, is in Northern Virginia, adjacent to Arlington National Cemetery.
§ Admiral William J. Crowe Jr., USN, served as Chairman of the Joint Chiefs of Staff from 1 October 1985 to 30 September 1989.
** Crowe was in the Naval Academy class of 1947, which graduated in June 1946.
†† Midshipman Louis H. Roddis Jr., USN, stood number one of the 581 graduates in the Naval Academy class of 1939. Midshipman Edward L. Beach Jr., USN, finished second.

Captain Schwab: Well, that was Beach.* Beach was the regimental commander during the fall set of midshipman officer assignments. I guess we had three sets then.† I was on the regimental staff in the last set. I was the regimental chief petty officer, which is the lowest you can get and still be on the regimental staff. But you had a lot of stars and stripes on your arm, and all the girls thought that was pretty good.

Paul Stillwell: What were your duties in that position?

Captain Schwab: I mustered the regimental staff. In the first set I was a two-striper; I had a platoon.

Paul Stillwell: What were some problems or highlights in your years at the Naval Academy?

Captain Schwab: All the way through the Naval Academy it was actually a lot of fun; I didn't have any real problems. Of course, the European cruises were the highlights. We had two of them then, battleship cruises in 1936 and 1938. In both of them I was always in the same compartment with Ernie Schreiter, so we always could go ashore together.

Paul Stillwell: In '36, which ship did you go in then?

Captain Schwab: In the *Wyoming*.‡ We went to Portsmouth, England, to Göteborg in

---

* On 30 October 1938, the day before Halloween, Orson Welles and other members of the cast of the Mercury Theater broadcast an adaptation of the story *War of the Worlds* on nationwide radio. The play was presented as if it were a live news broadcast of an invasion of New Jersey by Martians. Many listeners did not hear the explanation that it was fictional and thus believed it was a genuine news event. Midshipman Beach believed the invasion was authentic and offered the regiment of midshipmen to repel the Martians.
† In order to provide opportunities to a greater number of midshipmen, the Naval Academy rotated positions so that there were three different "sets" of leaders in the academic year—autumn, winter, and spring.
‡ USS *Wyoming* (BB-32) was commissioned as a battleship in 1912 and served in that role until being demilitarized as a result of the 1930 London Treaty on the limitation of naval armaments. She was redesignated a miscellaneous auxiliary, AG-17, on 1 July 1931 and thereafter served into the mid-1940s as a training ship for gunnery and for midshipman cruises.

Sweden, and then to Cherbourg, France, and we had a good cruise. But on the way over to England, a classmate by the name of Smith fell out of his hammock—we were still using hammocks then—and died in England.* From then on they were very careful about head injuries.

When we were up in Sweden, another classmate who went in the Marines—his name was Crowe—and I took a bicycle trip from Göteborg up to a little town called Alingsas.† Somehow, we got way up in the hills. Coming back, the road paths were about a foot and a half wide, and the center was a sandy rut. Suddenly there was this Swede coming up the hill and I was in the lead coming down. I never had hand brakes on a bike before. I used those, but the bike wouldn't stop in the sand, and my nose hit him right in the middle of the forehead. When I woke up, the front wheel of my bike looked like a pretzel, and the Swede was gone. We were wearing what we called a hiking uniform, which was a blue flannel shirt with blue trousers, white leggings, and white cap covers. My cap cover was all full of blood from my broken nose. Crowe was laughing. I said, "What's so funny?"

He said, "Well, I am trying to figure out how to fix the flat tire." It was an inner-tube tire, which he'd never seen before. He said all the directions were in Swedish. Anyhow, we got it more or less straightened out, and went back to the little hotel we were staying at in Alingsas. The proprietor had lived in the United States for some while, so he spoke English. His wife was horrified at my appearance. She washed my cap cover, fed me a bowl of beets "for my blood," which I think is another piece of mythology.

We already had dates with two Swedish girls that night. We went out there to the town fete, even though my nose was bent at a right angle. The next day was a Sunday, and we were supposed to go back to the ship in Göteborg. We knew that they were having a reception for all the local dignitaries in Alingsas. It was raining. I was very weak; I'd lost a lot of blood, I guess. We went to the local rail station, and there were two more classmates at the station. One had hurt his leg someplace, also on a bike. By pooling all our money, we had enough for the two injured ones to get on the train with our bikes and go to Göteborg. The other two rode back in the rain. When the two of us

---

* Midshipman Sidney P. Smith Jr., USN, died 28 June 1936.
† Midshipman John H. Crowe, USN, later went into the Army.

got back to town, we tried to turn our bikes in. But the bike shop was closed, so we left notes with them that we'd pay for damages. We'd taken some insurance; I guess it was all right.

We went back to the ship, and there was a reception going on; it had stopped raining. If you were on the ship, you were supposed to help escort the local dignitaries. My train companion had a bad leg, and my nose was all blown out of proportion. We decided to avoid the reception and ducked on board rapidly, cleaned up a little bit, and got ashore—illegally, because we weren't supposed to do that—and stayed until the reception was over. When we came back, we turned ourselves in to sick bay. Boy, I really was in trouble because of the head injury, since this other classmate by the name of Smith had died with one during the cruise.

We departed Göteborg for about seven or eight days cruising around, reenacting the battle of Jutland, things of that sort.* After that we were going to Cherbourg. The doctors put me on light duty, so I slept in the sick bay, got extra good food, and didn't have to do any of the normal deck work. All the first classman were angry, because they couldn't order me around—I was a third classman—and that was about it. My nose finally healed after being set. I still have a nice bump on my nose and a deviated nasal septum.

The second cruise was in '38.

Paul Stillwell: What ship were you in then?

Captain Schwab: The *New York*.† Oh, in '36, I forgot—the Spanish Civil War started.‡ We had started off with three battleships. I think we had the *Wyoming* and the

---

* The Battle of Jutland was the most significant naval engagement of World War I. Fought between the British Grand Fleet and the German High Seas Fleet, it took place 31 May 1916 in the North Sea, off the coast of Denmark. The British lost more ships in the battle but scored a strategic victory by maintaining control of the seas.
† USS *New York* (BB-34), lead battleship of her class, was commissioned 15 April 1914. She had a standard displacement of 27,000 tons, was 573 feet long, and 95 feet in the beam. Her top speed was 21 knots. She was armed with ten 14-inch guns, 16 5-inch guns, and eight 3-inch guns. She was eventually decommissioned in 1946 after service in World War II.
‡ General Francisco Franco was dictator of Spain from 1936 until his death in 1975. The Spanish Civil War lasted from 1936 to 1939. The opposing sides were the Republicans, who supported the established Spanish Republic and the Nationalists, a rebel group led by Franco. The Nationalists won the war.

Oklahoma, and I forget what the other one was, probably the *New York* or *Texas*.

Paul Stillwell: Well, the *Oklahoma* went to evacuate Americans from Spain.

Captain Schwab: Yes, that's right. We three ships all went into Bilbao, Spain. They also moved a group of Coast Guard cadets from one or two of their cutters onto the *Wyoming*, so we were really loaded up with people.

From Bilbao we came back to the States with two battleships, loaded with three sets of midshipmen and the Coast Guard cadets. We got to learn a lot about the Coast Guard Academy. As far as we could see from talking to them, that school was a lot tougher than the Naval Academy on the people. The first classmen treated their third classmen as if they were plebes. You know, we weren't youngsters yet, but we were third classmen, no "running" for us.

Paul Stillwell: What about the later cruise in the *New York*?

Captain Schwab: In the 1938 cruise, we went to Portsmouth and Copenhagen next. But we went to Le Havre this cruise instead of Cherbourg. She had reciprocating engines, and when she'd get up around 15 or 16 knots, you could hear "BLOOM, BLOOM, BLOOM." They called it the "honeymoon gallop."

Paul Stillwell: It was a definite thump.

Captain Schwab: It was very noisy. On the way back to the States, about a day out of our last European port, the starboard propeller shaft broke, right at a joint outboard, so it was hanging down vertically. By putting a diver out, they got a line around this propeller, and, with midshipmen hauling on the line, somehow pulled it back into the outboard strut bearing and secured it. But they were afraid that some of the watertight compartments down below were damaged. They didn't trust any third classmen to sit down there and keep a watch, so they put a first classman—'39, of course—way down at the bottom of a vertical access, right next to the broken propeller, and also the outboard struts. In case the hull started to leak, we were supposed to yell into a phone and then get out in a hurry after turning on a submersible pump that was down there. That was sort of an interesting experience. We limped back to Norfolk in 21 days. The other ships went to New York and had a great time up there.

In the *New York* coming back, we went right into Norfolk and went into dry dock right away, which was not bad. We were the only battleship there, and all the Norfolk girls were out on the pier with cars, and we had a great time. I guess the first classmen had liberty until midnight or 1:00 in the morning. The third classmen had to be back about 11:00, so we had a couple hours on them. In the morning, the first class would go under the ship and go back to sleep. Liberty would start about 2:00 o'clock. We did fire a short-range battle practice before docking. All the firing was on one side, because the lines holding the broken propeller shaft were obstructing the 5-inch battery on one side.

Paul Stillwell: Did you encounter a navigation instructor named Roy Benson on board that ship?

Captain Schwab: Roy Benson's an honorary member of the class of '39, as you know.[*] I don't remember him being on that ship. But he's another good friend of mine too. That's about all on the midshipman cruises. Oh, on second class summer, in 1937, we went on a destroyer cruise. We went to New York and Newport and saw the America's Cup races.[†]

Paul Stillwell: What ship was that?

Captain Schwab: It was an old four-piper; I know that. *Manley* sound right? I don't know. I've forgotten now.

---

[*] Lieutenant Roy S. Benson, USN, taught navigation at the Naval Academy. The oral history of Benson, who retired as a rear admiral, is in the Naval Institute collection.
[†] The America's Cup is a trophy awarded to the winner of match races between sailing yachts. In 1937 Harold Vanderbilt's yacht *Ranger* won on behalf of the New York Yacht Club.

Paul Stillwell: How would you compare the political climate in Europe for the two visits? By '38 you were getting very close to the time of the Munich crisis.*

Captain Schwab: Yes, that's right, because that was only a few months later. Well, the monetary thing was interesting. In France, when we were there in 1936, the franc was worth around four cents. And when we were there in 1938, it had gone down to two cents. But inflation hadn't occurred yet, so we were twice as rich as before. We had some money saved up that you could spend on the cruise, but not much. After you paid for tours and stuff, there wasn't much left, but the exchange rate change made us think we were rich.

In all of the countries we visited, everybody was very friendly. The French in particular were very helpful; we could do no wrong. We did all sorts of weird things. For example, there were about four of us in a taxicab with our heads through the top, singing "Anchors Aweigh," going up the Champs-Élysées in the middle of the day. The French all waved; they thought it was wonderful. If you had your uniform on, you could do no wrong. People would buy you champagne. They just liked Americans. Most of us in the fourth batt studied French, so we had no problems at all.†

Paul Stillwell: Can you talk shipboard duties? Certainly they were different when you were a third classman than when you were a first.

Captain Schwab: Well, when you were a third classman, of course you did everything enlisted men did. You lived exactly the same way; you ate the same food. In fact, the enlisted men bossed you around, because you didn't know anything. We holystoned the decks, and swabbed the decks, and squeegeed down—all those fancy words that you've heard about.‡ We tried to sleep as much as possible, because we were always either working or on watch. No matter when you were on watch, you always had to get up in

---

* Munich, Germany, became infamous because it was the site of a September 1938 meeting in which British Prime Minister Neville Chamberlain agreed to let Germany annex the Sudeten region of Czechoslovakia as the price of maintaining peace.
† Batt – battalion.
‡ Holystoning refers to the practice of cleaning a ship's wooden decks by scraping them with bricks pushed back and forth across the planks by means of wooden handles. It is a laborious operation.

the morning when you slept in hammocks, because you had to put the hammocks away. You couldn't sleep in. You slept anyplace and anytime you could; you learned how to sleep fast.

On the first class cruise, you theoretically were doing all the officers' jobs. You took turns as officer of the deck, for example. When maintaining formation—they didn't have radar in those days—we used a stadimeter to maintain distances.[*] You did a lot at sea, but not in critical maneuvers such as going into port. You did all of the normal, routine officer-like things; it was just a taste, though. It wasn't anything like actually getting out in the fleet.

Paul Stillwell: Did you find that you enjoyed the seagoing life?

Captain Schwab: Oh, yes. We left Annapolis right after June week.[†] The very first day out—or the second day out in the *Wyoming*—we really ran into some rough weather. None of us had ever been in weather where the ships really rolled. The *Wyoming* was rather high in the water because some guns and armor had been removed.[‡] We got deathly seasick. They gave us advice such as eating pickles and soda crackers, because they tasted the same going both ways. I forget the name of the captain of the ship, but when he saw all these midshipmen hanging over the side, he detailed several petty officers to get us going. The way he did it was to put us in groups of five or six or so, and we had to climb all the way up to the top of the foremast, and then come down and go back and climb up to the top of the mainmast and come down—all out in the open air. Going up and down those masts wasn't easy, and it was a little scary when the ship was rolling. By the time you'd gotten all the way up and down the mainmast, you had forgotten all about being seasick. That was all there was to it. From then on, I never was seasick again.

---

[*] The stadimeter is a mechanical device for measuring the range to another ship when the height of her mast is known.
[†] June Week was the term at the time for the collection of festivities surrounding the graduation and commissioning of the first classmen. Naval Academy classes now graduate in late May during what is known as Commissioning Week.
[‡] The *Wyoming* had been largely demilitarized as the result of the 1930 naval disarmament treaty.

We had a ship's paper, as they always do on cruises, and there was a little piece in there: "To make you appreciate life to the fullest, a person should be forced to be seasick one day a year." Silly things like that.

Paul Stillwell: What were the enlisted messes like in those ships?

Captain Schwab: We ate and bunked in a gun compartment for a 5-inch/51-caliber broadside gun.

Paul Stillwell: Those ships were built before the general mess concept.

Captain Schwab: Divisions ate separately; each division compartment had its own mess cook, they called them. They were people who went to get the loaded pots and pans from the galley and bring them back to the compartment. These were also the compartments where we slept. Our hammocks were all triced up with seven half hitches, and then they were folded and put in the lockers so you didn't see those. The mess tables were normally hung on the overhead when not in use. In fact, when you slept, you were underneath the mess tables. For meals we took the mess tables down, and the legs folded out. They were very heavy metal tables with folding legs, and they sat on the deck. I can't remember how we fastened them down. I don't know whether they sat in holes or what, but they didn't move around. Each compartment had its own set of mess tables, and where you ate you also slept. I don't know where the engineers slept; I was always in a gunnery compartment. We rotated around on duties, but I guess we always slept in the same place.

Paul Stillwell: Did you stand engineering watches?

Captain Schwab: You did everything.

Paul Stillwell: What do you recall of those watches?

Captain Schwab: They were *hot*. It was a joy to get down there when the weather was cool, but otherwise it was pretty hot.

Paul Stillwell: Were those reciprocating engines noisy?

Captain Schwab: Oh, yes, in the *New York*. I guess the *Wyoming* had reciprocating engines, too; I'm not sure.* At least they weren't coal burners. We heard from Roy Benson about loading coal; that must have been an awful thing.

Paul Stillwell: I think he claims to have been the last officer on active duty to have made a coal-burning midshipman cruise.†

Captain Schwab: That was apparently quite an all-hands evolution; everybody loaded coal. I don't think the engineering watches were much fun. There was a lot of wondering what was going on, because there were a lot of valves and things you didn't quite understand. You knew that there were certain needles that weren't supposed to go above the red or below the black or something; that was about it. There wasn't too much attention to explaining that sort of thing. But when you were up on the bridge, even as a third classman, it was interesting, because then you were a lookout or a signalman or something of that sort. That was more interesting, because you could see something going on. Down in the engine room you were sort of isolated.

Paul Stillwell: Did you have any operations in fog?

Captain Schwab: I can't remember any as a midshipman, no. We towed the fog buoys in my first ship, the battleship *Pennsylvania*. Each ship in column would tow a buoy astern. That was before radar, of course; we'd watch that buoy very carefully. The other ship was only a couple of hundred yards ahead, and we were going along at eight or ten knots.

---

* The *Wyoming*'s main engines were turbines.
† Admiral Benson retired in 1968.

It was sort of tricky. In fact, I don't know why they didn't have more casualties than they did.

Paul Stillwell: What would be your assessment of the caliber of an enlisted man from that late '30s era?

Captain Schwab: In those days, I don't think many enlisted men were married. They were all what the Army would call "lifers." They were in the Navy forever. They were all a pretty rough and tough bunch. I think they all took pity on the midshipmen; we didn't know very much. The ones that were on the deck force were very good seamen. That was all they'd ever done in their lives. I don't think many of them had been educated. Very few of them, I think, had been to high school as they are now; they were a pretty rough bunch. When they were in port, they acted like the old-fashioned tars in the movies. There were always certain ones who everybody knew shouldn't be allowed to go ashore by themselves. I even had some like that on my first ships. For example, on one of my submarines we had an American Indian who was outstanding at sea; he was a signalman, and he also manned a gun. But when he was ashore he went wild. We never let him go ashore by himself, because that firewater really hit him.

The chief petty officers and the first class petty officers were the ones who knew everything. Of course, when you first went out to the fleet as a brand-new ensign, if you didn't have the chief petty officers and the first class petty officers to let you know what was going on, you'd have been lost completely. The warrant officers kept to themselves, more or less, because they were neither fish nor fowl. The commissioned warrant officers, of course, were not Naval Academy, and they weren't enlisted men either.

Paul Stillwell: They weren't really accepted by the commissioned officers either.

Captain Schwab: No, they had their own warrant officers' mess.

Paul Stillwell: What were officers' living conditions in the fleet?

Captain Schwab: When we went out to the battleships after graduation, they split up the class. We were sent mostly to the larger ships. In the *Pennsylvania* we had 16 ensigns arriving all at once. The kind of room you got depended on how senior you were. Your signal number precedence was very important. You found this out right away. The lower numbers all were put in the junior officers' mess, which was just like an enlisted bunkroom, except it had fixed bunks and lockers. I graduated 100 out of a class of 500.[*] I was senior enough to be assigned to a little room with Allyn Ostroski.[†] It was second deck down and very nice. But there was no running water in it. When you wanted hot water for shaving, you pressed a button twice, and the steward's mate would bring the hot water. You pressed so many times for hot water. The room was about 12 feet long by six feet wide. One side had closets, and the other side had an upper and lower bunk, and that was it.

Paul Stillwell: No desks in it?

Captain Schwab: Yes, one little desk, and that was it. You didn't spend much time in there. You spent most of your time in the junior officers' mess or the wardroom. You didn't move up to the wardroom usually until you made lieutenant (junior grade) or were a full-fledged watch stander. We still had aviation cadets on board. They were not Naval Academy graduates. They wore midshipman stripes. Once in a while, one of them would get qualified as a full-fledged watch stander, and they'd have a cadet with a narrow stripe up in the wardroom. I don't think that happened but once.

We always used to razz the aviation cadets in the *Pennsylvania*. That's when they used to catapult the observation planes; we had two of them. We used to make the aviation cadets, who got extra pay because they were fliers, buy Coca-Colas at the movies, or we'd threaten to shoot them off on the down-roll. You didn't dare shoot any lieutenants off that way. I remember as an ensign, I thought a lieutenant—a full lieutenant with two broad stripes, two regular stripes—was God. You thought, "Gee, will I ever make lieutenant?" And a commander, of course, was way up there.

---

[*] Schwab stood number 150 of the 581 graduates in the class of 1939.
[†] Ensign Allyn B. Ostroski, USN.

Paul Stillwell: He was above God.

Captain Schwab: Not quite. The exec was a commander, and he was called "The Commander." He was the only full commander in the ship's company. The captain, of course, *was* God.

Paul Stillwell: Before we get into the *Pennsylvania*, I was wondering—you talked about how well the midshipmen were received over in Europe. What was the social status of a midshipman in this country, say, at home on your September leaves.

Captain Schwab: Well, all of your neighbors thought you were really something. To be at the Naval Academy was considered quite a thing. However, very few people knew what you did really. You always came home and showed off in your uniform. I remember once going to someplace on the subway in New York; I was going to meet a girl or something. I was wearing my midshipman uniform. A man on the subway platform looked at me, and he said, "Hey, Bud, what's the getup?"

You know the old story about a Midwesterner who went to the Naval Academy. He said his friends and family never knew exactly where he went to school. In fact, he was positive of it, because every year around Memorial Day they asked him for tickets to the auto races in Indianapolis.

Paul Stillwell: What do you remember about the town of Annapolis? It was much different then than it is now.

Captain Schwab: Oh, yes. Now it looks to be sort of a tourist resort. Then there were very few. Carvel Hall was the main hotel, and there was a group of greasy spoons and things of that sort for feeding the drags, one or two movie houses, and that was about it.[*] The main thing you could do was walk, because midshipmen weren't allowed to have any automobiles or even ride in automobiles, or drink anything alcoholic at all. Some

---

[*] "Drag" was Naval Academy slang for dating girls. A midshipman who dated seldom or not at all was known as a "Red Mike."

midshipmen knew places where they could get wine, usually with a meal in town, but not too many of them drank hard liquor that I know of. If they did, they didn't last long if they were detected.

Paul Stillwell: What do you recall about the social life at the Naval Academy?

Captain Schwab: Of course, plebe year, it was essentially zero.[*] The only time plebes got to drag there was to the shows and the NA Ten performances.[†] Plebes didn't go to any of the hops, except for the June ball; that was the first one plebes were allowed to go to. Plebes were allowed out of the academy grounds only on Saturday afternoon. On Sunday, if you had a relative, you could go out for lunch, and that was about it.

Once in a while they'd have what they call "tea fights." If you were a plebe, they had to be in the yard, and they were usually at the home of some senior officer. His daughter would invite other girls over, and you would go over there and actually have tea and cookies, and that was it. Youngster year, of course, you were allowed out—big deal—on Saturday *and* Sunday afternoons. You didn't have much to spend anyhow when you were a plebe. The first paycheck—the first pay I got—was supposed to be $2.00 a month out of $85.00 a month total.

Of course, they were putting it all aside to pay for their uniforms and everything, and build up for graduation. You were supposed to get $2.00 a month as a plebe, and they had not at that point in 1935 ended the Hoover years reduction of pay, so all we got was $1.80 on my first payday.[‡] I wrote something on a dollar bill—the first dollar bill I was paid—and sent it to my father. We got $1.80 that first time, but from then on it was $2.00 a month. We all lined up in the division passageway and got our money. You couldn't do much on that. When you were a youngster you got $4.00 a month, second classman, $6.00 a month. First classmen got a lot more, I think $10.00. When you were

---
[*] A midshipman in his or her first year is called a plebe; second year, youngster or third classman; third year, second classman; fourth year, first classman.
[†] NA Ten was a musical group comprised of midshipmen.
[‡] Herbert C. Hoover was President o the United States from 4 March 1929 to 4 March 1933. The Great Depression began during his tenure.

a first classman you could hire the corridor boys to take care of your room. I guess you know they called them "mokes" in those days.

Paul Stillwell: These were blacks.

Captain Schwab: Yes. They would clean up your room and make your bed. It was a first class privilege only. I guess second classmen were allowed out in town on Saturday, Sunday, and Wednesday afternoons. First classmen could go out any afternoon they wanted to, unless they were on restriction. The social life was not much.

We found out the little extra things you could do. For instance, I was on *The Log* staff and was excused from dress parades at times.* I was the editor of the plebe *Log* and then I stayed on *The Log* staff all four years. We had a competition before first-class year to select the editor in chief. I wound up as number-two editor, and Ted Siegmund in my class, now dead, was the editor in chief.† G. M. K. Baker was the other associate editor.‡ We all took turns editing. For example, here is a special issue of *The Log* from 1939.

Paul Stillwell: It used the format of *Esquire* magazine.

Captain Schwab: Yes, that was a special issue. We had permission from *Esquire* and other magazines to do things like that. I used to write regularly; every week I'd have something in there. In this issue I corresponded with the artist Petty. George Petty did all these curvaceous girls for *Esquire* magazine, drawings, not photos. He used his daughter as a model for most of them. *The Log* was a pretty good little magazine.

Paul Stillwell: Were there any other articles that you especially remember from your *Log* time?

---

* *The Log* was a midshipman-produced magazine at the Naval Academy. It was often humorous and satirical.
† Midshipman Theodore C. Siegmund, USN.
‡ Midshipman George M. K. Baker Jr., USN.

Captain Schwab: Oh, I wrote on about any subject. The very first one I did in my plebe year was on the library, because the library operated a little differently. You couldn't just go roaming around in it the way you could in the New York public libraries. You had to find things yourself in the card file. We didn't get much assistance. I wrote an article on the library and the varieties of books there. I guess the next one I wrote was about a math professor who had professor of mathematics as a rank. Then another one I wrote about how midshipmen food had changed at Christmastime throughout the years—things of that sort. All of them required some research. I had to go back into old documents, which led to me doing a lot of that kind of thing later on in life.

Paul Stillwell: *The Log* now has a humorous character to it.

Captain Schwab: It was humorous then too. It was always humorous. We had a literary magazine they called the *Trident*. I don't know if they still have that. And we had, of course, the *Lucky Bag*, which was the annual. And *Reef Points*, which didn't get revised much. I see they still have *Reef Points* but a much larger version.[*]

Paul Stillwell: That's revised annually now.

Captain Schwab: So *The Log* was humorous, and the main humor column was one that was usually in the center. It was called "Salty Sam." I don't know if they still have him or not.

Paul Stillwell: I don't think so.

Paul Stillwell: We're just back from a break, and during the course of it I heard a number of interesting tales about your predecessors. Why don't you go back to your great-grandfather and his immigration from Germany?

---

[*] *Reef Points*, a term taken from sailing ships, is the name of a small handbook issued to Naval Academy midshipmen.

Captain Schwab: Well, my great-grandfather came over to the United States, to Pennsylvania, from Germany, sometime around 1848. I assume he escaped whatever wars they were having or problems they were having in Germany at that time. I don't know much about him until he got into the Civil War. He was in a Pennsylvania volunteer cavalry troop. During the war, he was at the Battle of Gettysburg, dismounted, and was shot near the heart but didn't die. In those days they couldn't operate in that area, but he survived.

Maybe he was invalided out, for all I know. Right after the war he went to New York with a friend who was a former cavalryman from the Union Army. They started an ice cutting and carting business by leasing ice privileges from farmers out on Long Island who lived around Lake Ronkonkoma. They'd haul the ice into warehouses, where they packed it in sawdust in Brooklyn side, and then it would go over to Manhattan when needed. The ice would last, I guess, for the summer. Years after the war—at least five, and probably a lot more, because in the meantime my grandfather was born in New York, my great-grandfather was in a parade of Civil War veterans up Fifth Avenue in New York. He was a staff sergeant major in the cavalry. Instead of his horse continuing along with the staff that he was in, it kept on straight ahead to an area that is now Central Park. When they rode up alongside of him, he was dead in the saddle. So he died with his boots on. We have his sword and picture, in uniform, in this house.

Paul Stillwell: Was the conclusion that the bullet had moved around?

Captain Schwab: It had finally jogged loose. A *New York Times* account of the incident gave the whole story. There was an account of him coming over and starting his business and getting involved with horses. After my great-grandfather died, my grandfather took over the ice and trucking business. Unfortunately someone soon invented the ammonia process of making ice, so he used the horses for freight purposes and became the main hauler for the National Sugar Company. They made Jack Frost Sugar. They had places where they processed sugar both in Brooklyn and in Edgewater, New Jersey, so he more or less did the trucking for National Sugar around the New York City area. Ultimately, when motor trucks came into being, the horse trucking business died out. But my grandfather still had a comfortable income, at least for a while. He used to take my grandmother around in those little two-wheeled buggies. I have pictures of them riding in those things. Other relatives took over in the freight business.

Paul Stillwell: How did your father get into being a fireman?

Captain Schwab: Apparently my grandfather managed to spend much of the money that he was left by his father. I gather he was a bit of a playboy. So after a few years he wasn't in such great shape financially. It became a question of my father possibly working for another relative who was in the freight business. However, my father didn't like the trucking business, so he took the civil service exams in New York, both for the police department and for the fire department. The New York City Fire Department acceptance came through first. He went in the fire department and worked up to be a captain before he retired as a result of physical injuries. As I mentioned earlier, one of his colleagues in the fire department was Al Ryan, whose son was Al Ryan Jr., class of 1933. If my father hadn't gone in the fire department I wouldn't have known Al Ryan and probably wouldn't have gone to the Naval Academy, because I wouldn't have been invited down to look it over.

Paul Stillwell: Well, why don't you mention also the family connection that steered you into the French language instead of German?

Captain Schwab: On the other side of the family, my mother's side, my grandfather came over from Germany in 1890 from the Rhineland. The Schwab male connection was all Munich-based. My Grandmother Schwab's family was from Königsberg, up in Schleswig-Holstein. The Bavarian side, of course, were beer drinkers, and the side from the Rhineland were mainly wine drinkers. So there would always be big family arguments on which was better. Whenever the families gathered, they'd each have wine and beer separately; we always had to have both in the house. But one thing they were agreed on is that neither the Rhinelanders nor the Bavarian descendants liked the Prussians.

When I was about to go to high school, I had decided wanted to become a chemical engineer, although I had also thought about the Navy even then. But to become a chemical engineer, I would have had to study German. In those days, the Germans were the foremost chemists. When my two grandfathers found out about that, they told my father that on no condition was I going to study German, because the Prussians had made war on the United States, and that was it. So I studied French instead, which probably wouldn't have fit me to become a chemical engineer, and I wouldn't be in this interview right now.

Paul Stillwell: Well, you mentioned also that you had some other possibilities other than the Naval Academy.

Captain Schwab: Oh, yes. Well, in my last year of high school I already had tentative scholarships to Cooper Union and to Columbia University but hadn't decided exactly what to study there. As in the case of my father and the fire department, a firm Naval Academy appointment came through first, and that was it. Also, since the Depression was still with us, the Navy also offered employment after graduation.

Paul Stillwell: What do you remember about the academic side of the Naval Academy?

Captain Schwab: Well, most of the instructors were naval officers, except a rare few. There were even some officers teaching in the languages; we had a couple in French. It varied; one semester you'd have an instructor in French who was a naval officer and then shift to a civilian in the next semester. In mathematics it also varied. Then we had good physics and chemistry professors, especially one we called "Slipstick Willie."* But the civilian instructors, in most cases, were different, because they seemed to have a more lively sense of humor than the naval officers. The naval officers it seemed—except for Roy Benson, who had the best sense of humor of anybody at the Naval Academy—were all very serious and eager to get back to sea again.

---

* "Slipstick Willie" was the nickname given Professor Earl W. Thomson because of his prowess with a slide rule. He taught at the Naval Academy from 1919 to 1959. For details see *Shipmate* magazine, published by the Naval Academy Alumni Association, June 1982, page 13.

I discussed whether or not somebody should try to become an instructor at the Naval Academy with, I think, Roy Benson. He said he'd rather be out at sea. Oh, he enjoyed teaching, mainly because he enjoyed working with midshipmen, but he preferred to be out at sea and back in submarines. I understand it's a different attitude from the officer instructors at West Point. The Army has a more permanent set of instructors; once you become an instructor up there, you could become permanent. Benson said he would not like to see that happen at the Naval Academy, because one of the benefits of the Navy system was that we were getting a fresh input from the fleet all the time, into the midshipmen's minds. Whether that's good or bad, I don't know.

Naval officers were almost always the instructors in such things as ordnance and gunnery. In the Department of English, History and Government we varied from civilian to officer instructors. Carroll Alden was the head of that department.[*] Often you had Navy types. I understand now that they have mostly civilian instructors. Is that correct?

Paul Stillwell: Well, in those subjects. I think still in things like navigation and seamanship, you would have naval officers.

Captain Schwab: I thought it was a good system. The system, I thought, was fair because each midshipman had multiple chances of demonstrating whether he knew something or didn't know something. When you came into class, you drew question slips and manned the blackboards. It was strictly by chance what question you had to write on. The marks in class counted for two-thirds of the total, and I think exams were one-third. So if you passed the two-thirds with high marks, you probably could pass the subject, even if you failed an exam. The instructors had a pretty good idea of whether you knew anything or not. You had to demonstrate your knowledge continually; you couldn't just sit at the back of the room and take notes the way you can in some civilian schools. And, of course, all midshipmen took the same courses, except for foreign languages. Class standings were easy to compute, compared to now.

---

[*] Dr. Carroll Storrs Alden taught at the Naval Academy from 1904 to 1940. From 1925 onward he was chairman of the English Department, the name of which was later changed to the English, History, and Government.

Paul Stillwell: Did you notice a difference in the style of instruction between the civilians and the naval officers?

Captain Schwab: Not really. We didn't have the variety of courses that they have now, and as much concentration. Even then, the course was pretty solid. We didn't have much opportunity for questioning anything, especially with officer instructors. The main thing I noticed was that the naval officers were a little, let's say embarrassed at least—they were a little more reluctant to have you ask questions in class than the civilian instructors. The civilian instructors maybe were a little more sure of their subject, but, of course, it depended on the subject. If you had an assignment in navigation, for instance, how do you use Dreisenstock or Ageton, why, the answer would be cut and dried.* There would be no question of philosophical thinking or analysis of Anna Karenina's motives or why did Ibsen write "A Doll's House." That was what you'd get in English, and that used to lead to some interesting discussions. We usually didn't get that sort of thing, maybe because the naval officers didn't teach that kind of subject, as you pointed out.

Paul Stillwell: Did you have any problems with the disciplinary organization? Did you ever get sent to the ship?

Captain Schwab: Never to the ship.† I walked extra duty for minor offenses such as not having things stowed properly or talking in formation. But I never was sent out to the ship. That was for major offenses.

Paul Stillwell: Do you have any recollections of the superintendents or the commandants, executive officers?

---

* Dreisenstock is a method of celestial navigation that uses sight-reduction tables to convert sextant readings to lines of position on a chart. While an instructor at the Naval Academy, Lieutenant Arthur A. Ageton, USN, devised a method that simplified the process of solving a spherical celestial triangle to obtain a navigation line of position. His book *Dead Reckoning Altitude and Azimuth Table* was first published by the Government Printing Office in 1932.
† USS *Reina Mercedes* (IX-25), captured during the Spanish-American War, served as a station ship at the Naval Academy from 1912 to 1957. Until 1940, midshipmen being punished for various disciplinary infractions slept and took meals on board the ship but continued to go to classes ashore.

Captain Schwab: I never had to deal with them much at the executive or commandant level, except when I was one of the editors of *The Log*. They would call you in, and they'd say some article or something was a little unnecessarily raunchy. But we could usually clean that up in about two seconds. We didn't have much trouble, even then, on editorial censorship at all. They were very good about it. Of course, we did most of the cutting ourselves. The superintendents, Admiral Sellers and later Admiral Brown, were at rarefied levels and remote from contact with midshipmen.[*] Admiral Sellers was unique in that he had been CinCUS in 1933-34.

Paul Stillwell: "Raunchy" then would probably be very tame by today's standards.

Captain Schwab: Oh, yes. It was usually objectionable if we were a little too specific in identifying somebody who had girl problems. They didn't want you to do that in something that went out to families.

Paul Stillwell: There was no formal honor code then.[†] What was the teaching in that area?

Captain Schwab: That's right, we didn't have any honor code as such, as they did at West Point. From my observation of West Point, the cadets had all sorts of "honorable" ways to evade the honor code. For example, if a cadet put his name sign in a certain position that meant, "Don't ask me any questions." Cadets were supposed to turn themselves in. Midshipmen were told that honor was on top of the belt buckles. One line of "Anchors Aweigh" stresses "honor over all."

Paul Stillwell: What do you mean about the belt buckles?

---

[*] Rear Admiral David F. Sellers, USN, was superintendent of the Naval Academy from June 1934 to February 1938. Rear Admiral Wilson Brown, USN, was superintendent from February 1938 to February 1941. As a four-star admiral Sellers was Commander in Chief U.S. Fleet (CinCUS) from 10 June 1933 to 15 June 1934. As was the practice in that era, he reverted to his permanent rank of rear admiral when no longer in a four-star billet.

[†] The honor concept now in use was devised in the early 1950s. For details see the Naval Institute oral history of Vice Admiral William P. Lawrence, USN (Ret.).

Captain Schwab: Well, "duty, honor and country" was inscribed on the belt buckles that held your bayonet on parades. Honor was on top. I guess there was probably a remnant of the old southern tradition that gentlemen just didn't do anything dishonorable. We didn't need an honor code, because we were supposed to know automatically what was and wasn't honorable. Then, of course, a lot of us, I guess, went by the thought that if you didn't get caught it was honorable.

Paul Stillwell: Well, also the midshipmen have this inevitable temptation to beat the system. Did you get involved in some of those pranks or what have you?

Captain Schwab: No, nothing serious. The only ones I can remember involved quiz information. When they would have quizzes or tests early in the day in one battalion, the people in that other battalion, if your battalion was getting it later, would run over and tell you what the questions were. This was not considered dishonorable because it was considered stupidity by the authorities that they did it that way. But people used to do that. "Getting a gouge," I guess they called it. Usually only those having low marks would use this system, especially athletes. That's about the only thing. I don't know if anybody ever got caught doing that. I imagine all the instructors knew about it. In most cases, just to answer the daily questions on short notice, you had to study anyhow. You didn't gain much by that. Of course, final exams were given simultaneously for any given subject.

Paul Stillwell: Was there a real sense of competition fostered? You mentioned high school had really been competitive.

Captain Schwab: Oh, yes. We were told pretty early on that class standing was vital in the Navy. For example, it affected where you went as far as choice of ships, although that was partially a lottery in first-class year. Your choice of ships and your position on the ship, even your room on a ship, and date of promotion and so on, which of course then involved money, started off with your class standing on graduation from the Naval Academy. The higher you stood, the better off you were. On the other hand, they also pointed out that if you were a well-rounded naval citizen, both academically and on the athletic side, you'd probably do better in the long run than somebody who was all books or all athletics. We had to get out of our room every afternoon and go out and do something, either organized or disorganized, on the athletic side.

Paul Stillwell: What sorts of things did you do?

Captain Schwab: Well, I tried running, and I tried wrestling, and I tried fencing. But then I got so involved with *The Log* that I had little time between classes and study hours. Normally I would go out and run a little bit. Sometimes we'd go out and have a makeup game of softball or something of that sort, maybe just throw a ball around. You just had to go out and do something to get the air in your lungs, I guess. The people who didn't do anything, or avoided it, were called the "radiator squad." I don't know if they still call them that. As they say, some of my best friends were in the "radiator squad." A couple of the officers I already mentioned who made admiral never went out to do anything extracurricular. I always wondered about that, how it worked, but apparently their inactivity as midshipmen didn't make much difference. On the other hand, some who were football stars didn't rise very high either, so it must have been fair in the fleet, at least for my class. I know in some earlier classes, good football players often made admiral, but they were much smaller classes.

Paul Stillwell: Did you have any awareness at that time of the Green Bowl Society?*

Captain Schwab: I heard about it, but that was about it. I never had anything to do with it at all. We heard that once you got into the BuOrd gun club and the BuPers club, it was called Bureau of Navigation then—you probably would be in good shape for promotions

---

* The Green Bowl Society was a secret group of Naval Academy graduates who tapped promising young naval officers for membership and then allegedly aided them in getting favorable duty assignments as a means of enhancing their promotion prospects. The existence of the society became known throughout the Navy shortly after the end of World War II.

and assignments.* I don't know if that really was true.

Paul Stillwell: Well, the ascendancy of the gun club came to an end fairly soon after that.

Captain Schwab: Yes, the gun club was said to be the way to go. Also, the word was if you wanted to get a command early, the thing to do was go in submarines. And, of course, in those days there was the uniform appeal of the submarine service. In the *Pennsylvania*, for instance, they didn't wear dungarees as they called them then, blue jeans. The only time you wore dungarees was when you were actually in the dirty part of gunnery or the engineering spaces, that's all. The rest of the time, even for inspections, you had to wear blues or whites. Only submariners and aviators wore khaki.

When the *Pennsylvania* was in Pearl Harbor at Ten-Ten Dock we could see the submariners going out all wearing khakis.† They all looked sort of relaxed; and you were out there on the quarterdeck with your sword, and then later a .45. In Long Beach we had our full-dress inspections every Saturday with cocked hat, epaulets, and frock coat. They don't have those items anymore. When you were in a big ship—a battleship, flagship—and you were in a homeport such as Long Beach, they'd have formal dances once a month at a hotel ballroom. Then you got to use all your graduation outfit, tails, for example, and "railroad" trousers with gold stripes. The California girls really liked to be invited to these dances.

Paul Stillwell: Well, you were really on the tail end of that prewar Navy, which was a different style of living.

Captain Schwab: Yes, it was very formal. Your uniforms were always in good shape for inspection, because that was the only time you ever wore your frock coat, cocked hat, and epaulets.

---

* BuOrd – Bureau of Ordnance. "Gun Club" was a term used to describe the officers—particularly those with graduate degrees in ordnance—who served in battleships, cruisers, and destroyers. They felt that the warships' big guns were, and would remain, the predominant naval weapons. Once aircraft carriers came to prominence early in World War II, the influence of the Gun Club began to wane. The Bureau of Navigation made officer assignments to various duties in the years prior to World War II. In 1942 it was renamed the Bureau of Naval Personnel (BuPers).
† Ten-Ten Dock, which was part of the Pearl Harbor Navy Yard, was named because it was 1,010 feet long.

Paul Stillwell: What do you remember about the graduation ceremony in Annapolis?

Captain Schwab: Well, it was out in what they used to call Thompson Stadium. I guess it doesn't exist anymore.

Paul Stillwell: No.

Captain Schwab: It was the football stadium in those days—very small. Admiral Leahy, the CNO, gave the speech, in which he pointed out that the class of '39 was living in a period that was going to lead to tremendous changes in world history, and he was right.[*] I still have a copy of his speech around here someplace.

Paul Stillwell: How did you come to be assigned to the *Pennsylvania*?[†]

Captain Schwab: In our first-class year we were given a list of things we might want to do. If you wanted to go to a cruiser or a battleship or what have you, or an aircraft carrier, you put in your chit. I thought battleships—there were 15 of them—would be pretty good. I just put in for a battleship and in standing high enough in the class I got on the *Pennsylvania*. It was interesting, because I went through three CinCUSes, as the fleet commander was called them then: Admiral Bloch and Admiral Richardson, who was canned, and Admiral Kimmel.[‡] So I got to see all three of them.

While I was in the *Pennsylvania* I put in twice for Submarine School. The first time I put in for it, it was right after I had fleeted up to be secondary battery control officer, when all of the jaygees and lieutenants went off to the new destroyers and

---

[*] Admiral William D. Leahy, USN, was Chief of Naval Operations from 2 January 1937 to 1 August 1939.
[†] USS *Pennsylvania* (BB-38) was commissioned 12 June 1916. Following modernization in the early 1930s she had a standard displacement of 33,384 tons, was 608 feet long and 106 feet in the beam. Her top speed was 21 knots. She was armed with 12 14-inch guns and 12 5-inch/51 broadside guns and eight 5-inch/25 antiaircraft guns. The *Pennsylvania* was the flagship for Commander in Chief U.S. fleet, a four-star admiral. At the time that officer, whose title was abbreviated CinCUS, was the U.S. Navy's senior admiral in a seagoing billet.
[‡] Admiral Claude C. Bloch, USN, served as Commander in Chief U.S. Fleet from January 1938 to January 1940. Admiral James O. Richardson, USN, was CinCUS from 6 January 1940 to 1 February 1941. His relief, Admiral Husband E. Kimmel, USN, was designated Commander in Chief Pacific Fleet rather than CinCUS. Kimmel was relieved of the fleet command on 17 December 1941 in the wake of the Japanese attack on Pearl Harbor.

cruisers.* The first request was denied since I was the only officer on board who had ever fired a secondary battery practice. Hard to believe since this was the flagship of the United States Fleet in 1940. You had to be two years out in the fleet to go to sub school, but they had some exceptions then.

Later in 1940, I found another officer on a cruiser that was going down to Australia, a classmate of mine. His name was Curtis Spencer, and he had a girlfriend in Pearl Harbor.† That's where we were, of course, and Spencer said he could take my gun job on the *Pennsylvania* if I took his job on the cruiser. He wanted to stay in Pearl, since that was where the *Pennsylvania* was supposed to remain. The cruiser was the *Houston*.‡ I'd have been lost early in World War II.§ But he was supposed to be detached from the *Houston* anyhow to go back to one of the new destroyers. So we agreed to swap. Fortunately, my orders came in for Submarine School, and the swap was cancelled, and I stayed in the *Pennsylvania* for a few more weeks.**

Captain Cutts, my skipper since 1939, was just being relieved by then-Captain Cooke, Savvy Cooke.†† Both captains were submariners, so we all heard a lot about his submarines. The *Pennsylvania*, after the change of command, was due to go out to sea for one week or ten days of training. Captain Cooke decided to detach me in order to meet my sub school orders. The CinCUS staff in the *Pennsylvania*, many of them submarine officers, learned I was going to Submarine School. They said, "You know, if you are detached now, they'll probably send you back to the States on a tanker, and you'll stand watches all the way back to the West Coast. You should have a better trip than that on your way to sub school."

Lieutenant Commander Black was a submarine officer on the staff. He had some sort of temporary orders written, assigning me ashore in Pearl Harbor. He found out the schedule for all the Navy tankers going back and arranged my order dates for May 1941,

---

* Jaygee – lieutenant (junior grade).
† Ensign John Curtis Spencer, USN, was then serving in the heavy cruiser *Houston* (CA-30).
‡ The heavy cruiser *Houston* (CA-30) relieved her sister ship *Augusta* (CA-31) as Asiatic Fleet flagship on 22 November 1940 at Manila in the Philippines.
§ The *Houston* was sunk in the Battle of Sunda Strait the night of 28 February-1 March 1942.
** Spencer managed to avoid the fate of the *Houston*. He transferred to the battleship *Oklahoma*, which was sunk at Pearl Harbor, but he survived.
†† Captain Elwin F. Cutts, USN, commanded the *Pennsylvania* (BB-38) from 19 June 1939 to 27 February 1941. Captain Charles M. Cooke, USN, commanded the ship from 27 February 1941 to 3 April 1942.

so I missed them all. My orders were then written for me to ride back on the SS *Matsonia*, which was a Matson Lines liner. In order to do that, when the *Pennsylvania* went out, I had to be ashore. I was assigned to *Argonne*, Base Force flagship, but awaiting the *Matsonia*. During my waiting time, I was asked to go on shore patrol with the Army in Honolulu, which was another experience.

Paul Stillwell: I'd like to hear about it.

Captain Schwab: It was truly different from a usual naval assignment.

Paul Stillwell: What was different about it?

Captain Schwab: Well, in those days prostitution on Oahu was monitored by the Army. On Hotel Street in Honolulu was the main red-light area. They called it "Whore-tel Street." You probably saw the movie or read the book *From Here to Eternity*; well, that was pretty factual as far as those places were concerned.* I got to go make the rounds with this young Army officer. He had a book with pictures in it of the different girls who had been found to be diseased in the weekly or twice-weekly physical inspections. The ones that were suspected of having or actually had some sort of venereal disease had to leave. They were given 48 hours to get out of Honolulu. One of the Army officer's jobs, besides making sure enlisted men didn't get in trouble, was to check these places where the blacklisted girls were last known to have worked to see that they were gone. We had to look at all these pictures as identification.

One of the places was the same hotel that was in *From Here to Eternity*, and this beautiful blonde girl was in one of these pictures. I asked the Army officer, "God, why would she become a prostitute?"

He said, "Well, you know they make a lot of money. Then they go back to the mainland and get married or start a shop of some sort. The ones who are inevitably

---

* James Jones's novel *From Here to Eternity* (New York: Charles Scribner's Sons, 1951) was made into a popular movie in 1953. It contained a depiction of Army garrison life in Hawaii's Schofield Barracks in the period leading up to the Japanese attack on Pearl Harbor in 1941.

diseased go out to the Philippines or someplace in Asia, and they just go down the drain. You never hear from them again."

As it turned out, the *Pennsylvania* came in before the *Matsonia* sailed, so a group of my classmates—Rhythm Moore, J. V. Wilson, Don Furlong and four or five others from the *Pennsylvania*—took me out to Lau Yee Chai's restaurant in Honolulu for my last night.[*] Late that night they poured me on to the *Matsonia*. All my gear was on board already. I was in a two-man room, upper and lower bunk. I woke up in the morning, and there were a big bottle of 1,000 aspirin and a big bottle of Dewars White Label scotch on the side table. There was also a note that said, "Take whichever's the best." I woke up to getting-under way noises and I heard this groan in the upper bunk. It was from an engineer, a young fellow who'd been out in either Wake or Midway. They rotated him, and he'd been out there for some months and was on his way back to the mainland.

We got up just as the *Matsonia* was getting under way. On deck they a put a lei around your neck. You threw it in the water, and if it floated toward shore you were going back someday to Honolulu. My lei told the truth, because I did go back later on. My roommate looked awful. There was a little bar at the deck level. We went into the little bar, and I stuck a quarter in the slot machine. I hadn't played a slot machine in my life, and it hit the jackpot, which was guaranteed for $25.00. Now, now you could get a lot more, I guess. This $25.00 paid for all of my drinks for four days all the way back to Los Angeles.

Later on that day at sea, after we had something to eat, we were walking around the deck, and there was this familiar-looking beautiful blonde girl sitting in a deck chair. The engineer looked at her and said, "Boy, I'd like to talk to her." We walked around the deck a little bit more, and the next thing I know he'd disappeared. Suddenly, I saw him playing ping-pong with the blonde girl. I went back to the cabin to clean up for dinner. He came back and I said, "Hey, I remembered where I've seen her." And I told him about the book with the pictures of the diseased prostitutes.

---

[*] Ensign George E. Moore II, USN; Ensign John V. Wilson, USN; Ensign Donald Furlong, USN.

He said, "Oh hell." Then he said, "I've been out on that island so long, nothing can bother me." I didn't see him for the next three days. Never saw the girl either; I imagine they served all their meals in whatever room she was in.

Paul Stillwell: So he was getting professional treatment?

Captain Schwab: I don't know what he was getting, but, anyhow, to the best of my observation, that was the same girl as in the picture book. She never showed up again on the *Matsonia*. I don't know whatever happened to the engineer, but that's the story.

On the *Matsonia*, going back to the mainland, there were only two bachelor officers. One was going to flight school—he was a jaygee—and I was going to Submarine School. We met four young schoolteachers who had been out there for some vacation, so we had a great time all the way to Los Angeles. Then all the way across the country, the jaygee and I had a nice time on the train, also with the teachers. We went all the way across the country on the train in those days. I finally reached New York, and after a week or two of leave I reported to Submarine School. When I reported, Captain Cutts was the commanding officer, and he signed me in.* He had been my commanding officer in the *Pennsylvania* only a month before. That's sort of an unusual thing to have happen.

Paul Stillwell: Was he the skipper when you reported to the ship initially?

Captain Schwab: Yes, he had taken command only five days before I reported.

Paul Stillwell: What are your impressions of him as the captain of the *Pennsylvania*?

Captain Schwab: He was a very quiet officer and very aware of our inexperience. One thing I remember, he was very careful about: he didn't want anybody to become an alcoholic. You didn't go ashore in the battleships in those days after reporting unless all

---

* Cutts served as commanding officer of Submarine Base, New London, Connecticut, from 3 June 1941 to 14 January 1944.

of your equipment was there. In other words, if you didn't have all your full dress equipment and all your other gear, and if you hadn't checked out all the different check-off lists on the ship, you just didn't leave the ship. The railroads misplace baggage then the way airlines do now. I had one classmate, Jim Hingson, whose gear was lost someplace, and he didn't get off the ship for about six weeks.* But he finally found everything. He came from Alabama, and the railroad had sidetracked his gear down there.

Anyhow, after most of us qualified to leave the ship, Captain Cutts treated us just as if we were plebes. We were all invited out to his house after a week or so. He said, "We have a small bus to take you back to the ship after the reception at my house. What I want you to do, if you drink, is just keep drinking until you feel that you are tipsy. Then remember what the sensation was before that, and then in the future always stop before you get to that point." I remember that the soles of my feet would start tingling. From then on, the minute the soles of my feet would start tingling, I would stop drinking. It always worked.

Paul Stillwell: Did you have this system of calling on the skipper?

Captain Schwab: Yes. You called on all the ship's officers. You had your calling cards, of course, and you called on the skipper, and you called on your division officer and the head of the department at their homes ashore. You stayed only 20 minutes; you had one drink, and you talked. Lieutenant commanders and above, you called on only once usually, but the lieutenants were very kind to ensigns. There were quite a few of them who would invite us out in groups of four, and they'd have a poker party. We'd bring the pretzels, and they'd provide the beer. It was really a very family-type thing. They'd feed you—sandwiches and beer, pretzels. There were only a few difficult officers. Lieutenant Commander G. D. Linke, who was the gunnery officer, was one of the difficult ones.†

Paul Stillwell: In what way was he difficult?

---

* Ensign James M. Hingson, USN.
† Lieutenant Commander Gerald D. Linke, USN.

Captain Schwab: Well, if anything went wrong in your division, even something minor, you didn't go ashore the next weekend. No explanations were accepted. He was tough that way. I suppose he was trying to implant the principle of responsibility, whether we were there or not. That was about it, but we didn't appreciate his arbitrariness too much.

Paul Stillwell: Were there any special privileges with the *Pennsylvania*? Was it considered especially desirable to serve in the fleet flagship?

Captain Schwab: In the first place, when you were in ports where you had to use officers' boats, you had better, faster boats than anybody. They had a 35-foot motorboat that was beautiful—a great, big fast thing. And, of course, every once in a while you'd get to ride, maybe just by chance, in the admiral's barge, and that was considered a special event. I guess that was the era of simple pleasures. You always had the best anchorages. If in Pearl Harbor, for instance, we were at Ten-Ten Dock, which is the closest place you can just walk ashore from.

On the other hand, ship's officers came under the scrutiny of the staff too. I remember when we first went to Pearl Harbor in 1940.[*] Everybody said, "Oh, boy, aloha shirts." That lasted about two days before CinCUS orders officers to wear coats, ties, and hats when leaving ships to go ashore. Admiral Richardson was CinCUS. So what we'd do was take our swimming trunks and an aloha shirt. We'd go out to Fort DeRussy, put our coats, hats, and ties in a locker there, and put on our aloha shirts.[†] But when we left the ship and when we returned to the ship, we had to be wearing a coat and a hat.

Paul Stillwell: Was there a high degree of spit and polish in the ship?

Captain Schwab: Oh, yes, it was continual. Everything was in beautiful shape, old but in beautiful shape. But there was a lot more to it than spit and polish. For instance, I

---

[*] Fleet Problem XXI took place in the Hawaiian area in the spring of 1940. When it was completed, President Franklin D. Roosevelt directed that the fleet remain at Pearl Harbor rather than return to its bases on the West Coast. The idea was that leaving the fleet in Hawaii would serve as a deterrent to Japanese aggression in the Far East. Admiral Richardson protested, saying the fleet could best be supported on the West Coast, and the President fired him in early 1941.
[†] Fort DeRussy was the site of a coastal defense battery on Waikiki Beach in Honolulu, Hawaii.

rotated out of the gunnery department and became the assistant first lieutenant under Samuel P. Moncure.* One of the things that they started to do then, getting ready for war, was to be sure the ship could button up against poison gas. Memories of World War I, I guess. Everybody, I remember, was sure we were going to war but didn't know when. But junior officers really didn't pay much attention to things like that in mid-1939.

They'd have these movies after World War II started.† They came from the British, showing warfare, different types, mostly naval warfare for us, and they'd show them in the wardroom. We had so-called tactical lectures along with the movies. The war was all so distant. I don't think we had any sense of immediacy of the possibility of going to war. When the war did start in '39, I was playing cribbage in the JO mess with somebody when a classmate of mine came in and said, "Hey, the Germans are at war. They invaded Poland, and the British have declared war."

I said, "Ah, you're kidding."

He said, "I'll bet you a dime." So I lost a dime. I mean, that's how it was. We didn't have any real feeling for the crisis. There was no urgent sense of getting ready for war. This was the case, even though readiness directives came down from high, such as the one ordering readiness in anti-gas warfare. I was given the job to get ready. There were lots of barrels down in the hold of the ship, containing World War I gas masks. About half of them were in good shape. The material was disintegrating on many of them. But I had to train everybody in how to put on the gas mask on the ship. One time the captain decided, when we were out at sea, that they'd really button up, as if we were really going to be gassed. It was discovered, after an hour or so, that it gets awfully hot in the conning tower; that's the main battle command area. Nobody was up on the bridge; the command control people were in a sealed armored section under the bridge. There was no air-conditioning in those days. The captain said, "I know that on this ship there's a cooling system that's supposed to take care of the main control station."

So as the assistant first lieutenant, I was put in charge of finding and fixing the cooling system. It was like a refrigeration plant; it also had trays with chemicals that

---

* Lieutenant Moncure was in the construction and repair department, which was responsible for the material maintenance and appearance of the ship's exterior and also for damage control.
† World War II began on 1 September 1939, when German ground forces invaded Poland. Two days later Great Britain and France declared war on Germany.

were put in to reduce CO_2 levels. It was like a submarine, because it was a closed system. We never did try the chemical trays. I found out that when you tried to turn on the cooling plant, nothing happened. I eventually had to trace the whole system. I found out that a couple of valves had frozen shut and had it all fixed. There was very little control over temperature; the people in main control literally had to wear peacoats because it was so cold. We were only refrigerating the spaces, not air-conditioning. There was no way of carrying off moisture, so it was cold and damp. In the process of looking for gas masks, we had to check all of the watertight spaces. We found all sorts of things besides these gas masks that had never been listed on inventories. We found that some of the so-called blisters, when you went into them, had been used for storage.* Apparently this took place when the *Pennsylvania* was getting modernized, or getting tripod masts instead of cage masts, whatever they were doing.

On the other side of the dock area at Philadelphia was the USS *Florida*, which was going out of commission.† So some enterprising souls had liberated all the *Florida*'s wicker furniture. We found wicker furniture of all types, all labeled USS *Florida*. That all disappeared in a hurry—to where, I don't know. Of course, it wasn't on anybody's inventory.

Paul Stillwell: Did you find out that the watertight integrity was not very good?

Captain Schwab: No, we found that it was surprisingly good. All of the gaskets and fittings were in good shape. We just found extra things in the various voids and spaces that no one knew were there. There was an inventory list of ship's equipment in the first lieutenant's department. All the gas masks were on there, for instance, but nobody was exactly sure where they were in the ship. The compartment numbers were all blurred or something, but we finally found them. Things of that sort kept happening.

Paul Stillwell: Well, the first lieutenant was responsible in that era for damage control.

---

* The battleship *Pennsylvania* (BB-38) was modernized at the Philadelphia Navy Yard from June 1929 to May 1931. In the process her beam was widened with the addition of external compartments, nicknamed "blisters" that were to minimize damage if the ship was torpedoed.
† Under the terms of the London Naval Treaty of 1930, the battleship *Florida* (BB-31) was decommissioned 16 February 1931 and scrapped later that at the Philadelphia Navy Yard.

Captain Schwab: That's right.

Paul Stillwell: How much training and practice were there in damage control techniques?

Captain Schwab: Each department had its own damage control parties. It was a fairly good system. It was just a question of shutting the doors and valves. The damage control lockers had repair gear and breathing apparatus. Then all the passageways had these long beams of wood out there, in case you had to bolster up a bulkhead.

Paul Stillwell: Shoring.

Captain Schwab: Shoring, in case something started caving in. We had collision mats, submersible pumps, and things of that sort. I'd say, for that period it was probably adequate. There were a lot of watertight compartments on a battleship. There was a problem, however, because of all the weight, on all the battleships. Because of all the extra things that had been piled on, the side armor rode very low in the water. They began a big weight-reduction program. They started taking off all sorts of topside things: boats and so on. It didn't help much; you'd only get a couple of inches more freeboard out of it, at the most.

Paul Stillwell: She was not a flush-deck ship in that the stern weather deck was lower than the forecastle. Did you find that was pretty wet if you got in a seaway?

Captain Schwab: Yes, it was pretty wet, but you'd learn not to go aft in heavy weather. You could stay around right at the break of the deck and be all right. *Pennsylvania* was a very stable ship, actually. She didn't roll nearly as much as the *Wyoming* or the *New York*, but she was bigger.[*]

Paul Stillwell: Well, especially after they took the turrets off the *Wyoming*, that would be a problem.

---

[*] These were the ships in which Midshipman Schwab made summer training cruises.

What do you remember about the executive officer, Commander McCrea?[*]

Captain Schwab: Well, he was great. He was one of the finest officers I ever came in contact with, for inspiring us to do good work. He also had a great sense of humor. He had a slogan that he'd give to all the young officers at the end of any talk he'd give them. That was: "A little ginger 'neath the tail, will oft for lack of brains avail." We all remembered that. There's not an officer who was there then who doesn't quote that—if you'd mention John L. McCrea.

Most of the execs were pretty standoffish on the other ships, but McCrea would go ashore for group outings or games with the officers. During Fleet Problem XXI in April '40, for instance, we were moored off Maui, and he organized ball games. Maui is now a tourist resort, but there wasn't anything there then except a big beer hall with six inches of sawdust on the deck. But before any partying occurred, we'd always have a softball game. And it would be the officers versus the enlisted men. McCrea was always there playing. On each base there would be a keg of beer, and if you got to the base you could have another drink. You couldn't have a drink till you got to that base. I don't know how they kept it cool, now that I think of it. Things like that built up ship spirits. He'd also take us on different trips. We all went with him, a whole bunch of us, to explore the crater of Haleakala. That's where we learned about silversword, the plant that grows only there. He was interested in all such unusual things, and he made sure we got to see them. He also had a phenomenal memory for faces. Years later, when he was vice admiral, I ran into him in a Pentagon passageway. I said, "How are you, Admiral? I haven't seen you in a long time." He immediately knew my last name; I didn't have to tell him anything. I don't know how he did it, because I didn't look the same. He was a splendid officer of the old school.

Paul Stillwell: You mentioned the preparations for war. Certainly the war in Europe would have brought home the idea that airplanes were playing a big part in it. How capable was the antiaircraft gunnery?

---

[*] Commander John L. McCrea, USN. The oral history of McCrea, who retired as a vice admiral, is in the Naval Institute collection.

Captain Schwab: It was pretty bad, because we had trouble hitting anything. Even when they would tow floats behind very slow planes during firing practice, we had trouble hitting anything. All we had were 5-inch/25s for AA guns.

Paul Stillwell: Probably had some .50 calibers, too, didn't you?

Captain Schwab: We had .50 calibers, and then they put some 1.1 guns on there.* The 1.1s they gave us didn't work too well; they jammed up. They had many .50-caliber machine guns. I know when we were in port in Pearl Harbor, they always kept .50 calibers up in the fighting tops, and there were always two of them manned all the time when we were in port. They were manned on December 7, I'm sure. I don't know if they had the 5-inch/25s manned, but there wasn't much you could do with any of those. Our antiaircraft gunnery wasn't very good.

Paul Stillwell: You were with the secondary battery for a while. How often did you practice?

Captain Schwab: Oh, we had a whole series of practices each year. They had a regular gunnery year cycle we'd go through. There was individual gun practice, short-range battle practice, long-range battle practice, and then they'd have force practice with both the turret and broadside guns. They'd fire everything on one side at once. The whole ship would jump sideways about six feet or more. That was awe-inspiring. Have you ever been on one of the battleships when they did that—everything going at once?

Paul Stillwell: Not everything.

Captain Schwab: Yes, they had all the turrets and 5-inch/51s shooting to, say, starboard, and the ship just goes "kalunk." If you were up in the mast in force practice, it was really frightening. The mast actually whipped. Fire control was terrible. They had the Ford

---

* Early in World War II, a number of U.S. Navy ships were outfitted with 1.1-inch antiaircraft guns. But they were unreliable, prone to jamming, so they were soon replaced by better guns, the 20-millimeter and 40-millimeter.

Mark I range keeper for the secondary battery. It was very primitive: no electronics, of course, all mechanical analog gearing.

Paul Stillwell: Did you have any sort of director for the 5-inch guns?

Captain Schwab: Oh, yes, there was a director. There were directors up in the secondary forward and secondary aft, one atop each tripod mast. It was a follow-the-pointer system. The pointer and trainer on the gun had to match the pointer on the little repeater at the gun for director fire. They could also do local control. All short-range practice was fired with local control at the gun. Battle practice was director salvo fire.

Paul Stillwell: What would you have, let's say, for antiaircraft?

Captain Schwab: The antiaircraft battery had a little director, too, on the boat deck. There wasn't much to it; there was no fire-control radar. It was all by guess and by God. The battleships started to get so-called "bedspring" radars in '41, but they were for search only.

Paul Stillwell: Did the antiaircraft director compute a lead angle at all?

Captain Schwab: Yes, it did all that. I guess they hadn't come out with proximity shells then, but we heard that they were working on them at Columbia University.[*] That helped later.

Paul Stillwell: You really had to guess the range and set the mechanical time fuze for that.

Captain Schwab: That's right, exactly. As they did for surface gunnery, they tried to get a spread in there; they'd shoot around the target. Against a surface ship you'd guess from

---

[*] The proximity fuze for 5-inch antiaircraft projectiles was also known as the VT, or variable time, fuze. It contained a small radio transponder that detonated the projectile when it got near a target, thus eliminating the need for a direct hit.

your binoculars how far something was, and then you'd try to straddle by watching shell splashes. And when you straddled, you'd fire for effect, moving your fire back and forth over the target. That was about it—very crude. How we ever hit anything at long ranges, I'll never know. In our secondary short-range battery practice, though, we used to hit a lot; we did pretty well on that. Those 5-inch/51s had high muzzle velocity—3,500 feet per second, I think. Very flat trajectory, and they were accurate—like shooting a rifle. Whereas the 5-inch/25s, you know, the shells went out in a big arc. They hardly ever hit surface targets. They rarely hit anything.

Paul Stillwell: They had a parabola.

Captain Schwab: That's right; they were not much good. They had low muzzle velocity. I think they were around 2,400 feet per second—very low.

Paul Stillwell: Were you in the turrets at all during firing?

Captain Schwab: No, not on the *Pennsylvania*. But on one midshipman cruise I was in a turret. That was sort of impressive, even frightening. You know the way they ram those shells and powder home. In *Pennsylvania* I was a safety observer a couple of times in the turrets.

Paul Stillwell: Was there great emphasis on safety in handling the ammunition?

Captain Schwab: Oh, definitely, yes. They pointed out that one of the sure ways to get a new set of safety regulations was to have a casualty. That was where all the regulations came from, casualties, especially deaths.

Paul Stillwell: What are your memories of the three different admirals you had on board, the fleet commanders in chief?

Captain Schwab: Admiral Bloch was the first one. He was a white-haired, very distinguished, very staid gentleman. I don't remember him ever talking to anybody, especially the officer of the deck, except to salute when he left the ship. Admiral Richardson had a sense of humor. He talked a couple of times to all of us in the wardroom. He told us about things going on in Europe, which most of the young officers didn't pay much attention to. They wanted to get ashore probably. Besides, Europe was far away. We all knew that he'd gone back to Washington and had an argument with the President, and was relieved for that.

Paul Stillwell: Which he lost, yes.

Captain Schwab: Yes. He apparently told President Roosevelt that the fleet was a sitting duck in Pearl Harbor; it was no place for it to be.* The best place for it to be was on the West Coast. Roosevelt wanted to have it out there as pressure on the Japanese. That ended the argument.

Admiral Kimmel was a very strict. For example, if he came back to the ship at night and you were the officer of the deck you really had to practically do full honors, even if he was in civilian clothes. We thought he was rather pompous.

Paul Stillwell: Why don't you describe an officer of the deck watch in port?

Captain Schwab: Well, before the limited national emergency, we were always in the uniform of the day, blues on the West Coast and whites in tropical areas or Hawaii. You wore your sword, and you had a Marine bugler there all the time. Everything on the ship was run by bugles and boatswain's call, mostly the bugle. The buglers were the most interesting to have on watch. Most of them had been out in China, and you heard all kinds of good stories from them while you were standing watch.

---

* Franklin D. Roosevelt was President of the United States from 4 March 1933 to 12 April 1945. For details, see Admiral James O. Richardson, USN (Ret.), and Vice Admiral George C. Dyer, USN (Ret.), *On the Treadmill to Pearl Harbor: The Memoirs of Admiral James O. Richardson, USN (Retired)* (Washington, D.C.: Naval History Division, Department of the Navy, 1973).

You had a small officer of the deck compartment at the break of the deck, a little closet, actually. The quartermaster stayed there, and he kept the log. The main duty of the OOD was to run the boat schedule when you were anchored out. If you were alongside the pier, the main duty there was to make sure that people leaving the ship were in the uniform of the day. There was an officer of the deck and a junior officer of the deck. The officer of the deck, if you were at anchor, was always on the starboard side of the quarterdeck, which was the officers' side.

Alongside a pier, the officer of the deck was always on the side toward the pier. The port side at anchor was where the junior officer of the deck stayed, and he took care of all the enlisted men. On the junior officer of the deck side the enlisted men would go over in groups in motor launches after being inspected for the proper uniform. When the men came back to the ship, we inspected for contraband such as bottles of booze, things of that sort. If they were a little under the weather, why, you sent for somebody from their division to take them and put them to bed. You didn't do anything to them, usually. On the starboard side, as on both sides, you had to run the boat schedule. Then you had to watch for other ships approaching, for safety reasons.

Paul Stillwell: Render honors.

Captain Schwab: The OOD had to render honors to passing ships. When anchored, you had to take periodic fixes to make sure you weren't drifting. It was mainly a question of tending the house.

Paul Stillwell: Well, you probably relied a great deal on that bugler to see that the schedule was carried out.

Captain Schwab: Oh, yes, he was the schedule expert. In the morning and in the evening, on the *Pennsylvania*, a flagship, the band would do the honors, National Anthem, flag salutes, and so on. In port in the evening you had to make sure everything was rigged for the movie. The daily schedule was made out by the executive officer's office, and it was cut and dried most of the time; you knew what was going to happen. The only time any real planning was required was when there were change-of-command ceremonies, or when we were in a port where we were entertaining the locals. Then you had to rig awnings and also get tables with the ceremonial silver punch set out there and all that sort of stuff; that was fancy. Aside from that, it was routine. When we went to a limited national emergency, after the war started in Europe, we took off our swords and put on .45s. Most of us hadn't seen them except when we were in the Naval Academy and shot them.

Paul Stillwell: When was that, that you made that switch?

Captain Schwab: I think that was in 1940, if I'm not mistaken, I'm not sure. It was called a limited emergency then.

Paul Stillwell: The unlimited, I think, was in about June of '41.[*]

Captain Schwab: Yes, it was. Let's see, when was the destroyer *Reuben James* sunk?[†] That was in '41, wasn't it?

Paul Stillwell: That was around Halloween of '41.

Captain Schwab: Yes, that's when they went to unlimited, when the Germans started shooting at us. Well, of course, before that, when you were in port they had lots of little drills, where security testers would come around with fake bombs. We had security patrols constantly going around. We had our enlisted men patrolling in groups of two on the pier in Pearl Harbor. They wore black uniforms so nobody could see them. And they were wearing black or dark blue jerseys and uniforms and hats; they were supposed not to be too visible; all had .45s.

---

[*] President Franklin D. Roosevelt proclaimed an unlimited national emergency on 27 May 1941. He had previously declared a limited national emergency on 8 September 1939, shortly after war began in Europe.
[†] On 31 October 1941, the *U-552* torpedoed and sank the four-stack destroyer *Reuben James* (DD-245) with the loss of 115 lives. She was escorting a convoy from Halifax, Nova Scotia, to the British Isles and sank about 600 miles west of Ireland. She was the first U.S. warship lost to enemy action in World War II.

A few ships had dummy bombs slipped on board, and then they got bad marks from the fleet security officer. They didn't have anything like the SEALS or the underwater demolition teams then, but every once in a while they'd have swimmers going around and checking the hull. That was not often. In Pearl Harbor we had boat patrols every night. We had small boats with an officer and several enlisted men and submachine guns. And they'd roam all around the different lochs in the harbor and make sure the Japanese fishermen, I guess, weren't coming over to get you.

Paul Stillwell: Was there any concern about espionage on the part of the Japanese?

Captain Schwab: Civilians weren't allowed to roam around freely on the base, even before the limited emergency. But the hills overlooking Pearl Harbor had a lot of Japanese living up there. They could look down and see everything that was going on.

Before I left the *Pennsylvania* a Japanese local concessionaire for a liquor distributor invited eight of us to his house for dinner. He sent the word down to the flagship that he'd like to have eight young officers for dinner up at his house. He apparently wanted them from different ships, but on the flagship they decided that all eight would come from the *Pennsylvania*. So all eight of us went up there on a hill behind Pearl Harbor. There were six or eight Japanese men, very well dressed, and their wives or female relatives. We all sat in the regular Japanese stuff on the floor. Next to each one of us at the low table was a wife or a relative of some sort, and she did all the serving. But the women never said anything; they were just doing the serving. They weren't geisha girls.

The men discussed the affairs of the day, but nothing as if seeking information. They never asked us where our ships were going or what the Navy was doing. When we finished eating, they said the custom was that after dinner the host would tell a funny story—in English, of course. He'd tell a story, and then we all took turns telling little stories around the table. We either told simple jokes or told about some experiences ashore in Hawaii that impressed us. They clapped and laughed, even if the story wasn't very funny. The Japanese men then sang some Japanese songs, and we sang Naval

Academy songs, and that was it. After our return to the *Pennsylvania*, we were all interrogated by the intelligence people: "What happened?"

"Nothing." I don't know why the Japanese did it. I guess it was just a friendly gesture. They were trying to make us feel good, I guess. I don't understand why. Maybe they were hoping something good would come out of it.

Paul Stillwell: Well, there were a good many Japanese people who were loyal to the United States then.

Captain Schwab: Certainly, but we were told to be careful. There was a restaurant out in Waikiki owned by a German, either ex-German or actual German national; it was called the Wagon Wheel. A lot of us used to go out there, and that's where I learned to like mahi mahi, broiled in butter. As soon as the war started, they picked him up; he was a German agent. We didn't know that. You know, you'd talk about when your ship was going out next week. When you were at peace, what's the difference? Anyhow, the restaurant owner wasn't Japanese, so we didn't worry.

Paul Stillwell: You talked about the gas mask business and so forth. Did you see other signs of increasing readiness as you moved closer toward the war?

Captain Schwab: Well, as I said earlier, they went through an extensive checking of all the watertight integrity and made inspections of everything—much more than they ever had. We always had regular inspection check-off lists, but nothing as extensive as in 1940 and 1941. Of course, they didn't know when the war was going to start.

Paul Stillwell: I've seen pictures of the change of command, where Kimmel took over from Richardson in February '41, very impressive looking. What are your memories of that occasion?

Captain Schwab: Of course, I was in the one of back rows there. I was the editor of the ship's paper, too, so reported the ceremony. I don't remember anything about any speeches that they gave. In fact, I don't remember that they gave any speeches. I think they just had the normal reading of orders, as in any change of command. You'd read your orders, say, "I relieve you, sir," and that was it.

Paul Stillwell: Was there a general awareness among the ship's officers that Richardson had been fired?

Captain Schwab: Yes, even the JOs had a pretty good idea that's what had happened. Of course, it was mostly hearsay from the staff, the few staff people we talked to. There was a Lieutenant East in the staff, a communicator who kept us informed.* We got to know all the ones that are mentioned in *At Dawn We Slept*.† I can practically tell you what they looked like.

Paul Stillwell: Are there any memories of those staff officers, individuals that stand out in your mind?

Captain Schwab: Not particularly. I remember that East was short and red-haired, sort of stout. The thing is that all the staff officers ate in the wardroom mess or JO mess, except the senior ones who ate in the flag mess. The ones that ate in the wardroom or in the junior officers' mess became friends. We sort of forgot whether they were staff officers or not. So I can't really remember any specifically as staff officers.

Paul Stillwell: One who's become rather well known afterward is Admiral Layton, who was the fleet intelligence officer.‡

Captain Schwab: I didn't know him at all. If he was there when I was, he ate in the flag mess all the time.

---

* Lieutenant (junior grade) Walter J. East, USN.
† Gordon Prange, in conjunction with Donald Goldstein and Katherine V. Dillon, *At Dawn We Slept: the Untold Story of Pearl Harbor* (New York: McGraw-Hill, 1981).
‡ Lieutenant Commander Edwin T. Layton, USN. The oral history of Layton, who retired as a rear admiral, is in the Naval Institute collection. See also Layton, with Roger Pineau and John Costello, *And I Was There: Pearl Harbor and Midway—Breaking the Secrets* (New York: William Morrow, 1985).

Paul Stillwell: He reported to the staff on the seventh of December 1940, just one year before.

Captain Schwab: Well, I don't remember him at all.

Paul Stillwell: What do you remember about the Marine detachment on board?

Captain Schwab: The senior Marine officer on there was Major Wilburt Brown, a really big Marine with huge feet and hands.* He got the name Bigfoot Brown in Nicaragua in the '30s when they jokingly delivered replacement shoes to him one at a time, because the little observation plane couldn't carry more than one. But he was a great officer, great sense of humor, and I gathered had gone to the Naval Academy and left before graduation. He then went into the Marines, and wound up in Nicaragua, as I mentioned, where he made a name for himself.

A humorous exchange with him occurred when I had fleeted up to be secondary battery control officer and had control of eight 5-inch/51 guns forward. He had control of four Marine-manned guns aft; he was the secondary battery aft control officer. The forward officer, however, had control of the whole 12 in any practices. One time we were getting ready to shoot a practice. Brown called me on the sound-powered telephone and said, "You know, there's one thing that gripes me here."

I said, "What's that?"

He said, "Here I am a major, and I have to wait for a damn ensign to tell me to commence fire."—words to that effect. Would you like to hear about a boat incident involving Major Brown?

Paul Stillwell: Sure.

Captain Schwab: Well, in those days ensigns made $125.00 a month, and $18.30 subsistence, which wasn't much. You didn't have much money left for fun and games. So when you were in port, one of the nice but inexpensive things to do was to take a

---

* Major Wilburt S. Brown, USMC.

young lady out to the ship for dinner, and then take her to the movies on the ship. You were allowed at least one meal a week on your mess bill without any extra charges. And you could take your guest to the movie afterwards—it didn't cost anything—and then buy her a Coca-Cola for a nickel or so at the movies, and then take her back ashore again.

One night in Long Beach, California, when I was taking a young lady out to the ship, Major Brown was taking two ladies out to the ship. I imagine one of them was his wife. We were all in the officers' boat together, and about a third of the way out to the *Pennsylvania*, we noticed water coming up through the floorboards. I looked at Major Brown, and he looked at me, and he said, "Are you going to do something about that?"

I said, "Well, you're the senior officer present."

He said, "Oh, no, you're the senior naval officer present. I'm a Marine." So I had to take off my coat and roll up my sleeves, take off my shoes, and get down there in the bilges, find the drain plug that was loose and put it back together again. The enlisted boat crew didn't know what to do. Meanwhile, Brown had moved all the ladies up to sit up high so they didn't get their feet wet. He became a good friend.

Paul Stillwell: Did you have the feeling that they picked especially good Marines for the detachment on the fleet flagship?

Captain Schwab: I have a feeling that they were really handpicked. There's no question about it.

Paul Stillwell: What functions did they serve, other than manning those 5-inch guns?

Captain Schwab: Well, ceremonial functions primarily, and there was always a Marine following the admiral around. I guess this was a remnant from the old British Navy days, when people used to try to kill the admiral or mutiny. They'd follow the captain around too. They still do that, I think, on the flagships. The Marine follows the flag officer around. I don't think they follow the captains around anymore.

Paul Stillwell: Was there any idea that the ship might have to provide a landing party?

Captain Schwab: Yes, in theory. We did have landing drills with Marines and bluejackets. We had some sort of odd-looking little guns with big wheels on the sides. I think they were one-pounders. We used them in landing force exercises from 50-foot motor launches. There were ramps they'd throw over the bow and have gun-landing drill along with the landing party. Both Navy and Marine officers took part. The coxswains, of course, as I mentioned earlier, were all experienced seamen, so they knew what to do. We'd get the bow of the boat in as far as we could, and we'd drop an anchor over aft. And on the way in, we would drop another anchor. Then you were anchored fore and aft so you wouldn't broach in the waves. Then we'd run in on these anchors, keeping the boat lined up perpendicular to the beach. Then we would put the ramps over the bow and roll the guns over the ramps. It was really an old-fashioned exercise, something from the Mexican War days. I didn't mind being boat officer, but the worst thing was when you had to be in charge of part of the landing party and get your feet and uniform wet. That wasn't good for blues or whites. For the drills we actually wore regular service uniforms with leggings

Paul Stillwell: Did you go ashore then, ahead of a contingent of troops?

Captain Schwab: Yes, we did go ashore with bluejackets and Marines. The Marine officers led the Marines. We provided the boats for them. But we had bluejackets and naval officers in the landing party too. I don't know how effective they would have been against opposition, but used to do it that way. That's how they landed in Mexico and those places, in California in the 19th century.

Paul Stillwell: What do you remember about the aircraft on the ship?

Captain Schwab: We had floatplanes, SOC-3 biplanes.[*] They were replaced by metal-sheathed monoplanes in 1940.[†] They were launched from catapults. There was one catapult on turret number three, and one right at the stern. Before we went into port,

---

[*] The Curtiss-built SOC Seagull was a biplane that first entered fleet squadrons in 1935, primarily in a floatplane version to perform observation and scouting missions for battleships and cruisers.
[†] The Vought OS2U Kingfisher was the main floatplane used by battleships and cruisers in World War II.

they would fly in and stay at a naval air station. We launched them for observation and gunnery exercises occasionally.

They fired the planes off the catapults at sea. She ship had to be heading in a low-roll direction, and then we'd shoot them off into the wind on the up-roll. We'd tell the aviators, or particularly the aviation cadets, that if they didn't buy us a Coca-Cola at the movies, we'd shoot them on the down-roll. Catapulting was a risky business. And then when we had to recover them, they did what they called "cast recovery." The ship would turn and create a slick, and then the plane would land in that slick, taxi up and then the hook, from a winch, would be attached to a sling on the top of the plane, and a crane would hoist them back on board. Hooking the sling was a tricky operation. I never saw anybody get hurt or anything, though.

Paul Stillwell: What do you remember about the junior officers' mess? I imagine it was not as staid and formal as the wardroom.

Captain Schwab: Actually, I don't think the wardroom was very formal, but the junior officers' mess was a more democratic outfit. Of course, it was mostly all ensigns and aviation cadets; I don't think we had any jaygees there. Once you fully qualified as an officer of the deck, you moved up to the wardroom. We had a lot of fun in the JO mess. The meals were all good. We ate the same food as the wardroom. On Sunday it was nice, because everybody could sleep in, and the steward's mates served a continuous brunch, until noontime. We'd all chip in for extra equipment. All expenses were shared. On the *Pennsylvania* at first, we didn't have a wardroom record player or a radio. So we all chipped in, and we bought what was really something at that time. I can remember it well, a great big Philco radio/phonograph with a big speaker front on it, and it would take 12 records at a time. We played all sorts of records. classical and popular. Every once in a while somebody didn't like a record, and suddenly you'd find a broken record. Bing Crosby's "I'm an old Cowhand from the Rio Grande" was broken and replaced several times. They weren't the plastic records we have now; they were the old type, breakable ones, 78 rpm. It was pure democracy. They had a saying, "Rank in the JO mess is like honor among thieves." You sat in your own chair all the time.

Paul Stillwell: By seniority?

Captain Schwab: By seniority of arrival in the mess, not class standing. But it didn't make any difference; the food was the same for everyone.

Paul Stillwell: Did the blacks have any other role in the ship besides stewards?

Captain Schwab: No, the blacks were stewards and also room boys. Then we had a few Guamanians, too, who didn't do anything else.

Paul Stillwell: Did you serve as a division officer?

Captain Schwab: Yes. I started as the junior division officer in the secondary battery, the fifth division with the 5-inch broadside guns. I became fifth division officer before I was rotated to assistant first lieutenant. They rotated ensigns and jaygees through the departments. We were supposed to rotate every year. Of course, I was on there a little less than two years, so I was a year in the gunnery department and then almost a year in the first lieutenant's department. I guess my next year would have been in engineering, which I was just as glad to miss. You get enough engineering in submarines.

Paul Stillwell: What are some of the things you did in taking care of the needs of your men? Did they come to you with personal problems?

Captain Schwab: Well, most of them were bachelors, in the first place. They didn't have any family problems. I don't remember any major problems with the men at all. Minor problems existed, however. One of my men tended the incinerator. Behind the incinerator door he had a file, and he was running a bookmaking and money-lending operation. He was nominally attached to my division. He didn't have anything else to do; that was his number-one thing—running the incinerator. That became famous; that one's been written up by somebody. He had been on the *Pennsylvania* more than eight years. It was not unusual for enlisted men to stay on one ship for ten or more years.

Paul Stillwell: What was burned in the incinerator?

Captain Schwab: Oh, trash, anything that would burn, mostly paper, I guess.

Paul Stillwell: Presumably classified documents.

Captain Schwab: Classified documents, before shredders.

Paul Stillwell: You've talked about liberty in Hawaii. What do you remember about liberty in Long Beach?

Captain Schwab: In Long Beach officers went on shore leave at 4:00 o'clock. Enlisted men went on "liberty." In the first place, the official address of the *Pennsylvania* was San Pedro, which caused some confusion, because that was the naval station, address, but nobody ever went into San Pedro. It was just a little fishing village and naval depot. When officers reported out to the fleet, by mistake they always went to San Pedro, wondering why there were no officers' boats. Your first approach to your ship, in this case, was on a motor launch, because San Pedro was where they picked up the milk and supplies for the ships, and they used open motor launches. That is what I did. On the officers' boat you went in and alongside of a nice landing in Long Beach.

If you happened to have a car, which several of us did, or if you had several people owning one car, then you'd rotate driving days if the owners weren't on duty on the same days. There was a garage right at the head of the pier in Long Beach. We'd go up there and give our number, and then our car would come out. It would cost about $20.00 a month for storage and valet service for your car. You could leave it there as long as you wanted when you were away. After getting your car, you'd go into town. If you went ashore at the usual time of 4:00 o'clock, there wasn't much to do. They had something called the Army-Navy Club, which wasn't an Army-Navy Club owned by officers at all; it was a private enterprise. You could have a drink or eat there. I remember the Scotch and soda used to cost 35 cents. Everybody griped when it went up to 50 cents. I don't think it went up to more then 75 cents before 1940. It was very inexpensive. There really weren't too many things to do there. The main thing was to have a date and go over about 4:00 or 5:00 o'clock, pick her up, and bring her out to the ship for dinner and the movie. That was it. We really couldn't afford much else.

Paul Stillwell: Did you get up to Hollywood and Los Angeles?

Captain Schwab: Oh, yes. Another officer and I bought an old 1935 Pontiac, a great big sedan, very heavy. It cost $200.00, and it worked well, so we used to go up to L.A. on weekends, up there. The first weekend we went up there, they had a welcome aboard for new officers, ensigns mostly, in the Beverly Hills Hotel. This classmate, Allyn Ostroski, and I went up there to the Beverly Hills Hotel and met two nice girls. For weeks later, we'd go up there and see them. They all knew ensigns didn't have any money. The girl I was dragging was the daughter of a retired oilman who was well to do. Her brother was away at college, so I got to stay in his room at their house. I was even there for a couple of earthquakes, when the earth moved a little bit. The other officer did the same thing with a friend of the girl I knew. Then we'd invite them down to Long Beach to pay back, to the formal dances once in a while, and that was about it.

There was not much real raucous living, because in the first place, we couldn't afford it. You see, ensigns had a total monthly income, including pay and subsistence, of $143.30, and our mess bill was around $20.00, and our laundry bill was around $20.00, and then we had life insurance that was around $20.00. That was $60.00 right there. That left you $80.00 for all other expenses and incidentals: subscriptions to magazines, whatever you had. But you didn't have much money left, divided by four weeks.

Paul Stillwell: Was this a mandatory insurance?

Captain Schwab: Oh, no, everybody took government life insurance in those days, and it cost $20.00 a month for a $10,000 endowment.

Back to shore leave activity, several of us decided, two days before Christmas in 1939, to drive down from Long Beach to see what Mexico looked like. So Don Furlong, J. V. Wilson, and I drove down in the 1935 Pontiac, and we went down as far as

Ensenada. It was Christmastime. So we went back to Tijuana and looked around there, and that looked a little dangerous. So then we drove to San Diego to visit the father and mother of one of our Marine officers, a new Marine officer by the name of Bill Frash.[*] The father gave us some drinks that he called Rompope, which was sort of a rum cream drink.

Late in the day we decided we'd go back to Los Angeles, since we'd heard there were good restaurants, and we were going to have Christmas Eve dinner. On our way, when we were on Western Avenue in Los Angeles, we stopped for a light, and another car crashed into the rear of this great big old '35 Pontiac. J. V. Wilson was asleep in the back seat, and Don Furlong was awake in the front seat. J. V. Wilson had had several of those rum drinks, and I was driving. The crash woke him up, and he looked out the rear window. The woman who was sitting in the front seat of the other car had false teeth. She hit the dash or something, and her false teeth were going all over the place. For some reason that made J. V. Wilson laugh. This wasn't a good idea, because the driver of the other car was pretty well loaded. He got angry at that, and we had to restrain him from hitting J. V.

Just about two seconds later, a policeman arrived, who was a friend of the driver. The skid marks of the car that hit us went back a good 15-20 feet, and we were already stopped at the light. The back end of the Pontiac just had a little dent in it, but the whole front end of the Chevrolet that hit us had gone underneath our rear bumper. There was steam all over. The Pontiac was built like a battleship. The policeman then started giving us a bad time because of his friend. A man on the corner came over, and he said, "I heard you identify yourself as ensigns, and I'm a retired chief petty officer. I work for the real estate office on the corner, and I saw what happened. I'll be glad to be a witness." He said, very loudly, "Be sure to get the number of the officer." The officer looked at him as the former CPO wrote the number down too. Another person came over and said they'd seen the accident, too, and would be glad to help us. All this was out of the blue, in Los Angeles!

The former chief said, "There's a police station right down at the next corner. Why don't you go and report the accident there before anything else can happen?"

---

[*] Second Lieutenant William M. Frash, USMC.

There was nothing else for us to do at the accident scene, so we helped push the Chevrolet off to the side of the road and parked across the street from the police station. Right next to it was a three-story Sears-Roebuck building, and it had Christmas decorations in it; it was closed. It was now about 7:30 or 8:00 o'clock at night on Christmas Eve. We looked at the front of the Sears building, and I think it was J. V. who said, "There's something awfully funny going on there. It looks like a fire." We looked, and the second floor was burning. The draperies were ablaze. We ran into the police station, but there was nobody at the desk. We would hear some noise in the back, and the assistant police commissioner or someone at that level was going around giving the police stations a little cheer on Christmas Eve. We yelled, but nobody came out. So I picked up the telephone, called the operator, and said, "There's a fire here."

The operator said, "Where are you?" So I told them as far as I could figure out, "Police station on Western Avenue." The firehouse was only about the next block away, so they came zooming in and put their ladders up.

Meanwhile, the cops all came into the desk area and said, "How'd you get in? Why are you here? Somebody called us about a fire."

I said, "I came to report an accident," and they listened to my report.

I gave them the traffic officer's badge number and told them about the witnesses and they said, "Oh, forget it." They took it all down. We never heard another thing about the accident. But we probably would have been in trouble if witnesses hadn't come from that corner.

Paul Stillwell: That's right.

You just showed me a bound volume of the *Pennsylvania* ship's paper from that era, which is very interesting, *The Keystone*. How did you happen to get involved in that?

Captain Schwab: Before you leave the Naval Academy, they give you a questionnaire to send to your ship, listing all the different things that you might be interested in. In other words, the ships would like to know if you were a baseball player, or a football player, or a musician, or anything that might help your new ship assign you to collateral duties.

They also asked about what you particularly liked doing—gunnery or engineering or what have you.

I don't know if every ship did, but the *Pennsylvania*'s exec really read this questionnaire. One of the things I put down was that I'd been an editor on the *The Log*, the weekly Naval Academy magazine. I also wanted to be in gunnery, which I thought was a good thing when I was an ensign. So, when I got out to the *Pennsylvania*, I found out the first thing they assigned me to do was to be the editor of the ship's paper, and the second thing was to be in the gunnery department. It worked out nicely. That's how you get involved in things of that sort.

Paul Stillwell: How did you go about putting together the ship's paper? Where did the items come from?

Captain Schwab: Each division had somebody who was supposed to contribute items, and then the ship's chaplain was very active. His name was Ackiss, and he was always very active in organizing ship's dances and recreational things, and he would give us articles.* Then there was an enlisted journalist, and he would write a weekly column that he would get from various sources on the ship, mostly innocent gossip type things. Then all the ships exchanged their papers, so you would get information from other ships' papers, particularly jokes. There was always half a column or so of jokes. You just filled in, and you wound up with a weekly paper.

They had a good printer on the ship who helped. Remember, I had been the editor of a weekly high school newspaper, so I was used to frantic operation at the last minute. I'd have everybody turn in things on Monday and Tuesday, and then I edited it, and I'd get galley proofs on Wednesday. Then I'd paste up the paper on Wednesday afternoon, and the enlisted journalist helped. Then they'd print it on Thursday and distribute it on Friday, as long as it didn't interfere with the ship's operation. I don't know how it was paid for, now that I think of it. I think it was paid for out of government funds, if I'm not mistaken. We didn't get paid anything extra. Everybody enjoyed the paper. Everyone likes to see his name in print, so we made sure we printed as many names as possible.

---

* Commander Ernest L. Ackiss, Chaplain Corps, USN.

Paul Stillwell: I noticed another thing. It reported on sports results. What do you recall about the ship's athletic teams?

Captain Schwab: All the big ships, at least, had football teams, baseball teams, swimming teams, sailing teams, and rowing teams. The rowing part of it was more professional than athletic, akin to gunnery competition. All the big ships, the battleships especially, had basketball and football teams. And the football teams usually had, as players or coaches, officers who had played at the Naval Academy. The officers actually played in the games. The captain of the Navy football team in my class was Lucien Powell, called Pete Powell.* He was on the *Pennsylvania* and played on the ship's team, and others did, too. Rhythm Moore was on the baseball team, I guess. It was a ship-versus-ship competition.

Paul Stillwell: Where were the games played?

Captain Schwab: In San Pedro and Long Beach, they had athletic fields that the fleet used, so no problem there. I don't think they had any swimming teams. You'd think they would, but I don't remember any swimming teams.

Paul Stillwell: Boxing was very popular.

Captain Schwab: Yes, they had boxing quite often. The boxing that was more fun was when it was intramural, intra-ship boxing. That's when there'd be a lot of grudge fights. We'd gather after mess, and the enlisted men would get to take out their anger. Officers didn't fight.

Paul Stillwell: You mentioned, when the tape recorder wasn't running, that the ship made a visit to San Francisco in 1939. What do you recall of that?

---

* Ensign Lucien C. Powell Jr., USN.

Captain Schwab: In the summer of 1939, all the battleships went up and down the West Coast to visit various ports. We visited San Francisco and Seattle.

Paul Stillwell: The fair that year in San Francisco was on Treasure Island.*

Captain Schwab: That was it. Treasure Island. There was a world's fair in San Francisco and a world's fair in New York, two world's fairs in 1939. They also had something up in Seattle, called Potlatch Week, which was during the same summer. I can't remember whether we went to Seattle before or after San Francisco. I think we went to Seattle first, and we had Potlatch Week, meaning that the latch was out for everybody in the fleet. They invited all the officers to such things as the press club, you know, all on the house. If you were wearing your uniform, you got a free drink, or something like that, and that was fun. They had big beer parties for the enlisted men. In San Francisco they had a great big series of parties scheduled, except the Secretary of the Navy, Claude Swanson, died at that time.† So instead of having all these fancy, rather formal parties, we all wound up wearing our black bands on our sleeves and on our sword knots and so on. Unofficially some of the parties went on at several sororities over at the university. They invited all the ensigns over, so we wore our black bands but had a great time anyhow. They didn't invite any of the college boys, just the young officers. They even had a dance at the Mark Hopkins Hotel for us. It was sort of illegal; it wasn't supposed to happen during mourning, but it didn't bother the college girls.

Paul Stillwell: Well, this suggests also, as you were talking about your midshipman days, that naval officers had a good deal of social status.

Captain Schwab: Possibly. In those days, there weren't too many naval officers. Remember, the Depression was still with us, and naval officers had an assured income.

---

* Treasure Island is a man-made island in San Francisco Bay, located between San Francisco and Oakland. It served as the site of a world's fair in 1939-40, then was converted for use as a Navy base during and after World War II.
† Claude A. Swanson served as Secretary of the Navy from 4 March 1933 until his death on 7 July 1939.

Maybe that was part of our status. There were only 9,000 or 10,000 line officers when I joined the fleet. That's all. And now what do they have, 50,000 or something?

Paul Stillwell: I would think more than that.

Captain Schwab: More than that? I'm not talking about all types of officers, but the ones with the stars one their sleeves—line officers.

Paul Stillwell: Was the ship in the yard at all while you were on board?

Captain Schwab: In October of 1940, we went into the yard at Bremerton.* The main thing I remember about Bremerton was it rained all the time. I remember standing deck watches with high boots and long rubber coats, and sou'westers, and I was still wet when I came off a four-hour deck watch. We had a good time up there.

In November 1940 I went home on 20 days' leave, eight days of which were spent on the train. Two days before I went off on leave, Rhythm Moore and I drove the '35 Pontiac over the bridge from Tacoma to Seattle. It was called "Galloping Gertie," because it used to weave around in the wind. When we went over that, it was moving around, but they said it was perfectly safe, which was interesting. The motion made you seasick. The next day it fell down.† I went by in the train on leave, and you could see it in the water. I don't think anybody was killed, but they lost a car; a reporter's car went off. But that's how close you can be to things without having it happen to you.

Paul Stillwell: Yard time is usually a dreary period for a ship's existence. It's torn up, and you've got a lot of noise and so forth.

Captain Schwab: Yes, it was pretty dreary. But there was some social activity in Bremerton. They had parties going all the time. They had a private club there, which

---

* Puget Sound Navy Yard, Bremerton, Washington.

† The Tacoma Narrows Bridge opened for traffic on 1 July 1940. It collapsed into the water during high wind conditions on 7 November 1940, only a few months after it opened.

was always throwing parties for the officers. There were always one or two battleships in there, and we had a good time.

Paul Stillwell: I think the CinCUS staff moved to the *New Mexico* during that period.

Captain Schwab: I don't know. We dropped them off in Long Beach, I think.

Paul Stillwell: What do you remember about that fleet problem in the spring of 1940, when you went over to Hawaii and didn't come back?

Captain Schwab: Fleet Problem XXI? Well, we did know that Walter Winchell had said we weren't going to come back again.[*] I don't know how he knew that. It was just a normal fleet problem: exercises, running around, making believe we were having a war. Of course, I hadn't gotten into what kind of training we were doing for war out at sea while at Submarine School. That's interesting. I don't know if any other people have told you about that. Our training at Submarine School was strictly according to the book, the way the Japanese started using submarines at first. The rule was that the submarines would sink men-of-war only and be the "eyes of the fleet."

I went to Submarine School from July through September 1941. It used to be a six-month course, but they shortened it a little bit. We had these attack problems in the trainer there, where you'd put a periscope up and see ship models, instead of real ships. All the ship models were men-of-war. We had very little idea what a merchant ship looked like from those attack problems. Maybe they did show them for some later classes, but not in the one I was in.

All the maps and charts of the Japanese coast, for instance, were really antique. Things of that sort were constant. We were really not prepared for fighting, with informational things, either what the coast looked like or water conditions. I imagine it is that way in most wars. You never know in advance where or how you're going to fight. But now, with all of the things they have, such as mapping satellites, we probably should be better off. Of course, with all the attention paid to underwater formations since World

---

[*] Winchell was a prominent radio news commentator of the era.

War II, for sonar reasons, we should be a lot better off than we were then. We didn't have anything then that was equivalent of current high-powered sonar. It was all pretty bad stuff.

Paul Stillwell: Is there anything else to mention on the *Pennsylvania*, before we get into the Submarine School, per se?

Captain Schwab: No, it's just that the people stayed on the ships longer. I know a couple of people, one officer out of the class of '37, Charlie Burch, who was on the *Pennsylvania* through the whole war.[*] That wouldn't happen anymore. They'd rotate you out.

Paul Stillwell: And especially the enlisted men remained on board longer.

Captain Schwab: Yes, they stayed for years in those days. They got to stay; they owned the ship. In those days they called original crew members "plank owners," and many ships had them for their whole Navy careers. That meant you put the ship in commission, and you stayed with it. I don't think they have anything like that anymore.

Paul Stillwell: Well, nobody who would stay.

Captain Schwab: Besides, they don't have planks.

Paul Stillwell: What had impelled your desire to go to Submarine School?

Captain Schwab: In the first place, you get sort of tired on a battleship with all the spit and polish and being one among many. When the *Pennsylvania* was in Pearl Harbor, we would always tie up to Ten-Ten Dock. That was the choicest mooring spot in Pearl Harbor. The submarine base is right around the corner, and we'd see the submarines

---

[*] He was Lieutenant (junior grade) Charles A. Burch, USN, when World War II began and a lieutenant commander when it ended.

going out. Everybody looked really nice comfortable, wearing their khakis, which we didn't even have, let alone wear. Then I talked to a few of the submarine officers and found out that you could get command of a submarine when you were a lieutenant. You were not going to do anything like that in the surface Navy. For example, our exec, a commander, John L. McCrea, I guess, hadn't had command of anything, maybe a destroyer before that.

Paul Stillwell: He had some destroyer duty.

Captain Schwab: Yes, but that was it. But probably as a lieutenant commander. Although they did have lieutenants commanding way back in World War I. You didn't get a feeling from the battleships that you were going to get very far, very fast, and you were sort of one among a big crowd. Whereas, you knew on the submarines there were only five or six officers, at that time; during the war, they got up to eight or nine. And you got 25% extra pay, which was not for hazardous duty then. It was because you supposedly ruined a lot of uniforms in the battery acid. Well, it was true, you did get a lot of holes, and you sort of smelled funny all the time; the diesel fumes and the acid did smell a little bit. So going into subs seemed like a good thing to do.

Besides that, my first captain, Captain Cutts, had been a submarine officer and told us some of the things that went on in submarines, which were interesting. Captain Cooke had also been a submarine officer and also told us some submarine stories. So we had a good idea that submarine duty was interesting. Also, you were on your own when you were in submarines; you weren't surrounded by a bunch of other ships. You were independent operators. That also was attractive. And I didn't particularly care for aviation, because in the first place, we didn't see the carriers that much. All we got to see were our floatplanes; that didn't look so good. A few of the people I knew who had gone into aviation had left, because they didn't like it.

Paul Stillwell: What do you remember about the course of instruction once you got to Submarine School? How did it compare with that that you'd known at the Naval Academy?

Captain Schwab: Well, it had been compressed from six months to little more than three months. You studied long hours, and you were continually being quizzed. They weren't fooling around. Almost everything was of practical use, not academic. You were learning how to fight a submarine, and run a submarine, and balance it and all that sort of stuff. On the other hand, I think they weren't aware that they had to be more flexible than just fighting enemy men-of-war, as I mentioned earlier.

The whole emphasis was on submarines as eyes of the fleet. You went out ahead of the fleet, located the enemy fleet, sent your sighting message back, and then you became a kamikaze. Also, the estimates were that if you were held down by a destroyer, for instance, for more than half an hour or 45 minutes, you were a dead submarine. In all the war games, that was it. That's the way they scored. If a plane came over and dropped a dummy depth charge, or simulated a depth charge on you within five minutes or so after you submerged, you were dead. We found that wasn't true either. This led an awful lot of the early submariners who were very good in target practice at shooting torpedoes, to be super cautious in war, more cautious than they should have been. That led to some failures and reliefs of command.

Of course, the torpedoes were having problems, too, because of the unrealistic way in which had been tested. Using nets was the way to do it, because you could see actually how deep the torpedo was. Instead, they took the torpedoes' own depth gear, the Uhlan gear, to see how deep they ran. And for some reason that was inaccurate. They went too deep, which negated the benefit of the magnetic exploders. Well, you know that story probably. So that was that part of it. The submarines that we trained on, of course, were the old O-boats, from World War I or shortly thereafter.[*] They were falling apart; in fact, they lost one just before I went to submarine school, the *O-9* in '41[†]

Paul Stillwell: How much time did you spend in the boats and how much in the classroom?

---

[*] The early U.S. submarines were designated by letter-number combinations rather than names. *O-1* through *O-16* were commissioned in 1918.
[†] USS *O-9* (SS-70) was recommissioned on 14 April 1941. On 19 June of that year the submarine made a test dive off the Isle of Shoals, about 15 miles from Portsmouth, New Hampshire. She failed to surface, and the entire crew was lost, a total of 33 officers and men.

Captain Schwab: You got out in the boats at least one or two days a week. I can't remember exactly. The best thing was that you usually went out on the same boat, and I was fortunate to have Junior McCain as the captain of the one I was on a lot.[*] He would let you bring it in to the pier, which was unusual. In those O-boats you had to shut off the diesel engines and back down on the battery. I don't know if you've been in and out of New London on a submarine, but when you're going in for a landing, there's an awful lot of current across the face of the piers. You had to come in pretty fast and then back it down so you wouldn't crash the seawall. I remember when I was coming in once, and I had the conn.[†] McCain gave the student officers the conn coming in. I was coming in probably too fast, and he said, "Do you want me to get court-martialed, or are you going to back down?"—or words to that effect. He was pretty funny. He always smoked a big, black cigar. Knew him well all during the war and after the war.

Paul Stillwell: Do you have any other recollections about McCain from that period?

Captain Schwab: No, just as the captain of the *O-9*.

Paul Stillwell: What do you remember about your approach practices toward targets?

Captain Schwab: Well, they were standard submerged approaches, just as we did during the war. You went in there and took your normal approach course, and, of course, on the O-boats, you didn't have a torpedo data computer, what they call a TDC. You did it all with what they called an "is-was," which was a plastic slide rule.[‡] It was all by guess and by God. The main thing was that you could tell when you were on a collision course, because the bearing was constant. That was the normal approach course. You didn't want your torpedoes to hit at right angles to the target but just slightly off. Of course, they didn't have enough ships around for escorts either. We didn't get any practice on avoiding escorts as we went in to attack. Out in the boats, it was mostly one approach

---

[*] In 1941-42, Lieutenant John S. McCain Jr., USN, commanded the submarine *O-8* (SS-69). He eventually became a four-star admiral.

[†] The individual with the conn—normally an officer—directs the ship's movements in course and speed.

[‡] "Is-was" was the nickname for a circular slide rule that calculated a target ship's future track on the basis of where it had been.

against one ship. You got more practice, I think, on escorts and that sort of thing in the attack simulator. They also had a diving simulator that was fun. You had to simulate diving. The instructors would put the boat out of trim, and then you had to trim it for natural buoyancy.

Paul Stillwell: What about the escape tower? Did you train in that?

Captain Schwab: Oh, yes, we went through the escape tower, but that was before they did free ascent. We used the Momsen lung, and we went up with that, about 100 feet.[*] I guess they still do it with the lung, as well as free ascent.

Paul Stillwell: Well, the experience of the *Squalus* was still fresh in mind, so was that covered.[†]

Captain Schwab: Oh, yes; but in the *Squalus* they put down a bell, though. They didn't make any free or lung escapes, I don't think.

Paul Stillwell: No, you're right. But I'm wondering if that made the lesson pretty vivid, about escaping?

Captain Schwab: Oh, yes, sure. Well, there were people saying, "Well, it's better than nothing." The point is, that once you get away from the continental shelf, then you were too deep anyhow. But most of the submarine accidents until then had happened in the shallow water, especially collision accidents. The *O-9* happened right before I went to sub school. That was in the spring of '41. They didn't have a collision; they just

---

[*] Invented by submariner Charles B. Momsen, the Momsen lung was a breathing apparatus to be used when ascending from a damaged submarine to the surface. It did not have its own air supply but used the air already in a man's lungs.

[†] USS *Squalus* (SS-192), commanded by Lieutenant Oliver F. Naquin, USN, sank in 243 feet of water while conducting exercise dives on 23 May 1939 off Portsmouth, New Hampshire. Twenty-six men died, but 33, including Naquin, were recovered through the use of the McCann rescue chamber. The submarine later was salvaged, refurbished, and renamed the *Sailfish*. For details, see Carl La VO, *Back from the Deep* (Annapolis; Naval Institute Press, 1994).

flooded, I guess. I think they didn't get the main intake valve, main induction valve shut or something.

Paul Stillwell: Well, that was the problem in the *Squalus* too. Apparently the skipper, Captain Naquin, was trying to set a record for fast dives. It was carelessly done, and they didn't get the main induction closed.

Captain Schwab: My first submarine at Submarine School was the *Marlin*.* There were two submarines; *Marlin* and *Mackerel*, which were built because Admiral Hart wanted to have a new, small successor to the S-boats, and R-boats.† The captain of the *Marlin* was George Sharp, Red Sharp, who had been the captain of the rescue vessel that rescued the *Squalus*.‡

Paul Stillwell: I interviewed John Davidson, who was captain of the *Mackerel*.§

Captain Schwab: He had the *Mackerel*, yes. You talked to him? Did he tell you about the cruise of the two boats down to the Virgin Islands?

Paul Stillwell: I don't remember specifically.

Captain Schwab: Well, this was my first war patrol when we went down there. We didn't know anything. The weather was horrible, on the way back particularly. The German submarines were sinking ships all along the Atlantic Coast, and we were barely able to survive getting back to New London.

---

* USS *Marlin* (SS-205) was commissioned 1 August 1941 and the *Mackerel* (SS-204) on 31 March 1941. Their range was too short to serve the role that the fleet boats did in World War II, so these two were used primarily as training submarines. The Naval Institute oral history collection contains the oral history of Rear Admiral John F. Davidson, USN (Ret.), who had been the first commanding officer of the *Mackerel*.
† Admiral Thomas C. Hart, USN.
‡ Lieutenant George A. Sharp, USN, commanded the submarine rescue ship *Falcon* (ASR-2) from 1938 to 1940. He was the first commanding officer of the *Marlin* when she was commissioned 1 August 1941.
§ Lieutenant John F. Davidson, USN, was the first commanding officer of the *Mackerel* in 1941-42. The oral history of Davidson, who eventually retired as a rear admiral, is in the Naval Institute collection.

In addition to making a so-called war patrol, we were also making a test run to determine which of the two types, the *Mackerel* or *Marlin*, was better for production.* The *Marlin* had American locomotive engines, and I don't know what the *Mackerel* had, but no matter what, the American locomotive engines were supposed to be reversing diesels, which we'd never had before in small subs. They had a lay reversing shaft, but the whole ship was getting too heavy. So they had taken this heavy steel lay shaft and put some sort of aluminum alloy in there. The fourth time we backed down, the shaft broke, so we had to reverse on the batteries from then on. The *Mackerel* had a hydraulic clutch, which somehow they could reverse, but I don't know how that worked.

Also, we in the *Marlin* didn't have normal water-making facilities; they had some sort of things with pimples on them around the exhaust pipes, and they acted as the evaporators. It was a very experimental thing. We finally all got down to the Virgin Islands, but we weren't allowed to take water, fuel, or supplies on board since it was a test. We went into Charlotte Amalie, the submarine base there. We were allowed to go ashore and stretch our legs for a couple hours, and then we had to head back to New London after a short patrol in the Caribbean.

We went off separately into little patrol areas. One night I remember well. It was pitch black—like velvet—as it only gets in the Caribbean. I had the deck, and I saw this long shape out there, didn't know what it could be—no lights or anything. We had no radar then. Grouleff was on watch with me.† We stood watch one officer below and one topside. We were six on and six off; we only had four officers. Red Sharp was in New London, ill, and Grouleff was acting captain. He came charging up and looked and he said, "That looks like a submarine, and it's not supposed to one of ours, so we'll dive."

We dived, and just then this other thing dived. It was apparently a great big, long sub. We weren't sure who or what it was, and we didn't hear any propellers or torpedoes or anything, so we got away fast. It turned out that, we learned later, that there was one of those big Italian submarines over there, for some unknown reason. It never sank anything.

---

* Neither went into production because of her short range, which precluded long independent operations.
† Lieutenant Paul H. Grouleff, USN.

We headed back to New London and ran into really bad weather; it was horrible. The gyrocompass tumbled, so that was gone. The magnetic repeater compass, a new invention, was no good. We had following seas most of the time, which was fortunate; the water was fairly warm, even though it was winter. When it was rough, we tied ourselves into the wheelhouse. The *Marlin* looked like a German submarine, all closed in. You could tie yourself in there onto the wheel. We had a wheel up there still. The water would come in from aft and fill the wheelhouse. We were using the hatch for air, so we would close that and pop eardrums as the engines sucked in air. Sometime they would stop. You'd hold your breath when you'd feel the wave hit. Then it would gradually go down again, and we'd open the hatch. Your clothes were full of water. When all these compasses went out, the captain said, "Well, you don't have to worry about that too much, because we have this tank compass on a post down in the control room." But we didn't really believe that the tank compass was any good at all. Yet every night we'd look, and there would be the North Star where it was supposed to be, so all seemed okay.

We knew if we went north long enough, we'd hit the coast up off New London. So we kept going north. A couple of days later we were going along on the surface. It was still rough in the daytime. I had the deck. Suddenly there came this big Army bomber with his bomb bays opening up. I guess they still had the ASW mission then. Grouleff was down below in the control room, and I yelled, "There's a plane coming" as I pulled the emergency flares that we had. The Atlantic Fleet had several different identification systems. We had a U.S.-U.K. identification system and then we had Atlantic Fleet identification dual systems; it was all screwed up. I pulled these flares, and they didn't go off. They were all sopping wet. Grouleff, the acting captain, came up and took a look. The plane meanwhile had turned around—didn't drop any bombs—was coming back, we could see a guy in there taking movies.

Grouleff broke the American flag and was waving the flag madly, and we were blinking whatever the code was for that day at the plane. The movie man in the plane was looking at us, very low, right over the top of us. The plane never dropped anything, shut its bomb bay doors, and left. Grouleff said, "I'll have to get that movie sometime." We didn't really know where we were. There was a submarine sanctuary for us, but whether we were in it or not we had no idea. So we were lucky not to be bombed. We finally sighted the coast up near New London. I think we spotted Block Island, finally got in to the base, and tied up alongside the pier. We were all dented in from the weather. The black paint had flaked off from the sail. We had a lot of white aluminum showing; we looked just like a German submarine, even one little gun back aft. I went through the control room at that time and took a look. The tank compass was still pointing in the same direction, north, even though we were now headed northeast. It had been pointing at the stanchion the whole time.

How we got back to New London, I don't know. It's just that every once in a while, when it wasn't raining, you'd see the North Star up there where it was supposed to be. I went back to my locker to get dressed because they were having a welcome aboard party for the new Submarine School officers' class, and we were invited. Our electricians had opened the battery hatch but hadn't put the guardrail over. On my way to the party, I fell down the battery hatch and broke my nose. So I went up there and met my wife-to-be for the second time, with my nose all bent over. She was surrounded by all these new officers. I chased them away. They were saying, "There's a German submarine that was captured down at the pier."

I said, "What pier?" It was the *Marlin*, my submarine!

Paul Stillwell: What month and year did you make that trip down to the Caribbean?

Captain Schwab: That was February '42. Going back to before the commissioning of the *Marlin*, there was a funny incident. both of these new small subs were being built on a competitive basis. The *Mackerel* was at EB and the *Marlin* at Portsmouth, New Hampshire, and they were really in a race.[*] They actually commissioned the *Marlin* with sort of a cardboard conning tower because it wasn't finished yet. They wanted to have the government yard commissioning before the private yard, EB.

They began hurrying work at the end of the planned construction period. Somebody had painted in the pump room, which is below the control room on a

---

[*] EB – the Electric Boat Company, a submarine building yard in Groton, Connecticut. Portsmouth Navy Yard, Kittery, Maine.

submarine, and he had left a gallon paint can over in a corner with its lid on. Then somebody had gone through before an inspector came and spray-painted everything. The paint can, I guess, didn't have any bail, I guess you call it. The painter had painted it there so it looked like part of the ship's structure. Well, after the inspection they were running some airlines through the pump room, and they drilled through the bulkhead. As they came through, what did they run into but this paint can, which wasn't on the plans. But the pipe installers didn't know it was a paint can, and they didn't dare to move it, so they made junction in the pipe and came around the paint can and continued all the way through the compartment. So the paint can now appeared permanent. It could be moved, but no one knew that. Months later, we were down there and somebody happened to kick the can, that's how we found the mistake. Now we had a permanent, no-rattle place for a paint can.

The next *Marlin* story occurred right after the war started. Mayor La Guardia of New York was the air defense coordinator for the East Coast and decided to have a drill.[*] You have probably heard about that. So he put out the word to all the media and everyone that there was a flight of German aircraft coming across the Atlantic. The whole Northeast Coast was alerted. In Portsmouth the *Marlin* was alongside the pier. We'd had some problems with the periscope bearings, so the periscope was out, and there was scaffolding all around the shears. We'd had a place where we could mount a .50-caliber machine gun but couldn't do that because of the scaffolding. The gunner's mate and I were in charge. I was the officer of the deck and sonar officer. I was the only bachelor, and everybody else was ashore except for some enlisted men. When the alert was signaled, my gunner's mate rigged some sort of a gun mount on the bollard next to the ship, and we mounted our .50-caliber machine gun there, so at least we could shoot up in the air. The word was that the alert was serious, as far as we knew. We didn't worry too much at first, because they had just brought down a group of net tenders from Canada with those funny horns sticking out. Have you ever seen them?

Paul Stillwell: They do look like horns.

---

[*] The colorful Fiorello H. La Guardia gained national fame while serving as mayor of New York City from 1934 to 1945.

Captain Schwab: Yes, they look like horns. Well, they had about 20 of them in the yard, and we were surrounded by them. I don't know whether they built them in Canada or not. Each one of them had one of those real old-fashioned 3-inch/23s, single-manned gun with an arm that went around the gunner. The man stood in that, and I guess somebody loaded it, and then he shot all by himself. He was like a gunner in one of those old-fashioned airplanes. So the net tender people were all out there manning their guns. I looked over and said to an officer on one of the tenders, "Well, all we have is this .50-caliber, but we don't have to worry much because even if you can't hit anything with those 3-inch/23s, at least they put up a lot of shells."

He said, "Don't kid yourself. We don't have any ammunition!" The *Marlin* was the only ship that there could fire anything. That was really a funny period then, because nobody seemed to know what was going on.

Everybody can tell you where they were Pearl Harbor day.* Another officer and I were driving to Boston listening to some symphony or something on the car radio. They also had good classical music on a Sunday. The word came over that the Japanese were bombing Pearl Harbor, and all military personnel were to report to their stations. We went back to the Portsmouth Navy Yard. We arrived at the gate and said, "What are we supposed to do?" The guard at the gate didn't have any idea that anything had happened.

Then we went to the administration building, and there was big fuss going on. They were trying to get the safe open to get the war plans! Nobody knew the combination. Talk about "Keystone Cops." They finally got the safe open. Meanwhile we all put on our uniforms, and then we reported again and said, "What do we do?"

We were told, "We have nothing to do! Just sit." So we sat. After a while, we went up to the officers' club to sit; that was it. Overnight we all became jaygees; that was one thing that didn't go wrong.

Paul Stillwell: Did you have to take promotion exams?

Captain Schwab: Nothing!

---

* On Sunday, 7 December 1941, Japanese carrier planes attacked and heavily damaged American warships at the naval base at Pearl Harbor, Hawaii. The U.S. Congress declared war on Japan the following day.

Paul Stillwell: Back during the period you were in Submarine School, how much coverage was there in the classroom on the mechanical systems of a submarine?

Captain Schwab: Oh, that was quite detailed, particularly on the electrical systems. That was the main thing on subs. Everything on a submarine was explained to you, because in order to qualify in submarines in those days, an officer had to be able to do everything on a submarine. For certain emergencies, do it blindfolded, which is sort of silly. You had to take a sub out without assistance and dive it yourself. Of course, there was somebody standing there in case you goofed; you weren't all alone in the ship.

Paul Stillwell: What might you have to do blindfolded?

Captain Schwab: Well, the assumption was that all the lights were out for some reason. You had to know where all the different valves were for blowing the tanks to get to the surface again, and things of that sort.

Paul Stillwell: Well, that certainly is a conceivable emergency.

Captain Schwab: Yes.

Paul Stillwell: Who were some of your fellow students in that class?

Captain Schwab: Well, many of them are dead. There was Walt Sharer, out of '38, who's dead.[*] There were not too many of us; I guess 25. Chuck Nace, Bill Ruhe, Grady Reaves, Doug Syverson were all in '39.[†] Syverson was the first captain of the *Hunley*, which was the first tender for the nuclear submarines at Holy Loch.[‡] Was it the *Hunley*?

---

[*] Ensign Walter A. Sharer, USN.
[†] Ensign Charles D. Nace, USN; Ensign William J. Ruhe, USN; Ensign Henry Grady Reaves Jr., USN; Ensign Douglas N. Syverson, USN.
[‡] Captain Syverson, the commissioning skipper, commanded the submarine tender *Hunley* (AS-31) from 16 June 1962 to 15 September 1963. She first arrived at Holy Loch, Scotland, on 9 January 1963 to service Polaris ballistic missile submarines.

Paul Stillwell: Well, the *Proteus* was over there.

Captain Schwab: Yes, but *Hunley*, I think, was made especially to tend Polaris submarines.

Paul Stillwell: Well, the *Proteus* apparently was converted. The skipper who took her over there was Dick Laning, out of class of '40.*

Captain Schwab: Yes, well, this was Syverson, in my class, '39, who was the skipper up there.

About half of the July-September '41 class sub school class died during the war. It was pretty a big casualty rate in that class.

Paul Stillwell: Well, I've talked to men who went through the school in the late '30s, and they said that the incentive to do well in the class, was that you got your choice of duty.

Captain Schwab: Yes, that's right. I stood number five in the class.

Paul Stillwell: Out of 25?

Captain Schwab: It was 25 or 30, something like that. It wasn't bad.

Paul Stillwell: Why did you choose the *Marlin*?

Captain Schwab: Well, because I heard it was a new experimental submarine, and it was on the East Coast. Syverson and some of the others wanted to go to the Philippines, but I knew all they had out there were old R- and S-boats. I liked the idea of going to a new submarine. Since the *Marlin* had only four or five officers, it was more interesting than

---

* Captain Richard B. Laning, USN, commanded the submarine tender *Proteus* (AS-19) from 8 July 1960 to 25 August 1962. She was originally commissioned in World War II to tend diesel submarines. She arrived at Holy Loch on 3 March 1961.

going to one of the big fleet boats. I put in for a new submarine, and then they said, "How would you like the *Marlin*?"

So I found out more about it and said, "That sounds fine with me."

Paul Stillwell: Well, Admiral Davidson said just what you have, that Admiral Hart was the one who was pushing for this smaller submarine, somehow considering that more desirable than the fleet boats, although obviously . . .

Captain Schwab: For the Philippine area, yes.[*]

Paul Stillwell: . . . it didn't prove so in practice.

Captain Schwab: They were two new small boats that never went to war. The fleet boats were the best for that time, but Admiral Hart was worried that the fleet boats wouldn't be able to get into some of the smaller places. One thing you learned to do was stay away from confined places, especially where there were mines. We lost a couple, I guess, with mines.

Paul Stillwell: Well, and I think, too, that even in that era people didn't really know how the ships were eventually going to be used.

Captain Schwab: Yes, that's right. We really didn't know! During the war they didn't really tell you too much about subs being lost. I mean you found out about it by not seeing people anymore during refits. But they didn't tell you much about losses. I gather back in the States there wasn't too much publicity. It was just something about a sub being overdue and presumed lost, and that was it—period. They didn't say where they were or anything.

---

[*] Admiral Thomas C. Hart, USN, served as Commander in Chief U.S. Asiatic Fleet from 25 July 1939 to 4 February 1942. James R. Leutze's biography of Hart is *A Different Kind of Victory* (Annapolis: Naval Institute Press, 1981).

Paul Stillwell: Well, obviously it was a security measure, too, not tipping off the Japanese.

Captain Schwab: Yes. Some security lapses did occur, however. From hearsay, there were some politicians who were given commissions. One of them was interviewed when he came back on leave, and he was asked how come the Japanese weren't sinking many of our submarines. He said, "Oh, they're not setting their depth charges deep enough!"[*] I never did see the quote, but I heard it so many times. Right after that, we lost a lot of submarines. Have you seen the submarine calendar of all the losses? The Submarine Veterans of World War II put it out. It marks each day on which a submarine was lost. There was a loss of 52 submarines. There's the one I was "lost" on, the *Darter*. My wife thought I was dead for 12 days, until she found out that we were rescued by the *Dace*.[†]

Paul Stillwell: Some famous names on the calendar.

Captain Schwab: At first in the Pacific I worked under Lockwood, who relieved English.[‡]

Paul Stillwell: English died.[§]

Captain Schwab: Yes, he was killed in a plane crash. He was the one who was responsible in BuOrd for people fouling up the torpedo depth mechanism.[**]

Back to the calendar. There were 17 lost in '43 and 20 in '44. The interview about the Japanese not setting depth charges deep enough occurred right before those losses. I was in Submarine Squadron Eight. There were eight submarines in the

---

[*] Representative Andrew Jackson May, a member of the House Military Affairs Committee, revealed this in a press interview in June 1943. See Clay Blair's *Silent Victory*, page 424.
[†] Captain Schwab discussed details of the *Darter*'s demise in a later interview.
[‡] Rear/Vice Admiral Charles A. Lockwood, Jr., USN, served as Commander Submarines Pacific Fleet from February 1943 to December 1945. He was promoted to three stars in October 1943.
[§] On 21 January 1943, a Pan American Clipper carrying 19 people, including crew members, crashed into the side of a cliff near Boonville, California. All on board were killed, including Rear Admiral Robert H. English, USN, Commander Submarine Force Pacific Fleet. For details, see Clay Blair, Jr., *Silent Victory* (Philadelphia: Lippincott, 1975), pages 365-366.
[**] BuOrd – Bureau of Ordnance.

squadron. Eight went out on patrol, and the only one that came back was the *Guardfish* in 1943. The losses resulted from the sheer stupidity of that interview, I'm sure.

Paul Stillwell: Do you have any memories of the instructors in Submarine School, of how capable they were?

Captain Schwab: Oh, yes, they were all experienced submarine officers. There's no question about that. They did give you a very intensive psychological exam, before you went in. I don't remember what it consisted of, but it was long and probing. They wanted to know, I guess, if you were going to panic or have claustrophobia or anything like that.

Paul Stillwell: And you apparently passed the test.

Captain Schwab: I passed it, no problem. The only other one that approached it was when I went into the Foreign Service in 1965. They gave me a psychological exam, but that was more directed to whether anybody had anything they could pressure me on and make me unfaithful to the United States. The sub exam was mostly a question of how do you get along in close quarters and emergency situations and things of that sort.

Paul Stillwell: Well, I've gathered that another part of the submarine exam was that it had to do with aggressiveness too.

Captain Schwab: I don't remember anything about that. In fact, almost all the submarine officers I know who were very successful, were not particularly aggressive in their personal lives. For example, there was Burt Klakring, class of '27, captain of the first submarine I went to the Pacific on.[*] He was always extremely nervous, and sweating. He was probably scared; we all were. Of course, you know the old one about submarine patrols: 90% boredom and 10% intense terror. That's the way it was. In his case the

---

[*] Lieutenant Commander Thomas Burton Klakring, USN, commanded the submarine *Guardfish* (SS-217) from her pre-commissioning period in February 1942, through commissioning in May 1942, to May 1943.

10% terror was perspiration. He was a good officer, and he always knew exactly what he was doing. But I wouldn't say he was aggressive in a pugilistic sort of way. Maybe there were others that were aggressive. Johnny Davidson I wouldn't say was particularly aggressive, but he was a good submarine officer.

Paul Stillwell: No, but you had people like Dealey and Mush Morton and O'Kane.[*]

Captain Schwab: O'Kane wasn't that kind of aggressive. He was really a very nice guy.

Paul Stillwell: Slade Cutter who was a boxer at the Naval Academy.[†]

Captain Schwab: Yes, but actually they were all sort of easygoing people, I thought. Well, there were others who had good records who were really unaggressive when I knew them. Shirley Stovall, now dead, sank a lot of ships when he had the *Gudgeon*, but he was also heavily depth charged.[‡] He was the first captain of the *Darter*. He was just the opposite of aggressive. Dennis Wilkinson, first captain of the *Nautilus*, was the gunnery officer of the *Darter*, and I was, at that point, engineer.[§] We were in the conning tower during approaches. We would try to manipulate things to try to get close to the enemy more quickly. Stovall would tend to choose a less aggressive approach. I guess the *Gudgeon* depth-charging had influenced his tactics.

---

[*] Commander Samuel D. Dealey, USN, received the Medal of Honor for his service in command of the diesel submarine *Harder* (SS-257), which was lost in action on 24 August 1944.
Commander Dudley W. "Mush" Morton, USN, received the Medal of Honor for his service in command of the diesel submarine *Wahoo* (SS-238), which was lost in action on 11 October 1943.
Commander Richard H. O'Kane, USN, Medal of Honor recipient whose story is contained in his memoir *Clear the Bridge! The War Patrols of the U.S.S. Tang* (Chicago: Rand McNally & Company, 1977).
[†] Commander Slade D. Cutter, USN, commanded the submarine *Seahorse* (SS-304) from September 1943 to August 1944. The oral history of Cutter, who retired as a captain, is in the Naval Institute collection.
[‡] Lieutenant Commander William Shirley Stovall Jr., USN, commanded the diesel submarine *Gudgeon* (SS-211) from 11 July 1942 to 6 March 1943.
[§] Commander Eugene P. Wilkinson, USN, became the first commanding officer of the USS *Nautilus* (SSN-571), when she was commissioned as the world's first nuclear-powered submarine on 30 September 1954. The oral history of Wilkinson, who retired as a vice admiral, is in the Naval Institute collection.

Interview Number 2 with Captain Ernest L. Schwab, U.S. Navy (Retired)

Place: Captain Schwab's home in Potomac, Maryland

Date: Monday, 2 February 1987

Paul Stillwell: Captain, last week we talked briefly about the trip you made to the Caribbean in the submarine *Marlin*. Could you discuss some of the purposes of that voyage, please.

Captain Schwab: Right after the war started, the end of January and in February '42, SubLant sent both the *Marlin* and the *Mackerel* on a combination war patrol and evaluation cruise to the Caribbean. It was supposed to last one month, and we went out to test the suitability of the submarine for any kind of war patrol. The cruise was to go down the East Coast in submarine sanctuaries to the submarine base at Charlotte Amalie in the U.S. Virgin Islands. Then we were to come back again a week or so after a cruise period in the Caribbean, where a couple of German submarines had shown up. We were supposed to look for them. Of course, nobody on either ship had been on a war patrol. The Germans had been on quite a few at that point.[*] In fact, all the time we were out at sea during that month, towards the end of January and in February of '42, German submarines were sinking ships all around us, yet we never did see any German submarines.

Paul Stillwell: Was this considered as somewhat of a shakedown also?

Captain Schwab: Well, we'd already had a sort of a shakedown before the war. We'd gone up off Cape Cod and had all sorts of evaluation tests by the Navy Test and Evaluation Board—I forget what they called it in those days—and different tests of that sort. But this was more than a shakedown cruise; it was really an endurance test. We weren't supposed to take on any provisions or water or things of that sort in Charlotte

---

[*] German U-boats had begun their patrols when the war started in September 1939.

Amalie. We were supposed to be on our own. It was just go in there and let us rest for a day or so, and that was about the extent of that.

Paul Stillwell: What sort of role did you take when you got back to New London? The *Mackerel* was a school ship, for example.

Captain Schwab: Well, she hadn't been yet. Neither one of them had been at that point. They made them into school ships. The *Marlin* and *Mackerel*, I believe, both became school submarines. When I went to PCO school later on, after coming back from the *Darter* in 1944, *Marlin* was the school ship then; I don't know what happened to the *Mackerel*.[*] I guess she's long gone. The *Marlin*'s long been made into razor blades.[†]

Paul Stillwell: Did the *Marlin* serve in that role while you were on board?

Captain Schwab: No, no, we did not. We acted as training ships before the war or right at the beginning of the war. We went up off Newport and a few other places to train ASW surface ships.[‡] And we found there that the smaller Coast Guard ships and cutters were much better at antisubmarine warfare than U.S. Navy ships. They had a better sense of relative motion or something. We could hardly ever lose them, while we had no problem losing American destroyers.

Paul Stillwell: You thought it was because of the people rather than the equipment on board the vessels?

Captain Schwab: I don't know what it was. They just seemed to be better at ASW. Theoretically, they weren't supposed to be, but they did a very good job.

Paul Stillwell: What were the living conditions like on that small a boat?

---

[*] PCO – prospective commanding officer.
[†] The *Marlin* was sold in March 1946 for scrapping and the *Mackerel* in April 1947.
[‡] ASW – antisubmarine warfare.

Captain Schwab: Until the captain, George Sharp, went to the hospital with hepatitis I was number-five officer, and there were only bunks in the staterooms for four officers. So I slept out in the passageway, as number five, with the chief petty officers. My bunk was right opposite the chief of the boat. They had four chief bunks, and I had one of them. It was sort of crowded; all the things on there were. They had improvements. Instead of having to sit in the head in the engine room, they had an enlisted head and officers' head. In the R-boats and S-boats, when an enlisted man went to the head, they had the pedestal right out in the forward engine room. It was right out in the open for everybody to see. And we had a shower, which was about as big as a very small clothes closet. Living conditions were, for that period, all right.

We didn't have any conventional evaporator and condenser for making fresh water. We depended on some rig they had on the exhaust—the mufflers with evaporating metal spikes on them. The salt water would get processed that way. It seemed to be able to take care of the water all right, but, of course, if you were submerged, you couldn't run them, naturally, because you had to have the diesel engines running. So it wasn't as good as the setup we had on fleet submarines.

Paul Stillwell: Did you qualify for your dolphins in that boat?[*]

Captain Schwab: No, I qualified on the *Guardfish*. After we came back in February of '42 from the cruise down in the Caribbean in the *Marlin*, the captain of the *Guardfish* wanted a replacement for the communication officer that had been assigned. The captain's name was Burt Klakring; it turned out to be Thomas, but everybody called him Burt.[†] He had talked to my captain, who was Red Sharp, and he recommended me. So I was almost immediately shifted over to the *Guardfish*, which had not yet gone into

---

[*] The insignia for a qualified submariner is a metal pin worn above the left shirt pocket. The pin is gold for officers, silver for enlisted men. The design features a pair of dolphins and a portion of a submarine. An individual earns his dolphins by a rigorous qualification process.
[†] Lieutenant Commander Thomas Burton Klakring, USN, was the first commanding officer of the submarine *Guardfish* (SS-217).

commission.* And that's another interesting story.

One of the reasons that Klakring had trouble with the communication officer was that at Electric Boat Company, where the ship was still finishing, was a whole room full of publications and corrections to publications. It had completely overwhelmed the communication officer. I think he was a reserve officer; I'm not sure. He was always going in there crying on the captain's shoulder, and I'd already had experience as an operating communications officer, so I knew that we had a lot of things we were never going to use: all sorts of stuff dating back to 1938, corrections to publications. So I suggested to Captain Klakring—he went along with it—that we take out everything that was classified and destroy the rest of it. If anything was important, we'd hear about it. He said, "Sure, fine." So we did that. Most of the room's contents disappeared in whatever they used for incinerator or something at the Electric Boat Company.

Paul Stillwell: Well, was part of this reservist's problem that he just didn't have much experience?

Captain Schwab: Well, probably not much experience, and I think he also got a little overwhelmed by the size of the job. Because it would have taken him the rest of the war to make all these corrections. All of the ships had the same problems, because they were all started before the war began. They had just, following the automatic procedures, sent all of the books and corrections—things you would never need or never use during the war.

Paul Stillwell: What might be an example of something they sent that you didn't need?

Captain Schwab: Well, a lot of things were in relation to engineering practices and different kinds of examinations and training periods, and so on, which had all been thrown overboard with the war—and ways to assume accountability for everything.

---

* USS *Guardfish* was a *Gato*-class submarine commissioned 8 May 1942. She had a displacement of 1,525 tons on the surface and 2,410 tons submerged. She was 312 feet long, 27 feet in the beam, and had a draft of 15 feet. Her top speed was 20 knots surfaced and 9 knots submerged. She was armed with ten 21-inch torpedo tubes and a 3-inch deck gun.

Once you left to go to the Pacific, everything was wiped out. Nothing was accountable; it was written off as being expended.

Paul Stillwell: [Laughter]

Captain Schwab: Did you know that?

Paul Stillwell: No, I didn't.

Captain Schwab: Yes, that's the way it worked. At least part of the room full of documents consisted of accountability sheets for everything. But we found out pretty soon that these were meaningless, as well as all the corrections. So we just eliminated everything except the classified material. And a lot of that was outdated too. But you had to make a listing of what you destroyed there, so we just got rid of it all.

Paul Stillwell: What about the U.S. Fleet publications, the doctrinal things? Did you have to get those into shape?

Captain Schwab: Yes. Well, they were usually classified, and, of course, we still had "restricted" then. Most of them were restricted-type things. There was hardly anything secret except some communication documents—that's about it—and a lot of confidential stuff. Most of it had no bearing on the war.

Paul Stillwell: Well, the prewar doctrine really went out the window.

Captain Schwab: Oh, yes, especially when they declared unrestricted air and submarine warfare.

Paul Stillwell: Did the doctrine or international law at that point still specify giving warning to a merchant ship?

Captain Schwab: Well, they mentioned that. At Submarine School the training was all in accordance with doctrine at that time, with being the eyes of the fleet and sinking men-of-war. I imagine that changed as soon as we went to war, but I went to Submarine School July to September '41, so it was close.

Paul Stillwell: How much contact did you have with the yard workmen at Electric Boat on getting things done a particular way in the *Guardfish*?

Captain Schwab: Well, at both the Electric Boat Company and the yard at Portsmouth, New Hampshire/Kittery, Maine, all of the civilian workmen and all the military people there were extremely anxious to have us in good shape. Of course, especially, once the war started, you got priority on everything; there was no question about it. We had no problems at all. They just worked around the clock to get things ready. Because the surface fleet had been crippled to a great extent at Pearl Harbor, somebody realized rather early that about the only thing we could do in an offensive way was to run submarines out there, and that was the whole reason for pushing the submarine force. Luckily, they had started building all these things before the war, or we'd have been in trouble.

Paul Stillwell: In addition to the pubs, you were probably learning the systems in the boat also.

At Submarine School they did teach you fleet boat systems. You also had the actual operating of the boats we went out on for training, the O-boats, for instance. You found out that this was not the way it was. We went out on a couple of R-boats and S-boats, and the great big, funny-looking ones like the *Bass* and *Bonita*.

Paul Stillwell: The Navy had the *Argonaut* and the *Narwhal*.

Captain Schwab: Yes, well, they were a different class. The *Bonita* and the *Bass* had very peculiar hulls on them—streamlined compared to the fleet boats. They looked like surface ships, really, compared to them. And they were much bigger. The *Nautilus* and the *Narwhal* were huge.

Paul Stillwell: What do you remember about the commissioning? Was there any special ceremony?

Captain Schwab: First, of course, they had launching, going down the ways. Then the commissioning was the normal thing. The officers and men were all on the deck. They had the dignitaries there, read the orders, and that was it, nothing very special.

Paul Stillwell: There were, in the picture you showed me from *Life* magazine, seven officers in the boat.* Could you provide a description of each of those?

Captain Schwab: Klakring was really an old-school China sailor. I think he met his wife out in Asiatic station way back, and he'd been in R-boats and so on, and had been a music writer. He supposedly had written certain pieces of music, one of them being "Louise," that a French singer, Maurice Chevalier, had made popular. He also wrote quite a bit of music for different Naval Academy music groups. I guess this was his first submarine command. None of us on the ship had been to war, of course; you realize that. He was a very calm person. He was from Annapolis. In fact, when we came back after his big war patrols, they had a Burt Klakring day there. I think he played lacrosse at the academy.

As you said earlier, they seemed to pick submarine people on the basis of them being aggressive; well, he was not that kind of a person. I mean, he didn't strike you as that person. He was very careful to be polite to everybody. In fact, when he was interviewed by newsmen, they always commented that he kept calling them "sir," after coming back from three good war patrols.

Paul Stillwell: But he was a contrast, though, to the timid skippers who went out of their way to avoid contact.

---

* John Field, "West to Japan: U.S. Sub Patrols the Jap Coast, Watches Jap Horse Races and Sinks 70,000 tons of Jap Shipping," *Life*, 15 March 1943, pages 84-86, 88, 90, 93-94, 96.

Captain Schwab: He wasn't timid, no. There were some who appeared to be avoiding contact. I was with one captain like that. He had had very good war patrols in a previous submarine and had really been worked over and just barely escaped depth charging, so that might have had some effect on him.

Paul Stillwell: Sure.

Captain Schwab: But Klakring went out there and did his job. He had a pretty good appreciation of his job, that the job was to sink ships, and it didn't make any difference what kind they were. He did just that when we got out on our first war patrol, off the Japanese coast. We were the first sub in patrol area one, which was the northernmost one that extended from Hokkaido down to below Sendai on the northern Honshu Japanese coast. No American submarine had ever been there before, so that was good in that the Japanese didn't expect us. We sank two ships in about an hour.[*] We had some pictures from ONI, diagraphs, or whatever they were called, pictures of the coast somebody had drawn in 1890.[†] Fortunately, the headlands still looked the same, so that helped us recognize our position. Aside from that, we didn't have any really accurate info. Even soundings were meager.

Luckily the Japanese antisubmarine warfare wasn't much good anyhow, in my personal experience. I imagine later in the war, when they had the small *Chidori* destroyer escorts, they got better, but early in the war they were apparently short on destroyers and had very few air patrols. So we were lucky that way. We would have probably lost a lot more submarines if they'd been any place near our proficiency and the British ASW proficiency.

But Klakring was aggressive, to the extent that we kept very close to the coast all the time. We were operating on the basis that because the Japanese would probably be short of fuel, they would try to conserve time and take the shortest shipping routes. We did have the normal shipping route diagrams from the ONI publications, so we just stayed in those shipping lanes.

---

[*] On 4 September 1942 the *Guardfish* (SS-217) sank the 2,276-ton *Chita Maru* and the 3,738-ton *Tenyu Maru*. Later that day the *Guardfish* torpedoed and sank the 5,254-ton *Keimei Maru*.
[†] ONI – Office of Naval Intelligence.

The first week or so we didn't see much, and we finally went right in off the coast, and we ran into a bunch of fishing boats with a small escort. We tried to talk the captain out of surfacing to shoot him with the deck gun. We had a puny 3-inch/50 double-purpose gun that had been taken from an American Legion lot and refurbished. They ran out of new guns, so that was all we had. All we had was common ammunition. We shot up what appeared to be a small patrol boat, and there was also a couple of the fishing boats. The fishing boats didn't have any engines in them, and the common projectiles would go right on through, so they all jumped overboard. We were only, oh, less than a mile from the beach; they all swam ashore, I guess.

Paul Stillwell: Then you liberated their cache of fish.

Captain Schwab: No, we didn't take any fish from them. We tried to talk the captain out of shooting by saying, "We'll alert them that there's a submarine there."

But he said, "No, we have to do something!"

After the surface shooting, Captain Klakring said, "Well, maybe the best thing to do is to go up off Hokkaido, where the ore ships are." Supposedly, that was their mining area. Then they took the ores down south someplace, where the smelting machinery was. The first ship we sank was an unescorted ore ship, and you've seen a picture of it broken in half; it was just a great, big, empty ship.[*]

Paul Stillwell: Now, you took that photo, and it appeared in *Life* magazine.[†] What were the circumstances of the photograph?

Captain Schwab: We didn't have any special periscope cameras in those days. When we sighted that first ship, the captain was sound asleep. He was wearing blue silk pajamas that his wife had given him. We first saw the ship at very close range, and it was very hazy. He came up to the conning tower and went through the whole sinking wearing his blue silk pajamas.

---

[*] On 24 August 1942 the *Guardfish* sank the 3,109-ton passenger-cargo ship *Seikai Maru*.
[†] See "West to Japan," page 90 for Schwab's through-the-periscope photos of two sinkings.

On that first war patrol we sank six ships, and he put on the pajamas before each sinking. We had the largest number of sinkings early in the war, and I guess we overestimated the tonnages a little bit at 50,000 tons for six ships. I think they cut it down to 40,000 tons and six ships. On the very first ship, the captain was so pleased with the sinking that he called to the chief torpedoman in the forward torpedo room to come up and look at it through the periscope. The entire patrol party got a good look. I suggested taking a picture, and I had the camera up there with me.

Paul Stillwell: What kind of camera was it?

Captain Schwab: It was a Kodak Medalist, a good camera for that period. I just put it on infinity and got it on the ship and opened it up. All we had was Tri-X film; it had only a speed of ASA 100 instead of 400. And it worked fine; you've seen the pictures.

Paul Stillwell: Well, in the picture it looks like the keel had been broken, so that was a good use of the magnetic exploder.

Captain Schwab: Yes. Well, I've got to say more about Klakring before we get into the other officers. On our way out to Pearl Harbor in the *Guardfish*, after commissioning and our shakedown on the East Coast, we went down through Panama. There we had another training period at the Perlas Islands in Panama.

Whoever the training officer was down there—I guess he was the local submarine squadron commander—told Klakring that he wasn't going to do very well; he wasn't aggressive enough. That got Klakring angry. We finally got out to Pearl Harbor, and we had some more training. At that point they cut away a lot of our superstructure, which until then looked like an old bathtub. We didn't get a new gun, though. We had another little training period there, and whoever the commodore was there, who was in charge of training, told Klakring he wasn't aggressive enough, that he was going to have problems.

Paul Stillwell: Based on what? Just his approaches, or . . .?

Captain Schwab: The approaches that we made, I suppose. Remember, the Battle at Midway had just been finished when we got to Pearl.* And they realized that we had a whole bunch of submarines there but few sinkings. Most of the sub skippers at Midway had been raised under the old rules of training that if a destroyer held you down for a half hour, you were dead, or if you were sighted by an airplane within a few minutes of going down, you were dead. So they were very cautious and unaggressive. You remember the *Nautilus*, I guess, conducted approaches by sound and didn't do anything.

Paul Stillwell: She got in a shot on one of the carriers.†

Captain Schwab: The *Hiryu*, *Soryu*, or one of those. But normally, in most parts, the submarines didn't do very much. And they were in the wrong place to begin with.

Paul Stillwell: Well, the submarine skippers were criticizing SubPac and vice versa, for lack of contact.

Captain Schwab: But, also, they weren't very aggressive, according to all the stories. I guess the training officers had been told to take action. And, of course, as the junior officer on the ship, I didn't get to hear all the chewing out that commanding officers did. We went out on the war patrol with Klakring seething, that he'd been told, at least twice now, that he wasn't very aggressive. So he was going to be aggressive, no matter what! Remember, none of us had been on war patrol. In the officers' club at Pearl, there were several officers who had come back from war patrol already, and they had already experienced problems with the torpedoes. A couple of them had said that they fired them according to the doctrine but with poor results. Admiral English supposedly had captains

---

* From 4 to 6 June 1942, U.S. and Japanese naval forces fought a battle northwest of Midway Island in the Pacific. After Japanese bombers had struck the island, carrier-based U.S. dive-bombers attacked and sank the Japanese carriers *Hiryu*, *Soryu*, *Kaga*, and *Akagi* and the cruiser *Mikuma*. U.S. ships lost were the carrier *Yorktown* (CV-5) and the destroyer *Hammann* (DD-412). The battle was both a tactical and strategic victory for U.S. forces.
† On 4 June those on board the submarine *Nautilus* (SS-168) believed they had torpedoed the Japanese aircraft carrier *Soryu*, which was already burning. More recent research indicates the *Nautilus* fired a torpedo at the carrier *Kaga*, but the torpedo failed to explode.

replaced who didn't follow doctrine and said so. He had been a gun clubber and, I guess, responsible for a lot of the torpedo development.

Paul Stillwell: Well, I think Admiral Christie was the main one.*

Captain Schwab: Anyhow, when you went into the officers' club, all the captains got off in the corner, but we didn't know what they were talking about. We found later, that they were cautioning everybody about the torpedoes, that something was wrong. Nothing happened to fix things till after Admiral English was killed. When Lockwood came in, then they started that test of dropping them and so on.

Well, the first estimate was that the magnetic exploders just didn't work. They didn't know till later that the torpedoes were running too deep, and we didn't know either. But a couple of the captains had come in and reported in their war patrol reports that they had set the torpedoes for contact instead of magnetic. Two of them had been summarily relieved for disobeying instructions.

We were short on torpedoes, and, theoretically, the magnetic exploder, if it worked properly, would break the back of a ship, and then you'd only need one or two torpedoes. If the Japanese watertight compartmentation was any good, one torpedo hitting in the side wouldn't sink it, but one breaking the keel would. The captains returning from patrol suggested that the torpedoes be set for contact hits at 10 or 15 feet depth at the most, and not report it. That was the way it went then; it was pretty bad. So that's what we did. It turned out the torpedoes were still running too deep. The first one we shot ran underneath, and the magnetic exploder was close enough, so it worked, and the ore ship had its back broken.

We even started setting torpedoes shallower, because on one ship in the fog, again off Hokkaido, we shot three torpedoes, all of which failed. You were allowed to shoot three at a time, and then, if you didn't sink the ship, you were supposed to do an

---

* Captain Ralph W. Christie, USN. During the 1920s, as a junior officer, he was involved in the program to develop a magnetic influence exploder for submarine torpedoes. The result was the Mark XIV torpedo with the Mark VI exploder. During the early part of World War II, U.S. torpedoes were notorious for running deeper than the designed settings and for malfunctioning or poorly functioning exploders in cases in which the torpedoes did hit their targets. For details see David E. Cohen, "The Mk-XIV Torpedo: Lessons for Today," *Naval History*, Winter 1992, pages 34-36.

end-around and shoot three more, rather than shooting six and getting a decent spread. We shot three, and one of them hit the side of the ship and had a visible impact and noise but no explosion. We came up, because it was foggy, and there were no escorts around. We surfaced, and there was the body of the torpedo bouncing up and down in the water with no warhead on it. I took a picture of it. We came back from our first war patrol, and went into Midway, because we ran out of torpedoes in 40 days or so. The people in Pearl Harbor, when we came in there after our second patrol, didn't believe that this could happen, so we showed them the picture. I guess all these things built up until Admiral English died.

Paul Stillwell: He was killed in January '43.

Captain Schwab: Anyhow, all these things built up, so they finally had to test. There were no repercussions for showing them the picture. They couldn't say we were faking it. But that ship got away in the fog; we couldn't find him again. Of course, we didn't have any surface radar until April '43. All we had was something called SJ radar, which was just a little omni-directional thing, which, theoretically, picked up planes coming in from around 20 to 30 miles out. It never did seem to work. If the Japanese had radar detectors, it was a good beacon for them. I'll tell you a story about that later.

But that was about the business of the captains conferring. Of course, they were all lieutenant commanders. I don't think there were many commander captains in those days, and they were all rather senior people. Klakring was out of the class of '27. We didn't have any real young captains as we did later on, but as the older ones were either fired by the submarine admiral for one reason or another, or, because of rapid promotions, they suddenly became division and squadron commanders. All the young ones got commands. And all the young ones at that point had been out on war patrols, so it wasn't a question anymore of first war patrol for an older, more cautious person, which explains why the curve of submarine sinkings went up, I guess, to a great extent.

Paul Stillwell: Well, there were several factors: better torpedoes, better boats.

Captain Schwab: Well, better torpedoes didn't occur until the end of '43 or in '44. I'll tell you about that when we get to the *Darter*.

Paul Stillwell: Well, we were talking about your officers. Your exec was . . .

Captain Schwab: The exec was Herm Kossler, who was very nice.[*] He was out of the class of '34, and he was a real splendid gentleman. I guess he sank a battleship later on in the war.

Paul Stillwell: He later had the *Cavalla*.[†]

Captain Schwab: That's right. But he was a nice officer, and we had no problems with any of them.

Paul Stillwell: What characteristics do you remember about him? Did he serve as a balance wheel for the captain?

Captain Schwab: Oh, yes, yes. You sound as if you've heard about that. Well, Klakring would take off and start chewing out somebody for not doing something right, and Kossler would calm him down; that's about the way that worked. Did you talk to Herm Kossler?

Paul Stillwell: No.

Captain Schwab: Then he'd be a good one to talk to. But, yes, he was a good balance wheel. There was not a question of who was in charge; it was the captain, but Kossler was good. Of course, neither the captain nor the exec stood watches as we did on the

---

[*] Lieutenant Herman J. Kossler, USN.
[†] *Cavalla* (SS-244) was commissioned on 29 February 1944. On 19 June 1944, during the "Marianas Turkey Shoot," the *Cavalla* torpedoed and sank the *Shokaku*, one of the Japanese aircraft carriers that had taken part in the air raid on Pearl Harbor in December 1941. Kossler was then a lieutenant commander.

Marlin; everybody stood watches—two on and two off, six on and six off. We only had four officers on that cruise we made to the Caribbean.

Paul Stillwell: What kind of a rotation did you have then in the *Guardfish*?

Captain Schwab: Let's see, how many officers did we have?

Paul Stillwell: There were seven in that picture.

Captain Schwab: Yes, seven or eight. Well, we had five watch standers. There was always an officer of the deck and somebody down in the control room; they rotated around. I guess once in a while Kossler would stand a watch, depending on how tired we were.

Paul Stillwell: Well, to have two men in three sections, you needed six officers.

Captain Schwab: Yes, maybe we did. Maybe he did it during the day, because he was also a navigator. I think he used to hang out down there in the control room in the daytime, and that sort of relieved people that way. I forget exactly how that worked, but you did rotate around. I qualified in submarines in *Guardfish*. I guess I didn't qualify for command of submarines until I hit the *Darter*. They made you do more actual physical operation of things in those days. I don't know what the situation is now. To qualify, you had to make a notebook, all sorts of weird things, which I guess is by the board now; I don't know what they have.

Paul Stillwell: They probably still have something like that.

Captain Schwab: You became an expert on submarine history. Kossler was very gentlemanly, a very nice, soft-spoken person. Claggett was the third officer.[*] He was in the class of '35. He left *Guardfish*, I guess, after the second war patrol. He went back

---

[*] Lieutenant Bladen D. Claggett, USN.

and was in New London, Connecticut, when I got back to put *Darter* in commission as the third officer. I was the engineer on the *Darter*.

Paul Stillwell: What was his job in the *Guardfish*?

Captain Schwab: He was the first lieutenant and torpedo officer. They sort of went together. He was also very soft-spoken. He was from the Maryland Claggetts, a famous family name. No problem there.

Let's see, and then the fourth officer was Dick Bowers out of '38.[*] He'd been a lacrosse player, so he got along well with the captain. I don't know if he's still alive or not. But all these people such as Dick Bowers I'd met before someplace or other. And then I was the fifth officer, out of the class of '39.

Paul Stillwell: What was your job?

Captain Schwab: Well, to begin with, I was the communications officer and everything else: commissary and everything you can think of. That was the usual job of the fifth officer. The sixth officer was Don Bowman, who was a reserve officer.[†] The seventh officer was Gil Rohrback, who was also a reserve officer.[‡] He was one of those who left the ship early for some reason. Why he left I don't know. I can't remember how long Bowman stayed on there; Bowman was a very nice officer. He was married. I wasn't, of course, on the *Guardfish*, and Rohrback was a bachelor. Rohrback went on later to become sort of an oceanographic scientist out on the West Coast, and he got mixed up in electronics too.

Paul Stillwell: Were reserve officers relatively rare in submarine wardrooms at that point?

---

[*] Lieutenant (junior grade) Richard H. Bowers, USN.
[†] Lieutenant (junior grade) Don C. Bowman Jr., USNR. Bowman remained in the Naval Reserve after the war and eventually retired as a rear admiral.
[‡] Ensign Gilson H. Rohrback, USNR.

Captain Schwab: There were not too many of them. They'd rotate them out. As you know, in the old days the reserve officers were an unknown quantity. You didn't know what they knew. In submarines it was somewhat different, because none of the Naval Academy officers knew what submarines were all about either. So all your background stemmed really from Submarine School. All the reserve officers had been to Submarine School. So there was a little different feeling about them. If they did their job, that was it. It didn't take long during the war for any feeling that might have existed before the war about reserve officers to disappear on submarines. I don't know how it worked on surface ships, because I was in submarines all the way from the summer of '41 until July of '51, either at sea or ashore, in the submarine force.

Paul Stillwell: Well, you were really all learning together.

Captain Schwab: Yes, that's true. And we hadn't any more war experience than they had, so that was it.

Paul Stillwell: What do you remember about Bowman specifically?

Captain Schwab: He was a very friendly person, and he used to write letters to his wife constantly, a constant writer. I can't remember what job he had, or Rohrbach. I think they were all just assistants: assistant engineer or assistant something or other; that was about it. They were all nice officers, and there were no personality clashes at all. And we all got along well. The captain, Klakring, liked to play cribbage. Whenever he was sitting in the wardroom, if you weren't doing anything, you had to play cribbage with him. And he had all these old China Station tricks. When dealing, he'd flip it so the card would hit the cribbage pegs. We used to accuse him of cheating at cribbage, laughingly, but he didn't, I don't think. We'd play cribbage and keep records of it, you know, win $10.00 on a patrol or something like that.

Paul Stillwell: What was his technique on the cards?

Captain Schwab: Well, when he dealt the cards for cribbage, he'd hit the little pegs on the cribbage board, and they'd flip up a bit. And we'd say he did that so he could see what the card was. You know, he laughed at that. But we all played cribbage a lot; we didn't play too much poker.

Paul Stillwell: I've heard all these tales about the skippers of submarines staying awake for incredibly long hours. What was it like for a watch officer in rotation? Did you get enough rest?

Captain Schwab: Oh, you learned. Well, you learned how to sleep instantly and wake up instantly. You got enough rest when you were off watch, unless other things came up. For instance, if you were the communication officer, you always had a lot of decoding to do. And before we got any of the electrical coding machines, why, you had to do it with a strip cipher, and it was sort of a mess. Then you always had an argument with the captain about what something meant.

Most of the time the engineer, of course, had to do his normal inspections and checking of things, and the exec, the navigator, was taking his sights and trying to figure out where we were all the time. And the watches were standard Navy watches. You just stood them, you ate at normal meal times, and you slept whenever possible.

Paul Stillwell: How was the food?

Captain Schwab: Oh, outstanding! Well, we did have other good things too. Submarines had the first crack of all the movies, and we always had a movie machine, set up either in the after battery or the forward battery compartments, wherever the people weren't trying to sleep. And I guess they slept through the movies as well. But whenever you'd go into port, why, you'd always swap the movies, and you'd usually try to find the one enlisted man on board who knew somebody who was running a movie exchange. Then you'd get more than you were supposed to. There were all sorts of schemes to get more movies and some of the movies where they had people like Betty Grable or somebody in them in a bathing suit, why, you'd find that those pieces would be missing. People would splice them all together so you had movies of girls in bathing suits; that happened a lot. Then sometimes if the area was safe or something, and you ran into another submarine, one of the important things to do was exchange movies. Do they do that today? Did others mention that to you?

Paul Stillwell: No, not specifically.

Captain Schwab: We'd change movies out at sea. Well, there were movies, and then the crew played games, probably poker; I don't know. There was an awful lot of free time off duty, and we had lots of paperbacks. They were those very flimsy ones, not the modern paperbacks, but these were put out by the government. They were free. And we used to get box loads of those things: everything from detective stories to real good literature, history, everything. There was an awful lot of reading going on.

Paul Stillwell: How frequently did you get mail?

Captain Schwab: Well, you got mail only, of course, when you came in from patrol. When you first came in from patrol, you'd get a stack of mail. When I was married I'd get about 20 or 30 letters from my wife with pictures, when we had a child later on. And then, of course, a lot of the people out at sea—if they were married or in love or something—would write letters almost every day, a single letter, and save them up until they came in. Of course, there was no postage requirement; you just mailed them off.

Paul Stillwell: So you probably had to censor those.

Captain Schwab: You trusted the men, because it was their necks if they sent one off. But I can't remember any problems with censorship. You looked at the letters from your own division. You just wanted to be sure they weren't saying, "Well, we're going out on war patrol from Perth, or Western Australia," or something like that. That's the sort of thing; you didn't pay much attention to the personal stuff. Officers usually just initialed off on each other's; they got a censor's stamp on the front. You've probably seen some of the envelopes.

Paul Stillwell: Yes.

Captain Schwab: I can't remember any problems with that at all. Early in the war, most of the enlisted men, of course, were old-timers. They'd been around a long time, so they weren't going to do anything bad.

Paul Stillwell: What about outgoing communications? That was probably pretty limited, wasn't it?

Captain Schwab: You mean of a radio nature?

Paul Stillwell: Transmission, yes.

Captain Schwab: Once you left port, you didn't send anything. You received, and the only time you were supposed to transmit anything was if it was something in the nature of sighting a big enemy fleet, and you knew that there were other American ships, somebody or something, who would be able to take advantage of that. But, of course, early in the war we didn't have anything out there, where submarines were. Then when you left your patrol area, especially if it wasn't when you were supposed to leave the patrol area—as in the case of the *Guardfish* leaving early, because we'd expended all our torpedoes—then you sent a message just as you surfaced, at dusk. Then you'd run like hell in a different direction, in case they were tracking you. Normally, you would send a message that you were coming back, when you were somewhere near Midway, something of that sort—Wake, I guess.

I don't know what patrol it was on the *Guardfish*, first or second, we were coming back and sent the normal coming-home message, but not at night, as usual. On the surface we usually ran around 15 knots on two diesel engines. That was the standard speed going and returning, so you conserved fuel. That was the most economical speed for those boats.

Not long after we sent our message, somewhere near Wake Island, somebody in the control room picked up what appeared to be a plane on the SJ radar. We had rigged a push-button bell over the radar set display, which was in the control room. It was just a little circular cathode ray tube—and a bell up in the conning tower—so when a person saw what appeared to be a plane, he would push this button, and the bell would ring, and the officer of the deck was supposed to dive. So we dived, and, of course, that woke up the captain, Klakring. We came back up to periscope depth in a few minutes, and there was nothing in sight. As the communication officer and everything, I was also in charge of the radar.

We surfaced, and we went along a little bit further. And the enlisted man, whoever he was, on the radar set saw another thing he thought was a plane. So he pushed the button, and down we went again. This got Klakring really mad, because he was eager to get into Midway and get the rest period started. So we looked around, and there was nothing up there so we surfaced again. He said, "I don't want that damned thing to be rung again unless you actually see a plane!"

This time we were running along the surface another five minutes, and the bell rang again. There was a plane in sight. So we dived; this time we delayed a little too long, and the plane, whatever it was and where he came from—Wake, probably—dropped a depth charge on us, and it didn't hit us, but it pushed our nose down.

I remember I was, I guess, in my room writing something, and Dick Bowers was the diving officer, and he was sitting talking to me while I was writing. I don't know who was the officer down below and who had the deck. I've forgotten all that, but when the charge exploded, we took a *big* nosedive. The people in the control room were all thrown off their feet, and the wrenches that worked all the air banks, which you could save yourself with, went flying across the control room. Bowers ran in there and somehow got hold of a wrench and blew the forward tank so that we wouldn't dive all the way down. We backed full, because we were really going down. We were at a tremendous angle. It would have been the end of us, without ever being hit. And we finally surfaced. From then on we had no problems with Klakring and that bell.

Paul Stillwell: So it really had detected an airplane.

Captain Schwab: Oh, it had! If the sun was out, they'd come in at you from the sun, and you couldn't see them. So it really worked. But that's the only time I know of that it really worked.

Paul Stillwell: Were there other occasions when you were depth-charged in that boat?

Captain Schwab: Well, in the *Guardfish*, where I made my first three war patrols, we were lucky. On the first war patrol, when we sank the six ships, the first two had no escorts at all. And then off Sendai, I guess we got three of them in a matter of hours. We were inshore of them, and they had a couple of escorts on the seaward side. We were less than a mile from the beach, and we shot a torpedo or torpedoes at one and sank him right outside the entrance to the harbor. The second one zigged the wrong way, so we got him, too, about five minutes later. The third one actually got into port.

Herm Kossler was a pretty good navigator. We had very peculiar currents off the coast of Japan, so he had figured out, over a period of time, what the current situation was there and how much drift we could allow. The third surface ship went in and anchored in the outer harbor of Sendai, and you could see him. As he swung around, we had a broadside picture of this surface ship, and you could see his anchor chain pretty well on high power on the periscope. So Klakring and Kossler figured out how to fire one torpedo, long range, 10,000 yards or something like that—long shot—five miles.

Paul Stillwell: But you didn't have to figure any course and speed on him.

Captain Schwab: No, he was dead, but you had to figure on the currents. We fired, and the torpedo threaded its way in and hit this ship inside the harbor. Meantime, the one or two escorts that the other ships had with them had figured out that we were probably inside of the shipping lane instead of outside, so they were heading over and dropping depth charges. They threw a few over, but it didn't bother us any. Of course, we were some distance away, but the escorts were headed our way.

When we hit this other ship, that really confused the escorts. They headed into the harbor, figuring we were in there. That saved us from more depth charging. That night they had dozens of little antisubmarine or patrol boats out searching. We had to run out to sea to avoid them. They were trying to surround the sub they thought was in there; they never got us.

We didn't get too much depth charging on the first war patrol. It was mostly because of getting right in close to the coast; they didn't know where we were, and, also, the Japanese weren't very good on ASW.

Paul Stillwell: Was the experience with the plane the worst one you had?

Captain Schwab: Yes. That was on the first war patrol. Second war patrol was—let's see, what did we do on that one? We had to stop and look at different islands, too, for the different things that were going on.

Paul Stillwell: Reconnaissance?

Captain Schwab: Reconnaissance of places such as Eniwetok. Of course, because of my name Ernie, they called it Erniewetok. There were other interesting things that you may not have heard about. Captain Klakring liked fish, and when you got out in certain areas out there, you had flying fish. And so we learned at night we could rig a little sail, canvas or something, on the deck forward. And in the morning there'd be several flying fish there. They were reserved for the captain's breakfast.

On the second war patrol, we sank a couple of ships. The third war patrol we were actually operating out of Brisbane Australia. We left Pearl and went down there. That was when we got a destroyer. Who was it, you mentioned his name, the *Wahoo* captain?

Paul Stillwell: Morton.

Captain Schwab: Morton had gone into a harbor—Wewak, on the northern coast of New Guinea—and had claimed that he had fired down-the-throat shots at several destroyers, maybe two or three. So that was our patrol area on this third patrol, in that whole sector.

So Klakring said, "Well, if he could do it, we can go in there and see what's there." I wrote an article for that in 1947 for *Shipmate*. The title of it was "Too Good to be True."

We went into the entrance at Wewak. Everybody was very nervous, because it was a very small harbor. Klakring said he couldn't see how Morton could have gotten into this place because it was so shallow and narrow. We kept going in, and I don't think the water was any more than 90 feet deep. We were close to being aground. There were about seven merchantmen lined up. We didn't see any destroyers, but there were patrol boats you could see wandering around. We kept going in and in, and the captain said, "Gee, now, all of these merchantmen are lined up. We could fire about six torpedoes and probably get six of them." We were just about to fire the torpedoes when, WHAM! We heard this noise; a shore battery had spotted our periscope and was shooting at it. Of course, all the patrol boats headed for us. For some reason or other, all of the surface ships started swinging, so we no longer had an overlapping shot.[*]

Klakring said, "Well, we better get the hell out of here." And Kossler took a look at the chart that we were operating with. Apparently this had been charted, because it was a British possession or Australian possession. We were in a very tight situation. Backing out was almost impossible in a submarine. In order to turn and get out of that place, we had to actually twist on the propellers submerged. In a submarine to try and twist submerged, it's very difficult to maintain your equilibrium and trim. So we twisted around and headed out of the harbor. Of course, there were about four or five patrol boats dropping what appeared to be small, little depth charges. We started out through one little section of the harbor entrance and they stopped. Instead of coming in to attack us, they sort of paralleled our course, as if they were escorting. We got out of there without any problems. We found out later that we had been right in the middle of a

---

[*] Theodore Roscoe, *United States Submarine Operations in World War II* (Annapolis: U.S. Naval Institute, 1949), page 203, describes and incident that closely matches Captain Schwab's account. The book indicates the operation was on 27 January 1943 at Blanche Bay near Rabaul, New Britain.

minefield, and that was why the patrol boats stayed clear, and nothing had hit us! It was sheer luck. It was too good to be true that we could have gotten in there and out, never doing anything, but not suffering from the minefield at all. Sheer luck!

Paul Stillwell: Well, do you think Morton actually did what he said he did?

Captain Schwab: Well, he might—we didn't see—I don't know how, if he did it, going all the way into that place and actually attacking somebody in there with a down-the-throat shot. If he did that, it was really something. Of course, he didn't live to tell us all about it. Was that the war patrol he was killed on?

Paul Stillwell: I don't know.

Captain Schwab: Well, one of them, where he did three down-the-throat shots, which is the riskiest way to shoot a destroyer that I can think of, because he's lined up perfectly to get you.

Paul Stillwell: Well, and Sam Dealey did that.

Captain Schwab: In the *Harder*.

Paul Stillwell: Apparently, these guys would get away with this a certain number of times and think they were invincible, and they weren't.

Captain Schwab: Well, there were other techniques. When captains would share information—that was before we had surface radar—one of the things that was suggested was the "up-the-kilt" shot. Japanese convoys always were pretty slow, seven to ten knots usually. And early in the war, they had very few escorts. And if they had them, the escort ordinarily would be ahead. One captains said would find the convoy and come around from behind at night on the surface fairly close and shoot them up the tail with his torpedoes. He sank a couple that way. This happened very early in the war, before we got out there on patrol. This was probably why in the convoys we found the escorts were astern of the ships instead of forward.

Paul Stillwell: Did you read patrol reports to see what was working and what wasn't for other boats?

Captain Schwab: Yes, we'd read them, but, of course, each submarine, early in the war, was usually the first one in an area, and what would work up in area one off of Japan, off Hokkaido and so on, probably wouldn't work down off in the South China Sea or Singapore—places like that. You had a different problem in each area. Besides, most captains were individualists. They didn't pay much attention to what others did. They usually looked at the reports to see the kinds of things that went wrong, rather than how attacks were made. For instance, if they had a problem with the radar, they would be interested in what tubes you changed and things of that sort.

Paul Stillwell: Was the equipment generally pretty reliable in the boat?

Captain Schwab: Well, the propulsion equipment was; there was no problem to speak of with the engines. There were very, very rugged diesel engines on those ships. Submarines either had General Motors—Winton, I guess they were called—or Fairbanks Morse. We had Fairbanks Morse. The electrical systems and so on had duplicate, parallel routes on the boat, so you had a lot of redundancy, which helped. The fuel capacity seemed to be all right; we hardly ever ran out of fuel or close to it. I don't remember any patrols where we were really low on fuel. We always came in with somewhat of a reserve. The main problem on equipment, especially early in the war, was the torpedoes. And, of course, before we had radar we were sort of running in the dark, literally, at night. And so were the Japanese, fortunately. I can't think of anything much that was bad, that didn't work properly. They were very reliable submarines, luckily.

Paul Stillwell: Well, that helps when you're on detached duty.

Captain Schwab: We didn't start the wolf packs until later on in the war. I guess we got the idea from the Germans, and then we had *small* ones. I think the largest we ever had was about seven boats, and most of them were two and three.

Paul Stillwell: Well, that's because there were more boats to form wolf packs from.

Captain Schwab: And, of course, at the end of the war, there wasn't too much Japanese shipping left over, either. And they were doing it for different reasons. When Klakring, towards the end of the war, went out with six, I guess, or seven of them, called "Burt's Brooms."* They were supposed to sweep all the patrol boats away from the routes that the surface ships, would go into, actually to attack Japan proper. More typical was the *Darter* and *Dace* team, which was a two-boat wolf pack for various reasons, self-supporting.

Of course, as you probably know, at the beginning of the war, they'd more or less tell submarines what was going on in the different Pacific areas, even probable operations. Then they learned that when the Japanese would capture submarine officers, they would torture them. After the war that was confirmed. They would put matchsticks under their fingernails and burn them. They did that to a couple of people. They'd try to get information on what was going on so they could plan for them. In fact, one submarine that went down, the commodore was on board, and he had operational information.

Paul Stillwell: Cromwell in the *Sculpin*.†

---

* The wolf pack "Burt's Brooms," under Commander Thomas B. Klakring, USN, comprised the *Silversides* (SS-236), *Saury* (SS-189), *Tambor* (SS-198), *Trigger* (SS-237), *Sterlet* (SS-392), *Burrfish* (SS-312), and *Ronquil* (SS-396).
† On 16 November 1943 the submarine *Sculpin* (SS-191) attempted to attack a Japanese convoy but was discovered, depth-charged, and badly damaged. Her commanding officer, Commander Fred Connaway, USN, surfaced the boat and attempted to fight the enemy. He and other members of the bridge team were killed by gunfire. The senior surviving officer ordered the boat scuttled, and a number of the crew members were recovered by the Japanese and became prisoners of war. Captain John P. Cromwell, USN, on board as wolf pack commander, voluntarily stayed on board and died rather than face the potential of revealing classified information. He was awarded a posthumous Medal of Honor.

Captain Schwab: *Sculpin*, yes. Cromwell was the only one who knew future plans. He went down with the ship, so he wouldn't divulge them. But towards the end of the war, for instance, when the *Darter* and the *Dace* were out there in the South China Sea, Palawan Passage, we didn't know that we were there to possibly intercept the Jap fleet coming out to attack the landings at Leyte; we didn't know that. We knew that something was going on, because there was a lot of traffic. We had no information at all on that sort of thing; they just didn't tell you. We learned about Leyte from news broadcasts.

Paul Stillwell: When you were in the *Guardfish*, how much awareness, if any, did you have of Ultra?[*]

Captain Schwab: I don't think we really were getting it then, in the *Guardfish*. I think that came later.

Paul Stillwell: I see.

Captain Schwab: There were certain code words at the beginnings of the messages, which meant only the captain and the communication officer could read them. The communication officer had to do all decoding personally. We didn't know of any code name Ultra. We didn't know where this information was coming from. But we would get advance information—particularly on the *Darter*, we got advance information of convoys coming through and what their turning points were. Of course, the Japanese, as far as I could see, always used their peacetime shipping lanes, because they were the most economical ones, and they were short on fuel. See, especially when we sank their tankers and sank all their supply ships.

---

[*] Ultra—short for ultra secret—was a special security classification given by the British to information gained from breaking the code of the German radio enciphering machine. It has come to be used more broadly to encompass other information obtained from interception and decryption of German and Japanese radio communications.

Captain Schwab: The Japanese were short on shipping, always, for all their war purposes, because they were spread rather thin. And I think I mentioned where they placed their escorts. Early in the war, having few escorts, they put them ahead of the convoys, which were usually small; they were usually seven ships or fewer. They rarely had large convoys that I ever saw. And very early in the war, before we had surface radar to permit really good night attacks by submarines, why, a couple of the commanding officers were able to do up what they called "up-the-tail," "up-the-skirt" shots, by coming around behind a convoy at night on the surface and shooting torpedoes up the stern of the enemy ships until they hit one. Of course, the other ships didn't know they were being shot at until they got hit. Apparently this happened often enough so that the Japanese finally, instead of putting escorts ahead of the ships, they put them astern. That was one of the things that helped us in the *Guardfish* in sinkings off the port of Sendai.

Now, in the *Life* article that you mentioned, it said that supposedly we watched horse racing off the coast of Japan. On the chart, for what it was worth, there was an indication there was a racetrack on the right-hand bank of the entrance to this one port. It was on a Sunday, and we noticed an awful lot of trains and flags flying around this so-called racetrack. We figured they were holding races, but we couldn't see any of them, even though some of the newspaper accounts said we were actually placing bets on the horses. Of course, we couldn't see them at all.

But we noticed that on the bridge that the trains went over, to go from left to right, that there was a single-pedestal railroad bridge. We spent about two days trying to figure out how to hit that post with a torpedo. I think we fired one at it but missed. That probably gave us a little experience for shooting the ships later on when they went in the harbor. But that would have been an interesting one to knock out.

Paul Stillwell: Yes.

Captain Schwab: Well, one of our submarines, actually during the war, did send a landing party ashore and sabotaged a railroad bridge someplace.

Paul Stillwell: I think that was Gene Fluckey.*

Captain Schwab: I don't know who it was, but I remember reading about it.

Paul Stillwell: How did that article in *Life* come about? Did you go somewhere, and a reporter came and interviewed the crew?

Captain Schwab: Well, I had left the *Guardfish* down in Brisbane, after the third patrol. The orders detaching me put me on what they called the relief and retraining crew for a time. Normally, you were put on that if you were going to refit another submarine that was in and go out again. But in my case, I had orders to the *Darter* for the pre-commissioning and commissioning.

But the orders actually allowing me to go never arrived. I mean, they kept saying, "Well, they must be in the mail." We looked in the mail every day for them. We went to the races and did all sorts of interesting things in Brisbane. Meanwhile, the *Guardfish*, I think, instead of coming back to Brisbane, went back to Pearl Harbor, from that fourth war patrol, and that's where the captain and all the people were interviewed. I wasn't on board when this happened. I was already back, or on my way back, to New London to put the *Darter* in commission.

Paul Stillwell: When were you detached?

Captain Schwab: In the first part of April. That's another interesting thing, when you flew across Australia and stopped at all these different places. We got to Brisbane, this was April of '43, and we shifted to the equivalent of a two-engine floatplane—PBY

---

* On the night of 22-23 July 1945 the *Barb* (SS-220), under the command of Commander Eugene B. Fluckey, USN, sent ashore a party of crew members at Karafuto, Japan. The men planted explosives that wrecked a train. See Fluckey's memoir *Thunder Below: the USS Barb Revolutionizes Submarine Warfare in World War II* (Urbana : University of Illinois Press, 1992).

equivalent, except it was passenger configured.* Pan Am was still flying them with male stewards and everything, Pan Am men.†

Paul Stillwell: Was this one of the old Clippers?

Captain Schwab: No, no, it was a PBY; it was not a Clipper. It was a small, two-engine job. So we flew from Brisbane, and we sort of hit Noumea, New Caledonia, Canton Island, Christmas Island, and Fiji. We hit all the islands going back and finally got to Pearl. In Fiji we refueled with the natives with their orange hair. You know, they put lime on it, or lye on it, to make their hair orange. We hit all these places, and one place we were at, Noumea, New Caledonia, that was the headquarters for some admiral—Halsey, I think.‡

Paul Stillwell: Yes, it had been his South Pacific headquarters.

Captain Schwab: They had a big officers' club there; I can remember that very distinctly. The floor had a couple of inches of sawdust on it, just like the place in Maui and Lahaina Roads. All the officers there were fighting all the time. It was a hospital, I guess, there, and they were always fighting over who was going to take a nurse out. I remember that two officers—I guess they were doctors—had a big fight right at the bar, and somebody had to come in and calm them down. We were supposed to leave the next morning on the same PBY, and they had us sleeping in tents.

Another classmate of mine named Jim Hingson—he lives over in Virginia someplace—and I were sleeping in this tent. We'd both been on the *Pennsylvania* together. See, everybody's related. We'd been waiting at Brisbane for our orders; when they finally arrived, we were both sent back together. He was going to go to New

---

* The PBY Catalina was a twin-engine flying boat that performed extensive service before and during World War II.
† PanAm – Pan American World Airways, a commercial carrier that flew many international destinations.
‡ Vice Admiral/Admiral William F. Halsey Jr., USN, served as Commander South Pacific Area from 18 October 1942 to 15 June 1944. He was promoted to four-star rank in November 1942.

London to put another submarine in commission also.* So there we were lying, and we heard these two officers in the next bunks talking, and one of them was G. D. Linke, who'd been the gunnery officer in the *Pennsylvania*, so we got to talking to them. It was really a funny place.

G. D. Linke was a surface sailor, because he'd been on the cruiser *Helena* at Pearl when the attack occurred, and he was objecting.† He was talking the next morning to this other officer and griping about how he didn't get promoted or something. We didn't know what it was all about. But, anyhow, we introduced ourselves, and there was G. D. Linke. You'd always run into people you know. So the next morning we were supposed to get on the PBY to fly to the next island, which I guess was Canton; I forget what it was. They said, "Oh, we're sorry about you two officers, Hingson and Schwab. You've been bumped by these two doctors." I guess they were commanders.

So we said, "We have orders, we're supposed to put a submarine in commission. We've been out on war patrol."

They said, "We're sorry."

Just by luck a co-passenger on the plane was Sunshine Murray, who was captain going back to be chief of staff, I guess, to SubPac.‡ So he heard this, and he said, "Who changed these orders?" And they told him. He went over there, and he said, "You know, these two officers have been out fighting the war, and you guys have been sitting here fighting over nurses." He'd seen that episode, too, and he said, "They're going to go on that plane, or you're going to have to fight me." So we went back on the plane. It was a pretty good deal. Anyhow, we got back to Pearl, and there were no planes then.

I got on the *President Polk*, which was taking—they still had dependents there. This was a transport going from Pearl to San Francisco. And then you had to wait around, and I guess I flew from there. We had priority of some sort, putting new submarines in commission. Hingson stayed in San Francisco because his wife was an Army brat, and she was staying at the Presidio with her family.

---

* Lieutenant James M. Hingson, USN, a Naval Academy classmate of Schwab, served in the submarine *Batfish* (SS-310) from August 1943 to April 1944.
† Commander Gerald D. Linke, USN.
‡ Captain Stuart S. Murray, USN, served as chief of staff and war plans officer for Commander Submarine Force Pacific Fleet from April to November 1943. The oral history of Murray, who retired as a four-star admiral, is in the Naval Institute collection.

So I rode a plane, and I remember it must have been a DC-3 again, which I was used to from Australia. We stopped about three times going across the country. I had everything in a great big suitcase and a seabag, all my earthly belongings from the *Guardfish*. I was going back to get married and had all my better uniforms in the seabag. I don't know why I did it that way, but that's the way it was. So someplace along the line the seabag got detached from my belongings.

I wound up in New York, and then ultimately New London, with just the suitcase and getting married rapidly, on April 22, 1943. I didn't have time to get new uniforms or anything. I got married in a very shiny, blue service uniform. My new mother-in-law said she could practically see herself in the seat of the pants. But it was very good cloth, which I bought when I got out of the Naval Academy; those things still fit after four years. But that was about the extent of that little adventure. But I never forgot Sunshine Murray for getting us back.

Paul Stillwell: Where had you met your future wife?

Captain Schwab: Before the war when I was going to Submarine School, they always had a welcome-aboard party for new officers. Of course, I was an ensign, and a friend of mine, Oliver Bagby out of the class of '38, was in the preceding submarine class.* He was actually there getting ready to go to put the *Marlin* in commission. I didn't know any young ladies in New London, so I was there. Oliver said, "There's a nice young lady I'd like you to meet." So he introduced me to Betty Sandgren, and he said, "The only trouble is that she's engaged."† So we sat out on the balcony at the officers' club in New London, and talked for hours. And, finally, that was the end of it.

Paul Stillwell: Was this in '41?

Captain Schwab: This was in July '41. She told me later, after we were married, that she wondered why I never called her up for a date. I said, "Well, you were engaged."

---

* Lieutenant (junior grade) Oliver W. Bagby Jr., USN.
† This was Betty Ruth Sandgren.

She said, "Well, I'd just broken off my engagement." But Oliver Bagby didn't know that, or things might have happened earlier. Anyhow, I didn't see her again until we came in from the first patrol, so-called, of the *Marlin*, with my nose broken again, and sort of swollen, and with the rumors that we had a German submarine down at the pier, which was the *Marlin*. And there was my wife-to-be at this party, surrounded by a bunch of new Submarine School candidates. Her father was a supply officer, of the submarine force at New London, and also supply officer of the base.[*]

I recognized her right away, figured, well, she can't be married because she wouldn't be up there with all these young officers around her, so I went over. She didn't have a drink, and I said, "Won't any of these people buy you a drink?" Just took her away from them. There were about five or six of them. I took her over to the bar, and she remembered having met me. Well, this was now February of '42. So, of course, being a still unmarried officer in the *Marlin*, I was on night-on, night-off duty. Whenever your married officers had anything to do, I was stuck on board. I managed to get off every other night. I'd call her up a lot, and almost every other night took her out. You didn't do much in those days, because gasoline was already being rationed, and things were short.

So one thing led to another, and before I went off on war patrol on the *Guardfish*, we became engaged. So that was in June of '42, and when I was ordered back to New London, to put the *Darter* in commission, that was about the tenth of April '43. I had said, "Well, let's get married when I get back." So it was all set for April 22. I didn't have much to do about it! That was it. So we got married, and Claggett was my best man at the wedding. Of course, you didn't have classmates to speak of around, and he volunteered.

Paul Stillwell: So he had been detached by then also?

Captain Schwab: He left the *Guardfish* after the second war patrol and went back to put another submarine in commission. I don't know if he was commanding officer or not. I

---

[*] Commander Charles E. Sandgren, Supply Corps, USN, later captain. Betty's mother was Lillian Amelia Nelson Sandgren.

have the feeling he was the exec.* So he was back in New London, finishing up his submarine, and I rounded up a couple extra classmates around, Chuck Nace and a few others.

I stayed at Claggett's house when all this was going on. So it worked out very nicely. Another funny thing happened when I was still on the *Marlin,* after we came back. I knew they had dances every Saturday night at the officers' club, so after I found out she wasn't engaged I invited her to this one dance. I didn't know it, but George Sharp's female cousin was going to be in town. He said, "Well, you're the only bachelor on the ship. You've got to take my cousin to the dance."

I said, "Well, I already have a date."

He said, "Well, would you rather take my cousin to the dance or have the duty?"

So I said, "Well, I already have a date with the supply officer's daughter." That caused him a little problem.

He said, "Write her a letter and tell her that duty is calling you," something like that. So I wrote her a letter to Betty Sandgren and told her that for duty reasons, I would not be able to take her to the dance. And, of course, I went to the dance, and there I ran right into her, with this other girl, which sort of intrigued her. She said no one had ever broken a date with her before, so all these things led to where we finally had to get married to resolve everything.

Paul Stillwell: Did you have much of an opportunity for a honeymoon?

Captain Schwab: Oh, yes, that was another interesting story. I came back, and I had three weeks' leave before I had to report to Electric Boat Company and the *Darter.* I guess you reported to ComSubLant, and then they sent you down there or something—weird system. But I came back, and we got married.

We were from New York, and my father, a retired New York City fire captain, had been grabbed for lots of extra duty. He was the chairman of the draft board in the area we lived in. He also had some connection to the rationing board, not a direct one,

---

* Lieutenant Commander Claggett was executive officer of the submarine *Pargo* (SS-264) from 26 April 1943 to 30 November 1943.

but indirect. So he was always getting introuble with Mayor LaGuardia for drafting firemen. He told him, "My son's out fighting the war, so can a fireman go out and fight the war."

We came back, and just before the war started, I had bought a brand-new 1941 Ford for $950.00. I had sold an old '36 Ford I had from Submarine School. So that car was still in perfect shape, naturally. This was now 1943, but gasoline was rationed. So my father took me down to the rationing board with him, and I wound up with stacks of gas coupons—legally or illegally, I don't know—but I had more gasoline. So went back to New York to get all ready to get married, left New London, went back down there, and decided, well, we'd better go someplace on a honeymoon, even though the war was on.

I figured we might as well go to the best, and went into the Waldorf.[*] They were having a conference of newspaper editors, or something of that sort, and it was full—nothing there. So they said, "Well, try the Park Lane Hotel, down the street on Park Avenue." I went in there, and the resident manager had been in the Navy. His name was Brown—I still remember this. He took pity on me, and instead of just a room, he gave us a nice little suite. So we got married and wound up in New York at the hotel. We were going to be there a week.

The first thing I remember is that on Easter morning the WAVES had been to church or something.[†] About 9:00 o'clock in the morning, they went marching past in the street singing, waking us up, which is not a thing to do on your honeymoon. The next thing I recall is that my wife's mother and sister arrived in New York about three days into the honeymoon. Barnum and Bailey Circus was in town, even during the war, and they had tickets to take her to the circus! So we all went to the circus—another interesting thing to do on your honeymoon.

When we arrived at the hotel, on the way down from New London after we were married, in the room were flowers and invitations to a couple of receptions they were having in the resident manager's suite. In fact, one was the next night, and we went there. They had a bunch of Allied military there. I can remember that one was a great

---

[*] The Waldorf-Astoria is a posh hotel in Manhattan.
[†] WAVES—Women Accepted for Voluntary Emergency Service. Until the 1970s, when women ceased to have a separate organization within the Navy, the term WAVE was used to refer to a Navy woman. In 1943 Easter Sunday was on 25 April.

big Norwegian officer. I think he was in their air force or whatever they had at that time. He thought my wife was very interesting, a newlywed. I was about a foot shorter than he was, but I offered to take him out and beat him up if he didn't leave my wife alone. He put his arm around her and everything like that, so I still remember that I was about ready to kill him! Newlywed, my God! Maximum possessive period in your life.

We found out right away a very interesting thing, that when you were wearing a uniform, you got all sorts of discounts. We went to several good shows and restaurants, and if you were in uniform when you went to them, which I didn't want to do, because I was trained the other way—personal things, you didn't wear your uniform—you got 25 to 30% off on the room. That was even though we had a small suite but were paying the regular room rate. All sorts of goodies.

Towards the end of the week, we got a little tired of charging around New York, so we decided we'd go upstate. We called up there different places, and none of them were open, except we found out that after the next weekend, Beekman Arms in Rhinebeck, New York, was going to be open, and this was the oldest hotel in America. We slept in the same room where George Washington was supposed to sleep. And, of course, it was only a short distance away from Hyde Park.

The manager of the hotel was amazed that anybody would come up there. We had a real big, nice room, and they had good meals in the hotel dining room. And he let us have his bicycle built for two, which is not another thing you want to do on your honeymoon. But we drove all around on the bicycle built for two and had a great time. I can remember that every time we'd drive anyplace, there was nobody on the road. We were the only ones who had gas coupons, I guess. So, finally, we wound up back in New London and started our regular married life, but it was a very interesting honeymoon. No competition from traffic.

Paul Stillwell: Well, you must have fit in the normal honeymoon duties somewhere, because your son was born ten months later.

Captain Schwab: Yes, he was born March 1, '44.[*]

---

[*] The son is Commander Donald E. Schwab, USNR (Ret.), who aided in the editing of this oral history.

Paul Stillwell: Well, what went into getting the *Darter* ready for going to sea?

Captain Schwab: Well, the *Darter* had not yet been launched, as a matter of fact.* So we didn't go out to sea until October. This was the beginning of May, so it was quite a while there. The usual thing.

After the commissioning in September, we tested some torpedoes in the *Darter*. We went up to Bar Harbor, Maine, and fired a whole bunch of torpedoes at a cliff up there to see what would happen, because the contact exploders weren't working either, as you know. They were all made wrong, with aluminum pins or something in them instead of steel. So if you hit at a 90-degree angle, which you think would be right, it would crush the exploder, and it wouldn't go off. If you hit at about a 60-degree angle, for some reason, it worked all right. They didn't know any of these things early in the war. We didn't get electric torpedoes until, I guess, the end of '43 or '44, but they were much shorter range. We didn't like them too much; we liked the steam torpedo. The only thing good about the electric torpedoes, they didn't have any wake. But they weren't quite as fast or long range.

Paul Stillwell: What was your billet in the *Darter*?

Captain Schwab: I was third officer now—the engineer—fleeted up from five to three. The captain was Shirley Stovall, the exec was Buzz Gebhardt out of the class of '38, and I was the third officer out of '39.† Dennis Wilkinson was the first lieutenant and gunnery officer.‡ Eugene P. is his real name, but for some reason he liked to be called Dennis.

Let's see, I remember the other officers on there. Oh, we had Skorupski and Walter Price.§ Walter Price was out of the class of '42 from the Naval Academy.

---

* USS *Darter* (SS-227) was a *Gato*-class submarine launched on 6 June 1943 and commissioned 7 September of that year. She had a displacement of 1,525 tons on the surface and 2,410 tons submerged. She was 312 feet long, 27 feet in the beam, and had a draft of 15 feet. Her top speed was 20 knots surfaced and 9 knots submerged. She was armed with ten 21-inch torpedo tubes and a 3-inch deck gun.
† Commander William Shirley Stovall Jr., USN, commanded the *Darter* from her commissioning on 7 September 1943 to 15 June 1944; Lieutenant Charles R. Gebhardt, USN
‡ Lieutenant Eugene P Wilkinson, USNR. The oral history of Vice Admiral Wilkinson is in the Naval Institute collection.
§ Ensign Walter J. Skorupski, USNR; Lieutenant (junior grade) Walter W. Price Jr., USN.

Skorupski was a reserve officer. Then we had a former warrant officer named Bill Passler, who was really a solid citizen.* All his life he'd been involved in the Boy Scouts, and I'll get to that later. He knew all sorts of tricks of doing things with minimum of resources, especially when we would go to rest camp on the little island that no one had ever been on before. We built tents and things of that sort. But we had a pretty good group.

I came to find out that the *Darter* was the big poker ship, probably because of Dennis Wilkinson, who could remember everything. If you played five-card stud with Wilkinson, just from seeing the up-cards he knew what the frequency was on the down cards. He could tell almost *exactly* what you had.

Skorupski, who was from Hoosick Falls, New York, was another good gambler on board. His father had owned a tavern up there, where in the back room they had poker and so on. Skorupski was a small boy at the time, and he'd go out there and help serve them beer, I guess. And in the center of each table was a hole, he told us. When they'd bet, if they'd say, "Put $10.00 in the pot," you always put about one-tenth of it down the hole, and that paid for the beer and everything else. But he learned all about poker from watching there, and also about shooting dice and so on. He was very good at that but also erratic. You know, one game he'd win a lot, and another game he'd lose a lot. He was that way, whereas Wilkinson never won a lot, and he never lost. He always was level, a very, very clever player.

Paul Stillwell: Nobody would want to play with him if he always won a lot!

Captain Schwab: Well, it worked out that way. I wasn't on the same ship with him after the four patrols on the *Darter*, but I understand that later on, nobody would play poker with him because he never lost. He had been a mathematics instructor in San Diego before he went into full active duty in the Navy—a sharp officer. Of course, you know

---

* Lieutenant (junior grade) William T. Passler, USN.

his career: first captain of the *Nautilus*, and the first captain of the first nuclear surface ship, man-of-war, *Long Beach*.* He was an outstanding officer.

Paul Stillwell: Please tell me more about the skipper.

Captain Schwab: As I said, the captain had a tremendous record from his previous patrols on the *Gudgeon*. He had sunk quite a few ships, but also had received some horrible depth-charging.

Paul Stillwell: Was he the exec in the *Gudgeon*?

Captain Schwab: He was the captain, and he had received some horrible depth-charging on his last patrol.† In fact, the *Gudgeon*, I think, had to go back to the Navy yard to get worked over because it was so damaged. And that sort of made him a lot more cautious, not speaking any—he was a nice fellow. He was also very conservative and staid, and I'll give you an example. We started operating right away out of Brisbane, Australia. We didn't operate out of Pearl except to fuel up and so on, on the way out to the patrol area. We received not as much in the way of training as we had on the *Guardfish*. We had a little bit but not much, because they figured everybody on it had been on war patrol, except Skorupski.

Paul Stillwell: What about the enlisted men? Had they generally been on prior patrols?

Captain Schwab: Well, usually three-quarters had been. When you went in for a refit period, they took off a third or quarter of the crew to stay with the ship and answer questions from the big book that you filled out. And then the refit crew—the ones who hadn't been on the patrol—an unknown number of those would fill in. So everybody in the refit crew was going to do a good job, either because they'd been on the ship or they

---
* Captain Eugene P. Wilkinson, USN, commanded the nuclear-powered cruiser *Long Beach* (CGN-9) from September 1961 to September 1963. The oral history of Wilkinson, who retired as a vice admiral, is in the Naval Institute collection.
† As a lieutenant commander, Stovall commanded the *Gudgeon* (SS-211) from 11 July 1942 to 6 March 1943. He was awarded two Navy Crosses for patrols in 1942.

were going to be on the ship and they didn't know it. So there was a lot of incentive to do well. I think the Germans did the same thing, so we'd learned something from them. Maybe the British did; I don't know.

In one of our patrols, we were to take some Army rangers and land them on the northern coast of New Guinea. I forget the exact name of the place. It was preparatory for some sort of a landing by MacArthur's people there; they were popping around.* Before we went out on this, why, we had a British submarine officer who was rather famous. His name was Miers, and he was famous for having done all sorts of wild exploits in the Mediterranean.† He sank an awful lot of German and Italian ships, and would penetrate into an Italian harbor and shoot it all up, and then go out again in the submarine. He was the one that I'd seen written up many times. It was out there, somehow got out of place, and a bunch of British antisubmarine warfare ships picked them up and started depth charging him. None of his identification signals worked, so he surfaced and let out these typically British obscenities at the officer of the deck of the destroyer. Then they said, "It could only be a Brit." They absolutely didn't shoot at him. I won't tell you what he said; it was pretty vile.

But he had hundreds of stories, all of which were pretty obscene. He would tell us things till we were in hysterics with this guy in the wardroom. He was sent to get him out of the Med, because the Germans had put a price on his head. Anybody captured him got a big, special award.

Paul Stillwell: Was he liaison to your boat?

Captain Schwab: No, he was given permission to ride us and see how we did it, or maybe—I don't know why he was put on there, just to get him out of the Mediterranean. He came out, and I remember we went out to take these rangers out, and we had an awful lot of extra gear: rubber boats and all sorts of junk that we normally wouldn't carry. So the diving officer, and that was me, had a real problem compensating for everything. When we went out, we were sort of bounced around a little bit, had to go up and down

---

* General Douglas MacArthur, USA, Commander Southwest Pacific Area and Force.
† Commander Anthony C. C. Miers, Royal Navy, commanded the submarine *Torbay*. He was awarded the Victoria Cross for heroism while on patrol off the coast of Greece on 4 March 1942.

and finally got her leveled off. On the way down, something jammed in the hatch in the conning tower. We got quite a bit of water in there. Miers was standing next to me in the control room, and I said, "Doesn't that bother you?"

He said, "Ah, happens on our boat all the time." The British are very blasé about things of that sort. We finally got up to the section of the coast where we were supposed to put the rangers off, and they all got off in their rubber boats and went over there. They didn't know what kind of Japanese situation it was. They knew there were Japs there and trying to land on either side of them, sort of pincer them. They got on this one little thing, which was an island instead of a little spit of land with a road in between. They thought was a road was a dry riverbed, and it hadn't rained yet. They went over to reconnoiter, and I remember hearing the ranger who was back on the ship, talking to them on their walkie-talkies. One ranger was up in a tree watching the Japs. He said, "There's about 20 Japanese going by on the road, or river bed below. What should I do?"

The guy back on the ship said, "Shut up, and don't shoot!" I can remember that clearly. So apparently they were going to go ashore; they were going to plot the land out there and see where the Japanese were, and then rig it so that MacArthur's people would come in the proper place. Fortunately, the next day, it rained, and when they went over to take another look, what had been a riverbed was now a torrent. They would have been trapped on this little spit of land. So that never occurred. Whatever happened in northern New Guinea didn't occur right there—further away.

But getting back to what I originally started to tell, when Miers would be eating with us in the officers' mess, which is pretty small in a submarine, he would start telling. Then Captain Stovall would immediately get up and leave and go to his cabin. He wouldn't sit around for the stories, so he was pretty, pretty straitlaced that way. But we all thought Meyers was a wild character.

Paul Stillwell: Entertaining companion, probably.

Captain Schwab: Oh, he was something, yes. He had all sorts of stories about the Mediterranean. I guess the British submarines were a lot more primitive than our fleet boats at that point, so he was amazed at some of the stuff we had. I can't remember if we had the little anti-surface ship torpedoes, called "Fido," the Mark 46, and they would swim out of the tube. They called them "Fido" because you could scratch the little sonar at the nose, and it would wag its tail. That's the way the story goes. But we had four patrols on the *Darter*, and she's still out there on the Bombay shoal, where she's no longer visible.* But the first two patrols were with Shirley Stovall, and I don't think we sank anything. I can't remember.†

Paul Stillwell: Would you attribute that to his caution?

Captain Schwab: Caution and there wasn't much to sink. But we did a lot of reconnoitering of Truk, things of that sort.

Paul Stillwell: Was that before the big air raid?

Captain Schwab: Before the big air raid, yes.‡ They had several submarines watching. We spent a lot of time on various lines there, in case the Japanese wanted to reinforce or do something.

Paul Stillwell: Scouting lines.

Captain Schwab: Scouting lines, yes, but mostly it was boring stuff. We never did see anything. We were on the surface a lot during the daytime. In some cases, we'd be on a scouting line, and you'd go to one end of your line, you'd see an American submarine on the surface, and you'd go to the other end and there'd be another American submarine.

---

* During the Battle of Leyte Gulf, the submarine *Darter* (SS-227) torpedoed and damaged the Japanese cruiser *Takao*. The *Darter* and her sister ship *Dace* (SS-247) pursued the crippled cruiser through the channels of Palawan Passage in the Philippines. Just after midnight on 24 October 1944 the *Darter* grounded on Bombay Shoal. Efforts to free her were unsuccessful, so the crew evacuated to the Dace and rode safely to Australia. See the Naval Institute oral history of Vice Admiral Eugene P. Wilkinson, USN (Ret.), who was one of the crew members evacuated from the *Darter*.

† The *Darter* was credited with one sinking during Stovall's time in command, the 2,829-ton cargo ship *Fujikawa Maru* on 30 March 1944.

‡ On 17-18 February 1944, planes from nine carriers attacked Truk Atoll in the Carolines chain, and surface combatants later made a circuit around the atoll. All told, U.S. forces destroyed most of Truk's airstrips and sank a number of warships and merchant ships—a total tonnage of some 200,000. The *Darter*'s reconnaissance took place the month before the raid.

That's all you would see, American submarines. That's what Japanese were thinking about at that time too.

Paul Stillwell: What specific memories do you have of reconnoitering Truk? Were there a lot of Japanese ships there?

Captain Schwab: Oh, we did see a lot of tops; that's about all. That's as close as they wanted us to get. They didn't want to warn the Japanese. This was before the air raid.

Paul Stillwell: What was your purpose?

Captain Schwab: To see if it was worthwhile, I guess, to have a raid. We also stayed in position so that when the raid occurred, we were supposed to get the people who came charging out of there. They all went to different directions, and we never got a shot at any of them. We did see them coming out.

Paul Stillwell: What do you mean, different directions? Did they go out a different entrance?

Captain Schwab: Well, they didn't come anyplace where we could make an attack on them. We had sectors there we had to stay in; we couldn't go out of our own sector.

Paul Stillwell: Was part of the idea of you being there also that you could pick up downed airmen?

Captain Schwab: Yes, that would have occurred, if necessary, but we never got involved in any of that.

After that we had a rest period, and that was when my son was born, so it was around March 1, 1944. We were all in a so-called rest period at Surfers Paradise in Australia, which I understand is quite a resort now; I haven't been there since the war.*

---

* Surfers Paradise is a suburb of Gold Coast City in Queensland, Australia.

We were informed that Admiral Halsey and staff were arriving. I heard that he always brought his own toilet paper with him.

Half the hotel was civilian. In the center court was a small zoo, which would wake you up about sunrise. The other half was all U.S. submariners, with a big tank full of Australian imperial quarts of beer, and all the booze we could get. Admiral Halsey and his contingent arrived, including a great big, flat-sided suitcase, which was loaded with American toilet paper. If you ever used Australian toilet paper, it's twigs on one side and shiny on the other. It's the worst thing in the world. You could cause yourself irreparable damage with it. In fact, before I left the *Guardfish* to come back to the United States to put the *Darter* in commission—I guess I was third officer, engineer, then, why, we were in dry dock, and all the rest of the officers were off at rest period or some rest camp. To go to the head, after my first episode down there, I carried my own roll of toilet paper with me. That was awful stuff.

He was there, and, of course, I got the message about my son being born. They had a thing there, "I'm a proud papa," I had picked up someplace. I put that on and passed out cigars to everybody. Admiral Halsey and his staff were at a table in the little mess hall there. I tried to give him a cigar. He didn't smoke it; he gave it to his chief of staff or somebody. But I had a case of Old Granddad or something like that, and he drank that all right.

We were having a great time celebrating my son, and we didn't turn in till around 2:00 or 3:00 in the morning. It was right at the beginning of a rest period. I heard this noise at about 6:00, and I looked out the window, and there were Admiral Halsey and his chief of staff going down to swim. That guy was rugged but had funny, skinny legs, a very peculiar-shaped person, but he was really nice, a very friendly person.

Paul Stillwell: Was that first patrol kind of a letdown in that you didn't have much action?

Captain Schwab: Yes, of course, having been on the *Guardfish* when we had sinkings every patrol, it was a lot different. We came back and went into Brisbane again. Stovall was relieved—maybe at his own request—by David McClintock, out of class of '35,

Claggett's classmate.* Buzz Gebhardt, the exec, had some sort of stomach disorder, so I fleeted up to become exec and navigator. Dennis Wilkinson then became our engineering officer. We also kept him on the torpedo data computer, because he was good in that too, I think; things were sort of rearranged that way.†

Paul Stillwell: Apparently he was not only good but *very* good.

Captain Schwab: Yes, very good. It was on the *Darter* that we were told that there were several Japanese cruisers up in Davao Gulf of the Philippines. The *Darter* was attached to the Southwest Pacific submarines, and the dividing line between Southwest Pacific and Pearl Harbor submarines ran right down the center of this gulf. To the east of that were supposed to be Admiral Lockwood's submarines, and to the west, Admiral Christie's submarines.‡ Well, Jimmy Fife was at Brisbane.§ He was the deputy. By that time Christie was in Perth, Western Australia—Fremantle.** So we were told from some sources, I guess coast watchers or something, that there was a place up there where cruisers were refueling, and that there were three to five cruisers in there, and we should go up and stop them. This was being relayed from whoever the source was, to Australia, to Pearl Harbor, and back to Brisbane. Bellconnen, I guess, was the radio station that we got. So there was always a time lag and so on. I don't know if this was when Stovall was the captain or not, but it was the *Darter*. So we were sent in to keep on the left side of Davao, the western side, and some other submarine was on the eastern side.

We took position there waiting for the cruisers to come out. Finally, one day we saw what appeared to be cruisers coming out. Then we don't know what happened, but the submarine up ahead of us—to the right of us—had moved over and got out of position. That was the Pearl Harbor submarine, and he was getting depth-charged. So we took position, figuring which way these cruisers would go. It turned out they went

---

* Commander David H. McClintock, USN, commanded the *Darter* from 15 June 1944 until the boat was lost on 24 October 1944. Commander Bladen D. Claggett, USN, commanded the *Dace* (SS-247), 1943-44.
† The torpedo data computer was a piece of equipment that figured approach courses for torpedoes to take on their way to a target and set the torpedo gyros prior to firing.
‡ Rear Admiral Ralph W. Christie, USN, Commander Submarines, Southwest Pacific Area, from January 1943 to November 1944.
§ Captain James Fife Jr., USN, commanded Task Force 42 (later 72), 1942-44.
** Fremantle is the port for the city of Perth.

zooming off the wrong direction. Even before it was dark, we surfaced to try to tell somebody what was going on, to get some more submarines—there were submarines all over the place—to get them to intercept these cruisers.

Our message got down to Australia, and by the time it got to Pearl, to get back to Lockwood's submarines, it was too late. They were all gone. But it was horrible; we couldn't talk to each other. It was really a very bad situation. But I remember we were there lying at periscope depth, trying to get into these cruisers, and we couldn't do it, because of the way they changed course. Probably the other submarine attacked, and we never knew who he was; he was getting really depth-charged. Depth charge noise travels a great intensity for long distances. You think you're getting depth-charged yourself, and that thing can be miles away, a very weird situation.

I think Stovall was the captain then. With the next patrol, we sank a gunboat in New Guinea, with McClintock.* It was supposed to be rated a small cruiser; they gave us credit for a super-large gunboat. We sank that, and then there was the fourth and last patrol of the *Darter* was when *Darter* and *Dace* started the Battle for Leyte Gulf. We intercepted Admiral Kurita's fleet going up to Leyte Gulf and sank the flagship *Atago*.† The *Dace* sank the *Maya*, and then we put a couple of torpedoes astern of another cruiser, *Takao*, which was crippled, and that led to the *Darter* going aground. You don't want to get into that yet, do you?

Paul Stillwell: Well, no, not if you've got more to say before that.

Captain Schwab: Well, the *Darter* and the *Dace* had been put out on this patrol in Palawan Passage, with minimum information that anything was going on, because of the reasons I mentioned earlier, not wanting to have anybody tortured, and so on, to divulge U.S. plans. We'd been inside the Borneo Reef with the *Dace* and sank a couple of ships up there. In the process the *Dace*, on its way out, had been chased down by a plane and wiped off one or two sound heads.

---

* The *Darter* sank the 4,400-ton minelayer *Tsugaru* on 29 June 1944.
† The *Darter* torpedoed and sank the heavy cruiser *Atago*, flagship of Vice Admiral Takeo Kurita. IJN, on 23 October 1944.

The exec on the *Dace*, incidentally, was a classmate of mine by the name of Rafael Benitez, and he was the captain of the *Cochino* when she was lost.[*] So we were all related in submarines in one way or another. We got out there without any incident. The *Dace* caught up with us and told us that she had some sound heads gone, and her radar was out. I don't know whether she needed a part or what was going on, but after relocating ourselves on a patrol station in the Palawan Passage, why, we closed the *Dace* on the surface one night. We put a line over, and we were going to exchange movies and parts, and we also exchanged messages. The easy way to exchange a message was to put it in a condom and tie the top of it; it would never get wet. You could do anything like that—very useful in those days.

While we were on the surface, we picked up on radar this huge number of ships coming from the south. So we told the *Dace* orally, megaphone, what was going on, and said, "You go up to the north of us, and we'll stay south, and we'll coach you on," which we did on the surface using aircraft code. So, finally, just before dawn, why, we dived. A short time later, these ships appeared, and the *Dace* was about three miles to the north of us. These ships appeared, a huge number of ships. So, meanwhile, we'd sent off messages to everybody, warning them that there was a hell of a lot of ships coming. We counted 20 or 30 ships—I forget the exact number—big ones.

We took a look. We couldn't figure out which were the larger ships. There were several columns there, at least two. We lined up and hit the *Atago* with, I think, four or five out of six torpedoes, and swung around. We saw another cruiser, the *Takao*, and when we started hitting, the Japanese ships changed course a little bit. And instead of getting the *Takao* with our stern tubes, we just got her stern. We didn't sink her, but she stopped dead in the water. Just about two seconds later, one column had come over right in front of the *Dace*, setting up perfectly. Claggett supposedly said, "Let the cruisers by; we'll try the battleship." But he got a cruiser, too, the *Maya*. The *Maya* actually came down on top of him practically.

---

[*] Lieutenant Rafael C. Benitez, USN. Later, as a commander, he was skipper of the submarine *Cochino* (SS-345), which was lost off Norway on 26 August 1949 as the result of battery explosions and fires. For details see the Naval Institute oral history of Rear Admiral Roy S. Benson, USN (Ret.), and William J. Lederer, *The Last Voyage* (New York: Henry Holt and Company, 1950).

They had 16 or so destroyers with them, and they dropped quite a few depth charges by us, but when the *Dace* started hitting, that confused them. They left us and dropped depth charges on the *Dace*. They missed both of us, and we surfaced. I mean, we came back up to periscope depth sometime later. Right about this point, Captain McClintock and myself and Wilkinson—we hadn't been to sleep in, oh, say, 60 hours, because we'd been inside the Borneo Gulf, and then in contact and all that sort of stuff. We were taking Benzedrine pills, but they had absolutely no effect at all. We could hardly stay awake.

We were at periscope depth, and there was the *Takao* dead in the water with two destroyers. We blew up one of its screws or something. But when it was sitting dead in the water, all we had left were some short-range electric torpedoes. We didn't have any long-range ones the way we had on the *Guardfish*. That meant you had to get inside of 4,000 yards, two miles. We were making noise or something, because every time we'd go in, one of the destroyers would come over, right at us. So we'd go down, he'd drop one depth charge, and then he'd go away again. Sort of a cat-and-mouse deal.

They were getting short of depth charges, I guess, too. So we tried that a couple times and, finally, McClintock said, "You know, we're not going to get anyplace this way. We can't even get close enough to be sure we're going to get a hit with these things." So we stayed at periscope depth, at about 6,000 yards, and watched them. We worked around towards Manila. We figured that they'd go up there, because there was a dry dock. Instead, they finally got way on, about six knots, as it turned out—we measured it—and headed south. They got to Brunei Bay in Borneo, where we'd sunk a couple of things, and then they went to Singapore. So we had worked to the wrong way. We didn't know what happened to the *Dace*; we kept in touch with the Japanese on the periscope.

Now, you realize this was in October '44, change of the monsoon, and navigation there was tricky at best. We were in the Palawan Passage, which, because of either Palawan or the reefs, is about 20 miles wide, and we had a dubious navigational position all the time. Now, by this time we had surface radar; I forget the mark of it. We were able to tell from the mountains on Palawan roughly what our longitude was, but it was very hard to figure out what our latitude was, and especially getting any star sights, to keep in touch with this cruiser to be sure he wouldn't get away. We waited until it was really dark, and then we surfaced. If we'd surfaced earlier, he would have seen us, and the destroyers probably would have come over and done something to us.

Paul Stillwell: So you started making a run toward the south when you saw which way he was going?

Captain Schwab: Well, he was going six knots, and we had worked around to the north, figuring he'd go to Manila, because we didn't know that the Philippines were under that kind of an attack at that point. We didn't know why all these Japanese ships were all going anyplace. So when we surfaced, we finally ran around, and we got in touch with the *Dace* with aircraft code.

Paul Stillwell: What do you mean by aircraft code?

Captain Schwab: Well, we had a two- or three-letter code that aircraft used to communicate. If you used that then, theoretically they wouldn't know you were a submarine, but they could probably tell from other reasons. But it wasn't long; it was just a book with two- or three-letter meanings like, you know, a two letter meaning was "am aground" or something like that.

Paul Stillwell: How were you were transmitting these?

Captain Schwab: By radio, Morse Code. So we worked around, and we were on the western side of the cruiser track. We got in touch with the *Dace* and told them the situation as best we could, and arranged to make a combined attack around, oh, midnight or 1:00 o'clock in the morning. He would come in from one side, and we'd come in from the other, figuring that the destroyers couldn't get both of us, especially since we had no indication that they had any radar. They might have had a radar detector, but we don't know that. So we were all set to go in.

We were partially flooded down. We were making about 19 knots on the surface on one side. I don't know how fast the *Dace* was going on the other side. Just about, oh, a couple of minutes before we were supposed to turn in, we hit Bombay Shoal at 19 knots. And just before we hit, I told the captain, "You know, because of the change of the monsoon and the variations in tides here, I'm not sure . . ." We were traveling in about a 20-mile circle, because we hadn't had a fix for 30 hours or so, except longitude. "So I don't know where I am in latitude and not too good in longitude, but if we're in the right longitude, we're going to hit a shoal one of these minutes."

I'd no sooner said that than the captain said, "Well, shoals aren't any worse than depth charges," and Wham!—we hit. Skorupski had the deck, and the captain was up there on the bridge with him. They thought we'd been torpedoed, because it went just like that! So did the crew. All the watertight doors went shut automatically, and not a leak. But we were aground all the way back to the screws. We hit at maximum high tide, and we really hit!

Paul Stillwell: And maximum speed.

Captain Schwab: Well, we could have been going 21 knots if we hadn't been flooded down partially. That was it. So we sent out in the two-letter code, "Aground," to the *Dace*. The cruiser still had two destroyers with it. We both had them on our radars, of course. I guess Dennis was in working the TDC in the conning tower, and I was navigating, telling the captain I didn't know where I was. The *Dace* lost one of the destroyers on its radar, heading toward where we supposedly were. It turned out it had. He'd heard us go aground or something, because they were only going about six knots. We had two 4-inch deck guns, and quite a few .50 calibers, and I guess we had 1.1s or something.

We had all sorts of classified stuff, so we started burning. They had cleaned out, because they knew we were going in really shallow areas. We didn't have an ECM on board.* They had taken that off. We had a strip cipher, and that was about it. So we started burning all that stuff in the forward engine room. And we got the crew up there to

---

* ECM – electric coding machine.

sally ship. They were really going back to the old days; they had no success. We burned out the motors while we were trying to get the boat to back off. Finally, the *Dace* lost the Japanese ship. She still had some good torpedoes left, and they figured they'd come over, take care of the destroyer, and then rescue us and go.

Meanwhile, I put Dennis Wilkinson over in a rubber boat. He went all around and said, "It's horrible." We had a lead line; we were really in there. By the time he came back, you could see the coral heads coming up. So the *Dace* came over and put a line over to us and tried to tug us off, and no luck at all. So we started to abandon ship. By this time there was no moon or anything. It was cloudy or something; we couldn't see anything. We decided to abandon ship, set all the demolition charges, including the torpedo tubes and all that sort of stuff, the torpedoes.

Paul Stillwell: Did you make a conscious effort to destroy the TDC?

Captain Schwab: Oh, well, they had little things you put in there; there's a special metal that burns very nicely.

Paul Stillwell: Magnesium?

Captain Schwab: Yes, it was magnesium something that you stuck in there. I don't know whether it worked or not. That wasn't my thing. My thing, with the chief of the boat and the exec, he and I had to go through and set everything. I don't know what the captain was doing, but we discovered that seven-man rubber boats held 21 people! We got over 14, anyhow. Everybody got off with what they were wearing. I was wearing shorts and a baseball cap and sandals; it was pretty hot. I had a .45, so I put that on for some reason.

So the burning was going on, and the destroyer came over and stopped dead in the water about 1,500 yards away, heading right at us. We had two 4-inch guns, all kinds of ammunition on deck, and if he'd come any further, the deal was, with the .50-calibers we were going to wipe out his bridge and then hull him with the 4-inch, probably could have sunk him. Of course, we were a pretty small target compared to him. Probably would have killed us first. But he was stupid; he just stopped dead in the water and didn't come over. He couldn't see us—obviously didn't. We turned off our radar so we wouldn't be detected, and he finally went away. That's when the *Dace* came over.

Paul Stillwell: Oh, the *Dace* hadn't been there?

Captain Schwab: Hadn't been there yet. So the *Dace* came over and put a line over and tried to pull us off. Just before dawn, we got everybody over except the captain, McClintock, myself, and the chief of the boat. This time we were way out of the water; the screws were out of the water, everything. So we turned on all the demolition charges, and we had a couple of minutes to get off. We got off the stern, and I cut my leg on the propeller, which is how sharp it was.

The chief of the boat wasn't going to leave, and I said, "Well, you're going to leave." I had to pull my .45 out and tell him, "You're going to leave with me, or you're going to be dead on the *Darter*. I don't want anybody here that can tell anything!" So he finally came over. We got over on the *Dace*—two complete submarine crews, so McClintock and Claggett had a little conference, and I think Claggett had four torpedoes left.

He said, "Well, we tried. Better blow up the *Darter*." He sat back there and shot the torpedoes, and they all hit the reef; didn't bother the *Darter*. The demolition charges just went "bloop," and nothing happened. We saw white smoke come out of the conning tower, and that was it. So the *Dace* got its gun crew up, and they put quite a few holes in the *Darter*, including—you were asking about the TDC. I'm pretty sure they hit the TDC, because that was a pretty good target.

While they were shooting, this Japanese floatplane came over and they saw it. We had a complete submarine crew and everybody watching this. They all got down and figured, maybe they'll bomb the *Darter*. And they dropped a bomb, whatever—depth charges, but they missed the *Darter* by about 100 yards ahead and nothing happened. That's all he had, I guess. He went away. Of course, the *Dace* had submerged in the meantime.

About an hour later, here came this Japanese destroyer. Of course, now the *Dace* had no torpedoes. To show you how poor communications they had, they must have known there were two submarines. The destroyer went over there and stopped dead in the water and put a boat over and boarded. All they got out of it, as far as we know, was one quartermaster's notebook. We had taken all the quartermaster's notebooks with us except one, which had slipped down when we hit, or something, and that showed that—I remember, somehow from intelligence or reconstruction—when we were operating someplace where we stayed pretty shallow, it showed that we were operating at about 100, less than 200 feet, instead of going down to our full submergence, which was around 400 in that period.

Apparently this confused the Japanese, and they started setting their depth charges at a more shallow depth again, which helped. I don't think we lost too many submarines from then on, except to mines. We got a couple of mines in Balabac Strait, I guess it was. But the destroyer stayed there for about an hour. Meanwhile, Claggett was champing at the bit, but there wasn't anything he could do about it. The destroyer finally went away, so we decided we'd stay that night and put the *Dace*'s demolition charge on board. So I was going to go over myself with the chief of the boat, who was a chief gunner's mate, and another enlisted man. We had the rubber boat on deck. This night was clear; there was a moon.

So along about midnight we closed in fairly close to the *Darter*, had the boat all inflated, and suddenly out of nowhere this "ping, ping." You could even hear it from the upper deck where we were. Claggett figured, well, there must be some submarine or something around there, watching. It turned out there was a Japanese submarine that was sent to watch what went on; I guess he was trying to get a range to shoot. So we abandoned the whole project and buttoned everything up, and 12 days later we were in Perth, Western Australia, having eaten everything on board. I couldn't eat American cheese or canned corn for years. That was when we played poker all—in order to sit in the wardroom, you had to play poker with Dennis Wilkinson. So I didn't lose; Dennis won a lot. It was a very interesting trip down there.[*]

---

[*] See Wilkinson, "Abandoning the *Darter*," in *Submarine Stories: Recollections from the Diesel Boats* (Annapolis: Naval Institute Press, 2007), pages 183-185.

Paul Stillwell: I bet it was pretty crowded too.

Captain Schwab: Oh, two complete submarine crews! Yes, getting to sleep any place was interesting. Well, I had that .45 on, and I went to sleep up in the conning tower; it was the only place you could find room.

Paul Stillwell: Did you sleep on the deck?

Captain Schwab: Oh the deck, yes. When I woke up, the .45 was gone. We never found out who got it; somebody did. It was expendable. So we got into Perth, Western Australia, 12 days later. They had the usual board of investigation and all that stuff. We all had temporary clothing they issued us; everybody looked pretty bad. We had the *Dace* crew forward when we came in, all in their good-looking uniforms. We were all in our horror, just the way we were rescued. It must have been an interesting picture if anybody took pictures of it. They had the board of investigation. A classmate of mine was the navigational expert, and he was awaiting investigation for having run the *Nautilus* aground.

Paul Stillwell: Who was he?

Captain Schwab: It was Ben Jarvis.* My quartermaster's notebooks were all right, and you were able to tell—the way we kept them in those days—exactly where we were and what we had estimated the currents were, and from other people operating in the area, what they were. They all jibed; they agreed that when we hit, that I was operating in a 20-mile circle and didn't know where the hell I was. But there's a Navy reg that says you can't break off contact with the enemy just because you don't know where you are, or words to that effect. So we all were excused.

    Oh, there were a couple of funny incidents, though. Before we left—I don't know which port it was—one of my quartermasters on the *Darter* was taken ill. We had to

---

* Lieutenant Commander Benjamin C. Jarvis, USN, executive officer of the submarine *Nautilus* (SS-168). On 31 October 1944 the *Nautilus* scored 55 hits with her 6-inch deck guns while firing at the abandoned hulk of the *Darter* and reduced it to scrap.

have a good quartermaster who was good on maps and charts and everything, because we were operating in those old British things. It turned out that the quartermaster on the tender, who was also an old submariner, had never been to sea on a war patrol, but he was the one who was putting all these charts together. So he volunteered to go on with us. He came out, and he was my navigation assistant too. They talked to all the crew to find out what they thought of all the officers and whether they'd done a good job. I saw all the transcripts later, and they said to him, "What was your . . ." aside from all this technical stuff, which was apparently all right, "What is your personal opinion of Mr. Schwab as the navigator?"

He said, "I can say, without any fear of being wrong, and so on, that he was the best navigator I've ever been on a war patrol with." I was the *only* navigator he'd been on a war patrol with. I thought that was pretty nice of him, pretty sharp.

I guess the *Guardfish* got the Presidential Unit Citation for a big first war patrol, which got a lot of publicity, and that was in the article in *Life*. And the *Darter* got a Navy Unit Commendation. In both cases, the captains got Navy Crosses, and I guess Silver Stars. They give all sorts of decorations for that sort of thing. It was an interesting thing, but that was about it.

When the *Guardfish* made its war patrols, the captain got a Navy Cross, Herm Kossler got Silver Star, and that was it. They didn't hand out millions of decorations the way they did later. They worked it backwards, so I got a Bronze Star or something out of the *Guardfish*'s first patrol. I don't know what for; taking the picture, maybe, or just being alive. You can see the commendations up there, as a matter of fact. They were all highly classified. Of course, the Japs knew they'd been sunk.

Paul Stillwell: What do you remember about the enlisted crews in these two boats?

Captain Schwab: They were great. All the weak characters had been weeded out as you went along. A lot of people wanted to go out and do a good job, but something would hit them. We had one young fellow who was a—of course, when you're in battle stations, you have other duties—but he was really gung-ho. He was talking about all these wonderful things he was going to do. We went out in the *Guardfish*, and the very first time he got depth-charged, he immediately got into his bunk and covered himself up and pulled the zippers around and never came out again. They had trouble feeding him, and it got to smell quite a bit, because he never did anything except stay in that bunk. We fortunately got rid of him at, I guess, Pearl Harbor, and he became a chief petty officer cook. After the war, we all received announcements that he'd opened a big restaurant or a chain of restaurants in upstate New York and wanted everybody from the *Guardfish* to come visit him. Still have it around here someplace.

People reacted in different ways. People you wouldn't expect to be aggressive were and vice versa. We had one whose name Walt Stanowski. He was a ship's cook, and he didn't like to get depth-charged or anything like that. Obviously, nobody did. But in the *Guardfish*, when we first shot up the fishing boats and the escorts, whatever they had, he was manning a .50-caliber machine gun. In the process, he got his fingers fouled up and cut off his little finger in the mechanism somehow. Blood was spurting all over; it didn't bother him. He said, "Well, give me a shot of brandy or something." So he had a shot of brandy, and that was it. We had to grab him to get him away so he wouldn't bleed to death. I guess you don't bleed to death from your little finger, but it was a lot of blood floating around. He was so excited with shooting up something. It's a lot different when you do it yourself than when you're just sitting there receiving. I can't remember any officers having problems that way, where they actually went into a blue funk of some sort. I can't remember any of that happening.

Paul Stillwell: Well, really, you had gone through quite a few screening processes to get the men who were with you.

Captain Schwab: Yes. Well, of course, I understand now they don't even ask you. They just assign you to submarines these days, which doesn't seem to be the right thing to do, because you're not fighting a war now, either. They stay out longer than we used to, and it's *all* boredom now instead of a little terror thrown in. I can't imagine staying out all that long if they hadn't screened them for being used to close quarters. My experience is that you ate better in submarines. The people were nicer than you had on surface ships; you didn't have any real oddballs to speak of. You had the best movies.

One way I didn't want to fight a war was to go out and get wounded someplace, like the poor Marines. I had a relative in the Marines, and I wouldn't have wanted to do that. On submarines, one officer I know whose name was Brown, out of the class of '38, was the only one I know of who had an interesting wound.* They were shooting up something with a deck gun and a plane came over. He was a rather large individual; he got stuck in the hatch and got shot in the rear end. It must have been an interesting war souvenir, but that's the only one I know of, that kind of an incident.

Paul Stillwell: How would you compare the different places you went for rest periods: Australia, Midway, and Pearl Harbor?

Captain Schwab: Oh, well, Midway, of course, there were no women there, so the crew didn't pay much attention to that really, when you think of it. They griped at first, but there was plenty of beer and plenty of bourbon and stuff, and a nice softball field. We did all sorts of things like that. They had movies, and we watched the gooney birds that were interesting; they were there when we were there. We were only in there a short period too. Instead of having the normal three weeks, we were only in less than two, because we'd only been out on war patrol for 45 days. The average war patrol, I guess, was around 50 to 55 days, total. You were supposed to be able to stay out till 60, but very few people did.

Pearl Harbor was interesting, because your submarine rest camp was the Royal Hawaiian Hotel.† But they did have blackouts at night, so you were supposed to be back in bed at 10:00 o'clock or something like that. You couldn't wander around at night. There weren't too many things for the men to do there. We all were in the same hotel, enlisted men too. There was a lot of rivalry. You always had several submarine crews at once, and I remember our submarine crew, we had our own ship's songs and so on. They'd go down and start singing in the courtyard, and some other submarine would tell them to shut up, and there'd be a little—not fisticuffs, but a little fun down there.

---

* Lieutenant Commander Charles D. Brown, USN, commanded the *Razorback* (SS-394) in 1944-45.
† The Royal Hawaiian is a luxury hotel, still in business on Honolulu's Waikiki Beach all these years later.

Usually, if the shore patrol got involved, who weren't submarine officers, both the submarine crews would chase them away. You know, we'd fool around.

If you were on the east coast of Australia, most of the enlisted men had hotels in town they were sent to. The officers, when the weather was nice, you went to Surfers Paradise, which I gather is now a big tourist place. There was one hotel there that was still half civilian on one side, and the other half was submarine officers. When you came into port, after you'd turned over your big refit book to the relief crew, showing everything that was wrong and had to be fixed, you then had two weeks of so-called rest period. In Australia each officer got a case of Australian beer, which I think was 48 imperial quarts, and a case of American bourbon, which was 12. You took that out with you, and the imperial quarts all went into a large communal zinc chest full of ice. The first night out there, why, if you drank one bottle of the beer, you were sound asleep. By the end of it you could drink a couple, and it didn't bother you. It shows you how you can gain on that. Nobody gained any weight, because at Surfers Paradise, you were swimming all day, one way or the other.

The submarine officers more or less owned that place originally, and then they put other surface people in there. The submariners had tied up all of the Australian ale, which is very good stuff, so when the surface people came in, they had to go along and drink American Lucky Lager, which was sort of poisonous. Australian liquor was Old Coraio; they called it black death. I think it had skull and crossbones on it. But it wasn't very good, so they always tried to come into the submarine officers' club, and we guarded that very carefully. There were a lot of probably bad feelings there too.

The aviators, the Black Cats, would come down once in a while, and we were more friendly to them because they would bring in jugs of torpedo alcohol, which is, you know, 200 proof or whatever it is. So that was an interesting thing.

At Perth, Western Australia, I think they had a beach place there for the crews. I'm not sure, but the officers had a couple of places. One of them was called Birdwood, and it was owned by an Australian Army colonel, and so on, and his wife was a tennis pro. She ran the place for the U.S. submarine force, and officers would go there. The captains all had a different place; this was for everybody except the captains. If you knew anything at all about tennis, and if you were staying at Birdwood, every morning about 6:00 o'clock she'd wake whoever were the tennis players up and they'd all be out playing tennis. Sort of an interesting place. There was a pool right across the street from it, which was sort of slimy, but it was a real pool, and you'd go in swimming there. That wasn't as much fun as Surfers Paradise, I guess, but Perth was a prettier city, something like the West Coast of the United States—San Diego or Long Beach area compared to Brisbane, which was more like Brooklyn, New York. It was pretty. I don't know what they look like now. I gather they have both built up a lot.

Paul Stillwell: How hospitable were the Australian people?

Captain Schwab: Oh, fine, no problem at all. Even when the Australian Army contingents would go through, why, we had no problem. The only thing that they didn't like was the cigarette availability. Americans there were mostly sailors, of course. They had almost free access to all the cigarettes they wanted and the Australians didn't. There used to be little cigarette wars once in a while. But no problem at all that I could see.

Paul Stillwell: But the men could have dates here, where they couldn't at Midway presumably.

Captain Schwab: Yes, that's right, oh yes. The whole civilian population was there, to speak of, and there was no curfew to speak of, in Brisbane or Perth because it was so far away. I guess I was in every state of Australia except where Alice Springs is.

Paul Stillwell: That's in the interior, isn't it?

Captain Schwab: That's right in the center, yes. That's where MacArthur hid out for a while when he first got there. We hit every place there. The reason I was there was when I came back from the *Darter*, we stopped overnight, and you flew across in a

DC-3.* I didn't have to go on a train, which some people did, and that must have been awful. All you had to eat was apples or things of that sort, all the way across Australia. But you'd stop in each one of the major cities, Adelaide and Melbourne and Sydney and so on. When you were overnight, they'd put you in a nice hotel. That's when you'd learn all sorts of interesting expressions such as, "What time do you want to be knocked up in the morning?" "Do you want to be knocked up with coffee or tea?" That was how they'd ask what you wanted in the morning and what time.

When you took off in a DC-3, which was still manned by civilians, when you passed 1,000 feet, they'd break out the free Scotch; they still had Scotch, so you could drink that.

On one of our trips in the *Darter*, I guess, we left Brisbane and went through the Great Barrier Reef, and through that passage up there where all the old sailing ships are still aground. We wound up and refueled in Darwin, up in the upper left-hand corner of Australia. There's a place up there where all they had left was an old Army base and a few nurses. The Japanese planes would come down there and bomb them once in a while. So we went in there and refueled, and that was sort of desolate.

Paul Stillwell: What did you refuel from?

Captain Schwab: Right alongside of a pier, and they had the tanks there or something. I don't know how they got the fuel in there, though. But all they had there was an Army contingent and a small hospital, for some reason, with about five nurses. The crew was all on deck waving at them.

Then we went on our patrol. We went up through the Sulu Sea and that whole area in there. We hit all the little interesting shallow areas on the way.

Paul Stillwell: What was the quality of the charts that you were supplied?

---

* The Douglas DC-3 went into service in the mid-1930s as perhaps the first really successful commercial airliner. Designated C-47 by the Army and R4D by the Navy, the plane was a much-used transport and cargo plane during and after World War II.

Captain Schwab: Well, in the areas that had been charted by the U.S.—I guess we still had the Coast and Geodetic Survey or something—those were all right. It's when you got over in the South China Sea that you had problems, because we had never charted those. I gather that the Japanese fishing boats had charted them all pretty well, especially since the *Takao*, that cruiser that I talked about that we were chasing, had missed the Bombay Shoal that we ran aground on by only several hundred yards. They come right out of the water. If he'd hit it, it would have been interesting.

Paul Stillwell: Was that shoal on your chart?

Captain Schwab: Yes, the shoal was on the chart, but the chart was in two pieces, and when we were operating, it was a photographic copy of an old English thing from the 18th century. They had charted it, but they added some along the line, I guess. When we were at the top of it, we had to piece it together to line up the latitude, and we were down at the bottom, we had to keep moving the chart to be sure the pieces matched up, an interesting operation. Of course, if you're out in the middle of the ocean, it didn't make much difference anyhow, but when you're operating in 20-mile-wide passages, it's a little different.

    The coast of Japan was—that's what I was going to mention—on the *Darter*, when we finally had a surface radar, we weren't quite sure where we were. If you wanted to get in close and be there to get the shipping, of course, you couldn't stay on the surface and take sights. So you had to figure out some way, and several things helped you there. The Japanese radio stations usually stayed on the air; there was one station that played Strauss waltzes all the time. We never figured that one out. Somebody knew where it was, so we were able to get a radio bearing line on that; we had a little gadget that would take radio bearings.

    Also, when you got in close, if you did have some sort of a chart of the coast, and you knew roughly where you were, then you could take one of the old is-wases, our plotting devices. Using the center as where your ship was, you'd then mark off on the arm that would swing the ranges and go around on the different bearings from your surface radar to the nearest land. You could mark sort of a coastal outline, and then you could slide that along the coast and see what it came closest to and see how that checked with the radio bearing. Nine times out of ten, it was very close. Unfortunately, there was nothing on Palawan that we got with a straight line practically—not quite north and south, but almost.

Paul Stillwell: You've talked about your previous skippers. What kind of a portrait would you draw of McClintock?

Captain Schwab: Well, McClintock was a lot younger than the others; he was class of '35. He was a very calm person who knew his job well. He didn't impress you at all as being an aggressive captain. Have you ever talked to him?

Paul Stillwell: No.

Captain Schwab: You ought to talk to McClintock and Claggett. Both of them were very competent; they were great friends, I guess, at the Naval Academy and afterwards too. So there was no problem there of jealousy or anything. But McClintock had a dry sense of humor. He was from in the Midwest someplace. Interestingly, when I mention about the Naval Academy, when we had tea fights, one of the officers at the Naval Academy was named Patterson—I forget whether he was a commander or something.* His daughter's name was Kirby Patterson. McClintock had married Kirby Patterson, and I didn't know that. I was in his room there one day when I was exec, of course, and there was this picture of this gal on his desk. It looked awfully interesting, and I seemed to remember.

I said, "Gee, you know, I used to drag a girl that looked like that when I was at the Naval Academy and went to tea fights."

He said, "Yes, she used to be Kirby Patterson." They say that you don't ride around in submarines for very long without finding you're related just about to everybody without knowing it.

---

* Lieutenant Commander Theodore T. Patterson, USN, aide to the superintendent.

Paul Stillwell: Well, it's especially intriguing in that your best man, Claggett, was the one who rescued you after the grounding.

Captain Schwab: Yes, yes, that's interesting. Well, and then, of course, I didn't mention this, but, because they were getting more cautious on announcing anything about submarines, my wife was back in New London at the time, and her father was a supply officer of the Submarine Force Pacific Fleet in Pearl and also submarine base. She got word very rapidly that the *Darter* was—I don't know if they said overdue or just lost. That's all. They didn't say anything else. Somehow she got in touch with her father, and he finally got word back 12 days later that we'd all been rescued, but meantime, we were all dead. She was the exec's wife, and, of course, all the women in New London called her to find out what was going on. I don't know where McClintock's wife was at the moment; she wasn't in New London, anyhow. It was a very interesting period there for all the wives.

Paul Stillwell: A very distressing period.

Captain Schwab: Yes, to say the least.

Paul Stillwell: What do you recall about the administrative side of things as executive officer?

Captain Schwab: Well, there really wasn't much to do because everything was written off. There were very few disciplinary problems. The main job of the executive officer before the war was holding mast and being the bad guy on the ship, as opposed to the captain, who was supposed to be the good guy.

Paul Stillwell: What made the difference, that you didn't get liberty?

Captain Schwab: Well, liberty, yes, and when you fight a war, people just didn't have time to do anything bad, because, as you mentioned earlier, the selective process that went into submarines, very few people did anything wrong. And so your main job as the exec was the navigational part of it.

Paul Stillwell: What about correspondence and other paperwork?

Captain Schwab: Well, it wasn't too much. You didn't make too many reports. You had to keep your quartermaster's notebook, which was the primary source for the deck logs. And you wrote most of the war patrol report with the captain doing his editing and so on, one way or another.

Paul Stillwell: It'd be interesting to learn what went into the reports when Stovall was the skipper of the *Guardfish*.

Captain Schwab: No, it was factual. He put in there an error was made or something like that, we turned the wrong way. It was all truthful. They didn't say, "I purposely avoided it." Usually you blame it on the enemy turning the wrong way. You've seen war patrol reports?

Paul Stillwell: Yes.

Captain Schwab: They were all factual, and most of the thing was trying to point out problems you had and ways to get around the problems to help both your coming patrols and other ships. There was an awful lot of that. Sort of a self-help society in there. I imagine there were a lot of little self-glorification episodes in there, but I didn't run into too much of that. In the first place, too many people knew what went on on a patrol, and if they got questioned, there would be problems.

Paul Stillwell: Did you have a greater knowledge of Ultra in this assignment than you had previously?

Captain Schwab: We didn't know Ultra by that name. There was a code word, but I forget what it was. We got increasingly better information on where we might run into ships, as I might have mentioned already. In some cases we were even given positions to take, waiting for a Japanese convoy, and if they were late, we got a little annoyed. Sometimes they were as much as a half an hour late, but they were usually right on schedule.

Paul Stillwell: Did you get any sinkings as a result?

Captain Schwab: I can't remember whether we got any as a result of that. I think that the submarines up off in Admiral Lockwood's area did better on that, because where we were, there wasn't much left. They had to go out and look for things. Well, it got so bad there at the end—the last submarine I was on, the *Capitaine*, why, we were—after coming back from the *Darter*, I went to New London, and they sent me to PCO school, and then I was supposed to go flying back out to Pearl Harbor and get a submarine.

Randy Moore was a good friend of mine, an officer from the Naval Academy class of '38; he was married to Captain Cutts's daughter.* It was icy in New London and it was the winter of '45, I guess, and he'd injured his leg on the officers' club steps. So they didn't have any people who were available at that moment to become executive officer. An officer out of the class of '37 by the name of Pete Friedrick was the captain of this *Capitaine*, about to take it out.† She only had about a week to go to depart for the Pacific. I guess she was going to wind up down in Australia. So they asked me if I would go out on it, saying I would either get off at Pearl if they had another exec in there or down in Australia. Of course, by the time all this occurred the war was over, practically.

So I went out as the exec on the *Capitaine*, and to show you the difference, we had the radars, surface radars and the air-search radars, which had become progressively fancier and fancier. We went out with one with a great big antenna up there instead of a

---
* Lieutenant Commander Raymond A. Moore, USN. Captain Cutts was skipper of the *Pennsylvania* when Schwab was in the crew and later commanding officer of the New London Submarine Base.
† Lieutenant Commander Ernest S. Friedrick, USN, was commanding officer of the submarine *Capitaine* (SS-336) from 26 January 1945 to 4 June 1948.

little dinky antenna. I don't know what that was called, but it was a great fancy one for air detection. It had flooded the mast inside of it when it was going up and down. So off the coast of Indochina we surfaced in the daytime and requested a "Dumbo," which I guess was a B-24 cover, while we opened up the mast and took the whole guts out and dried it out and put it back together again. That shows you how confident we were. We were running the war at that point. This was just before the end of the war—really confident.

That was when we also got the word that some American airplane had gone down. I think it was a B-24 too. They gave an approximate location, and we were supposed to go look for them, rescue them. And they were supposed to be in a raft, and somebody else said they spotted a raft. We went there and there were four Japanese seamen on a raft, and they were pretty well sunburned. They'd been on a convoy that was going from, I guess, Singapore up to Japan. Some American submarine had gotten in there and sank several ships, including theirs. They'd all been burned a little bit in the process. They got out in this raft, and when we came up alongside them, we spotted they were Japanese right away.

They didn't move, so we went alongside, and we yelled at them, and nothing happened. So one of the officers or somebody fired a sub-machine gun in the water next to them; that made them move. They didn't know what we were going to do. So there were two young ones, one middle-aged one, and one old guy. I guess the young ones were merchant seamen, and the old guy must have been the navy type; he was a gunner's mate. He'd been on a gun on this—whatever ship he was on—probably all in the same ship. We got that from one of the young ones who was able to draw pictures; he did this all with drawing.

Paul Stillwell: I take it you got them aboard your boat.

Captain Schwab: Oh, yes, we got them on board, brought them up, and we'd heard that some of them concealed guns or hand grenades. We made them strip down on deck, and the pharmacist's mate wouldn't let us do much to them because they were burned. So we bandaged them all up and got rid of all their dirty clothing and took them down below.

The gunner's mate wanted to fight—the old guy—so we had to tie him down in a bunk, and then he finally calmed down. The two young ones were so glad to be rescued, that once they were away from that gunner's mate, I guess they would obey. The middle one was in bad shape; he wasn't going to fight anybody. We just put him in a bunk and let him sit. The two little guys, though, loved pancakes. I can remember that they ate pancakes with maple syrup or whatever we had for syrup.

Paul Stillwell: Probably pretty hungry after that time in the water.

Captain Schwab: Oh, they were, yes. I don't think they had any water; I don't know how they survived. They'd apparently been out on that for five or six days in this broiling sun. Our crew sort of adopted the two young guys, who must have been 15 or 16 years old, that's all. They gave the Japanese wire brushes, and they kept both torpedo rooms in shape. They loved to clean up this deck. That's probably what they did on their own ship. The middle-aged one had been the quartermaster's assistant, and he was so glad to be rescued too. I think they hated the gunner's mate; he probably told them it was good to die rather than surrender. So he drew a chart of the coast and showed the shipping lanes, which was interesting, and how many ships had been sunk. Some American submarine got in there and sank four out of seven.

We finally went into the Philippines; I guess we went into Subic Bay at that point.* We had told them that we had some Japanese survivors on board. We had them on deck, looking around. We came over alongside a submarine tender, and these huge Marines came out, and they put blindfolds on these poor guys. The Japanese thought they were going to be shot. They were scared then, but I don't know why they were blindfolded; they'd been in this port many times. They weren't going to go anyplace. But they led them away, and that's the last we heard of them. It was sort of an interesting episode.

We didn't sink anything or see anything. Coming back down to go back through Lombok Strait, why, you always ran into various things: shore batteries here, patrol

---

* Subic Bay is a protected anchorage on the island of Luzon in the Philippines. It borders the Bataan province and is about 35 miles north of the entrance to Manila Bay.

boats, and so on. So it was a question there whether you should go through submerged or on the surface. We had the same problem with the *Dace* too. But some people liked to go through on the surface, in which case [unclear] shot, but the currents through there were peculiar. You could go down to a certain depth and get assisted one way—something like going in and out of the Mediterranean.

That's where the last submarine sunk during the war, the *Bullhead*, was lost.[*] The captain was a classmate of mine named E. R. Holt.[†] He'd gone through there a couple times, and somebody had shot him up from the shore batteries, so I think he was going to go in there and take care of it when they got him; that's what they think.

Before we came back through Lombok, we went through Karimata Strait, which is shallow.[‡] We got the word there was a Dutch submarine, which was disabled, and he was at such-and-such a point. We would find him there, and could we help him? He needed some sort of a part. The Dutch submarines were O-boats that had all been built or finished in 1939-40. They were sort of stranded out there when the Dutch Indonesia was lost. A bunch of them wound up in Australia. They had a Dutch officers' club, all sorts of interesting things, which I'll tell you about.

We went looking for this Dutch submarine to help them out, and we found that this was a shallow area. The water depth was only around 90 or 100 feet. We found the Dutch submarine hooked on to a sort of a permanent buoy that was down to the bottom. He was just hooked on there, the crew was sunbathing, swimming, fishing. It didn't bother them a bit; they were wild people. So we helped them out. The boat was held together with baling wire and chewing gum, practically. Then I guess we followed him back down to Perth. As a result, all the officers were invited to the Dutch officers' club for a rice-and-curry dinner with all the side boys, and that was something. You'd drink all the good Australian beer—they had access to that—and other interesting Dutch things, and eat like mad. After the dinner you were supposed to pay for the bar, but they were so glad to be back there they chased everybody out, and it was all on the house. The Dutch

---

[*] USS *Bullhead* (SS-332), a *Ballao*-class diesel submarine, was commissioned 4 December 1944. She was the final U.S. submarine lost to enemy action in World War II. She was sunk by depth charges from a Japanese aircraft in the Sulu Sea on 6 August 1945, a little more than a weak before hostilities ceased on 15 August. Her location was off the coast of Bali, near the northern mouth of Lombok Strait.
[†] Lieutenant Commander Edward R. Holt Jr., USN, commanded the *Bullhead* for only a week, from 31 July 1945 to 6 August.
[‡] Karimata Strait, between Borneo and Belitung Island, connects the South China Sea and Java Sea.

were a good bunch of people there—really rugged seamen, I guess. I mean, they'd been gone from home since whenever they went out there—1939 or '40—with these new submarines at that point.

Paul Stillwell: I wonder what they did for logistic support.

Captain Schwab: Not much. They had to manufacture everything over on the beach, I guess. Perth was a city; they could do a lot of stuff. They didn't have a lot. Hadn't heard from the Queen in a long time.

Paul Stillwell: Did you have any disappointment that you didn't get a command before the war ended?

Captain Schwab: Well, I did. Right at the end of the war, I was ordered to command the—what was the name of it?—Doug Rhymes had it, and it lasted one day because the war ended.* He said he'd take it back to the States. I didn't even have written orders; I was just told I was getting it. Then the *Capitaine* was in there, and I was taken off to get a submarine; that was it, see, they did take me off in Perth, and so there was nothing else. Nobody wanted to turn over a submarine then when the war was over. So I was put on as the head of the submarine refit crew and retraining crew or something, and the overall commander was Chuck Triebel.† I guess he became an admiral. Did you ever talk to him?

Paul Stillwell: No.

Captain Schwab: So I was put with him, and I had about 300 men under me. I had this whole refit outfit. There were something like ten submarines in there. This was just before the war was over, and then I got all these orders to go. I was refitting the submarine I was supposed to command. Was it the *Bumper*? I think it was, yes. It was a

---

* Lieutenant Commander Cassius Douglas Rhymes Jr., USN, commanded the submarine *Chub* (SS-329) from 21 October 1944 to 1 October 1945.
† Captain Charles O. Triebel, USN, commanded Submarine Division 301 from August 1945 to April 1946.

one-day command I was told, and it was canceled. So we had a good time there at Perth before the war was over.

Then another officer and I were out listening to the Perth symphony orchestra rehearse when the word came in that the Japanese had surrendered. We didn't know what had happened, because they stopped their rehearsal, and the whole orchestra stood up and they played the "God Save the King." I guess he was still alive.* And they played the national anthems of all the Allies. Then they told us what was going on. The town went mad; everybody stopped work. Everything was free if you were in the service, of course, and everybody was, except the females, and a lot of them were too. You'd go into a bar, and you could have been perpetually drunk if you wanted to be. Nothing was charged for anything. All the people stopped working.

So they disbanded all this stuff, and some of the submarines were sent off for the Japanese surrender. I guess they sent a couple up there and then to Guam, and all the other places. I don't know if they were sure it was going to be over or not, but they weren't taking any chances. So I became the squadron engineer for Squadron Ten under Triebel, and we came all the way back to the United States through the Panama Canal on the USS *Clytie*.

There are all sorts of little interesting things you remember. On one war patrol I was on, I think it was the *Guardfish*, when we had that thing. I was going through a watertight door and had a tooth broken; the door hit me in the face. It didn't bother me, there was a pivot tooth stuck in there. At the end of the war, on the last war patrol, I was brushing my teeth one day, and I had some sort of infection in the gum.

We came into Perth at the end of the war, and the senior dentist on the *Clytie*—maybe it was the only dentist—took a look and he said, "Well, those things are bad. They have to come out. You're infecting your whole gum up here." He was an expert on this stuff, and he injected me there and pulled out all four teeth and put a temporary bridge in it. He rode back in the *Clytie*, too, so I had my teeth pulled out in Perth, Western Australia. Then I got the permanent thing in October '45 in New London, Connecticut, from the same dentist. Every time I go in for any dental work, which is often because they don't do much anymore, they always take pictures of it, because

---

* King George VI (1895-1952) was the British monarch from 1936 until his death on 6 February 1952.

nothing's supposed to last this long. He put a lot of gold in there. My head's worth more from that than anything else.

Let's see, now. We rode the *Clytie* back, and every place we'd stop—we came down between New Zealand and Australia, circled Pitcairn Island. We did all sorts of weird things like that. Panama Canal—we had a great big party there. We stopped in Norfolk and unloaded a bunch of people, and then finally got to New London, went to State Pier, and that was it.

Paul Stillwell: Did you get reimbursed for the gear you'd lost on the *Darter*?

Captain Schwab: Yes, you did. You had to make out a list of everything; that was all there was to it. There was no problem at all.

Paul Stillwell: Presumably, just uniforms though, not personal items.

Captain Schwab: No, you put everything down there. I got something like $900.00 back. Dennis Wilkinson had just bought a whole new set of uniforms—I don't know what happened to his previous ones—and he got about $1,200 back. It was all legitimate, nobody was trying to gyp anybody.

Paul Stillwell: Well, then you rode back on the *Clytie*. What happened at the end of that trip?

Captain Schwab: Well, the next thing, I was ordered to submarine base New London. I guess the first job I had there, I was the communication officer and officer in charge of the radio station. I was also communication officer for ComSubLant at the same time. It was sort of one of those mixtures because they were short of officers for some unknown reason, immediately. I remember that I had several officers working for me. You never knew who you were going to have working for you. I had two WAVE officers. One of them was Evelyn Hardart, who was an heiress to the Horn and Hardart family.* She was

---

* Horn & Hardart was a food service company that operated automats in New York City and Philadelphia.

a WAVE lieutenant. To start out, I guess I had four WAVE officers. One of them was the custodian of registered publications. You had to relieve everybody as they got detached; they got their points, or whatever it was. And I had a couple of male reserve officers, communicators there. In those days they called them the "ball-bearing WAVES," the guys who sat on shore all the time. Did you hear all about that one?

Paul Stillwell: No.

Captain Schwab: Yes, the male communicators ashore were called "ball-bearing WAVES." Anyhow, that was interesting. The radio station was part of my duty. I didn't know a heck of a lot about running a radio station, but I had a warrant officer and then a lieutenant (junior grade) by the name of Bill Jackson, who was the senior officer under me. He was a very nice officer, very soft-spoken, and he'd been a prisoner of war in Palawan. My roommate at the Naval Academy had been a prisoner of war in Palawan. I didn't connect him at first, but after the war there was some sort of a parade. We had a little marching detachment from the radio station and communication office. The number-two guy was supposed to be the platoon commander. You still wore white leggings and that sort of thing; I guess they still do. So he told me, "I can't do it." I guess I was still lieutenant commander then.

I said, "Why not?" He pulled up his legs and he had massive scars; some of them still not even healed yet. This was at the end of '45, I guess, the beginning of '46. I said, "Where'd you get those from?"

He said, "Well, in the prison camp they had Korean guards, and they weren't armed, but they had these long sticks with split bamboo on the end, and if you didn't do anything, they'd hit you in the leg or elsewhere."

So we talked about it, and I said, "Gee, my roommate at the Naval Academy was over in one of those prison camps. His name was Bill Hogaboom."*

He said, "Was he a Marine officer?"

I said, "Yeah."

---

* First Lieutenant William F. Hogaboom, USMC, died 19 December 1944 in the Philippines.

He said, "Well, he was in my death squad. He was the commanding officer of the death squad." You really do get involved. He had, of course, fought all the way down Bataan Peninsula to Corregidor.* He started in 4th Marines in Shanghai and then got to Bataan and then Corregidor, captured there, and was in the death march and everything. He was in a prison camp, and at the end of the war, when they were transporting some American POWs to Japan for, I guess, hostage reasons, and they found out somehow we were going to drop poison gas along—mustard gas and everything else—they started bringing them up there, and they were supposedly, according to what I've read, going to scatter them around and tell us about it so we wouldn't drop.

He was in one of these ships, several of them, and when we were on patrol in 1944, we'd sunk a couple of ships off Borneo, and then we didn't know where they were in prison at that point. But the *Queenfish* was in one of the upper positions, slightly to the north of us, off Palawan, and she'd sunk two of these ships with the prisoners on board. One of them with my roommate on board. They managed to break out and swim ashore. He was rescued by the guerrillas on Palawan and died about two weeks later of malnutrition and exposure. He used to send Red Cross postcards to his family, who'd send them to my family, who'd send them to me. Just about that time we came back into port, and there was a postcard from him saying, "The war must be getting over because the guards are really treating us nicely." But he was dead by then.

Let's see, where was I?

Paul Stillwell: Well, you were talking about the time in New London when you were running the radio station.

Captain Schwab: Oh, yes. This lieutenant said that Bill Hogaboom had been the head of his death squad. According to him, the Japanese told them that if anybody in that squad escaped, then they'd all be put to death. Apparently, in one of the other death squads some American officer had escaped and they captured him—I don't know how much later. They brought him out and they had the whole camp assembled and they eulogized

---

* In late 1941 and early 1942, the Allies suffered heavy casualties and lost many troops to prison camps during operations on the Bataan Peninsula of the island of Luzon in the Philippines.

this guy. They said, "Now this is what, when you're a prisoner, you're supposed to try to escape. This is an honorable man, and we'll give him an honorable death." So they got him over and cut his head off, which was honorable; otherwise, they'd shoot him. He went honorably.

He remembered Hogaboom particularly because after one beating he'd received, Hogaboom could see he couldn't stand much more of it, and the guard was about to hit him again. Hogaboom went over and knocked the guard down, which normally would have been the end of Hogaboom, but that didn't happen. He remembered that too.

Paul Stillwell: Was this kind of a slack period for you in New London?

Captain Schwab: Yes, well, other interesting things happened. The previous WAVE lieutenant or lieutenant commander had left. She was the custodian of the publications and apparently had not listed a lot of the numbers that she had permission to destroy. So when I had inventoried with her everything that was left, that list agreed with the list I signed. But then about six months later, whoever was in charge of publications in those days came to us saying, "What happened to all these other publications that you were supposed to have?"

So I didn't know, and she, meanwhile, had left the service. We called her back to active duty, to fill out all these affidavits to the best of her knowledge and belief. I was sweating blood there. I thought I was really going to get court-martialed, because I didn't know what had happened till, finally, it came out. Things like that happened all over, I guess.

Then after a while of doing that, then—let's see, Lew Parks was the executive officer of the base, I guess.* He was the one who brought back a Japanese yacht for his own personal use. He got it back on the tender, and nobody paid any attention to those things. There were tons of samurai swords and guns and everything else. That was before they had these problems with congressmen and so on.

---

* Captain Lewis S. Parks, USN, became executive officer of the New London Submarine Base in April 1946.

Ricky Haskins had been the first lieutenant, and he fleeted up to be, I guess, the chief of personnel.* I don't know what he was doing, but he moved up to some other office. So I was ordered to relieve him as first lieutenant and fire marshal, which was interesting, and which I did. Just about that time, I guess, Admiral Fife was the SubLant.†

So I remember in the middle of the winter, a very cold night, a call came to my house over in New London that SubLant headquarters was on fire. So I went charging over, and we finally got the fire out, but there were indications that it might not have been an accident. Of course, it could have been too. Admiral Fife was upset because the bag that he kept golf clubs in had been scorched slightly. Some enlisted man who had been on watch there apparently had reported the fire and had spotted Admiral Fife's golf clubs, which would have been burned otherwise, and rescued them. He was slapped on the back, and that was it. He didn't get promoted or anything like that. He was shifted somehow to the base and got into my outfit.

I, of course, as the first lieutenant also owned all the BOQs; we owned everything.‡ I was also deputy commander of the reserve fleet; I had more titles; I had 17 titles. It's in one of my biographies. I never had so many titles in my life. I was everything. I had my own car for being a fire marshal and everything else.

Well, that fire was over with, and Mike Fenno was out there, and we wrote a report.§ Everybody got congratulated for doing a splendid job, especially this young enlisted man. And then, oh, a few months later, a telephone call came in that the BOQ was on fire. So I went in there, and this time we'd called the state police fire arson experts, and there was an indication that something had been set up in an attic. We didn't know what to do about it. How do you catch an arsonist? This was an interesting thing. The arson experts sat down with everybody who was involved with the fire, including me, and I was home. And they made a list of all the heroes. And one of the heroes was the guy who'd rescued the golf bags. He was nominally on watch in the BOQ office.

---

* Commander Enrique D. Haskins, USN.
† Rear Admiral James Fife, Jr., USN, served as Commander Submarine Force Atlantic Fleet from 15 April 1947 to 1 June 1950. The oral history of Fife, who retired as a four-star admiral, is in the Columbia University collection.
‡ BOQ – bachelor officers' quarters.
§ Captain Frank W. Fenno Jr., USN, became commanding officer of the New London Submarine Base in 1947.

Now, the way they discovered the fire was that one of the black stewards, whatever he was, up in one of the wings of the BOQs—which is rather extensive in New London, had seen the flames and called down to the BOQ office, from which you can't see any of this, and said, "There's a fire up here."

So the hero from the other fire had been out getting coffee or something; that's when he set the fire. Then he came back and said, "I'll take care of it." So he called up the firehouse and told them where the fire was right away. Well, then they started putting all this together, the times and everything. He was the only one who had opportunity to go in, and he was the only one who knew where the fire was without ever being told, because the black guy up in the other wing hadn't even told him. He'd rung up and suddenly said, "Fire," and got the hell out. So they finally got him, and in the process I learned a lot of things. The first thing they do is check the heroes. He was angry because he hadn't been promoted or given more than just a pat on the back. Secondly, they check homosexuals. They checked this guy's locker and found letters from a couple others, one of them being a chief petty officer who was the head of the base football team—of all the letters. Well, everybody got cleaned out. Apparently, these things all go together, which I'd never heard of before.

Paul Stillwell: Did they suspect he set Admiral Fife's quarters on fire too?

Captain Schwab: I think that was accidental, but he did set the one in the other place. In fact, he had to set it twice; he had to go out for coffee twice, because the first time it didn't take. He set it in the attic, so all that burned was the roof; it didn't hurt anything else.

Lots of interesting things happened. Let's see, when was that all over? About '48, I guess. We stayed in New London forever. The next thing I knew I was ordered to the Naval War College in Newport, for the logistics course.

Paul Stillwell: Well, we're right at the end of the tape, so why don't we save that for next time? Anything else to mention about that New London time? You got a much different family life than you'd had aboard the boat, certainly.

Captain Schwab: Yes. That was nice. We were still living in rented houses at that point, and I guess at that point we'd also acquired all three children. They came in '44, '46, and '48—good timing.* Is that about it? The end?

Paul Stillwell: Yes, we're right near the end of the tape.

---

* Donald Ernest Schwab, as noted earlier, was born 1 March 1944. Holly Elizabeth Schwab was born 15 December 1946. Trudi Sandgren Schwab was born 21 April 1948.

Interview Number 3 with Captain Ernest L. Schwab, U.S. Navy (Retired)
Place: Captain Schwab's home in Potomac, Maryland
Date: Friday, 20 February 1987

Paul Stillwell: Captain, last time we talked about your experiences when you were at the submarine base at New London, and from there in 1948 you went to the Naval War College. Could you resume the narrative there please?

Captain Schwab: Yes. I don't believe I had volunteered to go to the Naval War College, but I was ordered up there to attend a combination of the senior course and logistics course, although the senior course was normally reserved for commanders and above, and I was a lieutenant commander at the time. It was the normal ten months' course at the war college, in which we had many interesting lectures. It was mostly a review of World War II lessons and the future with an awful lot of attention, interestingly, on the Persian Gulf and the possibilities of Russian invasion of Iran and what we might do about it. In the case of the course I was attending, much attention was paid to the logistics of the situation. We had all the strategy and no tactics, of course, at the Naval War College.

Paul Stillwell: Was this your first exposure to those subjects for the most part?

Captain Schwab: Well, we hadn't learned much of anything at the Naval Academy about the Middle East, except, actually about the Greeks in the early days of naval warfare, and that's about it.

Paul Stillwell: You probably hadn't learned much about logistics either.

Captain Schwab: No, there wasn't too much attention paid to logistics or economics or anything of that sort. The course at the Naval Academy was primarily nuts and bolts of very elementary things compared to today. There were no electronic situations; the furthest you got on the electronic side was the plain old vacuum tubes, things of that sort. But there were no transistors and, of course, no computers as we know them now.

Paul Stillwell: How demanding was the war college course, in terms of pace and the amount of study?

Captain Schwab: Well, the course was primarily to give the officers at the senior and logistics course level a broad view of national strategy and how the Navy would fit into it. There were officers there from the other services. Of course, by that time we had the separate Air Force. We had speakers from the State Department and the CIA, things of that sort.[*] So it really broadened our view on things. On the logistics and economics side we were fortunate to have as one of the lecturers and instructors Henry Eccles, who was well known.[†]

Paul Stillwell: An institution up there.

Captain Schwab: Yes.

Paul Stillwell: I've interviewed him.

Captain Schwab: It was very good to have a course under him. I guess, is he dead now?

Paul Stillwell: He died last year.[‡]

Captain Schwab: But he was an interesting character and had been around and that sort of thing forever, on logistics particularly.

---

[*] CIA – Central Intelligence Agency.
[†] Upon retirement from active duty in 1952, Rear Admiral Henry E. Eccles, USN, began a 25-year second career as head of the logistics department of the Naval War College; he was a prolific author.
[‡] Eccles died 14 May 1986.

Paul Stillwell: Well, he'd been on the Service Force staff in the Pacific so he'd had firsthand experience in that.

Captain Schwab: The other thing is that this was really the first time I got to talk to people who had a lot of experience in the air and with the surface warfare. Except for a while in battleships, I'd been all in submarines or in submarine-related activities. And, of course, that was their first time to talk to submarine people in most cases. We found out there was a lot of mythology to be dispelled about what went on, on both sides.

Paul Stillwell: What might be some examples of that mythology?

Captain Schwab: Well, for example, how submarines went about conducting their approaches and things of that sort. Most of them thought it was a lot more difficult than it really was in gaining a normal approach course and then firing a torpedo spread, things of that sort. They were also interested to learn that we never did know anything really accurately when we fired at a target. It was always estimates, which were supposedly taken care of by a torpedo spread. From the submarine side, we talked a lot about the Japanese tight schedules they had for their convoys and things of that sort, which I guess became unclassified later on, but at that time they were still classified.

Paul Stillwell: Were there any myths about the aviators that were dispelled for you?

Captain Schwab: No, not too many myths that way, I guess. They did have when they were in an area where other ships—I was surprised at the intensity of operations. They mentioned they were always going. I thought they were sleeping most of the time, the way you see in the war movies, and then they'd take off when somebody appeared. But apparently they were up a lot, as much as they could with the old propeller planes.

Paul Stillwell: There's been, in recent years, an emphasis on the rivalry between the three major communities: air, surface, and sub service. Did you see it in that era?

Captain Schwab: I didn't feel any rivalry there. Of course, the aviators were still in the ascendancy, but we didn't feel too much of the competition for money that occurred in the Washington area.

Paul Stillwell: Well, that was the area of unification.* Did you get any spin-off from that?

Captain Schwab: Well, all during that period, maybe just after it, the Secretary of Defense was Johnson.† Everybody referred to the cuts in the budget as the "Johnson deep." That just proceeded getting mixed up in Korea, so there was a surprise we were able to respond in Korea as well as we did; sort of put together in a hurry.‡

Paul Stillwell: Were there any Army and Air Force students at the war college?

Captain Schwab: There were Army and Air Force and they were very good; in fact, there were Army and Air Force on the staff too. They were very good at giving people what they thought about things. There was very little parochialism in it; there wasn't everybody saying, "My service is better than your service," see. They were all trying to look and see how things could be better under the new circumstances. Unification really wasn't advanced that much until the Key West meeting.§

---

* The National Security Act of 1947 became effective on 18 September of that year. It provided for the unification of the services under the aegis of a single National Military Establishment, which later became the Department of Defense. Previously the Secretaries of War and Navy had been Cabinet officials. Now there were three different departments at sub-Cabinet level: Army, Navy, and Air Force. As part of the act the former U.S. Army Air Forces became a separate service, the U.S. Air Force.

† Louis A. Johnson served as Secretary of Defense from April 1949 until September 1950. He cut back substantially on defense expenditures, a program that had to be reversed with the beginning of the Korean War in June 1950. He was removed as SecDef a few months after the war started.

‡ The Korean War began on 25 June 1950, when six North Korean infantry division and three border constabulary brigades invaded South Korea. The troops were supported by approximately 100 Russian-made T-34 tanks. In New York that same day the United Nations Security Council adopted a resolution condemning the invasion.

§ The policy paper "Function of the Armed Forces and the Joint Chiefs of Staff" became known as the Key West Agreement. It addressed the allocation of assets among the U.S. Armed Forces. The agreement was arrived at during meetings of the Joint Chiefs of Staff at Key West, Florida, 11-14 March 1948. It was approved by President Harry S. Truman on 21 April 1948.

Paul Stillwell: Well, the war college was probably your first exposure to officers from the other services, too, wasn't it?

Captain Schwab: Yes. We hadn't seen much. Well, during the war, I mentioned, we had some Army Rangers on the submarine, which we were taking to land on the northern coast of New Guinea, but that was about it. You didn't see much of the other services.

Paul Stillwell: What was the format for your study, that is: lectures, projects, papers? What did you do?

Captain Schwab: We had a combination of all those. There were regular lectures in which everybody attended: general, broad strategy. Then they had smaller ones for the people who were on the logistics and senior side. Then we also had the old way of playing war games: sort of mechanical on-the-floor-type things, dating back from the beginning of the war college, I guess. Then we had to write papers. You had a pretty good choice of things. My major paper I wrote was on the comparative war potential of the United States and the Soviet Union from the industrial, logistics angle, which would fit into the logistics thing. Interestingly, while I was at the war college it was the last time, I think, anybody had to take the promotion exam to go to commander. I took it, while going to the war college, I also studied and took the promotion exam for commander. By being at the war college I was able to eliminate part of it, but still had to take a promotion exam.

Paul Stillwell: Well, and it was probably more conducive to studying there than had you been on board ship.

Captain Schwab: Well, I don't know. Of course, we used to see people taking the exams for lieutenant (junior grade), and they were studying when they weren't ashore. Out at sea was a good time to do it on a battleship.

Paul Stillwell: Who are some of the instructors you remember?

Captain Schwab: Mostly Eccles; I don't know, that's a long time ago now.

Paul Stillwell: Do you remember any specifics about him?

Captain Schwab: Well, he convinced us—most of whom were pure operators to speak of—that it wasn't all strategy and tactics. Without logistics everything fell apart, and that was the main lesson I got from him, that unless you had prepared yourself to support operations, your operations had a slim chance of being successful in the long run.

Paul Stillwell: Well, he was right, of course.

Captain Schwab: Yes, of course.

Paul Stillwell: The operators sort of have a view that God will provide.

Captain Schwab: There was a lot of attention then on sealift and things, especially when we had to go do anything over in the Persian Gulf or south of the Persian Gulf. There wasn't an awful lot of attention given to Iran, which I think he still called Persia at the time.

Paul Stillwell: In these war games on the floor, were you re-fighting World War II battles?

Captain Schwab: Well, in some cases we were re-fighting World War II battles, but then we were adding what we would have done differently if we'd had the equipment. Of course, things really hadn't advanced that much then, but a lot of the World War II battles were fought without the advantage of radar and things of that sort. I guess we were starting to get jets at that point; I'm not exactly sure when the jets came in.[*]

---

[*] The FD-1 Phantom I, soon redesignated the FH-1, was a jet fighter built by McDonnell. Its first carrier operations, both takeoffs and landings, were on board the *Franklin D. Roosevelt* (CVB-42) on 21 July 1946. The Phantom first entered fleet squadrons in 1947.

Paul Stillwell: But you were working in the new technology?

Captain Schwab: Yes, that's right, as much as we could, particularly in defense against submarines. Of course the Soviet Union's always had a great number of submarines; so did Russia before that. They never seemed to use them too well during—of course, they didn't have to, I guess, in that kind of war. There was an awful lot of that, antisubmarine warfare emphasis and selection of sea routes if you had to resupply Europe or go anyplace else.

Paul Stillwell: How were the decisions made on how well the sides did in a given battle?

Captain Schwab: They really weren't right solutions or wrong solutions. It was strictly a learning process. Everybody got to say just about anything they wanted to; it was very loosely run. There were no school answers, in other words. It was whatever you got out of it; you were more or less on your own in many ways.

Paul Stillwell: Do you remember any prominent visiting speakers?

Captain Schwab: I can't remember any names. This was, of course, 1948 and '49. No, I can't remember any specifics. I have all the records somewhere; I guess I should have reviewed those.

Paul Stillwell: Was Admiral Spruance still the president?[*]

Captain Schwab: I believe he was, yes. I think it was Admiral Spruance who gave a talk on educating naval officers more in international affairs. He pointed out that the Air Force, and I guess the Army, had quite a few, or were getting quite a few officers who had had graduate education in those areas. Whereas, the Navy had essentially zero, and without knowing it. That's one of the things I went into later when I went to Fletcher

---

[*] Admiral Raymond A. Spruance, USN, served as president of the Naval War College from 1 March 1946 to 1 July 1948.

School as a result of his initiatives, Admiral Spruance. And I guess Admiral Burke, when he was a captain then, pushed that too.

Paul Stillwell: Did you have a chance to read other things than the required text, just to expand your horizons?

Captain Schwab: Oh, yes, you had a big reading list—mostly on international affairs and the role of the United States in global strategy.

Paul Stillwell: Well, how much of a chance did you have for leisure time or a social life in the Newport area?

Captain Schwab: Not too much, except that usually they had a some sort of a movie or a dinner thing on, say, a Tuesday night or Wednesday night. Every once in a while they'd have an informal dance at the officers' club or the war college grounds there. That would be usually on a Saturday night. I remember distinctly that there was a lot of reading that you had to do. We had no television or anything in those days, and I can remember I would sit up in one corner of the big room in the house we rented there. I had all my books stacked around. Along about 10:00 o'clock at night I'd say, "Let's turn on the radio for a few minutes." We'd listen to the news or whatever was going on, then I would say, "Now I'm going to take a nap for 15 minutes." Then my wife would wake me up, and I'd start reading again. I rarely got to sleep before midnight. It was an awful lot of reading, especially when I was writing things. It was pretty intensive for ten months.

Paul Stillwell: Are you able, on reflection, to see ways that that period helped your later career?

Captain Schwab: Oh, yes, it gave you a better appreciation of the role of the armed forces in the national well-being. And it broadened out your views from just looking out from a naval point of view.

Paul Stillwell: Was that a direct influence in your going into the Foreign Service and geopolitical things later, do you think?

Captain Schwab: No, I don't think so. I'll tell you later about my graduate study at the Fletcher School.

Paul Stillwell: Well, any more about the war college specifically, before we move on to your submarine command?

Captain Schwab: No, the war college was an eye opener on all the things. In the war we had our blinders on. I guess I wrote a little something once about that. The main thing as you get older is to realize where your blinders are and try to do things to keep shooting holes in the blinders, so you can see all the other things that bear on you. Of course, going to school is one of the blinder openers. But that was about it.

Paul Stillwell: Well, I'm sure you were delighted to get orders to command the USS *Toro*.[*]

Captain Schwab: Well, and it was doubly interesting because the *Toro* was in a new outfit under Roy Benson.[†] It had just been formed: one division in the Pacific and one in the Atlantic. This was in the Atlantic, based at New London, Submarine Development Group Two. The purpose was to develop antisubmarine tactics—using whatever available we had in regular submarines—against the perceived threat of Soviet snorkeling submarines. Of course, they didn't have any nuclear submarines then. The *Nautilus* still hadn't been launched at that point in '49.[‡]

So getting into SubDevGroup 2 and four submarines there, that was interesting, especially since I already knew Roy Benson. A classmate of mine, Rafael Benitz, was

---
[*] USS *Toro* (SS-422) was a *Balao*-class submarine commissioned 8 December 1944. She had a displacement of 1,570 tons on the surface and 2,415 tons submerged. She was 312 feet long, 27 feet in the beam, and had a draft of 15 feet. Her top speed was 20 knots surfaced and 9 knots submerged. She was armed with ten 21-inch torpedo tubes.
[†] In March 1949, Captain Roy S. Benson, USN, became the first commander of Submarine Development Group Two. The oral history of Benson, who retired as a rear admiral, is in the Naval Institute collection.
[‡] Construction of the *Nautilus* (SSN-571), the world's first nuclear submarine, began on 14 June 1952.

captain of the *Cochino*, and Robert Worthington had the *Tusk*.* Let's see, who was the other one? The other one was the *Corsair*; Lincoln Marcy of '39 was the skipper.† So I had two classmates there. And Ozzie Lynch was a staff member.‡

The main interesting thing in this was that Harmon B. Sherry was on the staff, and he had dabbled in electronics of different types, which was probably why he was on the staff.§ He had read some articles about some work that the Bell Telephone Company was doing on increasing the number of transmissions that could be carried on single wires and so on, and he was doing it by some sort of magnetic separation. I don't know if this is classified or not, but it's the basis for SOSUS.** At that point we didn't have any way of doing any magnetic separation, but we were experimenting with our submarines in listening to various frequencies to see if there was any special frequencies that snorkeling submarines produced that would travel long distances.

And, of course, as you can see from the picture of the *Toro* up there, we eliminated all our deck guns, and there was no railing or anything anyplace. They'd cleaned off all the superstructure, and made it as silent as possible. We'd even taken out one of the periscopes and actually put sonar equipment up instead of a periscope so we could try that. We did all sorts of thing. We'd lie on the bottom in various places, Long Island Sound and so on.

The *Tusk* and the *Cochino* were snorkeling submarines. The *Corsair* and the *Toro* were not. There were not too many of them, but we were thinking of using our remaining submarines that weren't in the reserve fleet—if things got tense—as sonar pickets up forward to detect the passage of their submarines, so we could put our ASW—we were still working on the basis of escort carrier type things.

So in this whole process Harmon Sherry somehow got hold of a German robot camera and necessary cathode-ray tubes and so on. He rigged them in the forward

---

* Commander Rafael C. Benitz, USN. USS *Cochino* (SS-345) was lost off Norway on 26 August 1949 as the result of battery explosions and fires. For details see the Naval Institute oral history of Rear Admiral Roy S. Benson, USN (Ret.). Commander Robert K. Worthington, USN, commanded the submarine *Tusk* (SS-426) from 15 July 1949 to 15 August 1951.
† Commander Lincoln Marcy, USN, commanded the USS *Corsair* (SS-435) in 1949-50.
‡ Commander Richard B. Lynch, USN.
§ Commander Harmon B. Sherry, USN.
** SOSUS – sound surveillance system, a seafloor network of listening devices used by the U.S. Navy to detect noises from transiting ships.

torpedo tube room on my submarine. And we suspended some low-frequency microphones in the superstructure; it was airplane bungee cord. Then we sat on the bottom in a quiet area, near Block Island, I guess, and the submarines would snorkel by. We kept varying the frequencies we were listening to with the sonar equipment and discovered that repetitive frequencies peaked at a certain range—I don't know if it's classified or not now—from the snorkelers, and we could track them out a long distance. We had no directional capability, but we could track them out a great distance that way. We knew about this because we took pictures of the cathode-ray tube with the robot. So this became something of a recommendation through Commodore Benson—he was captain then—and the SubLant staff to BuShips and others, and also to OpNav, the ASW outfit then—OP-03 something—to explore this further.[*]

We did this quite a bit, but it was interrupted to a certain extent by our cruises; we also were cruising. We made two big cruises: one in August of '49, and another one in February of '51. We went up as far north as we could get in August of '49. If I haven't mentioned this earlier, the *Toro* got up to 80°-17' north latitude, which—as far as we could find out—was the farthest north of any combatant ship up to that point. Of course, we didn't have nuclear submarines then.[†] I made Lincoln Marcy stay south of me so I would have the record.

Paul Stillwell: You must have been senior!

Captain Schwab: I was senior by a few numbers. And meanwhile, the *Cochino*—and we were also testing up there—we had various loops we'd rigged especially on the topside, to see what kind of low-frequency radio transmissions we could receive, looking forward to the day when we had, I guess, Polaris submarines. We were preparing for that; I guess that was already in the mill too. We didn't know much about that; I thought at the time, of course, that this was designed to see what kind of instructions they would be able to give to picket submarines; we didn't know. So we were up as far north as you could get,

---

[*] As the unit commander for the submarines in the development group, Benson was referred to and addressed by the honorific "Commodore" even though his rank was captain. BuShips – Bureau of Ships.
[†] On 3 August 1958, the nuclear-powered *Nautilus* (SSN-571) made the first successful submerged transit across the geographic North Pole. For firsthand details from her commanding officer see William R. Anderson, with Clay Blair, Jr., *Nautilus 90 North* (Cleveland: World Publishing Company, 1959).

singing "Way down south in Iceland," or something of that sort. And meanwhile the *Tusk* and the *Cochino* went up off North Cape, snorkeling, and that's when the *Cochino* had her battery explosion and managed to surface in very heavy weather. And the *Tusk* in the process of rescuing the *Cochino* crew lost several, six or so, of their own men somehow—I forget the exact number.* Benson was on the *Tusk*. I think it was his flagship; yes, it was the *Tusk*, he wrote that. He does a lot of writing on that. He probably told you all about it. So we didn't know much about that until we got further south; we weren't allowed to transmit up there, but the reception and so on was very satisfactory. And that was the main emphasis in 1949.

Paul Stillwell: Were there any special things you had to do for navigation that far north?

Captain Schwab: No, it wasn't bad at all. Surprisingly, the weather was very good up there in the summertime. Even though the water temperature seemed to be about 35 degrees, the air temperature was warmer. There was no wind right up against the polar ice cap, and we could go up there and sunbathe, even though the air temperature wasn't very low either, but it was a lot of radiant heat from the sun. I was surprised to see the polar ice cap went up about 60 feet or so, and it was just like a shelf; there was no icebergs or anything, which we found later off Greenland. But they don't break off the polar ice cap, apparently; they stay there. At least there weren't any problems with icing in it at all till you get down further south, I guess, where there are pieces floating around—the "bergy bites" and what have you.

The other interesting phenomenon was going north of the Aurora Borealis; I didn't realize where that was either. It's a frightening thing to see all those lights in the air. We didn't have too much problem up there, and we had—well, if you got a little cold we had equipment to knock—mostly from the British that told us about it—you had sort of rubber hammers to knock the ice off your antennas and things of that sort, but that was about it. We didn't have too much problem.

Paul Stillwell: Did you get to any ports on that visit?

---

* A civilian BuShips technician was swept overboard by a wave; six crew members of the *Tusk* were lost.

Captain Schwab: Well, we went into Portsmouth, England. We still had CinCNELM then; I guess they hadn't gone to the other designation.[*]

Paul Stillwell: Was that Admiral Conolly then?[†]

Captain Schwab: I don't know who the admiral was then. In August of '49, of course, four submarines went into Portsmouth. I guess the British call their submarine base Pompey. I must still have my little dolphin here someplace. The British submariners were all on vacation because they always tie up everything in the summertime. Here it is. You get one of these in your life, and that's the souvenir of being a guest to the mess at the—gee, there's a special name, Fort something. But, anyhow, it's on the left as you go into the Portsmouth Harbor, and you make a very sharp turn.

Going into Portsmouth Harbor there's a big clock there—looks like a big clock—and it has a black sector, and a green sector, and a red sector. It tells you the state of the current going through this narrow gap that you go in. I guess Fort Blockhouse is the name of the submarine base, and for some reason they call it Pompey. HMS *Victory* is only a short distance away.[‡] And then as you come in on the left there's a little swirl of water and there's a point of land right there, and the British officers call that Promotion Point, because if you hit it you don't get promoted! So we were warned about all this, and they sent out a British pilot to each ship to bring us in.

We went in with no problem, in the black period of this "clock." The black was for when anybody could go in and out, including their little submarines. The green was high-powered submarines, the big ones such as ours, and the red meant you were supposed to stay outside in the roads. So we had no problem getting in there; of course, as we went in, we tied up alongside the pier there. Most of the British submarines that were there were sitting in the mud! They put them in at high water, and then I guess they

---

[*] CinCNELM—Commander in Chief U.S. Naval Forces Eastern Atlantic and Mediterranean.
[†] Admiral Richard L. Conolly, USN, served as Commander U.S. Naval Forces Europe from September 1946 to November 1946, when the title was changed to Commander U.S. Naval Forces Eastern Atlantic and Mediterranean. In April 1947 the title was changed again, to Commander in Chief U.S. Naval Forces Eastern Atlantic and Mediterranean (CinCNELM). He remained in the billet until December 1950.
[‡] HMS *Victory*, a ship of the line completed in 1765, is the oldest commissioned ship in the Royal Navy. In 1805 she was flagship of Lord Horatio Nelson in the Battle of Trafalgar. She is now a museum ship in Portsmouth, England.

just had one watch keeper on each ship and that was it; maybe they didn't have anybody. In their usual hospitality, they had to have a big party for us, and so they rounded up all of the active duty people and reserve people they could and they put one on—I'm trying to think of the name—I know the next admiral was Admiral Raw, but that one I've forgotten. They threw us this big party and wanted you to pass the sherry around. If you could pass the bottle of sherry you passed up to the head table without them noticing—everybody cheers, then they have to buy sherry for the lower table. The British officers get up on top of the tables and tell jokes and so on, most of them pretty raunchy. No women. There was all sorts of fun, and then after the dinner, they were all wearing their dress uniforms and, of course, we were just wearing our blue service.

They had different contests: like beer-drinking contests and so on. Roy Benson did very well in that, incidentally. Maybe it's the Swedish blood that helped, but he did well. Then they had contests with different kinds of games; I don't know what we call them, but we call it "Buck-Buck." One person will get against the wall, and then the others will grab behind him and then the other team will jump on top to break them down. Well, in the process, the British officers there suffered a couple broken ribs—I mean, it was really rough—and the torn collars and everything else.

They really were beat up. From my ship we had Bob Kaufman, who was my engineer, and he was quite a rugged person himself.* He managed to disable two of the Brits. Then Bob Worthington, I guess, was also a gymnast, and he did a lot of things. We'd challenge them to all sorts of things such as walking on your hands and so on; he could do that, and Kaufman could do pushups from a headstand. He could do more with one arm than most people could do with two! All in all, we had an interesting night, and all the Brits were pretty well beaten up.

I don't know if Roy Benson went in to see CinCNELM or not. The officers went up to London, and we had a couple of nights there. We came back—all the officers did—and we took off for our northern voyage. Well, apparently not much information had been given to CinCNELM on what we had been doing or where we were going. I don't know what they thought we were doing. So when the *Cochino* was lost, this was somewhat of a shock to them and also to the Norwegians, who apparently hadn't been

---

* Lieutenant (junior grade) Robert Y. "Yogi" Kaufman, USN, later a vice admiral.

told very much about it.* When the *Tusk* started sending out radio messages—I guess this is unclassified now—the Soviets alerted their whole northwestern frontier, and that area didn't know what was going on.

The Cold War was just getting under way, nicely, in '49, and I guess we'd had a Berlin Blockade—it was over by then—maybe not.† But the *Cochino* crew, rescued by the *Tusk*, was taken in to Hammerfest, and I guess there was a Russian consul or something there, and he asked the Norwegian, "Did you know that an American submarine got in?"

"Oh, yeah, we knew about it all the time." That's the story; that's all "triple" hearsay. Apparently the Norwegians took care of it. NATO had just formed in April, so this was only a couple months later. There really wasn't any NATO as such, certainly no organization as we have now.

Paul Stillwell: Benson's facility with the Scandinavian languages helped.

Captain Schwab: Well, yes, I don't know. They all speak English up there—at least these people did. Of course, I didn't get in there. Meanwhile, in the *Toro*, we went off down past Greenland and checked that side over there. We went on the other side of Iceland and past Greenland, and I got a picture of my submarine. I guess you've seen that, against the iceberg. I made Marcy take that picture.

Paul Stillwell: What specific research were you doing that far north?

Captain Schwab: The research there was primarily to check communications capabilities: at what depth you could pick up different—we found out there were certain low-frequency communications from England, I guess Londonderry, Northern Ireland. We could hear them very well no matter where we were. From the United States it died out, so it was a question of, I guess, which radio station—I guess we had a U.S. Navy

---

* See Roy S. Benson, "Fire in the *Cochino*," *Submarine Stories: Recollections from the Diesel Boats* (Annapolis: Naval Institute Press, 2007), pages 216-219.
† On 1 April 1948 the Soviet Union began a land blockade of the Allied sectors of Berlin, preventing overland transport from West Germany. U.S. and British airplanes then began an airlift that flew food and coal into the city until the blockade was lifted on 30 September 1949.

communication station still in Londonderry.* I don't know if we have now or not, but that was primarily to test communications with submerged submarines. That was that.

So then we came back, did the normal exercises in different areas, and wrote up all our reports. The next big event, as far as SubDevGroup 2, involved two submarines: my submarine and the *Halfbeak*. At this time Phil Eckert had command of the *Halfbeak*.† I still had command of the *Toro*. This was February 1951.

This time the emphasis—besides the normal listening type of stuff and radio tests—was to test the food. A contractor by the name of Henry Sell was, among other things, the editor of *Town and Country* magazine, and he also had the Sell Food Products in the New York area. They still sell them, Sell's liver paté and other things. The company had contracted with the, I guess, Bureau of Supplies and Accounts through Bayonne, New Jersey, to provide a balanced, complete set of food for submarines to go on patrol with. The premise was—based, I guess, on reports of war patrols—that after you've been out on patrol for a while, appetites go down, the people get lethargic and disinterested in the food and energy levels go down, things of that sort. Plus the fact that when you load up a submarine to go to sea under the old system, every place you could think of as extra, there was food. If you've seen *Das Boot*, it wasn't as bad as that where they had sausages hanging, but you were pretty well loaded down.‡ The idea was to reduce the amount of loading by doing an awful lot of precooking—that's prefabricating the food—and also by finding ways to reduce the amount of garbage. Things that you had to dispose of over the side let submarines be tracked.

I guess the thinking was that if you were a submarine, or anybody on station, if you were staying in a general vicinity you'd give yourself away by throwing a lot of stuff over the side, which is true. So these were the efforts made by Henry Sell, and I guess he hired people too.

The *Halfbeak* went out with a conventional load of food, and we went out with this special stuff. In fact, we were allowed to try it for about a week before we went, so we had all kinds of pieces of roast beef in about 4-inch cubes that had been partially

---

* The U.S. Navy operated a communication station in Londonderry, Northern Ireland, from 1942 to 1977.
† Commander Philip F. Eckert, USN.
‡ *Das Boot* was a 1981 German film that depicted in fairly realistic fashion the claustrophobic lives of a U-boat crew in World War II. A dubbed English-language version, titled *The Boat*, appeared in 1982.

cooked and then quick frozen. The gravy that went with it was in little packages; it was all beautiful stuff, and there were instructions in everything. You'd put it so many minutes in the oven. We had special microwave ovens stuck on board for other things. It was a big difference from World War II food, which wasn't bad, but it was delicious.

They put a lieutenant commander reserve officer, who was the head of the dietetics department at the University of Washington—his name was Henry Kotschevar—and he went out with us to sea.* He brought a small suitcase along, which he kept in his cabin. I said to him, "What's in that?"

He said, "Oh, that's some special spices." What he had were spices plus different kinds of wine that you could mix with the gravies. Everything was great; it was probably illegal, but it was great stuff. We ate well, but, of course, this was the wintertime, and we didn't get up much past Iceland, just about up to Iceland, before we started running into problems with the weather.

On the way there we went into Portsmouth again. The commodore was Barney Sieglaff.† Just two submarines, and I was the flagship this time. And we went in in February '51, and the British were there in force, because they'd all heard about the fiasco in August of '49. Of course, we now had two submarines coming in, and they were all ready for us, except that a bunch of British submarines were going out on some exercise, and we had to wait for them to come out.

That big "clock" I was telling you about went from the black into the green, and it kept going and going, and right before it got to the red, why, they said, "Okay, you can come in now," so I zoomed in. I had this British naval officer with me, and he was supposed to pilot. I'd been in there once before, and I knew about Promotion Point and that stuff, and I'm not so sure he was so sharp. He said, "We'll go way back in there, you know, and then twist around and go in." So he told me when to start twisting, and I was coming back rapidly on Promotion Point. I knew that if I kept twisting, going sideways, I would go aground, so I immediately turned around, went ahead full to the right and

---

* Lieutenant Commander Lendal Henry Kotschevar, Supply Corps, USNR. Kotschevar was a prolific author, eventually turning out more than a dozen books on food- and drink-related subjects. His career was profiled in an article in the journal *FIU Hospitality Review*, Volume 19, Number 1, 2001. Included in the article is an account of his naval service during World War II.
† In August 1950 Captain William Bernard Sieglaff, USN, relieved Captain Benson as Commander Submarine Development Group Two Atlantic.

dropped my anchor right in the channel. It turned out I was right in the place where it says, "Do not drop your anchor because there's telephone lines." But having been swept sideways by this current, and the "clock" at this point was in the red—I couldn't see it anymore, but I knew it was in the red. And just at that point when I was ready to pull in my anchor and go way up and turn around and come in, the Isle of Wight ferry came out, and I was on the wrong side of the channel. So we turned on every light we could, put out a radio call, everything, and the Isle of Wight ferry went sailing by on my starboard side. Here I was, right next to Promotion Point, anchored. I had to keep my screws turning over at about one-third speed so I wouldn't drag the anchor.

Meanwhile, the *Halfbeak* was waiting outside, and the *Halfbeak* was on the right side of the channel coming in, near these mud flats. Then the Isle of Wight ferry came out on the wrong side of the channel about to collide with the *Halfbeak*! The *Halfbeak* couldn't go to the left because there was not that much room, and he could hit the ferry. He went over to the right and he had nothing sticking down below, so he just went aground and sat on the mud. There he sat, because the tide was going out, and he was out there overnight. Finally I'd twisted, and I'd told this British naval officer to go to the back of the bridge, and I got in all right. The British admiral was Raw, and he was sitting up in the tower up there, watching all the fiasco.* He called down after I got alongside, and he said, "Young man, you need a drink. Come on up." So I went up there, and he gave me a couple of sherries.

So we got all dressed up and, of course, the *Halfbeak* wasn't in at all. So the *Toro* officers—I had practically the same bunch I had the first time—we all had to go up there and defend the honor of the United States submarine force. And it was really something.

Later the commodore, Phil Eckert, and I had been ordered to go up to be up in Portsmouth at 9:00 o'clock in the morning. That meant we had to get up early, about 6:00, to catch the train and go on up there. So we left the party with everybody playing "High Cockalorum," which was the name they called it. We called it "Johnny, Johnny, how many fingers are up?" or something like that, and it was "High Cockalorum."

Back to the time we were having this problem of making an entrance there, Sieglaff was back on my cigarette deck on the *Toro*, talking to Arnie Schade, who was on

---

* Rear Admiral Sydney M. Raw, Royal Navy, served as Flag Officer (Submarines), 1950-52

CinCNELM's staff.* He lived in Wimbledon. They were back there and didn't even notice anything was going on until suddenly Barney noticed that the Isle of Wight ferry was coming out. He said, "What are you doing?"

I said, "Well, I can't hit the ferry; I have to anchor."

I remember he was completely shocked by not having noticed what was going on. Commodores don't pay any attention to the ship, the navigation, and that sort. So the *Halfbeak* had got in in the black section there. The three of us went charging off from the *Toro* to go over to the car to go to the railroad station. As we walked up the pier, the officers from the *Toro* were just coming back from this party, which had apparently gone on all night, and they looked bawdy. They said, "We won, Captain!" whatever that meant. There were apparently a lot of casualties, but not on our side—again, Kaufman contributing to most of them. So we went up there, and of course, the reception in CinCNELM headquarters up there was a lot different from the previous time, because they all knew about the loss of the *Cochino*. Geez, we had a whole day telling them what we were doing. We weren't doing anything except testing food, really. But it was an interesting time.

Well, we came back, and in the process we had discovered certain things. First of all, the crew loved everything, and the officers did too. We all ate the same thing, of course. The food was outstanding. There was 65% less garbage from the special stuff that Sell had put together. When we came in, there was nothing left over. It was just perfect; everything worked out nicely, and we were out there a good time. It was designed for that period of time. But there was no problem. I understand that the same techniques are used now on nuclear submarines. I've been out on one as an observer, but I've never had command or served actively in one.

Paul Stillwell: Was Kotschevar monitoring all this as you went along?

---

* Commander Arnold F. Schade, USN, undersea warfare officer and submarine liaison officer on the staff of Commander in Chief U.S. Naval Forces Eastern Atlantic and Mediterranean.

Captain Schwab: He wrote a diary every day on what went on in the food. We got to be pretty friendly on the trip, and he said, "What are you going to do when you come back in?"

I said, "Well, write up the report, and then I'm going to take my wife to New York. We've always wanted to see Mary Martin in *South Pacific*, and every time we were around we could never get tickets for any time I've available."[*] He wrote that down and didn't say anything. So he left the ship, and we were going to be in port during a refit period for a couple of weeks. A week or so later Kotschevar called from New York, and I guess Sell had already seen the reports. Kotschevar said, "Say, if you and your wife can come up here on such-and-such a night, why, Henry Sell is going to have a little dinner party for people: you, me, and our wives at the Pavilion in New York where Henri Soulé is the head guy." It was a very famous restaurant. He added, "There's a little surprise." I didn't know what it was.

Betty and I went up to New York and had dinner. We had unborn lamb that Soulé himself carved, because I guess Sell was quite a customer. About three-quarters of the way through the dinner, after commenting on how glad he was that we were so happy with the food and blah, blah, he said, "And here for you and your wife are two tickets to *South Pacific*. They're Mary Martin's tickets, and they're fifth row, center" or something like that. He said, "Be sure to wave at her, she'll be looking; I told her." He was apparently a friend of hers.

So the others sat there and finished off all kinds of stuff and we zoomed out. We got there just in the middle of the overture, so we didn't miss too much. We sat down and sure enough, we waved and she waved back when she got on stage. That was quite an experience. I told you before about staying at the Parklane Hotel on our honeymoon. Well, we stayed there again, I think. That hadn't been torn down yet; that's gone now. The manager, Brown, was no longer there, and we didn't get 25% off or whatever the discount was.

---

[*] James A. Michener (1907-1997) was a prolific American novelist. Many of his books covered generations of history in a particular location. He served as a Naval Reserve officer in World War II. One of his early works was *Tales of the South Pacific*, which earned him the Pulitzer Prize for fiction in 1948. It later became a Broadway musical.

When we first got command of the *Toro* in 1949, I bought a house in New London. I bought it from a lieutenant who had been an enlisted man. He bought it on the G.I. Bill; he paid $10,000 for it and it was in a nice section, not super section of New London, but not bad, off Ocean Avenue.* I took over his G.I. payments and gave him whatever he had paid on his equity. I remember I was in and out all the time there. The house had been built around 1928 and it had something like 32 windows in it; a nice piece of property—rose bushes and all that sort of stuff. In the process of owning it, I actually, personally, rebuilt 25 of those windows because the frames had rotted and I had to replace the old-fashioned cords in the side with sash-weights. I did all sorts of dumb things: insulated the attic. Your first house you do a lot. I painted it, did the attic, did all sorts of interesting things, little improvements to it.

So when I came ready to leave, an officer by the name of Gordon Nicodemus, now dead, had orders to relieve me.† He'd been a classmate but hadn't graduated with the class. He called me up from an ordnance depot someplace, and he said, "I have orders to relieve you. Do you have a house?"

I said, "Yeah."

He said, "I'll buy it, if you are going to sell it."

I said, "How do you know you want it?"

He said, "Well, if it fits you with three kids, I know you can afford it because you have the same pay I do, I'll take it."

So I said, "All right."

He had three kids and he had a cat. We didn't have a cat at that time; we had a springer spaniel. So he bought the house, and he was angry because I had also an old Model-A Ford that I had driven to the sub base and back. I'd sold that, I guess, to Phil Eckert. I guess those old Fords are still around up there. You can still get parts for them—never rusted—great big heavy-gauge metal. But he was angry because I hadn't saved that for him. But he took over the *Toro*, and I had orders—the next interesting part of this—to take over the Underwater Sound Branch at the Bureau of Ships.

---

* The G.I. Bill, officially the Servicemen's Readjustment Act of 1944, provided educational assistance and other benefits to all veterans honorably discharged with six or more months of active service after 16 September 1940.
† Commander Gordon K. Nicodemus Jr., USN.

Paul Stillwell: Before we get to that, I wonder if you could talk about the internal organization of your ship: your wardroom, your enlisted crew? And what were the satisfactions of command after having been in subordinate positions up till then?

Captain Schwab: Well, of course, it doesn't hurt to be in command of submarines, because you're on your own. Even when the commodore's on board, as I pointed out, you don't get many orders from above. That was especially the case in SubDevGroup 2, where everybody was eager to solve this problem of submarine versus submarine, using whatever assets we had. As a result of the Johnson funding cuts, we didn't have much under construction.*

Paul Stillwell: Did you have the "Guppy" technology?†

Captain Schwab: No, we did not. The *Toro* and the *Halfbeak* were specially picked, because apparently they were in good shape, not to have snorkels. And the *Tusk* and the *Cochino* had been—then the *Halfbeak*, because she took over from the *Cochino*.

Paul Stillwell: What officers do you remember from your wardroom?

Captain Schwab: Well, there's the first exec I had, his name was A. H. Clark, "Ace" Clark they called him; he was a rough-and-ready submarine type.‡ And I mentioned Bob Kaufman, and those were the main ones. The second exec I had was Francis Riley. I guess he's retired out on the West Coast now. He was a real typical Irishman. But Kaufman, I think, was the most interesting officer on there. Of course, see, he was my engineer, and he also fancied himself to be a good singer.

---

* Six fast attack diesel submarines of the *Tang* (SS-563) class were built between February 1949 and August 1952. The other boats in the class were the *Trigger* (SS-564), *Wahoo* (SS-565), *Trout* (SS-566), *Gudgeon* (SS-567), and *Harder* (SS-568).
† The term "Guppy" grew out of the initials for the postwar modification fitted to World War II fleet boats to give them greater underwater propulsion power (GUPP).
‡ Lieutenant Commander Alexander H. Clark Jr., USN.

I mentioned to you the trouble we got into on the very first trip in the *Toro* in August of '49. Our four submarines went up to operate up with the British submarines to see how they operated.

We went up to Rosyth, which is their submarine base, and the HMS something or other was their submarine tender. Rosyth is a Scottish summer resort. So we went out and operated with the British submarines for a little bit. I went out on a British submarine one day as an observer; I think it was the *Truant*. We went out to dive and I don't know why; maybe they were going to check to see if they could hear American snorkeling submarines go by. When they dived, the uppermost hatch in the conning tower was stuck or something and didn't shut all the way. Water was pouring in and the officer of the deck was a line officer—the white business instead of red and so on. And I said, "Aren't you going to do something about that?" Because in our submarines the officer of the deck pulls the [unintelligible].

He said, "I don't do that, that's not my job."

Anyhow, I was impressed by how, let's say, carefree they were about operating submarines. I don't know, maybe they lost a lot. I understand that they lost more submarines before we got in the war than they had submarines at the beginning of the war.

The other things I'd forgotten too, is that, on our way north, after we left Portsmouth we went into Londonderry. Londonderry was a submarine base, and we had to go up the River Foyle. For some reason they hadn't maintained the ranges on the rivers. I think this apparently has some bad twists in it plus shallow spots, and we were drawing about, I think, 18 feet then, and one of the shallow spots said 19 feet. I said to the Irish pilot on board, "Is that going to bother us?"

He said, "No, I'll let you know when you go a little faster when you get there." Which is bad, because then you tend to sink, but we sort of bumped over it and it didn't hurt anything. We got in all right; so all four of us were in there at Londonderry.

Another memory from the summer of '49, that was the year—whoever the British minister of agriculture was, they called him a bad name. He had said, "Oh, we have a surplus of chickens." So he gave permission to take chickens off the ration list—they were still rationing—but he forgot that chickens lay eggs! So I guess this happened some months before, and by this time they had very few eggs and very few chickens. We came up there, and we were told all about this. So for all of the wives and children we could find of the submarine outfit up there, we had them out to the ship and we fed them as much as we could spare. They hadn't had any good food in a long time. The same thing happened when we were in Portsmouth: we gave them some stuff there. They took us out; they gave us all their Scotch. They always liked to have guests, because then the King would pay for it instead of the ship.

They did all sorts of weird things. While we were in Londonderry, all our submarines were together. They said, "Well, you know that we are all going to some party or something tonight, but there's a duty officer on each submarine. And the usual thing is for visiting commanding officers to go visit all these and have a small drink with each one of them." There were about eight British submarines up there, the ones who weren't in Portsmouth. So Lincoln Marcy and I went together, and I don't know where the others went. But, anyway, we went and I was very careful because the brows on these British submarines are about two feet wide; whereas, we have pretty big ones on American submarines with railings. They had no railing at all; you had to sort of balance your way across.

So we got down to the next-to-the-last submarine. I looked at Lincoln Marcy, and I think he had a cold besides. I said, "You know, you don't look too good; maybe you better go back down in the ship."

He said, "No, I'm all right." We went on to the last submarine, and he fell off the thing right into the water between the ships. They fished him out, and he got all dried up. We went off to the party all right, but it could have been bad. Of course, he was drinking. I think it was a combination of that and the little brow, which was a little damp. The Londonderry thing was interesting because in 1951 we went in there, too, and this time we didn't have any pilot because the pilots were on strike or something. I'd been in there before and they said, "Do you want to go in there?" So I took it in. It was an interesting experience; we had no problems, though.

Paul Stillwell: Was there any increased emphasis on safety after the *Cochino*'s battery fire?

Captain Schwab: Well, a lot of things were learned by that, not so much by the battery fire, which can happen any time, but what happens when you try to operate when you have men running around topside. In a probably overzealous attempt to eliminate noise-makers, they had removed all the railings and everything you could grab onto on the *Tusk*, and, of course, on the *Cochino*—all of us. So when the *Tusk* was out there doing this rubber boat transfer, I gather it was pretty rough where they were. Off North Cape it's always rough, I understand. When they were making this transfer the reason the people on the *Tusk* were lost. They were washed over the side when the waves hit them, and they weren't holding onto anything.

The major thing that resulted there was they put tracks in the deck of the nuclear submarines and they put on safety lines, which hooked in and you could get on and off, also, things you could hang onto around the sail on the submarine. That was the main thing learned there, that you just couldn't let people stand on deck, especially on, of course, the nuclear submarines with their tumblehome; you had no room at all to walk around. That was the main thing, and also the so-called immersion suits that the *Tusk* people were wearing. When they fell in the water, something was designed wrong and several of the people were observed to turn upside down. Did Benson tell you about this?

Paul Stillwell: I don't remember that specific detail.

Captain Schwab: Turned upside down, and they died because they were upside down in this water, which was around 35 degrees. It was very cold and you don't last long. The immersion suit should have protected them, but they drowned. And the ones that, I guess, didn't drown that way would die from the cold, so it was pretty bad.

Paul Stillwell: What do you recall about the enlisted crew in the *Toro*?

Captain Schwab: They were great. There was still the draft, but everybody in submarines was a volunteer.

Paul Stillwell: You had a good bit of war experience still on board too.

Captain Schwab: Oh, yes, most everybody on there had been to war. It was only 1949; they were all career people, mostly, and there were very few people on there escaping the draft. There were several ex-reserve officers who were staying in. I don't want to mention his name, but the worst officer that we had on there was a Naval Academy graduate. He thought because he was a Naval Academy graduate he didn't have to do anything, to speak of. He was not the most junior, he was next to the most junior officer, but he was terrible. He wouldn't follow any rules or anything else. That was the first and only officer I disqualified in submarines, and his father was a naval officer, too, which is sort of sad. I talked to him many times. He used to do other weird things, such as when coming to the captain's house for dinner, he'd arrive late with some real babe he'd picked up someplace and proceeded to insult everybody. I never could understand him. All the other officers and the wives sort of disliked him. You know, it doesn't take so long to disqualify somebody for cause. I guess they still do that in submarines. The captain still has a little power problem there.

Paul Stillwell: Sounds like he had a professional death wish.

Captain Schwab: I don't know what happened to him. I see the same name, but it's not the same officer because it's so many years ago.

Paul Stillwell: Anything else to recall about the *Toro*?

Captain Schwab: Having put a couple of submarines in commission in New London, I knew about going under the railroad bridges there. You don't really dive, but you flood practically to the deck level, and you could get under the railroad bridge when it was closed. Some of the other submariners, after the war, had never done that, and so my submarine—we'd be out exercising, usually went out, say, Monday to Friday or something like that, and the crew of course was all eager to get in on Friday night and have a weekend at home when you were doing local exercises. There'd be maybe six or seven submarines waiting in line to go in, and I would flood down and go by all of them. We'd get in, we'd get the choice of the best pier, the easiest—of course, you know the current in New London is pretty bad on the Thames River, as they call it.* So that was a good thing.

Paul Stillwell: Well, then you went to the Underwater Sound Branch of BuShips.

Captain Schwab: Oh, yes, then I took over. The officer I relieved there was Steve Gimber out of the class of '34, a submariner.† For some reason they liked to keep a submarine officer in the Underwater Sound Branch. Even though I had never had any graduate training or education in that area that's where I went—and Gimber hadn't either. But the interesting part of that is that there, waiting for me when I arrived, were all their reports from SubDevGroup 2 about all the things you might be able to do on certain low frequencies. It had been noticed by the people there. They had about 40 engineers—civilians and six or seven officers—almost all of whom were engineering duty officers. I think I had been the only unrestricted line officer there. My number-one civilian assistant had been there forever in the Underwater Sound Branch, which was Code 845 in those days.

The general attitude was a lot different from being out at sea: that your senior and your more knowledgeable civilians really were running the place. I mean, they were doing all the work, and the people with gold on their sleeves were sort of window dressing. It was someplace to put them temporarily. But the civilians were really running it, and especially when you had a non-educated head of the outfit. I think they looked on you as—"What the heck's he doing coming here?"

But what you were supposed to do was to bring in the benefit of your at-sea experience. Although I had no surface warfare experience as far as ASW was concerned, which is mostly what the sonar branch was for, I had a lot of operational stuff and actually, you might say, experimental things with SubDevGroup 2. And I was well aware, because we used to have conferences with Roy Benson and Sieglaff on what to make of all these little things we were learning.

---

* Schwab's "... as they call it" refers to differing pronunciations of the river's name. In London Thames is pronounced so it rhymes with "hems." In New London the pronunciation rhymes with "tames."
† Commander Stephen H. Gimber, USN.

It was all there, and there hadn't been too much money spent on it, but fortunately Junior McCain—who became Admiral McCain—was captain. He was over in OpNav in whatever branch of OP-03 was involved in submarine warfare.[*] Admiral Frank Akers was his boss.[†] Akers, I had gathered, didn't like to make speeches too much about what we were doing about ASW, so he gave the job to McCain, and I made him a chart, I remember. I'd known him from submarines, of course, and he called me up and gave me a chart of what the different capabilities were in different things. I gave a circular chart: ranges here, ranges of detection of torpedoes, range of detection of this, that, and the other thing. And I also mentioned to him all these things that we'd learned in SubDevGroup 2, or seemed to have learned, and that interested him. Of course, I was a commander by that time. I got the people in BuShips interested.

I don't know who exactly was the spark plug on this, but we finally got Admiral Akers interested. Woods Hole Oceanographic Institute was also involved in this. They were helping us out on this sound business. We got a little bit of money to put some sort of microphones off Eleuthera Island in the British West Indies. I don't know what year that was exactly now, probably '52. There wasn't anything on Eleuthera Island then except one small hotel, which didn't have many people in it.

We somehow had Akers get together a group of admirals from CinCLant and from the Pentagon, and I guess there were a couple of civilians on there, too, and they somehow got permission to take people from Bell Telephone. The outfit was the one in downtown New York City, where they had their laboratory at that time, before they went over to Whippany or wherever they were in New Jersey. And we all flew down to Eleuthera. They had this very primitive shack and a line going out this, I think, cost $7,500, if I remember exactly—in the water, and they had a submarine set up. They knew where he was to begin with; I guess they had tested this before. He went out and with this primitive equipment on an oscilloscope, and they tracked him out to around 300 miles. It was an ideal area down there to do it. That impressed everybody.

On the way down all we wanted for the next phase was Bell Tel to try to introduce this magnetic business, separation into our stuff. We wanted to have $75,000;

---

[*] Captain John S. McCain Jr., USN, served 1950-53 as Director of Undersea Research and Development.
[†] Rear Admiral Frank Akers, USN, was Assistant Chief of Naval Operations for Undersea Warfare, a rarity for a naval aviator.

and that's all we wanted! That was based on all the expert civilians in the BuShips talking with the people from Bell Tel Labs; and on the way back they wanted to give us about $750,000—everybody wanted to get in the act. So the thing zoomed like mad; that led to SOSUS—Project Caesar.

A young man by the name of Joe Kelly was, I guess, a lieutenant at the time, and he had been a reserve officer on active duty or had been an ex-enlisted man, I don't know. He was an electronics "whiz," and he'd been over at Bell Tel. I don't know how he got designated as the only one we could have available as the project officer on this. He stayed in that thing right all the way through, and he was the one who really did it.

We had all sorts of problems in that. This is how fast it developed. I was there '51 and '54, I guess. I was only supposed to be there two years, and I'll tell you about that in a few minutes. And we went from zero money, $7,500, to right up to having all sorts of interesting problems, such as how do you lay cables? Since we had no cable layers then, we borrowed a cable layer from the British. All sorts of things that went on, and which probably would be illegal now. But we actually had a British cable layer, and we had to figure out on which ledges to put the microphones; the microphones had to be designed to fit inside these tubes so they wouldn't float away. And then they had to have electronic steering to get bearings; a lot of this technical stuff was way beyond me. Then they had to get permission from—I guess the 99-year lease on the British West Indies was still in effect from the destroyer deal.* Then we had all different stuff. But the thing went from zero to an operational system, in certain areas, overnight practically. It was amazing. Just because of this little experimentation by Harmon B. Sherry—I give him the maximum credit—and the fact that Ozzie Lynch, and Roy Benson also, noticed that this was something that should be explored.

Paul Stillwell: Would it be fair to say that was the origin of SOSUS?

---

* In September 1940 President Franklin D. Roosevelt concluded a deal with Prime Minister Winston Churchill of Great Britain whereby the United States transferred 50 destroyers to the Royal Navy for use against German submarines. In return the United States received 99-year leases to British bases in the West Indies, Bermuda, and Newfoundland.

Captain Schwab: Oh, yes, that *was* the origin of SOSUS. There was no question about it. If it hadn't been for Junior McCain having to have to give talks—I was able to tell him about these things, because—the whole thing stirred up. Nobody invented it out of the blue, but without all this concurrence of events it wouldn't have happened.

Paul Stillwell: Who was your immediate boss?

Captain Schwab: Oh, he's a white-haired, let's see—well, there was a Captain Bull, who was in electronics, but he wasn't the—let's see, I have some papers on all these things.

Now, while I was in the sonar branch of the Bureau of Ships, I noticed that many of the requirements for the development of underwater sound equipment were sort of vaguely phrased, coming from OpNav, and they were usually on the basis of, "Let's do the best we can for our boys," instead of recognizing that money was limited and you had to have some priority system, putting the money in the proper places with relation to a kind of challenge or threat it had to meet in a time period. So when I got further into this, I devised a system for the sonar branch in which the different engineers in charge of different functions such as: the sonar for surface ships against submarines; and submarine search, both for long-range search and for attack sonar; and then such things as even bottom navigation equipment; depth soundings; things of that sort. They would all be defined in terms of a minimum functional requirement phase-in time, where possible, defining the functional requirement in yards and degree of reliability, percentage of reliability. And, of course, this got a few of them a little angry because they'd never done that before. But after a while they began to realize it.

We discovered certain interesting things: that in the sonar branch, at that time, we were spending money on an underwater obstacle locator for the Marine Corps to use for some of their amphibious landing craft. We also were spending money on a mine locator for surface ships—for minesweepers, mine locating, and destruction ships. And we were also spending money on a relatively short-range attack sonar of the active variety for both submarines and for surface ships. When you defined all the requirements on the size of the things that you were supposed to detect, and the degree of reliability, and the ship's speed, and all that, you found out that almost all of these things were being designed for the same functional requirement, but we had four different projects, spending four different sets of money on these things.

After the technical people examined it, we were able to eliminate two of them. By concentrating the money, we got the mine locator and the attack sonar much faster. And then some of the money still left over went into developing a long-range passive listening sonar for submarines.

So we found out other things, such as, if you overstate the requirements for accuracy, you can get yourself into problems too. There was a so-called close-in attack sonar, passive variety, being developed for submarines. The requirement for its angular accuracy was something like 1/100th of a degree, but we found out that the feed into this particular sonar and its repeaters was from the ship's gyro, and the accuracy was only about 1/10th of a degree. So we were spending an awful lot of money to get a mechanical accuracy, with all special hand-ground bearings and gears and everything in there, to get this, which made no sense. If you couldn't solve it with accuracy on the detection and location end, then you had to move over into the other side of the problem, which would be on the weapon end, which, of course, made us talk to the Bureau of Ordnance.

If the sensors for detection and location couldn't be accurate, then the weapons had to go out towards the target and find it, which, of course, led us to recommend improvements in homing weapons, particularly against submarines. So that was the kind of different things that were brought about by making this kind of an investigation, and we built up a good relationship between the Bureau of Ordnance and BuShips on these particular subjects.

I was supposed to be the head of the Underwater Sound Branch for two years, which were '51-'53, and then go to sea again. And I didn't know where I was going to go to sea, but because of this paper I'd written, which ultimately got involved with the whole Navy planning system with a SecNav instruction, I was kept on for an extra year. I became the head of the Electronics R&D Planning Branch, which also made everybody angry.[*]

---

[*] R&D – research and development.

Paul Stillwell: What stimulated you to write that paper?

Captain Schwab: Well, the main reason for doing that kind of thing was that there's some virtue in intelligent ignorance. I didn't know what the hell they were doing most of these projects for, so I decided to find out. That was when I started asking them, "What was the specific requirement that led to such and such a project?" That was it, so it was purely a question of asking questions. I imagine if I'd been an engineering duty officer and had come in there—not to say anything about them—but if I'd come in there with a pretty solid knowledge of what they were doing, I would be probably snowed by all the technical language and not having been an operator, as I was, I would not have realized that maybe the operators who wrote the operation requirements really didn't know how to approach the project. So I was sort of in the middle, between being an operator—in position to get their support—and being on the receiving end. I wish I could remember some of their names now, but that should be easy to find out from BuShips register if you're interested, Code 845—I was able to get their support in making my people do it. There were a few rebellions in there, which I had to quell, but that was about it.

As a result of this, the Chief of Bureau of Ships directed that I stay on for another year and put this system of R&D planning through the whole electronics outfit.[*] Then it spread to all R&D planning in the Navy. So I don't know what effect that had on my seagoing, so instead of staying in submarines then, the next thing I knew I was out in command of a destroyer in the Pacific.

Paul Stillwell: Are there any more specifics to talk about from this planning phase: how you drew the thing together? Was it a matter of getting the requirements for research more rigorously defined?

Captain Schwab: Well, in the budget process, each sub-branch, particularly in R&D, would draw up its own requirements. Each figured that in order to gain a certain objective it would need so much money over such and such a period of time. It was all

---

[*] Rear Admiral Homer N. Wallin, USN, served as Chief of the Bureau of Ships from 1951 to 1953. Rear Admiral Wilson D. Leggett, Jr., USN, served as Chief of the Bureau of Ships from 1953 to 1955.

being done—as you'll see later—in a vertical sense. In other words, all the people who were working on, let's say, submarine sonar where there was long-range or short-range, were just looking at the sonar aspects and not how it would tie in with the weaponry that was going to be associated with it.

It was the same way on surface ship sonar: there still was an awful lot of attention being paid then—when I first got in there—to relatively short-range attack sonar for surface ships, which would permit accurate launching of depth charges or ahead-thrown weapons, such as Hedgehogs, things of that sort.* There was an awful lot of money being spent on that. There wasn't too much attention being paid to the fact our own submarines, and we would assume that the Russian submarines—if we ever had to use the stuff—would use small homing torpedoes against surface ships, and that the surface ships were vulnerable to countermeasures from the submarines. So if the surface ship got inside the homing range of one of these torpedoes—before it did something to the submarine—it was a good possibility it would be disabled or sunk.

The idea was then to say at what range you would have to do something to the enemy submarine before it would do something to you. We found out, from different things during that that period in history, if you could detect the enemy submarine out around 10,000 yards and track him in—it would be a good idea if you could do something to him before he got inside of a 1,000 yards. So you had a long tracking period. We kept moving that out as information on possibilities of their kinds of torpedoes they had, which were many, and I guess homing and all the other kinds too.

So just by looking at the problem across the board horizontally, rather than vertically, one of the things that was noticed by me, and by my senior assistants, was that while the BuShips Underwater Sound Branch was spending a lot of money on improving short-range attack sonar, the Bureau of Ordnance was spending a lot of money on long-range torpedoes to be launched from surface ships plus ASROC and things of that

---

* Hedgehog, developed in World War II, was a British-designed spigot mortar that fired its weapons out ahead of the attacking ship. It was the first ASW weapon that could be fired while the surface ship remained in sonar contact with the target. Its name came from the collection of spigots in the launcher; they stuck up like porcupine quills.

sort.* They were looking at ranges in the thousands of yards, and the sonar to direct them was just not around.

Again, by consolidating certain overlapping things, both in time and in functional requirements, we saved some money and got up to some of the longer-range lower frequency sonars that you still have today—SQS-53 and things of that sort. I'm not sure where bottom-bounce sonar, for instance, came from, but it was something noticed in SubDevGroup 2: that you did get some bottom reflections with certain things. The bottom-bounce sonar and the fact that you have annular rings of detection around a target—I think on the order of seven miles. That applies whether it's an active echo or sound actually coming from a target or a ship. These things all led into the long-, long-term, long-range surface ship sonars, which in turn had to tie in with the accuracy requirements for these new weapons that BuOrd was developing. So it all hooked together ultimately. That was one of the objectives of the research and development system: to open the blinders and get rid of the vertical constraints on the planning that was occurring at that time.

Paul Stillwell: Were there any requirements growing out of the advent of the nuclear submarine?

Captain Schwab: Well, no, not specific ones. In the first place, we didn't have any at that point. They were starting to worry that maybe nuclear submarines wouldn't make the same kind of noises that snorkeling submarines did. For ASW detection, it turned out that that wasn't too much of a worry, I guess, as far as Soviet submarines were concerned. They didn't have any nuclear submarines, either, for quite a while.† But there wasn't anything specifically—in the electronics R&D area—aimed at nuclear submarines, except to see what kind of noises they might make, and we didn't have any to listen to.

---

* ASROC – antisubmarine rocket. It entered the fleet in the early 1960s in new-construction ships and in FRAM I destroyer conversions.
† The *K-3*, designated "November" class by NATO, was the first Soviet nuclear-powered submarine. She was launched 9 August 1957 and commissioned 4 June 1958.

Paul Stillwell: Did your planning job get just into sonar-related developments, or did it go beyond that?

Captain Schwab: Well, my last year there I was the head of the electronics R&D planning staff with a splendid civilian by the name of Al Rubenstein, who's still with IDA.* He's down there and he's a real sharp person, and he's one of the few people that I know who, if he doesn't know something, he'll say, "I don't know." Really, he never tried to give you a snow job. That's hard to do lots of times for most people, not to have the appearance of knowing more than they really do. We had three people on this electronics planning staff, and the reason he was brought in as my number-one assistant was to implement the type of minimum functional planning, phased and time outline of requirements that developed for the sonar branch, and that was applied to all of the different segments of electronics R&D planning. In fact, that's how we found out, for example, that the Marines had a separate section, even though we were financing it. We didn't know what the Marine requirements really were. When we started checking these things, that's how we found out about it. It applied to radar. Communications was a little different, but most of the things that required sensors for detection localization were really affected; sonar and radar were the main ones.

Paul Stillwell: Do you remember any other specific programs you were involved with at BuShips?

Captain Schwab: No, those were the main things. R&D electronics were the only things we got involved in. Then, by talking to people over in OpNav, modifying the kinds of requirements that would come over, we'd have this horizontal tie-in in time. There's not much point in spending a lot of money on something to get completed seven years from now—with certain capabilities associated with it—when the enemy's or possible enemy's capabilities to overcome that will be better than that in three years. These things always depended on intelligence, and that's one of the rules we came up with. If you didn't have intelligence in what the enemy capability was that you were trying to counter, assume it's

---

* IDA – Institute for Defense Analyses.

the same as your own. So it's either going to be better or worse, probably, but if you didn't know you should assume that, because otherwise you were in the dark. You didn't want to get too far ahead—to say he was much better than you were—because then you were overdoing it and you'd never get anything done. That was our rule of thumb, which seemed to work all right.

Paul Stillwell: How good was the intelligence? Was there much available on the Soviet capabilities?

Captain Schwab: Well, apparently they had acquired over time a lot of information on the kind of noises their submarines made; they still have that. In fact, it's been written in unclassified press that they supposedly can even identify which submarine. I don't quite believe that, but that's what they say. Then they had information on their weaponry, torpedoes and so on. What happens over time is you forget how much of this is classified, and I don't know right at the moment how much is classified.

Paul Stillwell: Did you do any intelligence collection in the *Toro* by listening?

Captain Schwab: No, we didn't do any of that.

Paul Stillwell: So it was coming from other sources?

Captain Schwab: Yes.

Paul Stillwell: Well, that's got to be a feather in your cap, that BuShips thought highly enough of you to keep you for another year there.

Captain Schwab: That's probably why I made captain. Of course, nothing illustrious at that point had happened. Been involved in lots of things, but so had a lot of other people.

Paul Stillwell: It's surprising that that development on SOSUS was almost accidental, that your boss wasn't pushing you to get into something like that.

Captain Schwab: Well, you mean accidental in BuShips?

Paul Stillwell: Right.

Captain Schwab: Well, it came from all the things that had come in from SubDevGroup 2, which were there waiting. It was towards the end of that period, when I went in there, that was where they were. Plus the fact that we got support from Junior McCain. Also it coincided with the work of Bell Telephone Labs on magnetic separation of signals. If they hadn't done that enhancement—if that all hadn't happened at the same time we probably wouldn't have anything like SOSUS.

Paul Stillwell: Or at least not as soon.

Captain Schwab: You never know. Yes, that's possible. So many things happen by accident. I think it was more a fortunate accident with the people in there who were able to recognize and support it with money. I don't know who rigged the microphone at Eleuthera, but whoever it was probably did more than anybody to get the money, because from then on it was clear sailing.

Paul Stillwell: Well, it must have been, at least, something somebody had thought of before as a concept for submarine detection. Maybe it just hadn't been considered technically feasible.

Captain Schwab: Well, no. The only reason for the existence of SubDevGroupTwo was to explore ways to detect snorkeling submarines, and in doing this we explored the whole frequency range and discovered that a snorkel tube resonates at some certain low frequency. It wasn't accidental. We just happened to discover this by checking the whole frequency range, using Harmon B. Sherry's oscilloscope and German robot camera. Otherwise, we wouldn't have seen these things reinforcing all the time. I mean, when you're looking you're going to get a lot of noise in there, but then you got these little spikes at a certain discrete frequencies over and over and over again, which you would only recognize if you had a record of it, which he got from the camera. Take the record at certain intervals, and then there it was.

Paul Stillwell: You mentioned you went from that job on to the *Wedderburn*.* Was there disappointment going to a surface ship rather than a submarine?

Captain Schwab: Well, I'd already had a submarine, so I was getting too senior for a submarine. But they had decided that they would rotate submarine officers around the surface ships. I'd been on a destroyer for a couple of weeks in the summer of 1937 to watch the America's Cup races off Newport. But this was the first surface ship I'd ever had command of, and it was the first destroyer I'd ever run around in.† It was a lot of fun, because you have a lot more power to maneuver than you do on a submarine; you didn't have to worry about lots of things.

Well, the destroyer navy was something like the submarine navy. Of course, when you were operating on a division of four destroyers—it was pretty small—you were on your own as well. I even got off with another destroyer. Two of us went down to escort a carrier to Singapore. The commanding officer of the other one was Dan Bergin; he had the *Kidd*, and I had the *Wedderburn*.‡ This was 1955, and they sent an aircraft carrier down to that vicinity. I guess it was to check out certain operations that were occurring. There were Russian ships or something down there, but they were just checking out all the different aspects of commerce and Singapore being sort of a focal point. I was disappointed in Singapore; it wasn't as glamorous as I thought it was going to be. But the two of us went down there and operated together. It was just like being in

---

* USS *Wedderburn* (DD-684), a *Fletcher*-class destroyer, was commissioned 9 March 1944. She had a standard displacement of 2,050 tons, full-load displacement of 2,700 tons; was 376 feet long, 40 feet in the beam, and had a draft of 18 feet. Her designed top speed was 35 knots. She was armed with five 5-inch guns and ten 21-inch torpedo tubes.
† Commander Schwab was commanding officer of the *Wedderburn* from 30 October 1954 to 23 July 1956.
‡ Commander Daniel E. Bergin, USN, commanded the destroyer *Kidd* (DD-661) from 2 July 1955 to 17 December 1956.

a submarine, as far as that was concerned. Any small ship is better than a big ship, as far as I was concerned.

Paul Stillwell: Did you have to learn your way around the destroyer navy initially because you didn't have the background?

Captain Schwab: Well, I think some of the destroyer officers sort of resented a submarine officer coming in there and taking over command without ever having been on board. It wasn't too bad. Handling a destroyer came instantly practically. It was very responsive to everything, and I had good officers on board. There were no problems. You were more separated from the crew than you are on a submarine. I mean, you had a little more insulation in there. But all in all, I enjoyed it. You can't beat any kind of command. They say it's the best job in the Navy. You've probably been told that.

Paul Stillwell: Did you have to learn, specifically, destroyer tactics—antiair warfare, shore bombardment?

Captain Schwab: Oh, well, before you'd go to a destroyer they sent you down to ASW school. They sent me to ASW school in Norfolk, Virginia. The head of the school was Bob McNitt.[*] I guess he made admiral ultimately, and president of the Naval Academy Alumni Association. He was also very innovative on ASW tactics. At the school, besides going into the normal individual ship tactics, they had little machines that you practiced on, things of that sort. He had what I would call war games for ASW campaigns, the different situations of war—large, general war, or isolated instances. So it was very, very good; I learned a lot there.

Having been on the receiving end of ASW, even when we were operating with our own surface ships, I had a pretty good idea of what was required to counter a submarine. In fact, you probably had a better idea what the submarine was likely to do.

---

[*] Captain Robert W. McNitt, USN, was commanding officer and director of the Atlantic Fleet Anti-Submarine Warfare Tactical School from 1959 to 1961. The oral history of McNitt, who retired as a rear admiral, is in the Naval Institute collection. After his retirement from active duty, he was president of the Naval Academy Alumni Association from 1985 to 1988. Schwab attended the school before his duty as chief of staff to Carrier Division 20 in 1960-61 rather than before his command tour in the *Wedderburn*.

The main difference, of course, was in surface gunnery, which we hadn't had much of in submarines. I hadn't had any gunnery experience since I'd been in battleships. Of course, now we had radars and radar-controlled directors and things of that sort. It was a pretty old destroyer, too, not one of the new ones. I guess they didn't want to give a submarine officer a new destroyer. But we had a good outfit.

Paul Stillwell: Where was your ship home-ported?

Captain Schwab: In San Diego. That was nice too. That was before they put the bridge in, you see. You took ferryboats over to the mainland. It was a lot of fun. I was there two years on that.

Paul Stillwell: Did you make two deployments in that period?

Captain Schwab: Oh, yes.

Paul Stillwell: What are the highlights of the deployments?

Captain Schwab: During the deployments you usually went out as a division of four destroyers. You left the West Coast and went to Pearl Harbor, and you operated out of there a couple of days, something like going to war in a submarine, actually. Then you went on to Japan. The first port that you hit in Japan was Yokosuka. The highlights out there were mostly just operating with the Seventh Fleet.

Of course, in that period we had the various retrenchments by the Republic of China, as opposed to the People's Republic, which we still called Red China.[*] We didn't have any diplomatic relations, I guess, at that time. There was considerable worry about the possibility of an assault on Taiwan from the mainland, or other kinds of things that might occur there that would spark off hostilities.

---

[*] In 1979 the United States shifted diplomatic recognition from the Republic of China (Taiwan) to the People's Republic of China (mainland).

I don't know where the initiative came from, but they did evacuate such things as Tachen Islands, and I was the senior destroyer officer at the Tachen Island evacuation.* It was mostly an amphibious operation, with a few units of the Chinese Navy helping. They evacuated all the people with no incident. The Chinese military didn't interfere at all; they were probably glad to get them out of there. Of course, there had been an awful lot of problems then with Quemoy, Matsu, and the Tachens.†

But they got them all over the island, to Taiwan, without any problem. I remember the Chinese admiral who was the nominal head of the whole thing. He threw a big luncheon or a dinner for us in Keelung, in a big warehouse. They had magicians and dancers and it was good. The senior amphibious officer was a U.S. Navy captain who had been in charge of the amphibious ships. I was the senior destroyer officer, and the Chinese admiral was a destroyer officer, so we got along real well, and he didn't like the amphibious captain, whoever he was. To me he said, "You drink what I drink, and we'll get him something special." He was drinking, I guess, rice wine—it looked like bourbon—and he found out that the captain liked whiskey of some sort. So he had him served whiskey all the time.

Of course, in a Chinese banquet we were arranged in tables. I guess there were about eight of these tables—a whole bunch of tables—and all of the officers, Chinese and American, had been involved in this. At the end of each little course that was served then you had a toast, and you had to compete or to put it upside down on your head to show it was empty. After about four or five courses—these were pretty good shot glasses—this captain here was no longer with it. We were on backless stools. He fell off his stool, and that was the end of him, which the admiral thought it was pretty funny.

Paul Stillwell: What was the role of the destroyers in that operation?

---

* The small Tachen Islands, north of Formosa (as Taiwan was then called) were subject to attack from mainland China in the early 1950s. On 7 February 1955, on the advice of the U.S. Government and with the assistance of the U.S. Seventh Fleet, the Nationalist Chinese evacuated the Tachens.
† On 23 August 1958, Communist China began an intensive artillery bombardment of the offshore islands of Quemoy and Matsu, which were held by the Nationalist Chinese government. The Seventh Fleet escorted troop transports that carried forces to protect the two islands. The aircraft carrier *Essex* (CVA-9) supported the operation.

Captain Schwab: Just to monitor everything. We had orders to watch any planes; it was mostly airplanes we were worried about, I guess, approaching us in a hostile fashion. We were to shoot them down in a friendly fashion, I guess, if we were worried. It was sort of peculiar. The rules of engagement were as usual, you know, political. If you didn't shoot it down, and it was going to attack you, and then if you got hit you were in trouble. And if you did shoot it down and it wasn't going to attack you, you were in trouble.

The Nationalist Chinese aviators were crazy. They'd come flying up and down in the straits there, and they'd come right in at you as if they were going to attack, and then they'd zoom away. Well, we locked and loaded on these guys all the time. You didn't know who they were; you couldn't see any markings when they were coming right at you. Well, they've got blue and gold, I guess, with the sun on them.

Then the other thing was that at night our division was scattered out, and we were patrolling the coast. We were staying outside the 12-mile limit; they told us to stay outside; we were a little farther than that. But these Red Chinese fishing boats would come out, literally by the *thousands*. It was like a solid mass of them over there, and some of them had engines and some didn't. I guess they towed a lot of them out there, and they were fishing away. We'd run up and down and watch them; they never came out past whatever their limit was. Then we were supposed to identify all the merchant ships that were running up and down. Of course, we were at darkened ship; it wasn't war, but it was like it.

These were mostly British ships running up and down there, with non-British crews, but British officers on deck. We'd turn our running lights on, come up alongside, challenge them, try to talk to them. You'd get some good choice words back from the Brits. They wanted to know, "What the hell are you blankety-blank Yankees doing here anyhow? You think you're running the goddamn ocean?" That sort of stuff. But we'd usually get what the name of the merchant ship was, and where they came from, and where they were going, and once in a while they'd tell you what they had on board. I don't know what they used that for, but it was sort of a check. It was sort of an interesting thing.

We'd get into Hong Kong, of course. On the second deployment, I guess, we went into Nagasaki for the Harbor Festival. It was the occasion of the anniversary of the

300th opening of Japan to trade; then it closed again until the Americans got back with Perry.* We had a great big thing there; I don't know how many destroyers were in, two maybe, and I was one of them. I had, of course, to wear my uniform with the submarine insignia and stuff on it—I was still a commander.

Paul Stillwell: And your ribbons for beating the Japanese.

Captain Schwab: Yes, for beating the Japanese. Of course, Japanese defense forces were sort of meager; right near us they had a bunch of old harbor mine craft. That was the extent of the navy they had in Nagasaki. My host sitting next to me was—I don't know whether he was a commander or captain in the Japanese Navy, but he had no insignia, no decorations at all. So he looked over and he said, "Oh, you were in submarines, weren't you?"

I said, "Yeah." He talked English very well. He pulled his coat back and all this stuff was inside; he was a submarine officer too! He said, "They never let us do what we should have done, which you did, attack everything." He said they were mostly told to attack combatant ships. Apparently they obeyed all the rules—more than we did anyhow.

Paul Stillwell: It sounds as if there was a hospitable relationship.

Captain Schwab: Oh, yes. We really had a good time there. That's Madame Butterfly's town and all that sort of stuff. There was no problem there. One of my commodores was John Harllee, who was one of the original PT boat people.†

Paul Stillwell: He was the division commander?

Captain Schwab: He was the division commander on the second deployment, the second division commander we had. I remember once the four commanding officers and the

---

* On 8 July 1853 a U.S. Navy squadron of side-wheel steamers and sloops, under the command of Commodore Matthew E. Perry, USN, entered Edo (Tokyo) Bay to establish relations with Japan.
† Captain John Harllee, USN, commanded Destroyer Division 152 in 1955-56.

division commander were in port at Kobe, Japan, for about a week. We decided we'd go for a weekend to Lake Biwa-ko, which was the largest inland, fresh-water lake in Japan. It was in the wintertime—we were always over there in the wintertime—and we were supposed to go over on a Friday and come back on a Sunday night. It snowed so all the passes that we went through were filled in, so we were up there a couple days extra. But that was an interesting thing. There's a mountain there, which they call "Little Hell" or something like that, and it has all these sulfur jets coming out. We didn't realize, it was probably ready for a volcanic eruption. All the Japanese people were there in force; they wandered up and down. Bergin was my roommate for that little adventure. But that's about it.

The destroyer episode—I don't think I learned a lot, except I had a lot of fun maneuvering a destroyer. We did all sorts of weird things, such as transferring people by highline. I took millions of pictures. The main difficulties that I had were recovering boats in rough weather. For some reason we were always sending boats out, and I really smashed up a whaleboat once. It just happens; they swing against the side and then you have problems. I don't think the caliber or the experience level of the enlisted men in the destroyer navy—their incentive, because they weren't getting any extra pay—was the same as on the submarine navy.

Paul Stillwell: They hadn't been through as rigorous a screening process, either.

Captain Schwab: They were a lot younger, it seemed, too. That's right. But they all tried to do their best; it was just that you didn't have the same feeling of confidence. You had to check a lot more. When I would be asleep, for example, on a submarine, and we were running along even on the surface, I had a pretty good idea that if anything occurred, why, they'd call me in a hurry before it got out of hand. They would certainly call me. Whereas, I was not so sure about whether destroyer people would recognize something that far ahead of time. Of course, you had a little sea cabin up there, so you always sort of slept with one ear open.

If you were in a formation, of course, you always had the problem of the possibility of colliding with another ship, and you did an awful lot of weird ship maneuvers, which are cut-and-dried things. I won't mention its name, but we had one destroyer there where no matter who the commanding officer was, it was always getting itself in trouble, turning right when it should turn left. We always used to have one officer come up when we'd have these high-speed, close-in maneuvers, to watch that ship, to make sure that we didn't have any problems with it. It was always having problems; we didn't know why. It just seemed like the psychology of the ship.

Paul Stillwell: What do you recall about the material condition of the ship?

Captain Schwab: Well, in every job, no matter where you are, there's always something you can find, because of your background, that you might be able to correct. One of the things I noticed in the *Wedderburn* was that when I made captain's inspections and so on, there was always "the list" of what was wrong and what should be corrected. Of course, the captain didn't inspect every place on a ship during a captain's inspection. The areas were notified where the captain was going to go, so they'd make a special effort. They sort of rotated that around so they wouldn't go nuts, except you'd hit that place again, and an awful lot of things wouldn't be corrected. You don't know whether it was because they didn't have time, or forgot, or just sloppiness. You didn't know.

So I wrote up a thing for, I guess, the destroyer force. I must have a copy of that here someplace. In suggesting how to minimize the forgetfulness and emphasize things, I advised three kinds of shipping tags. It was a red shipping tag, which is emergency; the green one was do it right after the emergencies; and a white one for when you have a chance, maybe in the next upkeep period. That was a smaller tag.

Now, when I would go around, I'd have my senior enlisted man, whoever he was, with me, and he'd have a pocket full of these tags, see. Then I'd see something, maybe some sort of a valve which looked important, that I wanted fixed, and I'd have him put a red tag on that. Right on the tag was this penciled mark of what had to be done. And then he had the record for that; he'd write down the name of the compartment, what it was. He had a red-tag list, a green-tag list, and a white-tag list. On a red tag, all those things were supposed to be repaired within 24 hours; then the tag would be taken back into the repair shop office. The green ones within a day or a couple of days, maybe less than a week. The white ones, maybe the next upkeep period. It worked pretty well.

When we first put it in, I wrote it up, and quite a few destroyers were using it. The funny thing is the first time we did it—before I wrote up the article—I found so many things that when we went out, we looked like a Christmas tree. I got a signal from the tender, which was *Dixie*, I think, "What are all the funny things jiggling on your ship?" That's when I wrote the thing up. That was sort of an innovation. As your ship got larger, of course, you couldn't do that, but a destroyer was a good place to do that.

Paul Stillwell: Did you have any untoward incidents while you were skipper that involved the *Wedderburn*?

Captain Schwab: Well, I'm trying to think who relieved me on there.[*] We were in San Diego when I got relieved, and my relief actually had already come aboard, and we were doing all the inventory baloney that you do, documents and so on.

Well, before all that, we had an incident where one of the boilers had tubes that ruptured or something of that sort, and, of course, you always have to investigate. The general idea in any part of the Navy—not just the destroyer navy—was that if you can show that you had carried out the requirements as far as inspections and maintenance and training of whatever piece of equipment it was—training the men who operated it—you were okay because materiel failures do occur. Fortunately, I had all the records, and there was no problem there. I don't know if it was the same boiler or not that this occurred on, but while my relief was there waiting to take over, why, I got a call in the middle of the night saying that one of the boilers had really burned up again. They checked over, and I had practically the same papers ready. But he took over with that, even though it was not in good shape.

The only other thing was that I had trouble with my condensers making water all the time; I was always glad when Dan Bergin would—he made admiral; he's dead now—and the *Kidd* was next to me. We were always together, because we were in a

---

[*] Commander George Oliver Atkinson Jr., USN, relieved Schwab of command of the *Wedderburn* on 23 July 1956 and remained in that billet until 4 August 1958.

subdivision, and he knew my condensers were bad. A couple of times in San Diego we were supposed to go out on an exercise or something, and I couldn't make any water at all; he would give me water so I could go out. You had to have extra water for your boilers and everything too. So there was always a problem there, and we always had problems. The ships were getting old, and I don't think the maintenance was all that great. It's not as critical on surface ships as it is on submarines. I mean, you can't afford to have anything go wrong on a submarine. My generators were always going haywire too—things of that sort. Typically, the problems were mostly material things. You don't know how much of it's due to the personnel capabilities and how much is due to just lack of money to maintain things.

Paul Stillwell: Well, you got a cram course in steam propulsion then.

Captain Schwab: Yes, it was something. I mean, you're the commanding officer, so you had to crawl around unless you wanted to get in trouble. I'd crawl in those damn boilers and every place else, which is sort of interesting. I don't think I'd want to do it now; I had on my dirty coveralls that I went in there with. It's always an interesting thing to get inside of a boiler.

Paul Stillwell: Was there a great emphasis on good behavior by the crew in these overseas ports?

Captain Schwab: Yes, that's an interesting one. Of course, in submarines, as I mentioned, we had a few people who couldn't go ashore by themselves because they would get in trouble—particularly the one Indian quartermaster I mentioned. We'd always have him go with somebody. But when we were in these different ports, why, you'd always have a pep talk before we went in that we were "ambassadors" and that sort of stuff. The main thing we tried to encourage was that nobody go ashore alone. Go in groups of two or four or more, and even numbers. There's another advantage, because if you had an even number then you don't have one guy being left out or something. They'd usually pair up somehow. So we tried to do that, and that worked well.

When we were in upkeep periods, I had discovered in submarines that—the first thing—your crew morale soars if you were, for one reason or another, by skullduggery or something, able to get your ship in ahead of the others.

I also found that when you were in port for an upkeep period, that it was a good idea, no matter whether you were on deployment or not, that when they were in port the crew wanted to get off the ship. They didn't want to sit on the ship as if they were out at sea. So instead of having the normal, you know, 8:00 to 11:30 and then 1:00 to 4:00 working hours, I'd just ask everybody how would they like to have something like 8:00 to 2:00 without any time off for lunch? You know, besides that, you saved a lot of money for your commissary. So they all voted for it; they thought that was great. So at 2:00 o'clock, when all the other ships would still be busy working, all my crew were going ashore. We had one commanding officer on another ship who complained to the commodore about it. He said, "He's letting all his men go early. It's hurting morale on my ships. All the enlisted men on the *Wedderburn* are leaving."

The commodore said, "Well, the ship's being maintained all right, and why don't you do it?" That was the kind of thing that we would do, and all these things that made the people feel that their ship was operating a little bit better, a lot more fun than the others, anyhow. You get a lot of ship spirit; in the submarines and the destroyers, whenever we'd have parties where the officers, would be there. There was always a table for your officers, and we had even the commanding officers from other submarines come over to sit at our table, because they said they liked our officers better than their own, which is sort of bad. They didn't tell their officers that, but they told us.

Paul Stillwell: What recreational outlets did you provide for the crew of the *Wedderburn*, both under way and in port?

Captain Schwab: Well, in port, wherever we were we'd organize little tours or so on. You'd have a division chaplain that was on the division flagship usually. He'd arrange some sort of tours in port. You didn't really have too much time in port. Mostly you went over shopping or whatever they were doing, but there was no real emphasis on organized things the way you did when you came in for a rest during the war. When you were out at sea, if weather permitted and so on, once in a while we'd have a steak cookout on the fantail, crazy things like that. There wasn't much to do, and most of the time that the crew wasn't actually standing watch or so on, they were either lying down or reading, playing cards or something of that sort. There's not too much you can do on a ship, especially because we seemed to be out in a lot of rough weather all the time.

Paul Stillwell: Did you arrange sports events in port?

Captain Schwab: No, we didn't do too much of that; I don't remember any sports events at all, now that I think of it.

Paul Stillwell: How did you communicate with the crew, mostly—through the 1MC?[*]

Captain Schwab: Well, when we'd have our inspections, the exec and I would team up, and we'd go around to all the different divisions and give them a little talk on what was going on, in person. Then we had a ship's bulletin we put out, mimeographed or whatever it was, and that would explain, as best we could, what we were doing and where we were going. As far ahead as we could, particularly for the married men, we'd try to give them a schedule, so the family would know roughly where they were; they'd tell them what to buy. Not too much attention was paid to morale, I guess. I don't know what they do now, but living conditions on destroyers aren't that great. As a matter of fact, I thought they were better in submarines than on destroyers.

Paul Stillwell: They're certainly better in destroyers now than they were then.

Captain Schwab: I imagine they are.

Paul Stillwell: You said Singapore didn't live up to your expectations. How so?

---

[*] The designation of a ship's general announcing system is 1MC.

Captain Schwab: I don't know; it just looked a little shabby. Well, among other things, we went to the Raffles Hotel, which I thought would be a real glamorous place, and it wasn't. I understand it's been beefed up. Of course, this was in the 1954 to '56 period there. I imagine that it's a lot better. Hong Kong was just what I thought it would be, a big shopping mart. Then, of course, I enjoyed Yokosuka; I got up to Tokyo once or twice there. Leo Treitel had been my head of the sonar branch. His brother was a Marine lieutenant colonel then, and he lived near where the big Buddha is.*

Paul Stillwell: Kamakura.

Captain Schwab: Yes, Kamakura. He organized a little trip for me and one of my officers. Three or four of us went up to Tokyo on one trip and saw a sumo wrestling match. Then we had a brunch at the Frank Lloyd Wright hotel—what was it, the Imperial Hotel?†

Paul Stillwell: Yes.

Captain Schwab: And had champagne—what do they call it? French 75, champagne and brandy, I guess, for brunch and we ate like mad. Also had a dinner at the best German meal I ever had at something in Tokyo called Irene's Hungarian. Good German beer. It was as if you were living in Germany, but it was Hungarian. Once we went on a train, I guess, and another time we drove. When we came back from Tokyo the second time, I guess there were just three of us in the car. One of the sumo wrestlers, who spoke English—I guess he'd been in exhibition things someplace in the United States—wanted to go down to Yokosuka, too, so Treitel said, "Okay, hop in." I don't know whether he had an official car; it must have been his own private car. We looked around, and Trietel was pretty big, so they were in the front seat, and this was not a very big car. That left

---

* Lieutenant Colonel Paul S. Treitel, USMC.
† Tokyo's Imperial Hotel, designed by American architect Frank Lloyd Wright, opened in 1922. The building was undamaged by the Great Tokyo Earthquake of 1923. It closed in November 1967, was demolished shortly afterward, and was replaced by a high-rise building.

me in the back seat with this sumo wrestler. I practically didn't breathe the rest of the way. He was *huge*. That was an uncomfortable ride. Things of that sort happened.

Another time when we were on our way to Lake Biwa-ko with Harllee. We had a big car, and in it were three or four commanding officers and the commodore. The commodore wanted to pick up a stone lantern for some admiral who had asked him someplace, and so we went wandering around looking for this address out in the back roads of Kobe. He had the address written both in English and in Japanese; we didn't know where this place was except roughly. So we'd go down a road and there'd be men working at the side of the road. You knew enough Japanese to say, "Where is this?" or whatever.

He'd look at it and say, "Yes—hai."

Then we'd say, "Do you know where it is?"

"Hai."

Then we'd say, "Where is it?"

"That way," see, and we'd go that way and it wasn't that way at all, but they'd always tell you something, because, otherwise, I guess they'd lose face if they don't know where someplace is. We finally found the place.

Kobe is where they have this beer-fed beef; it's the best beef in the world, I guess. We saw the way they shoved the bottles down and force-fed them—pretty cheap beer, I guess. It's delicious; you can cut it with a fork. I have a picture of it too. Kobe was a place where the British operated a lot. I don't know, it's not that the British Navy was there anymore, but the British merchant marine, I guess, were still there, and the place that we ate at was called the Queen's Arms. There was a big picture of Queen Elizabeth over the fireplace, and you had your beer or whatever you had there, and they had these *big* things of bitter that they'd give you, beer. All of the waiters, of course, and the bartender were all Japanese, but they all spoke with a British accent, which was funny. We'd eat a delicious roast beef and British-style fried potatoes. They looked like French fires, but they were skinnier. I always like horseradish with my roast beef, so I asked for some horseradish, and this stuff came out like coleslaw, almost, but a little thinner than that, and that was Japanese horseradish. Let me tell you, if you want to clear a head, that'll do it! Have you ever been over there?

Paul Stillwell: Yes, but I haven't had any horseradish.

Captain Schwab: That's rough, yes. That's the sort of thing we did. Most of the commanding officers ran around together when they were ashore. The officers at the different levels would sort of stick together; the same way with the enlisted men—of course in their own ships. It was a pretty good, friendly atmosphere.

Paul Stillwell: How did the incidence of mast cases compare with what you'd known in the submarines?

Captain Schwab: I don't really remember too many disciplinary cases on the submarine at all. In the first place, you had a different kind of hierarchy. You had the chief of the boat, and he was God, as far as the enlisted men were concerned. I'd say 99% of all infractions were handled at the petty officer level, in other words. I'd hear stories, not on my ship, but stories about somebody who had done something wrong, and the next day he was seen with a sort of real bruise next to his head. "How did that happen?"

"Well, I fell down a ladder." Supposedly the petty officer had told him, "Would you rather see the captain at mast or what?" He'd get a little bit of back talk and WHACK, that was it.

I don't remember many disciplinary cases; as I said, only one officer I disqualified because he was just impossible to handle and we didn't have time to fool around with him. It wasn't a reform academy. On the surface ship it was mostly questions of absence over leave, things of that sort. I don't remember any insubordination-type things, which would have been serious.

Paul Stillwell: Was the punishment pretty much cut and dried in those UA cases?[*]

Captain Schwab: Oh, yes, just keep them on board for four or five days, or something like that. It depends on how long they were gone. Sometimes they had good excuses too. If they had a reasonable excuse, you gave them a warning.

---

[*] UA – unauthorized absence.

Paul Stillwell: That's where the imagination really comes into play sometimes.

Captain Schwab: Well, you could check on them, see, because your main dependence was still on your petty officers. Before you go there, of course, your exec was the one who told you what was coming up. He'd come in your cabin and tell you what the mast cases were, if you had any, and what their records were like. He'd already checked out with their division officers; then the division officers had checked out with the petty officers. Of course if the guy was a real troublemaker, then he was in trouble all the way up the line. But if it was a slip, which can happen, I guess, to the best of us, then that was it too. You had to trust everybody down the line, or you were in trouble. If you didn't trust anybody, then you might as well quit.

Paul Stillwell: How much did you work with aircraft carriers during your deployments?

Captain Schwab: We were always working with aircraft carriers in the Seventh Fleet. We were always either on the ASW screen or doing lifeguard duty right behind them; you were always there. Never had anybody go in the water that I had to rescue. I saw a couple of helicopters go in; well, later on when I was the chief of staff in a carrier division, they used to go in fast. It was scary.

Paul Stillwell: And these ASW screens, that's where learning those surface tactics was useful.

Captain Schwab: Well, yes, and of course your sonar wasn't so great in these things. When you were on an ASW screen, you were fanned out, bent-line screen mostly, but that was good against World War II submarines. But you mentioned nuclear submarines. They were already starting to think then that as submarines got faster and faster, particularly nuclear, that you weren't safe in the rear anymore. An old submarine couldn't catch much of a target that was going 15 knots. Couldn't do it submerged, anyhow. It had trouble on the surface, too, to get out ahead and run. But with the nuclear submarines able to get up to 30 knots or whatever, then you had as much chance of an attack from the rear as you did from the bow. Probably more, in fact, because your sonar equipment wasn't as good looking back through your propeller wakes and all that noise back there. This led to the invention of the new techniques of having big circular screens and using a lot of things *not* dependent on towed sonar, such as a helicopter with a dipping sonar. That was all coming on then, because at that point we still didn't have any experience with nuclear submarines.

Paul Stillwell: What sort of operations were you in with these carriers? You mentioned the Tachen Islands' evacuation. Any other specific things you remember?

Captain Schwab: No, just strictly training exercises, and then once in a while you'd see them shooting at towed targets. It was strictly routine stuff; we didn't do anything close to any hostility situations. In fact, we stayed well away from the shore of Red China. It was a lot of fun there, refueling from carriers and so on, because they'd always send over a great big jug of ice cream for you and things of that sort. Then from the various oilers that we'd go alongside, everybody had a pretty good time. We'd practice a lot on highline transfers.

Paul Stillwell: That was another thing you had to learn going to a surface ship.

Captain Schwab: Yes, I guess that was the trickiest thing I learned: maintaining station for fueling or highline transfers. That was different because you don't do that in submarines at all. There's an article in something about fueling a submarine at sea in one of the magazines, one of the *Shipmate*s.

Paul Stillwell: So it was mostly a matter of just practicing till you got some experience at it.

Captain Schwab: Well, you learned fast, because, in the first place, you're the commanding officer. My execs were all destroyer officers, so they were always up there, and the first time I did it, of course, they were out there saying, "Well, you may be getting in too close," or something. But after a while you learned. Once or twice and you've got it. You got a little more dashing as you went along—like coming up, you know, at full speed and then "pssst," backing down, and then going ahead again. You had to be sure of yourself, because you didn't know where that stern wa going to go, and learning how much to use in the way of rudder and revolutions to maintain station, about getting trapped by his bow wave and things of that sort. It was all sorts of little tricks that you picked up. The main thing was to read *Knight's Seamanship* and all the other books on ship handling before you went to it. I was a little concerned before I took over command, how was I going to do on handling something of this sort? If you don't have any casualties, I guess, in the first few months, why, you're okay.

Paul Stillwell: Well, that builds your confidence certainly. The Navy now has a great emphasis on taking care of dependents. How much was your wife a mother hen for the people back home during a deployment?

Captain Schwab: Well, all the ones who were married lived in San Diego or in Coronado. Most of the officers' wives lived in Coronado, and my wife would keep in touch with them. There wasn't too much attention that I remember being taken care of the enlisted men as family units there. I don't think so.

I know when we were in submarines, the wife of the submarine's captain was not in New London. When I was exec on the *Darter*, my wife was in charge of keeping everybody informed at the end when we were supposedly lost for 12 days. But there wasn't too much attention. If anybody had any problems when they were in there and San Diego, the DesPac flagship was there and they had chaplain and all this stuff, and the shore establishment, I guess, had something.* If a wife had a problem, she could call up the local district commandant's office and get assistance. But there wasn't anything organized as far as the ships were concerned, that I know of.

Paul Stillwell: Well, probably a lot lower percentage of married enlisted men in that era too.

---

* DesPac – Destroyer Force Pacific Fleet.

Captain Schwab: I don't know how many. I really don't know how many were married. There were quite a few of them that were married.

Paul Stillwell: Any other things to recall about the *Wedderburn* before we move on?

Captain Schwab: It was much more of a personal on-board struggle on maintenance than it was in the submarines. When you were out at sea in a submarine, everything was working—in peacetime, particularly, I'm talking about. In wartime, of course, you had a casualty you had to fix it out there by yourself. The materiel failures on submarines, as opposed to surface ships, were a lot fewer. Submarines were probably better maintained at all times than the surface ships.

Paul Stillwell: How would you account for that?

Captain Schwab: Well, in wartime the people doing the maintenance were submarine people, and they had to go out too. Of course, after the war the money was short. In other words, instead of replacing something that went bad you'd try to repair it, and sometimes it didn't work.

Paul Stillwell: How much choice did you have after that on what your next assignment would be?

Captain Schwab: When I had command of the *Wedderburn*, a request came out for an officer of the rank of commander with certain experience and time and so on to go to a course in the social sciences. Preferably he would be a graduate of the war college. I figured this would be a good way to get a graduate degree in something, which wouldn't hurt. So I put in for it, thinking it had to do with personnel. The next thing I knew, my orders came, and it said just "Tufts." I didn't even know where Tufts was, only that there was Sonny Tufts the movie actor. I guess we were back to the West Coast by that time, so I called up BuPers and asked what it was. They said, "You volunteered for it, and you got it." They had one aviator and one non-aviator.

I think the aviator's specialty was in ASW patrol planes. His name, surprisingly, was John Wayne, not the movie actor.* We were there together; we were the first two two-year people at the Fletcher School.† I think we were the first two altogether paid for by the Navy. I think there had been a couple of naval officers on their own or something prior to that, but who paid for them I don't know. I passed all the exams for a doctorate, but then I immediately got involved in the Navy. I did about half of my research for my dissertation and never bothered to finish it. Didn't have time.

I got to the Fletcher School of Law in July of '56, I guess. The interesting thing about that was that both Wayne and myself were much older than the other students. We were about the professors' age in some cases—not all of them. The Fletcher School now has gotten a lot more money than when we were there, so it has a bigger area for people to hang out. But we used to bring our lunch from home. Wayne and I would sit in this little library, which was only about twice as big as this with a bench all around there, and we'd discuss what was going on and how much we didn't know about economics, things of that sort.

Once we were discussing about something that had happened in the days before Pearl Harbor, about the destroyers for Britain and stuff, what we got in return and what effect that had and so on. One of the young civilian students there, also going to the Fletcher School, said, "That doesn't sound right to me, because I read such and such and such and such." Then he looked and he said, "But you must know, because you were there, and I wasn't even born yet or alive or even thinking about things like this." But they suddenly realized that we were a lot older. I thought there'd probably be a lot of anti-military feeling, since this was shortly after the Korean War.

If you want to compare courses, at the Fletcher School I'd say the intensity was at least twice as great as at the war college. There were no "school answers," but there were so many things there I knew practically nothing about: for instance, international economics. They realized this, and they wanted to have the Navy happy with the place. So for people who didn't have too much background in economics they set up a special course on Saturdays under a professor by the name of George Harm, who spoke with a

---

* Commander John B. Wayne, USN.
† The Fletcher School is part of Tufts University in Medford, Massachusetts.

heavy German accent. I couldn't understand him too well in class, but when there was just a couple of us on Saturday I could ask questions, and I guess Wayne went with me too. There's a reluctance to look a little stupid there, especially since both of us had very little experience in economics. But we could ask questions there, and since we were much older than the rest of the class and we were also professional naval officers we felt a little funny about asking questions. We weren't paying for ourselves where all these civilian students there were. So it was a good idea to have a separate course that didn't hurt anything.

We also had to take examinations in foreign languages; both of us had had French before; there was no problem on that. But then to be qualified for a Ph.D., you had to have two languages, and they allowed Spanish. So instead of taking the summer in between the two years at Fletcher School, we both studied with the head of the Romance Language section. His name was Simches, and we learned Spanish.* The emphasis was not on speaking so much, although we did speak it, but the emphasis was on translating from international law, history, and economics and things of that sort. To pass both the French and whatever the other language you took—in this case Spanish—exams, you had to translate something about, I guess, 250 words from some text in each one of those areas. You were allowed only three substantive errors in each thing, which was very interesting because there were a lot of opportunities for substantive errors. They've changed the rules there now, but we both wound up with two master's degrees, and I took the orals before the board and so on and passed that, but Wayne didn't bother. I don't know whatever happened to him; he got out of the Navy. He didn't like the course too much; he said it ruined his career.†

Paul Stillwell: Did you have to write a thesis for your master's?

Captain Schwab: The first one was on the Turkish transformation. I picked on purpose the emphasis on international affairs relating to NATO and to the Middle East.‡ I always considered the Middle East, or Near East, depending on what you call it, to be a key area

---

* Seymour Simches, professor of modern languages.
† Wayne retired as a captain in 1965.
‡ NATO – North Atlantic Treaty Organization, which was established in 1949 as a means of coordinating defense against a potential attack from the Soviet Union.

in the world, which it still is. That was gained a lot from my logistics information at the war college on oil and things of that sort and the increase of oil production by Saudi Arabia. At that point the United States was still the number-one oil exporter, but you could see the handwriting on the wall. And so that was on the Turkish transformation: how Turkey went from a theocratic state, sort of going downhill all the way from 1774 to when it's finally finished after World War I.

Paul Stillwell: To Mustafa Kemal?

Captain Schwab: To Mustafa Kemal and how that developed.* That was the first one, the Turkish transformation.

The second major paper I wrote was on the decisions taken in World War II on going into unrestricted air and submarine warfare, in which case, I have a letter here from Admiral Stark, which among other people, I wrote him.† You were writing papers all the time there.

Paul Stillwell: Do you remember any of your conclusions about that paper on the submarine warfare?

Captain Schwab: Well, of course, we were signatories to a 1936 treaty that we wouldn't do that, and as far as I could find out no one had ever consulted—when the order went out in the Navy, it was all done strictly at the operational level. It wasn't referred to the White House or the State Department. According to Admiral Stark, it seemed like about the only thing you could do at the time. They just sent out, "Execute unrestricted air and submarine warfare against Japan." That was it. It's sort of an amazing thing. Couldn't happen today probably, because you have all those civilian lawyers in there. Well, the conclusion I came to was that despite all the rules and regulations that you might have of an international nature, when your vital interests are at stake you use whatever you have

---

* Mustafa Kemal Atatürk served as the first President of Turkey, from 29 October 1923 to 10 November 1938. His government replaced the old Ottoman Empire, which was defeated in World War I.
† Admiral Harold R. Stark, USN, served as Chief of Naval Operations from 1 August 1939 to 26 March 1942. He was CNO when the U.S. Navy began unrestricted submarine warfare on 7 December 1941.

available, which, of course, doesn't look so good for nuclear warfare business. Because if you're about to go down the hill, you probably would drag everybody with you in that case—that sort of conclusion.

Eisenhower, as a former general, was President then. The Fletcher School at that time sort of had a, I think a sort of pro-Democratic Party, pro—what do they call it in England, the liberals or something? They used to get a lot of speakers from the Democrats, and while I was there I was the senior naval officer present, of course, there were only two of us. And then more came on. The second year we had another bunch of two.

Dean Acheson gave a three- or four-day series of lectures on his experiences plus future looks and so on.[*] With the dean of the school—his name was Stewart—we went out to meet him at the train.[†] He came in on train to one of the Boston stations there, and he was in the sleeper. He'd come out overnight, I guess, from Washington. We got out there and we were about to drive back to the Fletcher School for a lunch at Stewart's house, and Acheson said, "I've lost it. I've lost it; I don't have it."

We said, "What?"

He said, "My lucky silver dollar that I got in April '49. President Truman gave everybody a silver dollar for forming NATO."[‡]

I said, "Where could you have left it?"

He said, "I don't know, but it might be on the train." So I went back on there, and the steward was cleaning up on the train. There was the silver dollar over the little sink that folded down, so I got it back for him. He always carried that as a good-luck charm. He was quite a character too.

Paul Stillwell: Anything else you remember about him?

---

[*] Dean G. Acheson served as Secretary of State from 21 January 1949 to 20 January 1953.
[†] Robert Burgess Stewart was dean of the Fletcher School from 1945 to 1964.
[‡] NATO – North Atlantic Treaty Organization, which was established in 1949 as a means of coordinating defense against a potential attack from the Soviet Union.

Captain Schwab: Well, he had an interesting way of trimming his mustache; it was sort of a wild one. He was a good speaker—very sure, of course, that he was responsible for just about everything good that happened.

Paul Stillwell: You said that was a much more demanding regimen of study than you'd known at the war college?

Captain Schwab: Yes. Well, in the first place at Fletcher School you had to get a B or better or get thrown out. I mean, I volunteered to go there, and it would have been a great thing to get thrown out of my first and only graduate school course, so I had to work hard to be sure I'd get better.

I had a little problem with that, because part of the courses I took were over at Harvard; I took courses on the Middle East, a lot of them, at Harvard. The professor there was Kirk, and he was a Brit. He must have been about, I don't know how tall, but he was very short, and he wore solid leather heels. I guess I was the only one taking that course; I don't know what Wayne was taking. You could hear him coming down the passageway in this old Harvard building, going clank, clank, clank all the way. Then he was very anti-military, surprisingly; I don't think he liked me very well. On my first marking period with him he gave me a C, which would have meant I'd have been thrown out. So I went back to my advisers at Fletcher School and said, "These are the papers I wrote."

I gave them all my stuff, and they looked at it, and they said, "They looked all right to us." So they went over and they talked to him. He reluctantly raised it to a B. I thought I had a B. He didn't give anybody a B, as far as I know, in the whole class. It was a gentleman's C at Harvard, I guess. But that was one little episode.

Paul Stillwell: Did you wear your uniforms?

Captain Schwab: Oh, no, no, civilian clothes. But there were other interesting things there. They were starting a course over at Harvard on political-military policy and things of that sort. It was under Edward L. Katzenbach, who was, I guess, a Marine Reserve lieutenant colonel.* That's the one that Henry Kissinger took over later on, former Secretary of State.†

I guess after that course was on about six months, but the Navy had sent word to the head of the ROTC unit at Tufts—his name was Asserson—that they wanted the officers who were going to the Fletcher School to attend this course over there and see what this Katzenbach was teaching.‡ The head of the department that he was teaching for—it was the law department—and the head of the department was a general in the Air Force Reserve named Leach. So they wanted to see what kind of propaganda was being put out at Harvard. I guess Harvard still had its ROTC then.§ It's been on and off, and now it's on again, I guess. So it was nothing. Katzenbach was a gung-ho Marine in the reserve, and they had no problem at all there. He suddenly was replaced by Kissinger. In that same class was Al Haig, which is how Haig got to know Kissinger.** So it was really—all these things—again accident. I don't know how the Army sent him there. There's his book, there's Haig's book over there, which mentions it.††

Anyhow, this was right at the beginning of my two years at Fletcher School, and I suddenly found out that I was snowed by all the reading and writing and everything else I had to do. This course with Kissinger was two nights a week. I think you started at something like 3:00 o'clock and got out at 5:30. I lived about 45 minutes to an hour away in Westwood, Massachusetts, in a bedroom community. It just got too much, because you were supposed to do an awful lot of reading and writing for that course, too, and it wasn't one of the required courses at Fletcher School. I don't know how Wayne got out of it, but, I guess one of us they wanted to go and report on it, so I went up to Asserson and told him it would wreck my chances of getting good marks at Fletcher School if I went to this other course, which was extracurricular, really. He gave me a big argument, so finally I had to call up BuPers and tell them what his problem was, and they

---
* Dr. Edward L. Katzenbach Jr. was associate director of the Harvard University Defense Studies Program.
† Dr. Henry A. Kissinger was on the faculty at Harvard University in the 1950s and 1960s; he served as Secretary of State from 22 September 1973 to 20 January 1977.
‡ Captain William C. Asserson Jr., USN.
§ ROTC – reserve officers' training corps.
** Colonel Alexander M. Haig, USA, was an assistant to Kissinger when the latter was President Richard Nixon's National Security Advisor. Haig, who retired as a four-star general, later served as Secretary of State in 1981-82.
†† Alexander M. Haig, *Caveat: Realism, Reagan, and Foreign Policy* (New York: Macmillan, 1984).

overruled Asserson, so I didn't go. It probably would have been Al Haig, see. You never know.

Paul Stillwell: How much exposure did you get to Kissinger yourself?

Captain Schwab: Oh, practically nothing, because he had just arrived when I put in my—I didn't know who he was, only that he had written a book on nuclear war; that's all I knew about him. That's all he had done, I guess, at that point. But that was really a compilation; that wasn't his own writing. He compiled from some study group he was with and then put his own personal comments, I guess, on it. But Katzenbach was good.

Let's see. Oh, one of the papers I wrote, my last *big* one at Fletcher School, was a history of the Navy League. That was for a professor there whose name was Ruhl J. Bartlett.* I have a couple of books by him here. He was great on diplomatic history, and as a young man he'd been with Wilson to the peace conference.† He was one of the writers for going over there. So all these things tie together. He wasn't pro- or anti-military; he was very skeptical of the military. He disliked a lot of people; like he disliked Andrew Mellon.‡ He would never set foot in the Mellon's museum in Washington. He thought that Theodore Roosevelt was one of the best, greatest liars we ever had as a President, which is probably right, because they say he exaggerated everything to make himself look better.§

He was very certain that you needed the military, but that the military had to be under much better "civilian control" than it really was. He said all this business about military being under civilian control is—well, he didn't say mythology—but not really. He says the way everything is organized they can do things without any civilians ever knowing, and there's a lot of truth in that. So he was very skeptical.

He was interested in particularly that period after World War I, between World War I and World War II, particularly all the hearings in 1935—merchants of death and things of that sort. He said, "Now you're in the Navy. This is for your big paper for the

---
* Dr. Ruhl J. Bartlett was chairman of the Tufts Department of History.
† In 1918-1919 U.S. President Woodrow Wilson was the nation's lead delegate to the post-World War I peace conference in Paris.
‡ Andrew G. Mellon served as Secretary of the Treasury from 1929 to 1932.
§ Theodore Roosevelt served as President of the United States from 14 September 1901 to 4 March 1909.

second thing," the second year, MALD, the "bastard PhD" they called it because you didn't have to write the dissertation.* He said, "What I want you to do is to check into the Navy League and what effect it had on any of these things we've been talking about." So I did and found out it had essentially *no* effect. It was interesting; I have that around here someplace, too, and that's a great big fat one. He always wanted me to put that together and expand on it for a dissertation. I'd say, of the references in there, about one-third were originals, and then others were secondary and tertiary.

The way you got those was interesting. We had access, as Fletcher students, to the Widener Library, which is huge, in Harvard. There's one whole section there that was a donation from Theodore Roosevelt's heirs. That has a complete thing on naval history, if you're interested, including a bunch of vertical files with old newspapers and old Navy League pamphlets and stuff. A few of the old ones there—I don't know what kind of paper they were on—when I opened up one of them, it just crumbled; it hadn't been looked at. They had told me if that happened what to do. So they called them and they took some sort of a plastic thing with stickum on it and very gently pushed it all together, and very gently put that on top and "squozed" it all together. That was it. From then on, they looked at everything before I did. I found an awful lot of stuff. I also—to my amazement; I should have known it—found Theodore Roosevelt wrote a tremendous amount of stuff. Did you ever see the stacks of books he wrote? When did he find time?

Paul Stillwell: I don't know.

Captain Schwab: I mean, being President and writing like that! And he did it all himself; it wasn't like some of these other people, like Tip O'Neill's going to write a book "with the assistance of . . .," you know, but that's different.† Roosevelt wrote all that stuff.

Paul Stillwell: Well, as Churchill did in England too.‡

---

* MALD – master of arts in law and diplomacy.
† Thomas P. O'Neill, Jr., a Democrat from Massachusetts, served in the House of Representatives from 3 January 1953 to 3 January 1987. He was Speaker of the House from 1977 to 1986.
‡ Sir Winston Churchill had served as Britain's Prime Minister from 1940 to 1945 and from 1951 to 1955. He was born on 30 November 1874. He was a prolific writer.

Captain Schwab: Yes, I've got them all over here. There's a whole stack there of Churchill. Let's see now. Do you have any more questions about Tufts?

Paul Stillwell: I was wondering how much you got into current events. During that period, for example, there was the Hungarian revolt, the Suez crisis.[*]

Captain Schwab: Exactly, that was great. Gee, the names go clicking off. Norman J. Padelford was the professor of international organization that we were studying under.[†] And, of course, we had the Suez crisis when we were there, which was very interesting. We had to write papers on that, how we would first handle that if we were Secretary of State, how we would handle it if we were the U.N. representative, all that sort of stuff. That was a good one. How we would make France and England compensate for the damage in whatever they did, and Israel and so on? That was a very good examination in which he was highly critical; now he was interesting, because Padelford was one of the original writers of the U.N. Charter. You ran into all these original people all the time, especially in a school like Fletcher School. I'm trying to think who the number-one author was that he mentioned. I'll think of his name in a minute—some eastern European name. So we had that particular occasion.

What was the other one you mentioned? The Hungarian thing; that was in '56?

Paul Stillwell: Right.

Captain Schwab: Well, we didn't discuss that one very much, as I remember. I think the United States was sort of ashamed of not doing anything there. I noticed my son Don, who was born in '44, so he was 12 years old. He read everything; he was just horrified

---

[*] The Hungarian Revolution of 1956 was a spontaneous nationwide revolt against the Communist government of Hungary and its Soviet-imposed policies. It lasted from 23 October 1956 to 10 November 1956 before being crushed by the Soviet Army.
On 26 July 1956 President Gamal Nasser of Egypt announced that his country was nationalizing the Suez Canal Company. Israeli forces invaded Egypt's Sinai Peninsula on 29 October 1956. Britain and France then intervened militarily on behalf of Israel in an unsuccessful attempt to secure the Suez Canal, which was damaged and closed to traffic. Rather than support the British and French, the United States asked for a United Nations resolution to end the fighting. A cease-fire took effect on 6 November.
[†] Dr. Norman J. Padelford was professor of political science at the Massachusetts Institute of Technology in Cambridge, Massachusetts, from 1945 to 1971.

by that whole thing. I don't know what he expected; he was horrified that the United States didn't do anything. Did he ever mention that to you?

Paul Stillwell: No, I don't remember that.

Captain Schwab: Yes, he was really upset by that whole experience, now that I think of it.

Paul Stillwell: The Sputnik, the following year, caused a great national trauma.[*] What do you recall about that?

Captain Schwab: I remember getting out in the morning and watching it go over, right outside our house there in Westwood, Massachusetts. Well, the main thing there was that we felt a little disappointment that the Navy Vanguard had collapsed.[†] Well, we figured that sooner or later we'd do it. I don't know how the Russians managed to do it without us doing it.

Paul Stillwell: Did the Navy, through BuPers, express to you any specific ideas on what they attempted to get out of sending people to this school?

Captain Schwab: No. The reason, as I mentioned earlier, was that Admiral Spruance, way back when he was at the war college, he's the one who apparently sparked the thing, of going there, and I know that Burke had something to do with it. He was in OP 23, the one that was doing the admirals' revolt.[‡] He was one of the revolters. He didn't get

---

[*] On 4 October 1957, the Soviet Union launched Sputnik I, the first artificial earth satellite. It caused great uproar in the United States, which had expected to be first in space.

[†] Project Vanguard was the U.S. attempt to launch an artificial earth satellite in the wake of the Soviets' successful launching of the satellite Sputnik in October 1957. The test on 6 December 1957 was a failure because of problems with the rocket's propulsion system. The first successful U.S. satellite was Explorer I, launched on 31 January 1958, followed by Vanguard I on 17 March 1958.

[‡] The Navy and Air Force were involved in an acrimonious struggle in 1949 over the future of U.S. military aviation. See Paul Schratz, "The Admirals' Revolt," U.S. Naval Institute Proceedings, February 1986, pages 64-71.

caught; they got rid of Denfeld instead.* But, anyhow, the idea was that—outside of all the people who knew strategy, tactics, and logistics and materiel things—they needed people to—the reason for existence of all these things was the international arena. They wanted people who would add a note of some sophistication there to whatever papers, I guess, went into the JCS from OpNav. It was primarily for the Navy; they weren't training naval officers for purple suits and the Joint Staff; it was for the Navy staff.

Right after I graduated, in '58, was when they were going to send me to Lebanon, to the American University, for six months, because they were always concerned with that area. Of course, Lebanon was then the "Paris" of the Near East. But, of course, all that trouble came up with Chamoun and so on, so instead of going to Lebanon I shifted into the—I'm trying to think, when did we have landings in Lebanon?†

Paul Stillwell: That was in the summer of '58.

Captain Schwab: Yes. Well, before that, they sent a whole bunch of us who were going to OP-60 and -61, over on a so-called blue-plate special over to tour all the NATO headquarters, which I did. That was mostly getting briefed by EuCom and CinCSouth, and what have you.‡ Then we came back from that, so by the time that occurred I had the U.N., Middle East, and North Africa desk. Admiral Burke was the CNO, and I'm trying to think who the OP-06 was; he was a real tough guy.§ Well, anyhow, Admiral Burke was the one I talked to mostly, because I was the briefing officer. I had four officers working for me. For that same outfit they now have about 20 officers doing exactly the same thing. It was Africa north of the Sahara. When the crisis occurred, when Chamoun asked for help, we had a joint agreement—I guess this is all unclassified—with the

---

* Admiral Louis E. Denfeld, USN, served as Chief of Naval Operations from 15 December 1947 to 2 November 1949. He was fired as CNO for supporting his naval aviation program.
† On 15 July 1958, at the request of Lebanese President Camille Chamoun, U.S. amphibious forces landed at Beirut to support Chamoun's government, which was threatened by both civil war and the prospect of foreign invasion. Two of the Sixth Fleet's three battalion landing teams went ashore within 24 hours. For details see the account of the U.S. ambassador to Lebanon, Robert McClintock, "The American Landing in Lebanon," *U.S. Naval Institute Proceedings*, October 1962, pages 64-79.
‡ EuCom – U.S. European Command; CinCSouth – Commander in Chief Allied Forces Southern Europe.
§ Admiral Arleigh A. Burke, USN, served as Chief of Naval Operations from 17 August 1955 to 1 August 1961. His oral history is in the Naval Institute collection.
Vice Admiral Robert L. Dennison, USN, served as Deputy Chief of Naval Operations (Plans and Policy), OP-06, in 1958-59. He retired as four-star admiral, and his oral history is in the Naval Institute collection.

British on something called Operation Blue Bat. Does this get checked by the security people?

Paul Stillwell: Not necessarily.

Captain Schwab: Anyhow, Operation Blue Bat, which was a joint U.S. plan in case of hostilities in the Middle East, mostly any attack on Jordan, for instance, by exterior forces, let's say. I don't know if it had too much to do with Lebanon, but they had the communication plan in there. When the crisis came up there, you had to stay there overnight. They started to send all the ships over there. They had this Blue Bat thing in a locked briefcase, and you carried it around; it was locked on your wrist. It never got implemented, because there was no attack on Jordan, per se. But the British, as you'll remember, sent in paratroopers, airborne troops, into Jordan. We landed the two Marine amphibious units there in Lebanon, off Beirut. Well, the interesting thing about that was that Admiral Pirie was OP-05, with the beard.[*] The landing went off; it was all being done through the Navy. It wasn't handled at all the way they'd thought, through SecDef or JCS. The Navy did all this directly through CinCNELM and CinCSpeComME.[†]

Paul Stillwell: Admiral Holloway.

Captain Schwab: Yes, Holloway. In fact, he was in Washington when the order came out to go over and surround Chamoun's palace. So he had to fly all the way back and fly all the way down the Mediterranean, not knowing how well it was doing. I remember a submarine captain with the amphibious squadron commander who landed there. The ambassador's name was McClintock.[‡] McClintock said, "Well, you can't come in here," blah, blah, blah, and "I'm the ambassador and I represent the President." The submarine

---
[*] Vice Admiral Robert B. Pirie, Jr., USN, served as Deputy Chief of Naval Operations (Air) from 26 May 1958 to 1 November 1962. His oral history is in the Naval Institute collection.
[†] Admiral James L. Holloway Jr., USN, served as Commander in Chief U.S. Naval Forces Eastern Atlantic and Mediterranean (CinCNELM) and USComEastLant from February 1958 to March 1959. For the Mediterranean operations in 1958 he had the additional title of CinCSpeComME – Commander in Chief, Specified Command, Middle East.
[‡] Robert McClintock was U.S. Ambassador to Lebanon from 1 January 1958 to 29 August 1961.

with the amphibious commander came back and said, "Well, how do your orders come from the President?" So they landed.

But, anyhow, then McClintock, and Holloway, and the Lebanese general rode with the tank column—you know that whole story—so they wouldn't get shot at. It was a good thing we didn't land from the planes. They probably thought we were Russians or something. They were afraid of everything. But the thing I remember mostly is that we were all standing around-the-clock watches. I didn't come home for about a week. We were sleeping on canvas cots and everything else. We were really monitoring this, with no augmentation of staff or anything; it was strictly a naval operation.

Okay. What time is it? Oh, quarter of one?

Mrs. Schwab: It seems to me you ought to shut your mouth for a while.

Captain Schwab: So I'll finish this little episode, that's on your tape. So we were there, sitting around having some sandwiches or something one evening, and Admiral Pirie came running in wearing a tuxedo. Just about two seconds before that, the British officer, from the British liaison group, had come up and he said, "Do you gentlemen know that we're sending some troop carriers to Jordan?"

We said, "No, we haven't been told that here."

He said, "Well, better get the word over to the Sixth Fleet, because as far as we know, where your forces are, they're going to fly right over them."

Pirie came in just at that moment, and he said, "Oh, my god, they'll shoot them down, because they'll think they're Russian planes." So we did everything: we sent messages by every route known to man, and none of them got there in time. This was interesting. But what happened was that the Brits had to overfly Israel, and they were coming from Crete. The Brits had talked to the Israeli Defense Forces and told them what they wanted to do.

The Israelis said no. They said, "But if you'll allow us to send a token opposition in, we'll come down again." So that delayed it about six, seven hours, the whole thing. When the troop carriers arrived, they sent up a token interceptor, and he went down again, I guess this was for some reason that I don't know.

Paul Stillwell: "We tried to resist."

Captain Schwab: Yes, and then they went in, but without that it might have been—by that time the message had gotten through. God, what a possibility for disaster there. Like shooting them down going in Italy during the war. Remember they shot down a bunch of troop carriers? Maybe we better stop now, as my wife so kindly suggested

Interview Number 4 with Captain Ernest L. Schwab, U.S. Navy (Retired)

Place: Captain Schwab's home in Potomac, Maryland

Date: Thursday, 7 May 1987

Paul Stillwell: Captain, the last time you were talking about your experience in OpNav following your study at the Fletcher School. We discussed the Lebanon operation in 1958, so we are ready to resume at that point.

Captain Schwab: Yes. Well, aside from the operational things, one of the more interesting things about my time in OP-61—really, OP-611 was my exact code number—was that besides with three other officers handling NATO Europe, Africa north of the Sahara, Middle East, and disarmament, I understand there are about 40 officers doing similar things now, with several codes, in a different part there. We had a special arrangement with the State Department that had been made by Secretaries Webb and Lovett years before.[*] The State Department would pass over to the different parts of the Defense establishment—I assume all the services had the same arrangement, and I assume that the Secretary of Defense had the same arrangement—would pass over nominally closely held messages that would be of interest to whichever department they sent them to, on the understanding that these messages would be restricted in their distribution and just sent to the Secretary of the Navy and the Chief of Naval Operations.

OP-06 was more of less at that time the office of Chief of Naval Operations linkage with State. We still hadn't been directed to go only through ISA.[†] In fact, Admiral Burke said, "Don't bother. Do whatever you have to do." OP-611, in particular, for Europe, was the recipient of these things. As they came in, we had to paraphrase them. You couldn't use the exact language for, I guess, security reasons. But we'd paraphrase them, and they were called, in slang, "M of I," memorandum of information, to the Secretary of the Navy.

---

[*] Robert A. Lovett was Deputy Secretary of Defense from 4 October 1950 to 16 September 1951 and then was Secretary of Defense from 17 September 1951 to 20 January 1953. James E. Webb was Under Secretary of State from 28 January 1949 to 29 February 1952.

[†] ISA – Office of the Assistant Secretary of Defense (International Security Affairs).

They went just to the Secretary of the Navy and to the Chief of Naval Operations, being hand-carried. I don't know if that system still exists or not, but that was something called the Webb-Lovett Agreement. Otherwise, all the political ramifications of what the United States was doing overseas and in the areas we were most interested in would have been unknown. We wouldn't have known what the State Department was thinking about it, so it was a very good linkage. Maybe if they had something like that now in current problems, why, we'd be less in turmoil.

Paul Stillwell: It sounds like it was a mutually beneficial arrangement.

Captain Schwab: Yes, and then we had other things that happened in there. For instance, every time there was a Berlin crisis, we had a Berlin task force, which was over in the State Department, of course. The Berlin task force had its U.S. components, and I was the U.S. Navy member. Tim Stanley, who became the director of force planning at the U.S. mission in NATO years later, was the OSD member.[*]

Anyhow, we would go to the State Department, and we'd have a preliminary meeting of U.S. representatives, including several from State. Then we'd meet in an international group. There would be a British member and a German member—all of the members of NATO who had interests in Berlin. Without getting into any classification things, but one of the things that was always discussed was what kind of countermeasures could be taken—both at sea and anyplace—when the Russians or the East Germans would block the access to Berlin. It was very interesting how on at-sea matters, which I was in, the United States was always ready to do various nasty tricks, provided they could be interpreted as accidental and things of that sort: such as delaying passage of ships through the Panama Canal, which actually comes under the Secretary of the Army. I talked to Mr. Vance about that once; I guess he was Secretary of the Army.[†]

Paul Stillwell: Would Soviet-bloc ships use the canal all that much?

---

[*] Timothy W. Stanley served in the administrations of four Presidents. He was an assistant to Secretary of Defense Robert S. McNamara in the 1960s and was later an advisor, with the rank of minister, in the U.S. Mission to NATO.

[†] Cyrus R. Vance served as Secretary of the Army from 5 July 1962 to 21 January 1964.

Captain Schwab: Oh, yes, Russian ships were always going through there, so you delayed them. You didn't want to make an international incident, but you hoped they'd get the message that blockage one place leads to blockage in another place. Of course, they always camouflaged their blockage as other reasons too.

Paul Stillwell: Well, that was an appropriate tit-for-tat kind of thing.

Captain Schwab: That's right, yes. In that regard, speaking of tit for tat, Admiral Arleigh Burke had a good one there. It had nothing to do with the Berlin thing, but it had to do with when General de Gaulle was acting up about NATO, and he was upset because the United States wouldn't share nuclear information with him as it had with the British.* So he started doing nasty things and various interruptions for naval exercises—or any kind of exercises. So some staff officer at a CNO briefing said that we should probably give de Gaulle tit for tat. Admiral Burke said, "You've got to forget that de Gaulle has control of much more tit than we have tat." [Laughter] I notice the way other people you've interviewed tell weird stories like that, but Admiral Burke was always very funny in these things.

He always liked to put on the guise of sort of the country boy, as if he wasn't really as sharp as others. He really was, but when he was down in the Tank at a Chiefs' meeting—and things were always in doubt as to which way the ultimate red-stripe decisions would go with respect to the Navy interests—he would arrange to have someone send down a message to him.† It really said nothing, blank paper. He'd send down a message, and he knew the timing and somehow the signal was passed. And this messenger would come down, and it would be passed in to him. He'd open it up and look around knowingly, and he said, "Well, I'll have to . . ." You know, he made some remark that would either delay the proceedings or make it go in his direction. Usually there was nothing on the paper; it was just strictly an act. It was very cleverly done. But I'd say most of the time the Navy did pretty well on things.

---

* Charles de Gaulle was a general for the Free French in World War II. In 1958 he was called upon to form a government. He served from 1958 to 1969 as first President of France's Fifth Republic.
† "Tank" refers to the room in the Pentagon in which the Joint Chiefs of Staff meet on a regular basis.

Paul Stillwell: Would these retribution-type things have to be cleared with the State Department before they could be implemented?

Captain Schwab: Oh, yes. Well, State was in there. That's right; it was always agreed—and also the White House. Eisenhower was President. I remember standing out in the anteroom there while Tim Stanley, who went over to tell, I guess, Eisenhower what was going on. I got a glimpse through a crack in the door of Eisenhower standing there with the veins pulsing in his head. He was angry about something—I don't know whether about the suggestion or about what the Russians were doing. He sort of looked pretty red; I gathered this has been noticed by other people—that he had prominent veins that pulsed.

So the OP-61—did I mention about the possibility that the British troop carriers going to Jordan might have been attacked by the Sixth Fleet? Did I mention all that?

Paul Stillwell: I don't recall it.

Captain Schwab: Well, just to go back, in case I didn't cover it, it had been known that there were difficulties in Lebanon with the government, and that President Chamoun was in danger of being overthrown, or a military coup might occur. There wasn't as much feeling about Communists then as the insurgents who were friendly to other unfriendly countries there—maybe the Soviet Union.

But when the Marine landings occurred—in the summer of 1958, not too long after I'd gotten there—the preparation for that had been in the nature of joint U.S. and British planning called Operation Blue Bat. All of these joint U.S. and British plans were in a valise that you could carry around. Whoever had the duty in OP-61 had the charge of this.

Unfortunately, the way the situation developed there, the U.S.-British communication plans and so on were never activated. So the U.S. went separately, and the British went separately. Part of the British separate plan was to send, I guess, paratroopers into Jordan to help there, while the United States was about to do something in Lebanon. The United States had two squadrons of amphibious ships there, because one hadn't gone home. They had approached Lebanon, and the carriers weren't there at that point. I can't remember whether the Marines landed before the carriers got there or not. I think they did, and the carriers sent cover planes from way out.

Well, as the Sixth Fleet approached, one night I had the duty in the Navy command center, let's say. A British officer, who was detailed to the Pentagon, came in and he said, "I suppose you chaps know that we're sending these troop carriers into Jordan. They're supposed to go in at sometime early in the morning." We asked him what the track was, and he indicated it. It would have gone right over where the Sixth Fleet would be, and coming from the north.

We tried to get in touch with more senior officers to tell them what was going on. Admiral Pirie was OP-05 at that point, and just by chance, at that moment he came in. He'd been at a dinner party someplace and was wearing his dinner jacket—you know, beautiful beard and so on. We told him, and he sort of turned white and got on the horn to CinCNELM and tried to tell them what was happening. There was a delay in communications; it never did really get through in time.

Fortunately, as we discussed last time, the British had to overfly Israel to go into Jordan. They had told the Israelis. The Israelis said, "Well, we are determined not to allow anything to reduce our feeling of sovereignty here, so we'll send up a fighter and turn back your first tentative pass. Then we'll say okay," or something like that. It was an arrangement between the Brits and the Israelis, which we didn't know about. Fortunately, this delayed the passage of the troop carriers long enough so that the word got through to the Sixth Fleet. Otherwise, we might have had another of those things where the—as they did in Italy during the war—shooting down troop carriers, thinking they were bombers. That would have been an interesting experiment.

Well, let's see. That Lebanon thing—of course, as you know—was resolved with the Marines getting out rather rapidly, and I guess the Army went in too.

Paul Stillwell: I'm not sure.

Captain Schwab: Yes, the Army went in and relieved some of the Marine units. From then on, we in OP-61 got involved in all sorts of things. We were in everything that had to do with Africa north of the Sahara—my area there. And NATO Europe was in it, because the French were starting problems then, which didn't get resolved till '67.

Paul Stillwell: Did the Congo problem come up on your watch?

Captain Schwab: Yes. That was, of course, south of the Sahara, but we had all this business of what we should do about going up the river and things of that sort. But mostly there, we were involved with discussions with Belgium about what they might do. But I don't remember too much about that; that was somewhat out of my field.

We got into almost everything in OP-61; in fact, that was part of the problem—sorting out what was useful and what wasn't. You were asked to do odd jobs for the Chief of Naval Operations. For instance, I was asked to write a couple of papers, which were really nothing to do with my job there, mostly because I had been at the Fletcher school for two years.

I was asked to write a paper on the nature of democratic governments, for instance, and how all the revolutions were really, first, revolutions from something. But, really, if they were gong to be useful, they had to be revolutions to do something constructive. So I had to write a paper on that, about what the basis was of the U.S. principles and what attitude of the United States should have towards other countries which had not achieved, let's say, relative freedom of speech and religion and all that sort of thing.

That was put in a paper that Admiral Burke said he wanted it to be like something you would read in *The Saturday Evening Post*. This was in the nature of an extension of the national security policy and with an understanding of what the United States's attitude should be towards developing nations. I've got a copy of that here someplace. That was fairly well received, and apparently pieces of it were used by the President's speechwriters in some speeches. It's hard to identify, because they were getting so many inputs.

The other kinds of things that we were asked to do were to make estimates of how other countries might react to U.S. initiatives here and there. Most of those are still classified probably; I don't want to get into them. But we were asked to do all sorts of odd things that you wouldn't expect naval officers to be involved in.

I personally participated in a lot of political-military war games. In fact, Ronald Spiers, who's now the Assistant Secretary for Management of the State Department, was then a young Foreign Service Officer.[*] I guess he was an FSO-3, maybe -4. He was not senior to a captain at that point, about the same level. He was the State Department representative at a big war game, with representatives from Defense and all the services. He was the State Department man.

We went through the whole decision process at that level, and I was particularly interested in Spiers at that point, because he was one of the few people I've known in my life who didn't put on a false air of knowing everything. In other words, if he didn't know something, he asked a question about it right away. He was particularly emphatic in finding out what all the acronyms meant. You'd be surprised when you start asking people—you ought to do it sometime. They use acronyms, but ask them what they mean. A lot of them don't know. They know what the outfit does, but they don't know what the acronym means, which is sort of silly. So he was very impressive in that, and I've corresponded with him—not often, but every couple of years we'd exchange a letter and let him know what I think about something. Whether it has any effect or not, I don't know. But Spiers was very impressive.

The only other person—well, there are two other people. Al Rubenstein, who was my assistant in BuShips, when I had the electronics planning staff there, was another person who never put on any pretense. He would ask questions and is probably the most honest person I know.

Now, the other one was Ambassador Harlan Cleveland in the U.S. mission in NATO, which I went to much later.[†] He was different. The other ambassadors always come in with an aura of knowledge of everything, or they'd been at such high levels, such as Cleveland's successor, associating with the White House—that they felt embarrassed by not admitting things. As a result, instead of getting the benefit of a large and fairly knowledgeable staff there, they tended to reduce all of their thought discussions,

---
[*] Ronald I. Spiers was Under Secretary of State for Management from 1983 to 1989.
[†] Harlan Cleveland served as U.S. Ambassador to NATO from 1965 to 1969.

brainstorming and so on, to a small group, where their lack of knowledge in something wouldn't embarrass them as much. Or maybe they felt they would lose prestige or influence with the larger staff. It didn't bother Cleveland at all. He used to hold meetings. Everybody would come into the meeting, and one person who was engaged in something of interest would be asked to stand up and give a talk on it. Then everybody else would ask questions of him, including the ambassador. We all got to know everybody else's business.

As a result, besides everybody knowing what he was doing vertically, you had the horizontal coordination, which is what I mentioned when I was in BuShips. We found a lack of horizontal coordination in knowledge there. The same thing, I guess, exists in most government places. Not with Cleveland, so much. Ambassador Finletter, who was Cleveland's predecessor, had been Secretary of the Air Force, and there really wasn't much he *didn't* know.[*] So he didn't have to ask too many questions, except on the business of force planning, which I hadn't gone into yet, because I was still not in the ISA.

So in OP-61, while I was there, I learned how individuals really contribute greatly to policymaking and that staff work is great. But usually staff work is on the end of implementation of decisions, but the decisions themselves—a single man can influence those tremendously, which makes it important that you pick the right single man: the people who are not only intelligent but also knowledgeable and not afraid to ask questions. I think that's important. I gather that Jimmy Carter was one like that; he probably got everybody annoyed by asking too many questions.

Paul Stillwell: How much interchange was there between 60 and 61?

Captain Schwab: Well, OP-60 concerned itself more with the strategic—strictly military—stuff and interaction that way with the other services, whereas OP-61 was strictly political-military; it did everything. Also, we dealt on all the matters that were

---

[*] Thomas K. Finletter served as Secretary of the Air Force from 24 April 1950 to 20 January 1953. He was U.S. Ambassador to NATO from 1961 to 1965.

going in to the Joint Chiefs or in to the Defense Department. We dealt directly with people in ISA, which is probably how I wound up being in ISA later on.

There was an officer there who later relieved me when I became a civilian over in the U.S. mission to NATO. His name's James Tyler; he's retired now too.* He retired not too long ago, but he was an Army colonel at that time in ISA, and he was the one who passed around all of the position papers that were going to be discussed at the Joint Chiefs and then ultimately go as recommendations to the Secretary of Defense. So we got to be very friendly on that. His career had all been Army, but he was an avid reader of every kind of international thing. He's the only person I know who used to read *The New York Times* cover to cover every morning, which is sort of a feat in itself.

His influence, personally, grew as he went along; he became one of the prime people back in ISA when I was director of force planning in the U.S. mission to NATO. He was the one who generated stuff back there, and we'd exchange things; we'd generate things over there and bounce them off. Because of the growing interest in other parts of the world, and potential for arms control, and other kinds of crises, the U.S. mission to NATO almost acted, at times, as an autonomous organization.

We'd generate things, especially under Ambassador Cleveland, and he had a lot of weight back in the White House and State Department. People didn't want to argue with him too much, because he was knowledgeable. He'd tell them, "That sounds nice, but that's not the way it's going to work, because of this." He knew also how to maneuver, and this is a trick we used in OP-61 too. If you came up with a plan of action which was, say, controversial, but according to your lights—wherever you happened to be, OP-61 or U.S. mission to NATO—you thought that this would be the way to proceed, something that should be done, you would send out what the Navy calls a UNODIR message, which means "unless otherwise directed."

You would hold up this message. Let's say that the decision had to be made, or the position that the United States or the Navy would have to take on something—say you knew that ten days in advance, so you could get all your papers and arguments in order. But you wouldn't tell the people who were supposed to make the decision until, say, three days in advance. You'd say, "We have this meeting on umpty-ump three days

---

* Colonel James E. Tyler, USA.

from now, and unless otherwise directed, this is the position we're going to take." You sent it, of course, to everybody, but you were certain that the ones on the distribution list were ones who were going to have different points of view. Of course, they couldn't resolve those in three days. So, since in most cases whatever you said was correct anyhow, the variations on the theme were sort of meager.

Paul Stillwell: Do you remember any specific cases when that was used?

Captain Schwab: No, I'd rather not get into any of those, but that was a real good tactic for—that's a problem right now. I'm starting to get into areas of classified material that I'm still not supposed to talk about.

Paul Stillwell: You were selected for captain during this tour, I presume.

Captain Schwab: Well, actually, I was selected for captain, I think, when I was at the Fletcher School.

Paul Stillwell: Oh, I see.

Captain Schwab: See, I was selected in '58, just before I left, as opposed to being selected for commander when I was at the Naval War College and had to take an exam. I didn't have to take an exam for captain.

I left OP-61 in the fall of 1960 and went to be chief of staff in an ASW carrier group, CarDiv 20. The flagship was the *Lake Champlain*, the last axial-deck carrier in the Navy.* Admiral Magruder Tuttle was the head man, and then he was relieved by Sunshine Reedy, Admiral Reedy.† Tuttle was out of class of '32, and Reedy out of '33.

---

* USS *Lake Champlain* (CV-39) was an *Essex*-class aircraft carrier, commissioned 3 June 1945. She had a standard displacement of 27,000 tons, was 888 feet long, 93 feet in the beam, and had an extreme width of 148 feet. Her top speed was 33 knots. She had 12 5-inch guns and could accommodate approximately 90 aircraft. Later in her career she was converted to an antisubmarine warfare carrier and reclassified CVS-39 on 1 August 1957.
† Rear Admiral Magruder H. Tuttle, USN; Rear Admiral James R. Reedy, USN.

The important thing about the first part of the *Lake Champlain*'s trip on there and my duty as chief of staff was that she was one of the ships that went down to possibly assist the insurgents against Castro, in the Bay of Pigs crisis.* Our normal complement of ASW aircraft had been sort of reduced and supplemented by fighter aircraft. So we were down there in the vicinity of the action but were never cleared to go in and do anything. This happened shortly after Kennedy took over; it was his first month or something.†

Paul Stillwell: Well, that spring.

Captain Schwab: That spring. Apparently, there was another communication lag in there, so by the time that the word got back to Washington that the insurgents were in difficulty and needed some air support, it was all over. The decision was made, right then, before they knew it was all over, to release the fighters so we could go in and assist. We knew more about what was going on, for some reason, than the people back in Washington, so it never happened. If they had released them earlier, it might have been a different story. That was the information I had, being chief of staff in this carrier division.

The *Lake Champlain*, of course, participated in all sorts of ASW exercises, naturally, in the Atlantic Ocean, of course, and the Caribbean. In preparation for taking over here, I went to Norfolk for ASW school. The current president of the Naval Academy Alumni Association, Bob McNitt, was the captain who was the head of the school.‡ I kept running into him over and over. That was one of the finest schools I've ever gone to; he really ran a good course. Of course, he ultimately became the head of the Postgraduate School in Monterey, so he was very good in that. And at the Naval Academy he was the director of admissions. He's really been good on the education side.

---

* In mid-April 1961 a force of 1,400 Cuban exiles, secretly trained by U.S. personnel in Guatemala, landed in the Bay of Pigs, on the southwestern coast of Cuba, in an attempt to overthrow Fidel Castro, that nation's Communist dictator. The invasion attempt was a disaster. President John Kennedy decided that U.S. naval intervention would worsen the situation, so ships and aircraft offshore were prohibited from taking part.
† John F. Kennedy served as President of the United States from 20 January 1961 until he was assassinated on 22 November 1963.
‡ Captain Robert W. McNitt, USN, was commanding officer and director of the Atlantic Fleet Anti-Submarine Warfare Tactical School from 1959 to 1961. The oral history of McNitt, who retired as a rear admiral, is in the Naval Institute collection. After his retirement from active duty, he was president of the Naval Academy Alumni Association from 1985 to 1988.

Except for the Bay of Pigs episode, most of the things were uneventful on the *Lake Champlain*. On the various trips of President Kennedy and his wife over to Europe, when they flew across, why, we were in charge of a whole series of ships out in the ocean there, in case the plane had gone down. The word was, you know, save Jackie first, instead of Jack. [Laughter] It was an enjoyable trip. I don't have a picture; of course, it wasn't my ship.

Paul Stillwell: Did you get involved with any of the astronaut recoveries in that ship?

Captain Schwab: Well, we trained for all of it. This was an interesting thing. We trained for all that business, and it was always delayed. We trained to recover one of the chimpanzees they shot up. And then just before that occurred, they shifted us off to some other planning job ashore; the whole staff would go at once. They put another staff on, and they went out and recovered the monkeys. The *Lake Champlain* was the one who recovered Shepard.* That was the ship, but we weren't on there either, so we just got shifted around.

Admiral Tuttle was quite a character. Both Tuttle and Reedy had been captains of their football teams, so then they succeeded themselves in this ASW outfit. Now, they kept a non-aviator as chief of staff in these ASW carrier divisions, which exist no longer. They kept usually a submarine officer or a destroyer officer as chief of staff, and I was both. Also, having had the Underwater Sound Branch, I had really quite a broad background for that sort of thing. It was very interesting duty.

Paul Stillwell: Could you describe some of the exercises and how you'd go about prosecuting one of those?

Captain Schwab: Well, most of the exercises were what you might call canned exercises. You knew when it was going to start, and where the enemy was, more or less, and most

---

*On 5 May 1961 Commander Alan B. Shepard, USN, became the first American astronaut to fly into space. He completed a 15-minute sub-orbital flight in a Mercury spacecraft. After splashdown he was recovered by a helicopter and landed on the deck of the aircraft carrier *Lake Champlain* (CVS-39). He was later commander of the Apollo 14 mission, which reached the moon in 1971.

of them were exercises in communications and coordinating the forces, as opposed to actual war games. We didn't really get too much of that. We supported other units of the fleet from a distance, but that was about it. I don't think the realism was that great in the exercises, but people did a lot of things that were dangerous. I mean, we lost some aviators. The helicopters of that period were not—well, when they went down, they *really* went down. They kept going, so usually you lost one or two crew members, and we did several of those. That was before the advent of the current crop of ASW aircraft. We just had the S-2s.[*]

I did an awful lot of flying back and forth on the modified S-2, which was called the carrier on-deck COD plane.[†] All the admirals liked to fly in from sea on a little dinky helicopter, which I didn't think was too safe, but they always insisted. We were based, nominally, in Quonset Point, Rhode Island, so that was where we'd go home all the time. But we'd come in and spend time in Norfolk, bounce up and down the coast.

One of the more interesting things that we did was off Puerto Rico, I guess. We picked up a whole slug of Latin American presidents and dictators, including Somoza—we had him on board—and they were all in their uniforms. One thing I remember about Somoza, of course, was that he was a West Point graduate. I don't know which Somoza this was, but it was a relatively young one.

Paul Stillwell: Anastasio, probably.[‡]

Captain Schwab: Anastasio, probably, and he came on board rather plump and oily and so on, looking well fed. He had two bodyguards with him, both of whom had large bulges under their coats. They were sort of shocked when the Marines removed their weapons on board the ship. But we had everybody. We had people from Haiti, from every one of the Latin American countries. We did a big demonstration of ASW things,

---

[*] Grumman S2F Tracker propeller-driven, carrier-based antisubmarine planes first entered fleet squadrons in early 1954. In 1962 the Tracker was redesignated S-2. The S-2E version was 44 feet long, wingspan of 72 feet, gross weight of 26,867 pounds, and top speed of 253 miles per hour.

[†] The Grumman C-1 Trader, a variant of the S-2 antisubmarine aircraft, was used for carrier on-board delivery flights.

[‡] Anastasio Somoza Debayle (1925-1980) served as President of Nicaragua from 1 May 1967 to 1 May 1972 and from 1 December 1974 to 17 July 1979. He graduated from the U.S. Military Academy at West Point, New York, on 6 June 1946.

and then we would tow astern a sled, and then the planes would come in and dive-bomb. All sorts of other planes, not just ours. They'd shoot them up with rockets. Then there were demonstrations of napalm. This was all, I guess, to impress them with. We were an ASW carrier, not an attack carrier, but it was something, and they had a pretty good time doing that.

Paul Stillwell: Well, those ships on occasion were used as attack carriers.

Captain Schwab: Oh, in the war, yes, but once they got the angle-deck carriers, the *Lake Champlain* was no longer useful.

I know there was one interesting event. I'm trying to think of the name of the captain; he had a French name. When the *Lake Champlain* was up in Boston, it went into dry dock for some reason or other, to check something. They had a bunch of people underneath there, walking under the ship—civilians, newspapermen, I guess. They were mostly interested in the *Lake Champlain* because of the recovery thing, and the captain was explaining to them the different parts of the ship. They didn't seem to be particularly interested in what he was saying. They were saying, you know, that old business about, "Why is this red-leaded down here?" So it won't be mistaken for a carrot or something like that, I don't know. He said to them, "You know, you don't seem particularly interested in the ship, but I notice you have trouble keeping your eyes off her bottom." See, they were looking up there. It doesn't make a good story; it's not a very good story, but that was his story.

While I was up there, I was able to have a couple of my professors—Ruhl Bartlett was a favorite one, American history—to the *Lake Champlain* for luncheon and so on. In fact, I just got a letter from him out on the West Coast. He must be in his 90s now. He was, you might say, one of the predecessors of these political whiz kids. He accompanied Wilson. He was one of the staff people who went over with Wilson to the peace conference.[*]

Paul Stillwell: That goes back a ways.

---

[*] U.S. President Woodrow Wilson attended the post-World War I peace conference in Paris.

Captain Schwab: Yes. He loved Woodrow Wilson, hated Theodore Roosevelt. He didn't think Theodore Roosevelt ever told the truth. Anyway, aside from that, I was ordered from the—

Paul Stillwell: I'd like to cover a little more on that. What do you remember about the leadership styles of the two admirals, Tuttle and Reedy?

Captain Schwab: As I say, they were both football players. Tuttle had been involved with Point Mugu or something, with the rocket business out there on the West Coast.* So he was well known by the various manufacturers: Thiokol, for instance, and companies of that sort. So while I was in the *Lake Champlain*, we were always invited to all these rather fancy affairs in New York, and I always had to go. We had to take our wives and wear full dress and so on. A big industrial thing, and they had a whole bunch of military, and we were invited, mostly because of his Thiokol connections.

He didn't really like to do any public speaking, and so usually, whenever the occasion required public speaking, I always got dragged along and told to prepare the main part of the speech. He would get up and say a few words, and then he'd give some excuse why he couldn't continue, such as, "On this particular thing, my chief of staff is well-versed on this. He's been especially educated, and so I'll let him carry on. Especially he's had experience in submarines and antisubmarine destroyers, and so on." He'd lay the reason why I should talk. That occurred almost all the time, but he was very easy to get along with—no problem at all.

But I remember once we were in Willemstad.† We went ashore, and the Dutch had scheduled a television program for the American admiral and his chief of staff to talk. So we went in there, and he did the same thing, so I got to do all of the interviews. I don't know whether that ever came out. Well, the Dutch speak English, very close. That was a fine example, there. I had no problems with him at all; he was great.

The funny things that happened with him—apparently when he finished his active athletic period, he had gained a tremendous amount of weight. But he was on a very

---

* From 1958 to 1960 Admiral Tuttle was Deputy Commander of the Pacific Missile Test Range, Point Mugu, California.
† Willemstad is the capital of Curaçao, an island in the Caribbean Sea.

strict diet, and he had to exercise continually. When we were out at sea on the aircraft carrier, why, he had to walk so many miles a day on the deck. He always had his Marine orderly with him, of course. Then he'd always try to talk some of the staff officers into walking. Of course, out at sea, no matter what speed you're going on a carrier, there's a lot of wind on that deck, and it was quite a task. He had probably the best-exercised Marine orderlies in the United States Navy.

We always tried to figure out something else to be doing, or the admiral would come over and grab you. Every lunch we had was health food lunch on there. We all wound up in good shape. When we were in port and he wasn't able to walk there, we had to go over to the swimming pool at whatever base we were at. And we had to swim laps with him; all of us went over and swam laps with the admiral. And you'd be surprised. If you were in the same port for, say, ten days or so, after about four days you get so you don't even mind it anymore. He was very slow; we'd make a couple while he was making one. Then we'd go back and eat a diet lunch. We were all in good shape; our stomachs were gone. That was the main thing. He was always a jolly person; I liked him quite a bit.

Paul Stillwell: How was he as a commander at sea?

Captain Schwab: Oh, he had no problems at all with that. I think he and Sunshine Reedy had both had most of their experience in the big boats—the flying boats, not on the little ones, which caused a little problem there. But you've got to realize that most of the stuff is done by the staffs. All the admiral does is make the larger decisions, and there really aren't too many decisions to make. Most of the stuff is canned. The main problem I had with those exercises—and I've written something about it someplace.

I think Admiral Kidd, later on, when he was CinCLant, did something about it.[*] It seemed to me that because of the rapid churning of officers in rotation all the time, that you kept doing the same things over and over again and not knowing it. Because all the reports would go someplace, but the people who wrote the reports would disappear, and

---

[*] Admiral Isaac C. Kidd, Jr., USN, served as Supreme Allied Commander Atlantic, Commander in Chief Atlantic Command, and Commander in Chief Atlantic Fleet from 30 May 1975 to 30 September 1978.

then the people who were going to receive them—not knowing what was the reason for the exercise—would figure, "Well, we better schedule our own exercise, because we want to know what happens under these circumstances." So there was no real attempt that I could see—maybe there was—to organize both the methods of carrying out the exercise so that you weren't doing the same thing over—sometimes you have to do the same things over—but that you weren't doing it excessively. And second, to match up results with the exercises—for the bad results in particular—so you could take corrective action in the next exercise. That didn't seem to occur.

I understand that Ike Kidd, who was out of the class of '42, made an attempt—whether he carried through or not—to computerize these things, so that on one hand you would get a list of all the different kinds of things that were being attempted, and then you would get some sort of a feed out. Then, when they would schedule a new exercise, you would have a reference point so that you wouldn't be doing too much. That was one of the things that we tried to avoid, in our small way, in the ASW Carrier Division 20.

Paul Stillwell: The nuclear submarines were still relatively new then. How did they perform versus the diesel boats in your exercises?

Captain Schwab: I don't remember any direct contacts with nuclear submarines. If we did have them, it was probably that we didn't do much about them. When you were in that kind of an organization, it was mostly a question of organizing when you were en route from one place to another: organizing your screen properly and then diverting your aircraft to the places where contacts had been made. It was mostly a problem in management of whatever assets you had available, as opposed to war gaming. In other words, if somebody picked up a contact over here, and another person picked up a contact, then you had to figure out which one was the greatest threat to whatever you were protecting. That was the sort of thing.

Paul Stillwell: Did you get involved in hunter-killer group operations?

Captain Schwab: Well, that's what we were. We were a hunter-killer group thing. We didn't have much to do with any SOSUS-type things. I think that came under the land-based air mostly.

Paul Stillwell: How much did you have in the way of support ships? Was there like a division of destroyers with you?

Captain Schwab: Oh, yes, we always had a *squadron* of destroyers.

There was sort of a real separation on the ship. Everybody supposedly in the crew's mess ate together, but the aviators all ganged together, and all the surface people who were not aviators ganged together. Of course, in the staff you're sort of in an exalted position when you're on an aircraft carrier. You normally ate with the admiral in the staff mess, which was pretty fancy. But I had my own palatial quarters there, with my own—I could eat by myself if I wanted to. I had a great big brass bed, which I never had before. I had a whole suite; it was really different.

The one thing that I was going to mention—an interesting, odd occurrence on there, as I started to say, was that Admiral Tuttle had all these weight problems, and back problems as well. Apparently, with all this attention to diet and exercise he had overcome the problems of a fatty heart or whatever he was developing. That was all right, but the back problem persisted, and I didn't know anything about that.

So he had a rule with me. As the chief of staff, I used to knock on the door to go into his cabin. He'd say, "No, you can come in any time you want to." So one day a message came in that we were supposed to do something; we were out at sea. I went in, and there was the admiral hanging from the overhead. I thought, "My God, he's committed suicide." He looked at me and laughed. He had some sort of a gadget—a brace—and he had a hook put in the overhead, and he would hang up there for so many minutes a day to take the tension or something off his spine. But it was rather a frightening thing to see.

Paul Stillwell: What do you remember about Admiral Reedy?

Captain Schwab: Well, the name Sunshine Reedy described him. He was a very, very jolly person all the time. He went on to get the antarctic command, which is another rather interesting thing. I wasn't with him as long as I was with the other admiral. He was quite a character, and he had—let's say there was no real problem there of any difference in the method of operation. He was a lot more willing to talk; he had no problems there.

I gathered he knew a lot of people. He had been connected somehow with some publicity movie or something, so he knew some movie people. I wasn't on the staff any longer when they were over in the Mediterranean, but I understand that for some reason, he had gone off in a boat and had a whole bunch of movie people there, including Gina Lollobrigida, in the boat with him. But that's hearsay. The whole time I was on the *Lake Champlain* was very nice, and I went from there to the *Mount McKinley*.*

The *Mount McKinley* was interesting, because it was one of the amphibious force flagships. It was the one that would be going over for six months out of the year to the Mediterranean and getting involved in the whole area of the Middle East, which had been the focal point of most of the stuff I was doing in OP-61.†

The *Mount McKinley* was an interesting ship, because it had—and later it was even improved—a tremendous communication capability. It was nominally the flagship of an amphibious group of various types of amphibious ships and Marine battalion—a Marine amphibious unit—when it was deployed. On the deployments, of course, I went over six months at a time, and nothing really important happened during those times except we had exercises with the Spanish. We took Spanish people out so they could see what we did. We made landings in Greece; in fact, I relieved in Greece in the middle of an exercise.

We charged up and down the Mediterranean, trying different types of scattered dispositions so that the Sixth Fleet attack forces—strike forces—supposedly wouldn't be able to identify us as being "make-believe" enemy forces. There were all sorts of things going on of that sort. We never got involved in anything in North Africa, for example, or

---

* USS *Mount McKinley* (AGC-7), name ship of her class of amphibious force flagships, was commissioned 1 May 1944. She was 459 feet long, 63 feet in the beam, maximum draft of 25 feet, has a standard displacement of 12,560 tons, and a top speed of 15 knots. She remained in service until decommissioned 26 March 1970.
† Captain Schwab commanded the *Mount McKinley* from January 1962 to March 1963.

in Lebanon, but we went off the coast a lot. We spent a lot of time in Greece and in Italy, and all those different places.

The deployments were always in the non-touristy part of the year. We'd go over in the winter, I guess, and come back in the beginning of the summer, so we never got to see any of the bathing beauties on the beach. Oh, a few of them maybe, but that was about it.

Paul Stillwell: Who was your embarked admiral?

Captain Schwab: Well, we didn't have an admiral on that; we had an amphibious commodore. They changed almost every couple of weeks. They rotated around. I can't remember . . .

Paul Stillwell: Were these the squadron commanders?

Captain Schwab: Squadron commanders, yes, of the amphibious group.

These deployments were not particularly noteworthy, but other things that we did in *Mount McKinley* were interesting. At that time, for some reason, they wanted to have what they would call a national command ship, away from Washington. On that ship they'd put sometimes a high-ranking civilian, usually a high-ranking naval officer—admiral. We'd go off to some isolated place. Well, we went into the Dominican Republic right after Mr. Bosch was taken over, the gray-haired gentleman.[*]

We'd go into Bermuda. We'd go to Nassau—different places, all by ourselves, with the idea, I guess, that if something happened, we would be a focal point for communications, which we could handle. I never could understand what that was all about, but that's what we did, and I was the commanding officer. That was interesting, because once I was able to have my wife fly to meet us in Bermuda. We would stay in for a week or so, and then we'd come back again.

---

[*] Juan Bosch was President of the Dominican Republic from 27 February 1963 to 25 September 1963, when he was overthrown by a coup.

But the most important thing that happened during my time in the *Mount McKinley* was the Cuban Missile Crisis.* We were the flagship for the western invasion force, if we had invaded. Admiral Rivero had just taken over as Commander Amphibious Force.† So we were heading out on the exercise that occurred at the same time as the missile crisis. It had been planned for months and months and months ahead of time. Admiral Rivero was on board as we left Norfolk to go south with all the Marines. We went off to Camp Lejeune to pick up the Marines there. In the midst of all this very vague information on what was going on in Cuba, we also had a developing hurricane as we were heading south to conduct landings and bombard Vieques and all that sort of stuff. So I remember I had run into Admiral Rivero when I was in OP-61 somehow, and also I had talked to him about Spain. He ultimately became the U.S. ambassador to Spain.

He was having a staff meeting about what to do about getting all these ships past the hurricane, and I suggested instead of turning in towards the shore that we get way the hell out at sea. He called me in as the commanding officer of the flagship; with all that staff, it was sort of embarrassing. I said, "Let's go out to sea," and we did. If we'd gone in to shore, it would have disrupted the whole operation. We wouldn't have been in position to threaten Cuba at all. It might have even caused damage.

But we went down there, and I gathered, from having seen it later, that there were pictures of the *Mount McKinley* and a couple amphibious ships out there with captions that said we were guardians, a blockade force. We weren't blockading anything; we were just getting ready to land if we had to.

The *Mount McKinley* had just been fitted with some very high-speed, on-line communication equipment. In fact, it was faster than what they had back in Norfolk. Well, the first thing that happened was we got down there and heard President Kennedy's speech, which turned all the admirals white—the one admiral, anyhow. I've never seen

---

* The Cuban Missile Crisis was triggered in mid-October 1962, when a U.S. reconnaissance plane photographed a Soviet nuclear missile site in Cuba and the presence of Soviet bombers. On 22 October President John F. Kennedy went on national television to announce a naval quarantine of Cuba, to be implemented on 24 October. On 28 October Premier Nikita Khrushchev of the Soviet Union notified President Kennedy that he was ordering the withdrawal of Soviet bombers and missiles from Cuba.
† Vice Admiral Horacio Rivero Jr., USN, served as Commander Amphibious Force Atlantic Fleet from October 1962 to September 1963. The oral history of Rivero, who retired as a four-star admiral, is in the Naval Institute collection. He later served as U.S. ambassador to Spain from 1972 to 1975.

people really looking as concerned; they must have had more information than we had. So the next thing we knew, we were directed to return Admiral Rivero to Norfolk; we picked up another admiral to take him down to be the western group invasion force commander.

We went back down there again and started with our messages, one way or another, to overload the facility. So we were told to go into Mayport, Jacksonville, and hook up to the landline, which they could handle, so we did that. It's a wonder that Florida didn't submerge with all the people. I've never seen so many people: Marines jogging around in their combat uniforms; there were Army, Marines. The place was *solid* with people. If the Cubans had any kind of spies over there, that must have worried them quite a bit, because I think we could have really gone in there.

Paul Stillwell: How detailed was the planning for an invasion during that period?

Captain Schwab: Well, of course, they have this kind of intervention plans; they're *always* existent. In this case, I suppose all they had to do was change the landing plans from the exercise to actually go into Cuba. They were not going to go into Cuba; I mean, they move around. They also sent a landing force around from the Pacific, as you know. That was the other side, the eastern part; we were the western force.

I joined the *Mount McKinley* in Greece, and I left her in Greece. I flew each time. Each time, of course, I would stop off in Naples. On the way to join the *Mount McKinley*—it's not an important episode—I was told I was going to relieve her at sea. I didn't know exactly how that was going to happen. But I arrived in Naples, and I was told to shift into uniform. This was in January of '62.

Paul Stillwell: So you had just about a year in the carrier staff.

Captain Schwab: A little more than a year. You don't stay much longer than that. I left, and I was flying over in the wintertime, and they told me to shift into my blue service uniform in Naples, because I had civilian clothes with me, and to be sure I had my sword with me. But this caused a little problem on the plane. I didn't want to put the sword in the baggage, because they tend to get either lost or banged up somehow. I always had to have the stewardess put the sword someplace. They were very impressed with this sword on the plane.

So in Naples they shifted me into the equivalent of a COD plane to fly to Pilos, is where they were having this exercise, in the bay there, where Agememnon lived and so on. So they flew into what you might call an abandoned airport, with a whole bunch of mail. It was really a mail flight. I got all my stuff over there, and there were two Marine helicopters. They were going to take me out to the *Mount McKinley*.

So I loaded everything in there, mailbags all around, a couple of enlisted men. We were all crammed in like fish. The other helicopter was from another amphibious ship with a helicopter platform on it. We got about 50 feet in the air, and just everything quit. We came down. It wasn't high enough or anything to do any of the auto rotation. We hit! Luckily, I was all tied; they had to dig me out of the mailbags; that's all. They finally moved everything over to the other helicopter and got over to the ship.

Finally, they sent a boat for me from the *Mount McKinley*, and everybody was ashore having a cookout. They were in between exercises. They had a little beach there; all the officers were out playing softball against the enlisted men, or whatever it was. They had cooks, and somehow each place they went, they had a way to get hold of beer and things. They had cold beer and hot dogs and hamburgers and steaks and everything. So I arrived. I changed into khaki and got over there and joined in with the festivities. The interesting thing there was that Greek people always—as they do in Malta—have big smiles on their faces. Little kids were there; somehow they gotten on this spit of land on their burros. They apparently had experience with the Marines before, and they ate most of the hot dogs and hamburgers. And so it was quite an experience. We came back and had our change-of-command ceremony.

Paul Stillwell: Bet you had to sign for a lot of registered publications on there.

Captain Schwab: Oh, yes. You go on for days. Well, it took a week to do it. But, anyhow, the *Mount McKinley*, besides having all those amphibious exercises, the most interesting part of that was in the Cuban Missile Crisis episode. Then the various little visits as a national command ship. That was about it.

Paul Stillwell: You had served in the fleet flagship 20 years before. How did they compare in terms of the communications capability?

Captain Schwab: Oh, well, when I was on the *Pennsylvania* the really important thing there was what they called TBS, talk between ships. That had just arrived, the first time we'd used radio of that nature. Everything else was the old dit-dah hand-keyed stuff. In fact, first in submarines we still used that during the war. It was an entirely different world. I guess we got a bed-spring radar on the *Pennsylvania* just before I left, and that was it. I guess that was for air defense; I don't know which.

Paul Stillwell: Yes, the CXAM, an air-search radar.

Captain Schwab: Yes, great big thing. It was horrible. The captain didn't like it, said it didn't make the ship look good. It probably didn't work very well either.

Paul Stillwell: Who was that, Captain Cooke?

Captain Schwab: Yes, Savvy Cooke, C. M. Cooke. He didn't like the looks of that.

Paul Stillwell: Was there emphasis on spit and polish in the *Mount McKinley* because of her flagship status?

Captain Schwab: Yes. Of course, we had a very fancy Marine outfit. It was a well-kept ship, as you can see up there. That painting is like one that was hanging in the wardroom. Some previous visit of the ship to Naples, an Italian artist named Mario had copied a picture of the ship, but what he did wrong. He had painted the ship as it was alongside the dock there, and it had its awnings rigged. See, well, you don't leave your awnings rigged when you're under way. So it's sort of a little inaccuracy there, and it has a dent in it someplace. I kept admiring this picture in the wardroom, and I didn't know it, but before I left they had another one made by the same guy. So when I left, that was my parting gift as the commanding officer. Silly thing to do.

Paul Stillwell: How large a wardroom did you have on that ship?

Captain Schwab: Oh, well, of course, I ate in my own cabin all the time. We had the Marine group on there, the staff officers, and so we must have had 100 officers eating there. It was a big wardroom. It was a good bunch.

Paul Stillwell: Your main battery was the communications setup.

Captain Schwab: Well, we had a 5-inch gun on there.

Paul Stillwell: But that wasn't your main purpose.

Captain Schwab: No, no. The purpose was communications and command.

Paul Stillwell: Were there any aspects of that that were off-limits to you?

Captain Schwab: Yes, there were. In certain parts of the communications system—I guess the on-line crypto stuff—I was not allowed in there. It's sort of weird to be the commanding officer of a ship and not get in.

Paul Stillwell: And they also probably had an intelligence setup on board, too, didn't they?

Captain Schwab: I don't recall any specific area of that sort, but I know that certain communications things were—everybody was barred, except some people with special clearances.

Another interesting thing—you may or may not realize it—but the tactics of that time on amphibious landing was that one of the first ships that went in to make the landing was the command ship. You went in close, right away. That worried me. I said, "My God, you know, if you get wiped out, the whole coordination of the thing goes."

Paul Stillwell: What was the rationale?

Captain Schwab: Just had to be in there to see what was going on. I guess it was still depending on eyeballs.

Paul Stillwell: How was she to handle? She was a bigger ship than you'd had before.

Captain Schwab: Yes, single-screwed, but if you read all these various books that the past experts in ship handling write, I mean, it's obvious when you're backing down in a ship, your stern's going to go one way or the other way. You had to be very careful on the turning radius, things of that sort, especially depending on which way you were going. I didn't have too much problem with her. I found that in some areas the pilots didn't know what the hell they were doing; they were supposed to do it.

For instance, where were we? In Malta. It is a fairly small, enclosed harbor there, and the pilot sort of panicked. He was going to back us right onto a breakwater. Based on my previous years before, experience in submarines, the first thing you do is drop the hook and stop the ship. Of course, you don't slow her down too much with the screws on these big things. It takes a while to turn the screw in the other direction.

Then my wife actually watched me leaving Bermuda, where the pilot got a little screwed up. We were backing away from the naval station there, which is just a small place. In Bermuda you had to be careful. Despite the fact that the pilot supposedly is in charge, you're really still the commanding officer, except the Panama Canal, which we never went through.

Another interesting thing happened in *Mount McKinley*, on one of the command ship visits to Bermuda when my wife appeared. We were tied up to the naval station pier, but in preparation for the trip we borrowed two small sailboats from Norfolk. The plan was that one of the sailboats was going to be for the captain, and the other sailboat for the rest of the crew. So I had a boatswain's mate on there who said he was really an expert in sailing. So after we'd all settled down, I had my wife come over to the ship. We were able to stay at the commanding officer's guesthouse there, which was nice—very small, about as big as this room.

I had the boatswain's mate rig both of these sailboats, and then after lunch decided to take my wife out for a little sail of Hamilton Harbor, I guess it's called. We got in the boat, and he assured me that everything was fine. But somehow the main sheet had gone under and was in between the rudder and the boat. So it was all jammed up down there. We cast off from the ship with the wind not quite setting us onto the breakwater that was there.

Suddenly I found that I couldn't either use the main sheet or the rudder because of this jam. So I managed to drop the sail right away, to minimize the movement of the boat. The only way I could figure out to get out was to actually lift the rudder out of the gudgeon and pintle back there. So I lifted it out and got the sheet out, with my wife holding onto the mast so it wouldn't hit me in the head. [Laughter] There I was, hanging over the stern. It's hard while the boat is moving to get the rudder pins back into those two sockets again. I guess it's the gudgeon and the pintle.

Meanwhile, the whole crew was lining the side of the *Mount McKinley* to watch the captain sail. I guess they noticed right away that I was in trouble. We finally got it all resolved and went sailing out, and we heard this big cheer—like we'd won the Army-Navy game or something. It was a very interesting little episode. So we sailed around a while and came back. The next thing that happened—my wife can't even remember the name—we had so many admirals then. I can't even remember the—do the other people have trouble remembering all these things?

Paul Stillwell: Yes.

Captain Schwab: Well, I have records around here someplace. You can see my files. I have tons of files. I ought to go through it and pick all those names out.

But a cruise ship came in while we were there, and among other things we suddenly discovered that the pastor of our church—the Lutheran church here in Maryland—was on this cruise ship. I guess he got a free passage to be the chaplain for the cruise. So we invited the pastor and his wife over for lunch, some days in the future, while the cruise ship was still in there.

The reason we couldn't have him right away was that was the day that there was a ceremony over at the other end of Bermuda. I guess it's St. George's, not Hamilton. It's the other end, St. George's, where, in the War of 1812, one or two American seamen—naval types had been buried there. I think one was a midshipman; I don't know if the other was an enlisted man or not. Of course, the Bermudans liked or favored the United States rather than the British—for some unknown reason, I guess because of trade. So they had a ceremony every year, and I don't know where the admiral was. He didn't go to it, but I went over there with my wife to represent the current U.S. Navy.

There was this distinguished-looking gray-haired gentleman and his wife. It turned out to be Van Wyck Mason.[*] He was both sort of a fictional historian and a detective story writer. I guess when he wrote historical fiction he was F. Van Wyck Mason. When he wrote detective stories, Van Wyck Mason. So we got talking to him, and he had a nice house on a little inlet in Hamilton Harbor. He suggested that we all come over to his house some evening for drinks and dinner. So I, in turn, invited him on the same day as the pastor of the ship.

On my ship we had the luncheon first with Van Wyck Mason and his wife, the pastor and his wife, and my exec. So we had a real big luncheon, and then that night or the next night we went over to Van Wyck Mason's house on my gig, which was pretty big, 26 foot long, and nicely done. With everybody going over there, it was quite an interesting experience. Going alongside the little dock at Van Wyck Mason's was tricky, because the water was about six inches below our screw, so I was worried about that. We had a great time there, and Van Wyck Mason's wife was very good-looking. She adopted my admiral, the admiral on board, as her "aide de camp," she called him.

---

[*] Francis Van Wyck Mason (1901-1978) was a prolific historical novelist. During his career he wrote 78 novels. After his first wife Dorothy died in 1958, Mason married Jean-Louise Hand, his secretary.

There were all sorts of weird things happening in those things. Another time in the *Mount McKinley*, I think with a different admiral, when we were in the Dominican Republic, and John Bartlow Martin was the ambassador, a Kennedy appointment.* He was a newspaperman. I have a book of his here someplace. He was off in New York having an operation, so we found out that Mrs. Ambassador—I don't know if this is a good thing—thought she was the ambassador too. So she insisted on setting up all the different things that we were supposed to do in the Dominican Republic, including meeting Mr. Bosch, the white-haired guy, who I guess was taken over later by a triumvirate there.

It was a very difficult period in the history of that place. We had our own cars in the *Mount McKinley*; we had a whole bunch of vehicles on there. I remember distinctly that when we went around town, besides our driver in the front, we had a local soldier riding shotgun in the front with a semi-automatic—not the Uzi, but the predecessor. Every street corner you passed through, besides having a soldier directing traffic in the center, each corner had a soldier on it. It was a very interesting experience, but we never had any trouble. Nothing ever happened to us.

I remember one of the nights that Mrs. Ambassador had set up some sort of a little reception for us at one of the local hotels. Afterwards she insisted that we look around at the gambling room and so on, in which she proceeded to borrow $20.00 from me so she could gamble; she had no money with her. She paid it back ultimately, but she lost it all. But then we all had to go out—and this was the admiral, who was getting more and more bored by this whole thing. We had to go out and look at the swimming pool, because it was supposed to be especially beautiful. It had nice trees around it, but I guess with all their political upset there, no one had cleaned it, so the thing was full of slime. It was terrible, disgusting. I guess she hadn't seen it in years. But that's the sort of thing that happened on these different cruises; you got to talk to the local people and so on. That was about it.

Paul Stillwell: Do you remember any particular amphibious exercises during that time?

---

* John Barlow Martin was U.S. ambassador to the Dominican Republic from 1962 to 1964.

Captain Schwab: We had little ones going all the time. The ones in the Mediterranean were the most interesting, because you were landing on different beaches, mostly in Greece. The Greeks were very nice. I don't think we ever landed in Turkey, but the Greeks always wanted us to. They were always eager to get a lot of arms assistance—as they still are—and they cooperated quite well.

Paul Stillwell: How big a part did the helicopters play in getting the troops ashore?

Captain Schwab: Well, the ones that we had were not capable of lifting a very heavy burden. I think that we saw a couple that could pick up a small field weapon, or something, or maybe a Jeep or something like that, but that was about it. They didn't get used. We used regular landing craft. Of course, the *Mount McKinley* didn't land anybody. It was all done from the APAs and the LSDs and LSTs.* We only usually had one LSD, and usually an AKA, and one APA.† There were only about four or five ships in the whole squadron and an LST. But most of the landing was done in the old World War II fashion. I guess the helicopters mostly transported the officers and things—moved people around in a hurry, but there was not much emphasis on that as there would be now. Of course, we had no air-cushion vehicles or any modern sort.

I don't think there was much—if there was any difference at all, it was minor between what we were doing and what had happened in World War II. It was a big difference from what the landings that we would do from the *Pennsylvania* before the war. We used 50-foot motor launches and bow ramps. That was different. No, this was World War II style.

Paul Stillwell: What are your recollections of the enlisted crew on board the *Mount McKinley*? How capable were those individuals?

Captain Schwab: I haven't really run into any poor quality enlisted men or officers, with certain individual exceptions. I think I mentioned one officer on the *Toro* who was

---
* APA – attack transport; LSD – dock landing ship; LST – tank landing ship.
† AKA – attack cargo ship.

completely resistant to any kind of direction, even though he was a Naval Academy graduate. He thought he was always doing the proper things. We got rid of him. But I can't remember any really bad examples anyplace.

Well, I'll say, one of my principles was always—on any ship, even one as large as this—to talk to the individual divisions in turn and acquaint them with who *you* are in the first place and the fact that you expect them to do things in the old Nelsonian tradition.[*] Schwab expects every man to do his duty—that sort of stuff. It helps if you can establish some sort of a personal rapport. See, if you get people like Captain Cooke in the *Pennsylvania*, I don't think he talked to anybody except himself, whereas, Captain Cutts was different; he talked to everybody. Personalities have a lot to do with it.

We had, in the *Darter*, my submarine, Captain Stovall, now dead, who was the commanding officer, of course, he was very reticent to talk. He apparently had had a successful patrol on the *Gudgeon*, but he had been depth-charged heavily. And so that made him very cautious in the *Darter*, so we didn't do much. I think we sank one little, maybe two little things. But he didn't talk to many people. Whereas you got Dave McClintock, who relieved him, he was gregarious and that sort of stuff. You go to other things, such as my first captain in the Pacific, Burt Klakring in the *Guardfish*. He talked to everybody. He was quite a musical type, and also I think he'd been a lacrosse player.

Paul Stillwell: Did you model yourself on any of these skippers you'd had?

Captain Schwab: No, I was impressed more early on by John L. McCrea, I guess, who gave me that quote I gave you about the, "A little ginger 'neath the tail will oft for lack of brains avail." He was the one who, I think, got to me more than anybody, and Captain Cutts, about having a good rapport with your officers and your men. I guess there used to be a tradition of the captain being isolated and unapproachable, but they weren't. They organized things that led to everybody knowing everybody, as opposed to sitting back and doing nothing.

---

[*] Lord Horatio Viscount Nelson (1758-1805), British naval hero of the Battle of Cape St. Vincent, 1797, Battle of the Nile, 1798, Trafalgar, 1805.

Paul Stillwell: Did you make it a practice to walk about the ship and go in the various spaces?

Captain Schwab: Oh, yes.

Paul Stillwell: Did you feel some sense of isolation from the crew because it was a larger ship?

Captain Schwab: Yes, well, you weren't as close to them. You never do get used to hearing yourself referred to as "the old man," even when you're in command of a submarine, but you're always "the old man."

To give you an example of that, at a recent submarine reunion in Baltimore last year, my wife was there. We have an annual reunion—I don't go to all of them—of the *Darter* and the *Dace*, and the *Dace* rescuing, and the *Menhaden*, which is the successor to the *Darter*. While we were all socializing there, I learned that an awful lot of the enlisted men have done very well. A lot of them are rather wealthy. This one man, who was in charge of all the arrangements, has the nickname "Shanghai." He puts out a newsletter every few months. We were sitting there, and the matter came up about how I was about to turn 70. He said, "You mean you're only 70 now? You mean you were only a year old than I was, and we called you 'Sir'?" It's hard to think back that way. But they thought that all the officers were much older and so on than they were. I guess that's the feeling they get. I never went along with the custom of some of the submarines, particularly the really old ones, the S-boats and so on. Sometimes the officers on them were on a first-name basis. That died out, but I never did any of that stuff. You had to maintain a little decorum in there, but on the other hand, if you're a cold fish, that's the kind of reaction you get too. That's no matter what ship you're on.

Paul Stillwell: What kind of material condition was the *Mount McKinley* in?

Captain Schwab: Well, considering that the ship had been built in 1944 and was converted into a command ship from a merchantman, it was, I would say, in fair to good condition. But it was a constant struggle to keep it going. We kept finding problems here and there as we went along. The maintenance crews were at a constant going over, and, of course, with these amphibious ships, being deployed six months out of every year to the Mediterranean, where there was not much opportunity for refits, they did have a maintenance problem in that fashion.

I guess the amphibious force ships, along with the mine force ships, were sort of at the low end of the totem pole as far as maintenance funds—upkeep funds—were concerned. So you had to really go in right to the force commander's material officer to fight for your own ship if you were the commanding officer. Otherwise, if you just handled it in a routine fashion, you would never know what was going to happen.

Paul Stillwell: What impressions did you have of Admiral Rivero from the time he spent on board?

Captain Schwab: Well, I knew Admiral Rivero before and again later when he was ambassador to Spain.[*] After he came back and had retired as ambassador to Spain, and he was giving us information on the study I was doing for the Institute of Defense Analyses.

Admiral Rivero was probably one of the smartest, most intelligent men ever to go to the Naval Academy. I would say, though, because he was so intelligent and smart, he was also aware of all the things that could go wrong in almost any situation, which during the Cuban Missile Crisis episode made him extremely nervous. Now, I don't know whether he had privileged information as to how vital this whole thing could become to the future of the United States and Soviet Union, but he was extremely nervous at that time.

Paul Stillwell: Well, if there's a possibility of nuclear war, his nervousness was justified.

Captain Schwab: Yes, well, of course. Of course, he wasn't the one making that decision. He had just taken over from Admiral Ward as the amphibious force, and I

---

[*] Admiral Horacio Rivero Jr., USN (Ret.), served as U.S. Ambassador to Spain from 1972 to 1974.

guess Admiral Ward went up to be Second Fleet just the day before we left practically, change of command ceremony.* So this was a new assignment, and considering the limitations on consultation with Washington and wherever that you have on board ship, as opposed to ashore, I think he probably calmed down when he got to Norfolk. He was able to handle things a lot better there than out at sea, where you're so isolated. I mean, you can't have any personal closed-circuit communications with anybody.

Paul Stillwell: What was the reaction on board the ship when you found out that there would not be an invasion, not a confrontation?

Captain Schwab: Oh, we didn't know that there wouldn't. We were kept at maximum readiness forever, it seemed. We were never sure when it stopped; in fact, it never has. The word spread. After President Kennedy made his speech, we didn't tell the crew anything about that.

Paul Stillwell: Why not?

Captain Schwab: Because we were told—well, not the speech—before that we had an idea that something was going on. The newspapermen that were out there to cover the exercise were not allowed to communicate with anybody. That was something of pre-Grenada type exercise, you might say.† The reason was that since out at sea there was probably a sense that something was going on. I mean, they could look around on the different ships and see the Marines out there sharpening their knives and getting all their gear together, so they knew it wasn't just for fun, and I guess people talked a little bit. So the real, official announcement didn't come except with the President's speech. That's when they really started sharpening and everything. I've never seen so many Marines sharpening their knives in my life. This was on the flagship, where they

---

* Vice Admiral Alfred G. Ward, USN, commanded the Second Fleet from October 1962 to August 1963. The oral history of Ward, who retired as a four-star admiral, is in the Naval Institute collection.
† In October 1983 the United States mounted a joint-service operation to occupy Grenada in the Caribbean after a Marxist military coup overthrew the island's government. The overthrow and subsequent developments led to concern about the safety of approximately 1,000 U.S. citizens on the island.

probably wouldn't even get ashore. But everybody was really gung-ho about doing something about Cuba.

Paul Stillwell: Well, there was some point in which there was an announcement made that the Soviets had decided to take their missiles out. Was there a sense of relief at that point, or was there a sense of letdown?

Captain Schwab: Yes, that's a funny thing. I guess it was probably a sense of relief. I think most everybody there wasn't too worried about what was going to happen to us. The concern was probably that if there had been a nuclear war, what was going to happen to our people at home, is what they were more worried about, because I can't imagine dropping nuclear weapons on Cuba for any reason.

Well, there were other things that we didn't know about. I gather it's come out since then that they had ways of telling whether there were nuclear weapons on a ship—some sort of sensing equipment—but we didn't know about that except guess it, I guess. But I don't think there was a period of real trust that the resolution that had occurred was anything permanent, especially when the word came out about the removal of missiles from Turkey and so on, things of that sort. Yes, I'd say there was a feeling of relief. Nobody—least of all, military men—I don't think they like to fight wars that much. It's part of the job. A fireman doesn't like to fight a fire either, but he has to. A policeman doesn't like to shoot anybody; in fact, most of them don't.

Paul Stillwell: Well, there are probably some exceptions in all those cases.

Captain Schwab: Well, probably, yes. I can't imagine firemen liking to fight fires, my father having been a New York City fireman. But I can understand some policemen not minding shooting, especially if they've been subjected to things.

Paul Stillwell: What were the satisfactions for you as the commanding officer in having a deep-draft ship like that?

Captain Schwab: Well, the first thing is the fact that you have a big ship indicates that somebody, someplace, has some measure of confidence in you; otherwise, you wouldn't have it. It supposedly was—I guess they've changed the rules now, ever since Zumwalt—that you're supposed to have a deep-draft ship to be considered for higher command or to be selected to flag rank.[*] I guess now they have commodores, see.[†] They still call them commodores?

Paul Stillwell: No, rear admiral lower half.

Captain Schwab: Oh, they don't call them commodores anymore?

Paul Stillwell: No, that was temporary.

Captain Schwab: Oh, but they have only one broad stripe?

Paul Stillwell: Yes.

Captain Schwab: Whereas, it used to be rear admiral lower half with a one and a half stripes, a big one and a little one.

Well, that was the first thing. Secondly, is any time you finish any kind of a job and you come out smelling well, it makes you feel good, especially if you know what your fitness report looks like, and I had all good fitness reports from it, so I had a sense of accomplishment.

On all the ships I had—I'd say particularly on the submarine—we did an awful lot to advance the cause of submarines versus submarines in ASW. Well, I mentioned earlier, on the forerunners of SOSUS and the low frequency using cathode ray tubes and cameras. Harmon B. Sherry took the pictures, and we used all that. And then building

---

[*] Admiral Elmo R. Zumwalt Jr., USN, served as Chief of Naval Operations from 1 July 1970 to 29 June 1974. He changed the rule so that a major shore command could qualify for selection to flag rank.
[†] For many years the U.S. Navy used the O-7 one-star rank only in wartime. Otherwise the individuals in that grade wore two stars and were known as rear admirals. In 1982 the O-7 rank was changed to "commodore admiral" with the individual wearing one star. In 1983 the rank's designation was changed to just "commodore." Later in 1983 the O-7 title was changed again, this time to "rear admiral, lower half."

on what's gone before, using that stuff, which was in BuShips and in conjunction with Junior McCain over in the ASW outfit, and CNO getting the support from Eli Reich.[*] Being able to build on what's there and come out with some sort of a result—in this case it was SOSUS—or using other kinds of things, such as sheer imagination: looking into ways to defeat the capability of a submarine to go below thermal layers and avoid detection from hull-mounted sonars and going to variable-depth sonar.

Several of us in BuShips came out with that idea simultaneously, and that's, I guess, still used now. Or being able, in the same area, to realize this lack of timing versus requirements on different types of equipment and trying to concentrate resources, whatever they are, since they're not unlimited, on the things which might be more fruitful. Such as, instead of wasting—frittering—a lot of stuff on things which wouldn't be realized: overly accurate attack sonars, as opposed to accurate homing weapons. When you can't do anything very accurate with sonar, because there are limitations on the gyro, which is basically the controlling force on how accurate the sonar is, as opposed to a radar, which may be, I gather, more accurate. I'm not sure about that.

But to take the money away from the things, which from analysis appear to have less payoff in the time when they need it, and concentrate on the ones that have more, so that way you could accelerate the development and production of something like that SQS-23 or the BQR-4—things of that sort, which otherwise you would have been frittering money away on mechanical accuracy on a submarine, instead of going into longer range detection with enough accuracy to permit you to launch a long-range, smart weapon. So any time you manage to solve what at that period appears to be a problem--and whether it's in day-to-day managing of a ship or coming alongside a pier in a high wind which setting you up—any of those things, which are just sort of little achievements, which all add up into a big sense.

That's why commanding a ship, I think, is so great, because the commanding officer ultimately gets all the pats on the back for having accomplished something. He also gets kicked elsewhere when he's done it wrong. So he's ultimately responsible. That's probably the only reason why I can see anybody being President. If you do well,

---

[*] Rear Admiral Eli T. Reich, USN. The oral history of Reich, who retired as a vice admiral, is in the Naval Institute collection.

you get credit, and if you don't, you're in trouble. It's about the same thing as a captain of a ship, unless you're very skillful at evasion. It's more difficult to avoid responsibility when you're commanding officer of a ship, because it's a tangible, limited thing.

Paul Stillwell: There's no question who did it.

Captain Schwab: Yes, whether you were there or not.

Paul Stillwell: Well, from there where did you go?

Captain Schwab: Well, I left the *Mount McKinley* in early 1963. At that point I was due to go back to shore duty again, because it was quite a long time at sea.

I came back—and what the heck was the name of the admiral? Anyhow, there was an admiral working for Henry Rowen, who was the Deputy Assistant Secretary of Defense in ISA, under Mr. Nitze, who was Assistant Secretary for ISA, International Security Affairs.[*] ISP is International Security Policy, which has just changed hands. They hadn't split at that time. Rowen was the honcho for NATO affairs. Next door, under Rowen also, in the next office to me, was Zumwalt, who was a captain. He was junior to me at that time. He was the honcho under Rowen and Nitze, of course. He was the disarmament expert and didn't have much to do. Well, I'll get into that in a minute.

This admiral—I'll add that name later—and I had run into each other when I was in OP-61—and he knew I was a Fletcher School graduate and so on.[†] So he requested me to be under him in ISA—the policy and plans of NATO is what it really was. And Jim Tyler was already there. He was a West Point graduate, class of '40. Nothing much of interest occurred early on there, in that particular outfit, because the RAND Corporation had started a program over in the U.S. mission to NATO, over in the NATO political headquarters, which were in Paris at this time.

---

[*] Henry S. Rowen was Deputy Assistant Secretary of Defense (Planning and NSC). Paul H. Nitze was Assistant Secretary of Defense for International Security Affairs from 29 January 1961 until 29 November 1963, when he became Secretary of the Navy.
[†] Serving under Rowen was Rear Admiral John M. Lee, USN, Director of the Policy Planning Staff.

The RAND Corporation was starting a program to harmonize forces, resources, and strategy for NATO, because up until that point—although they had what they called an annual review. All the countries were saying what they were going to do, and then not doing it, or reporting that they'd done something, and no one ever checked on it. So it had become sort of a ritual war dance, where everybody said how wonderful they were. That was supposed to impress the Russians, I guess, but there was no real coordination of what the forces were supposed to do versus the declared strategy. Now, you've read all the books on Maxwell Taylor and all that, and McNamara, and the Whiz Kids.[*] They were impressed with the fact—first of all—that if we could maintain enough nuclear strength, unless the Russians were completely irrational, the chance of a nuclear war was pretty low.

Paul Stillwell: Mutual assured deterrence, I think it was called.

Captain Schwab: Whatever it was. Yes, M-A-D. Before that, though, with Eisenhower we had a different policy, which was nuclear war right away from the start. Mutual assured deterrence was after the Russians got theirs. Before that it was nuclear weapons right from the start. So they decided that it was in the interest of both sides not to have a nuclear war. This is probably in the history elsewhere, but I'm looking at it from the standpoint of a peon.

So they decided that, largely due to people like Maxwell Taylor and so on—*Uncertain Trumpet* and what have you—that there was a need to harmonize the conventional forces with nuclear capability, both of the strategic and short-range and battlefield variety.[†] The nation had to come out with some sort of a coherent strategy, as opposed to all or nothing at all, or never use anything. That led to the so-called flexible defense, which doesn't say that you don't use nuclear weapons first. It just says you use first whatever is necessary to meet what's happened.

---

[*] General Maxwell D. Taylor, USA, served as Chairman of the Joint Chiefs of Staff from 1 October 1962 to 3 July 1964. Robert S. McNamara served as Secretary of Defense from 21 January 1961 to 29 February 1968. "Whiz Kids" was the nickname for the group of young civilian officials whom McNamara appointed to key positions in the Department of Defense hierarchy.

[†] General Maxwell D. Taylor, *The Uncertain Trumpet* (New York: Harper, 1960). The book criticized the Eisenhower administration's doctrine that emphasized the use of nuclear weapons and neglected conventional weapons.

A lot of the Europeans, particularly the Germans, were against it at first because it implied to them that we were going to make Germany a conventional battlefield before we'd ever use nuclear weapons. It finally sunk through, after a while, that that wasn't what the intent was. The intent was to be flexible in your choice so the other side didn't know what you were going to do right away.

The whole basis of any kind of deterrence is uncertainty as to the outcome, which is the reason for any kind of anti-ballistic missile program. I don't think that anybody expects, if they have any sense, that you're going to stop all nuclear weapons. It's just that the other side doesn't know what percentage you're going to stop, or which ones they are, and what the effect ultimately will be. So the uncertainty is the basis of everything. If you were certain about the outcome of everything, why, then you would go to war—if you were sure you were going to win. I guess we've done that before, or other countries have. For instance, the Germans, several times, have been certain the United States was never going to participate. Of course, that was their problem in the end.

On the European thing, though, NATO, the U.S. ambassador at that time, was Finletter, who been a Secretary of the Air Force. He was a very articulate person, written several books, pro-Air Force, looked at the capabilities of the U.S. NATO delegation, which is sort of just a ritual war dance. Report both ways: report what the U.S. Government told it to report, report back what the other countries said—and convinced McNamara that in order to do anything to reform NATO's planning system, there had to be extra push, extra people of some intelligence and persuasive capability.

Being Air Force, they—and the RAND Corporation in Santa Monica, California, being originally Air Force oriented—it had actually been a part of an Air Force manufacturer before it separated and they got the task assigned. They sent over, under an economist by the name of Burt Klein, about 9, maybe 11, RAND Corporation people of all different things.* One of them is still the intelligence honcho in the Pentagon, but, of course, he hasn't been with RAND for a long time.

They did all sorts of things. They managed to convince the NATO council and so on that they should organize themselves, put double hats on, and become something called the Defense Planning Committee. The Defense Planning Committee would look at

---

* Burton H. Klein, who had worked on the Strategic Bomb Survey following World War II.

defense problems, and the council would look at political problems—the council being still the senior citizens there. Of course, this was now all in 1963, and this sort of stumbled along there for a while.

Paul Stillwell: There were negotiations on the nuclear test ban treaty. Did you get involved in any of that?

Captain Schwab: No, that was handled elsewhere. We got involved mostly in reporting back to ISA what the NATO attitudes were, but that was about it. I didn't have anything to do with that. I don't know, but I don't think the military particularly liked that treaty too much; I'm not sure on that. On the NATO side, towards the end of '63 they had sort of organized the effort to harmonize, they called it. Later it became rationalization of forces, resources, and strategy, and they had come up with something like seven studies.

One was the whole inventory of everything. Before you could do anything, you had to see what you had in all the conventional forces. It was only conventional forces. Secondly was to take a look at the ground force problems, what they constituted. Study number three was a naval study, and 3A was ASW; this was of interest. Study number four was logistics; study number five was air; study number six was communications. I forget what study number seven was, I forget, but that was something weird.

So they had all these study groups, and in each study group was a member of the U.S. delegation; in most cases it was a RAND Corporation person. They'd also gotten special permission to implant four or five RAND people in the international staff, so they could introduce them into the United States planning, programming, and budgeting system.*

Paul Stillwell: Which was McNamara's brainchild.

Captain Schwab: That's right. And the Whiz Kids all loved that stuff. The thing was met with a lot of resistance from the Europeans, because in the first place it required

---

* PPBS – Planning, Programming and Budgeting System, which was started in January 1961 by Secretary of Defense Robert S. McNamara. For details, see Gordon G. Riggle, "Looking to the Long Run," *U.S. Naval Institute Proceedings*, September 1980, pages 60-65.

work, and also required—there were ways to double-check, when you did all these studies, on whether it was truthful or not. In other words, a country would report they had X number of divisions, let's say, on the ground. But then when they had to start listing what these divisions had in the way of armor and anti-tank and chemical warfare defense, all this sort of stuff that got into the nuts and bolts, most of the countries thought was nobody else's business except their own.

But if you're going to match up—if people are in a defensive front area, and one country has each of its divisions with X number of tanks and no anti-tank weapons or very few, and the next one has twice the number of tanks and a lot of anti-tank, if the enemy has any intelligence he's going to go in the right place. The same way with air. I mean, you had to know what the relative ranges were, the different airs, where they were based, what their supplies were. It was quite an extensive survey, and it started, I would say, toward the end of '63. In '64 the thing was starting to roll, and I think the civilian, the RAND Corporation person, though, in regards to this effort, it was not looked upon with favor by the Navy.

Meanwhile, the admiral in ISA who had asked for me was relieved by an Air Force brigadier general. Then he became part of an arms-control trio; I'll think of his name. I should have been doing this research before you came here. So I was now working for an Air Force officer, and Jim Tyler was my senior. Even though he was in the class of '40, his rank was a year earlier than mine. He was a year older and ranked a year earlier. So he was my nominal superior there, but I was doing all the NATO stuff. He was doing other things. A younger colonel in the Army was detailed to be sort of the shuttle between Washington and Paris, to keep track of what was going on in what they called the force planning exercise.

Paul Stillwell: Did you get to Europe yourself much?

Captain Schwab: Well, I'm getting to that. So in the process here, a lot of things combined. The civilian from RAND who was doing the antisubmarine warfare part of it was getting no cooperation from the United States Navy or anybody because of the sensitivity of the subject. He wanted to have detailed specifics instead of relative ranges of capability. So he was getting zero support, and the Navy would keep calling me down, saying, "What the hell's going on? Why are we getting all these questions from NATO headquarters? We don't even tell Defense some of these things." So the RAND civilian objected; he said, "I'm not useful in this."

Andy Marshall is a big shot still in intelligence.[*] He's sort of the overall coordinator of U.S. defense intelligence, I think, in the Pentagon, so it was a peculiar position. He's in charge of net assessment. Anyhow, he's quite a character and a very private. Now, to talk about somebody who never talks to anybody—he never talks to *anybody*. God I don't think he talks to. Maybe he talks to Him; I don't know.

The lieutenant colonel was sent over there on a trip and then was going to come back and write his report. He visited, had dinner with some friend not too far from the Etoile, and was walking back to his hotel, and somebody came out of a storefront and whacked him over the head. So he didn't show on his plane the next day; they didn't know where the hell he was. He was in some Paris hospital there, and had suffered a concussion; he was in bad shape. He was a smart officer and was in line to become a general, he told me. So he had to retire from that.

He ultimately came over and became the defense adviser after Ralph Earle, who was Tim Stanley's successor.[†] Ralph Earle was the son of the governor of Pennsylvania and supposedly had presidential ambitions, but I haven't seen his name mentioned. Now, all these, up through Ralph Earle, had been ministerial rank, a State Department thing. I guess this last guy didn't get that rank; they downgraded it a little bit. But as far as I know, he's still there; he's been there forever. And Tyler just came back about five years ago; he was there a long time. Tyler came over ultimately, and I'll tell you about that.

So the next thing you know, we got a call from over there saying that they didn't have a liaison man anymore. Simultaneously, the ambassador to the Netherlands—his name was Van Dyle or something like that—was a good friend of McNamara's.[‡] This Burt Klein of the RAND Corporation was an intelligent but aggressive and abrasive little

---

[*] Andrew W. Marshall has been director of the Defense Department's Office of Net Assessment since 1973. In the 1950s and 1960s he was part of a "cadre of strategic thinkers" in the RAND Corporation.
[†] Ralph Earle II Served in 1968-69 as Principal Deputy Assistant Secretary of Defense for International Security Affairs.
[‡] John S. Rice was U.S. ambassador to the Netherlands, 1961-64; William R. Tyler held that post from June 1965 to June 1969.

guy. He had somehow taken it upon himself—with Finletter's permission—to go around talking to all the different ambassadors. At some point he apparently went in and—according to this Netherlands ambassador—had insulted him or called him stupid or something. That made the ambassador angry, so he called up McNamara and complained about it.

So I had specific orders, in person from McNamara and Rowen, that from then on Klein was not to go to any meeting of any kind without me along with him, to sort of hold him down, or at least report on what actually happened, one or the other. I didn't have trouble holding this guy down; he was the kind of person who had, say, 30 ideas in one day, five of which were good. The question was which 25 you rejected; he would spout all the time.

Very sloppy personally. He smoked a pipe all the time, and in his office was a small, nicely finished table that arrived when he was put in there. In a couple of weeks it was pitted with match burns, where he'd dropped the matches on it. And he was always borrowing tobacco. If he ran out of tobacco in the big NATO meeting room, he'd borrow cigarettes from people and stuff them in his pipe, filter and all. It was *awful*.

Once I arrived at the meeting a little late after I'd been someplace else. Everybody was there. The RAND group was sitting behind where we were talking; the defense planning working group was subordinate to the defense planning committee. They had a defense planning working group, and that made a working area that reported to the DPC, and everybody looked at me and smiled. I was wondering what they were smiling about. What happened was he'd forgotten all his pipes, left them at home or something, and so he'd gone in my office and took one of my pipes, which he was smoking. That's like using somebody's toothbrush. It was sort of weird. I gave it to him.

But, anyhow, forgetting that, he was notorious. He was really an absent-minded professor. He'd been in the Air Force during the war, and he was famous for being the navigator of a squadron that was supposed to fly to Italy, and he wound up in North Africa. [Laughter] That's true too. He would do other things. The group of us, Klein and everybody else, would go out to lunch and wander around that section of Paris and so on, but every once in a while, he'd take off and go someplace else. One day we missed him. He got lost and got on the wrong metro and went—God knows. It took him hours to find his way back to NATO headquarters, though we were only a couple blocks away.

But the funniest one—well, two funny ones on him—these are all good anecdotes for if you're writing about absent-minded professors. We had a little train that ran past NATO, a peripheral train. It used to go all the way around Paris, but now it started down one station past where he lived, and I was two stations up. I only lived one mile from NATO headquarters, so I used to walk all the time when it was nice weather.

We used to work late, and he got on the train one night. In these NATO meetings nobody started till 10:00, and then you'd knock off for lunch at about 1:00 or 1:30, and nobody would be back from lunch till about 3:00. That always was a slow process, because all the Europeans would have had a bottle or so of wine. You wouldn't finish till 7:00 or later. So he got on this little train to go home and fell asleep. Instead of getting off at his stop, he got off at the last stop and walked out of the station and didn't know where he was. He finally had to go to a phone booth and call home and tell his wife where he was, so she could come and get him. He had no idea.

The *really* funny one was one morning he came into NATO headquarters, and his wife called from their apartment. They were very security conscious, so it had a key lock inside and outside. She said, "You jerk, you took all the keys with you, so I can't get out of the apartment. It's locked."

So he said, "All right, dear." So he went all the way home—on the train, I guess—walked up to the apartment, and knocked on the door. She said, "You dope, if I could open the door, I wouldn't have called." She told us all this stuff. Now you've got an idea of what kind of a guy he was. Pretty soon it became obvious that his personality was not helping.

Well, he and his wife took Betty and myself out to some place called the "Dance of the Jaws." It was a restaurant, not much wider than this room is long, and it had sort of a three- or four-piece band at the end, very loud. All of the wine came out to the table from tubes; you filled up your glass with a tube. I don't know what the problem was. Anyhow, we were talking away, and we were only about five feet away from this band, and it was going like hell. You could hardly hear yourself talk or think. He fell sound asleep right at the table. His wife kept nudging him.

Finally, with all these things going on, they requested that I be sent over there, and I was. I went over there in the summer of '64 with my whole family in the SS *United States* for one year, supposedly, as a Navy captain.* On the same ship was Russ Dougherty, who had just made brigadier general. He is now the president of the Air Force Association. He became SACEur's deputy, but his last big job in the Air Force was Strategic Air Command.†

Paul Stillwell: What do you recall of the SS *United States*?‡

Captain Schwab: All of us rode over, which was delightful; they really take care of you that way. When we arrived in Paris, first of all we were put in sort of an apartment hotel for a month until the civilian who was leaving from the U.S. NATO staff, who had been part of this study over there, but he was not RAND. He was with the defense division.

We got his apartment, which was charming: a three-bedroom apartment in an old building that had been built around 1870 or so and modernized. It even had an elevator about as big as that chair. About two people could barely fit in it and so on and so on. So we moved in there and had a nice break. Of course, not much goes on in Europe in the summertime. July and August in particular are dead. So we traveled around, but as soon as September came, we got into this business. I relieved Andy Marshall as head of the ASW exercise as a Navy captain. With a Canadian captain and a Netherlands commander, I guess, we devised a system that would permit all of the countries to report ASW capabilities without divulging anything secret. We did it by using ranges, divided everything into categories X, Y, and Z. So X would be sort of the antiques, and Y would be things that could—X would handle, you know, old submarines, conventional submarines. Y would be things that could handle snorkeling submarines, and Z the things that might be able to handle nuclear submarines. And you also Did X, Y, Z on

---

* After one year, Captain Schwab retired from active naval service and joined the Foreign Service. He remained in Paris, doing the same job as in his final Navy year. The State Department had taken over NATO force planning from the Department of Defense.
† General Russell E. Dougherty, USAF, served as Commander in Chief of the Strategic Air Command from 1 August 1974 to 31 July 1977.
‡ SS *United States* was a 990-foot-long passenger liner that went into service 1952. At 53,329 gross tons, she was the third largest liner in the world. Her top speed of more than 38 knots was considered a potential military asset. She was removed from service by the United States Lines in late 1969.

detection ranges and reliability. The people would be able to give you things in those categories, both the surface and submarines. This is everything: surface ship detection ranges and so on it did.

So we finally came out with a report which showed what was a very, I think, revealing statement of the category of ASW, as far as NATO was concerned. It also showed certain areas where you were lacking. It resulted in some of the countries improving their sonars, when they saw how weak they were compared to other countries and how weak they were compared to the kind of threat. So that study was successful; in fact, it was the first study finished. It was finished early in '65.

Paul Stillwell: What was your personal role in the study?

Captain Schwab: I was the director of it, taking over from Marshall. I mean, the United States was really in charge of all the studies, except I guess the air study was run by a British aviator. It was all at the captain/colonel level as far as the military was concerned. As I say, there was a lot of reluctance, so they finally did all that. Just about that time, in '65, why, this then led to a generation of a new type of planning, a rolling type of plan. You've had three- and five-year rolling forward stuff so you'd get an idea of here's where you stand now, and this is what your objectives were for three years, and then what your long-term objectives were for five years.

So to go back to that sonar planning stuff I had in BuShips, it was similar to that. You would try to relate what your capability should be to what the intelligence arm showed the Soviets might be doing or whoever—that's the only ones we're going to fight, really. So we had a rolling program, and then the reports every year would be reports of progress. If intelligence or any other information changed, we would change. We would roll forward on the requirements too. There was always a gap between what you had and the requirements.

The whole thing was sort of artificial in the sense, you see, that your people should do—you were trying to figure out what percentage of national income and so on the different countries—you see those sort of figures every day now—what percentage of their national income they were spending on defense. We even broke it down to what percentage of defense spending was spent on these different elements, to see how that balanced out. The general emphasis then was try to convince the Europeans that they should emphasize the local, the ground forces which they had, and so on, and the things in defense of their own territory. We would take care of the overseas-type stuff, the long-range nuclear weapons stuff and mobile forces to go around. It hasn't quite worked out all that way, but that was the general intent.

Paul Stillwell: How cooperative were the other nations?

Captain Schwab: Well, I think all of them understood what we were trying to do. I think they sort of resented it. There was a feeling that the United States had the attitude that it knew better than anybody else what to do, which, of course, was resented, particularly by the Brits and Germans. They all participated. How, let's say, eager they were was always a question. The fact that all the information had been gathered made it difficult for them to wiggle out of things. Without that nobody knew what they had. They could just say, "Oh, yeah, in the old game we promised that we would improve our forces in this area," but nobody knew what they had to start with.

Paul Stillwell: Well, there's an element of self-interest in there; these were their own countries they were defending. You'd think that would be something to motivate them.

Captain Schwab: Yes, but they have grown so used to the nuclear shield protecting them, at minimum cost, that they're still reluctant to realize that the Soviets have a nuclear weapon. That nuclear shield works both ways now, but it isn't as protective as it used to be. In conventional forces they don't necessarily have to match the Soviets, but you have to make it so unlikely that they would have a quick and easy victory without tremendous additional expense.

Our big thing in our favor there is that the Soviet logistics system, and resupply system, and so on, is, I guess, still rather primitive compared to what it should be for the size of their front-end forces. So unless they're able to defeat conventional things on the western side very rapidly, they sort of run out of steam. If you could hold them for a month or two, you would really be in good shape. And whether you can hold them or not, of course, depends on how much warning you have and how much reinforcement you can get over ahead of time.

This is one of the things that in my later RAND studies we were going into—the reinforcement of Europe. That was another outgrowth of all these things. This was under President Carter and Robert Komer, when he was the head of these studies, and then he went over to become the number-three man in the Defense Department.[*] But everything that's been done in NATO since, say, 1964 is a result of this force-planning study. Of course, they modified it and expanded it, but as far as I know, they are still using the same type of reporting and rolling forward, probably because everybody's reluctant to get involved.

That was a hell of a lot of work, all that stuff. I don't think they've ever worked so hard. The international staff, of course, which is used to being a number-shuffling outfit—reproducing documents given to them and that sort of stuff—really resented having to do all this work. So that the main thing there was to make sure that the wishes of the administration were followed. Oh, I forgot to mention, I was in ISA when Kennedy was assassinated.[†] A lot of people in there knew him. It was really a tremendous shock.

Paul Stillwell: A tremendous shock to the whole country.

Captain Schwab: Well, I mean particularly there, because there were one or two civilians who actually knelt in the passageway when they got the word. They were praying right in ISA. I'd never seen that done before. That was it, and, of course, my wife and I and my daughters stayed up all night to try to get into the Capitol. They stopped the visiting just before we got there. But, anyhow, forgetting that's ISA.

---

[*] Robert W. Komer headed the U.S. pacification program in Vietnam in the 1960s, later worked for the RAND Corporation, and served during the administration of President Jimmy Carter as Under Secretary of Defense for Policy.
[†] President John F. Kennedy was shot and killed in Dallas, Texas, on 22 November 1963.

Paul Stillwell: How cooperative were the French on this study? They've been not too cooperative on NATO.

Captain Schwab: Well, the French were very—now, there were side studies going on all the time. One of them I was involved in was called a NATO-wide study of improving the reinforcement of NATO's flanks, and particularly Greece and Turkey.

The people who were most interested in that, of course, were the Americans; if they had anything, the Brits; the Italians; and the French, because they can cooperate that way. So, among other things, I had to go down there with representatives of those countries and talk to the Greeks and the U.S., of course, contingent from both places, and the Turks—first to try to identify what they thought might be a reasonable reinforcement to add on to their forces, how to merge, the timing, the locations and what have you.

There was a French colonel by the name of Bergere; of course, he was from Alsace. He went down with us, but he was allowed to travel only on Air France. He was very cooperative. On the ASW study we had a French Navy captain who was extremely cooperative. He was so cooperative that when the study was three-quarters finished he was summarily relieved [Laughter]. We gathered—we never knew, of course—that their French Ministry of the Marine were a little peeved at him for being too cooperative. We had all the dope on the French stuff, which wasn't bad, as a matter of fact. At that time it seemed better than the Brits.

Actually, I'd go out and visit with ambassadors and so on from time to time, and the French operating forces always cooperated very well with NATO. There was no problem at all. They allowed—I understand—I didn't see it, but they allowed the U.S. naval aviators, to use bombing ranges in France and everything, even though France was nominally out of the integrated command structure. France is in NATO on the political side, and it cooperates with the military side, but it has separated itself from the integrated structure. It doesn't make all these reports everybody else does, which leads to the next thing.

So when France did all this, in '66 and '67.* They gave a time lag, warning that by such and such a date, '67, they'd be over. Two things happened. First, all of the NATO headquarters, and U.S. headquarters had to move out of France. They moved into Germany, and Belgium, and the Netherlands. The political headquarters at Port Dauphin there, they didn't say anything about that, but then NATO—and the rest of them—got together and said, "Well, if you're not going to have the military headquarters here, we'll get the hell out of it too." That's why they all moved to Brussels in October '67.

That was a fascinating movement. Closed for business on Friday, whatever that week was in October '67, and opened in Brussels in these buildings, which were supposedly temporary, on Monday morning, as if nothing had happened. It took them only six months or so to put them together. I mean, it's amazing how all the people found housing and everything else; it was fantastic. But all the people moved, and it was just as if nothing had happened.

The French sent observers—pretty nasty setup—but they don't do anything in that way. Every once in a while we'd ask for a report or something, and they'd provide it. They were aware that they were there on sufferance and also under the shield of NATO, when you get right down to it. Of course, they are a part of NATO. But de Gaulle was pretty nasty.

Paul Stillwell: Yes. The Standing Naval Force Atlantic was coming into being.† Did you have a role with that?

Captain Schwab: Yes. The Standing Naval Force Atlantic and the Naval On-Call Force Mediterranean came right out of the U.S. mission to NATO, and the force planning outfit, of which I was the director, along with the admiral down at SACLant headquarters. You had to get permission down there to talk to them, and that came through. The role we played was to generate ideas that some kind of naval forces of that type, of an integrated,

---

* In 1966 and 1967 French Prime Minister Charles de Gaulle gradually withdrew his nation's naval and military forces from NATO because he believed the United States had too much control over those forces. He also demanded that all NATO headquarters, bases and troops be removed from France by October 1967, which was done. France remained a member of NATO politically but not militarily.

† Standing Naval Force Atlantic, a multi-national group of ships that operated together under the auspices of NATO. Rear Admiral Richard G. Colbert, USN, initiated the concept paper on the subject in November 1966. NATO approved the concept, and the force of ships was activated in January 1968.

multi-national thing, was necessary. In the Mediterranean we couldn't get everybody to do it on a permanent basis. I guess they didn't want to call the standing naval force "standing." All we could get there was Naval On-Call Force Mediterranean, called NavOCForMed, which the Dutch said was a dirty word in Dutch. That's all we could get down there, but that was one of the few tangible results, besides U.S. commitments on Marines from the flank-reinforcement structure. That was one of the things. The On-Call Force in the Atlantic was a very interesting thing, because that really is an offshoot of the multilateral force, which they were going to have. Do you remember that one?

Paul Stillwell: Well, they were going to have mixed manning in ships.

Captain Schwab: Mixed manning in ships, and also before that, they were going to have mixed manning of missile-bearing ships. That was the real MLF. The mixed manning of ships; they named a destroyer after him.[*]

Paul Stillwell: Claude Ricketts.

Captain Schwab: Ricketts, that's the one, yes.[†] He was the honcho on that. And so that's where the Standing Force Atlantic basic idea came from. And the main part that I played, and the U.S. mission played in that, was talking it into the Defense Planning Working Group and the Defense Planning Committee to authorize it. And SACLant, of course, helped.[‡] SACLant didn't mind; he had command of it.

Paul Stillwell: Well, isn't that still largely a symbolic thing, though?

---

[*] DDG-5, commissioned originally as the USS *Biddle* on 5 May 1962, was renamed *Claude V. Ricketts* on 28 July 1964. For pictorial coverage of the multinational experiment, see "The Mixed-Manning Demonstration," *U.S. Naval Institute Proceedings*, July 1965, pages 87-103. The issue has a painting of the USS *Claude V. Ricketts* on the cover.
[†] Admiral Claude V. Ricketts, USN, served as Vice Chief of Naval Operations from 1 November 1961 until his death on 6 July 1964.
[‡] SACLant – NATO's Supreme Allied Commander Atlantic.

Captain Schwab: Yes, but it's good, because it can expand or contract as necessary. My son was in it when he was still on active duty in the Navy; he was in a destroyer.* When the Russians have exercises, the multi-national force can go and sort of observe, the way the Russians are always observing, with so-called trawlers and things. It is symbolic, but then what isn't?

Paul Stillwell: Well, that's the essence of deterrence sometimes.

Captain Schwab: Yes. It shows that you're unified. They do learn a lot from each other. You find out that the Dutch and the Brits and the Canadians are superb seamen, even though sometimes their equipment isn't that great, although sometimes it's better. They're pretty good. When I was in the *Marlin,* probably in peacetime, we were training American ships, and we had a Canadian cutter. The American destroyers and so on were not too great on maintaining contact. This was a little submarine, and we had no sophisticated ways of evasion or anything; we just got away from them.

We had a *hell* of a time getting away from the Coast Guard cutter; their understanding of relative motion or something was great. We couldn't get away at all from the Canadian destroyer; it was really good, whatever the name of it was. It was outstanding. I don't think their sonar equipment was any better. We're probably getting into restricted stuff. It was probably powerful but not very good on reception. Now, that's the sort of thing they learned. Of course, they all use English: the Dutch, everybody.

Paul Stillwell: Convenient for us.

Captain Schwab: Yes, and, of course, all the aircraft of the world use English too. But all those things were great; over a period of time you built up this tradition of cooperation and coordination, and it works. Another important thing that we discovered in all this was the horrible hodge-podge of communication equipment in all the different countries,

---

* Donald E. Schwab, a Naval Reserve officer, served on board the destroyer *Vesole* (DD-878), a FRAM I version of the *Gearing* class.

including the United States. I think it may be corrected by now, but for instance when we were having that supply operation to Israel, way back, we found that the Air Force planes couldn't communicate with the Sixth Fleet.

Paul Stillwell: In 1973.*

Captain Schwab: Yes. I mean, there were things of that sort.

We should have learned from World War II, when Submarines Southwest Pacific couldn't talk to Submarines Pacific. You had to go back through Bellconnen, Australia, to go to Pearl Harbor. I mean, that resulted in the *Darter* and other submarines missing about five cruisers in Davao Gulf, because by the time we got the word, we couldn't get close to them. But if we'd had the word earlier, we might have. There were other submarines behind us that could have gotten to them, but the word had to crisscross Pacific. In order to get the word, we had to go back through Bellconnen in Australia, and then go to Pearl Harbor, and then come back, and by that time it was too late. Horrible tactical, to have submarines from two forces in the same gulf. It's a good thing we didn't shoot each other.

Paul Stillwell: Well, the worst case of all on that was the Battle of Leyte Gulf—not for submarines but for overall forces. The Seventh Fleet and the Third Fleet couldn't work together.†

Captain Schwab: I didn't know about that.

Paul Stillwell: Well, that was when Halsey went off and left San Bernardino Strait unguarded.

---

* The Yom Kippur War started on 6 October 1973. Egyptian and Syrian forces began major coordinated ground offensives against Israeli positions, seeking to improve territorial claims in the wake of the Six-Day War of 1967. Supported in part by weapons supplied by the United States, Israeli forces counterattacked and drove back the Arabs. A cease-fire finally took effect on 25 October.
† On 25 October 1944, during part of the wide-ranging Battle of Leyte Gulf, Admiral William F. Halsey, USN, left San Bernardino Strait in the Philippines unguarded, and Japanese heavy warships came through toward the invasion beaches at Leyte. Japanese gunfire sank two American escort carriers and three destroyer-type ships.

Captain Schwab: Well, the *Darter* sent out the word on the attack and the forces coming, which was the first indication that there was a big force coming from the south. And that got to Halsey's outfit, because they attacked with planes. We were Southwest Pacific, so that went to Australia and back to them, I guess. Halsey, of course, as an aviator admiral was going to go after them. He wasn't really basically an aviator admiral.

Where'd I go?

Paul Stillwell: Well, we were over in NATO, and you were talking about your study, and I gather that talked mostly about hardware. Did you get into combined planning, combined intelligence?

Captain Schwab: Yes. Well, what happened on that side—not on this study—this was primarily forces; what we had, resources, how much money was available, and the strategy connected with it. The strategy side was where the French caused the problems, because we were trying to go from the bombs away right away to a so-called flexible response strategy in which you had sufficient conventional strength to delay, at least, the other side till you could make up your mind whether you wanted to use nuclear weapons or not. You could use nuclear weapons in the onset, depending on the nature of whatever the tactical situation was.

So that was the type of thing we were doing and were trying to change, and the French balked at that. It wasn't until 1966-67, when the French withdrew, that that went through. So that was the main thing, and, of course, that was slightly after the move to Brussels. From what I hear, though, the NATO force-planning thing has gone back into sort of a ritual war dance again, but it can't be worse than it was before. There were a lot of entrenched civil servants on the international staff who loved the other system, see, because they didn't have to think; all they were doing was regurgitating numbers and tabulating numbers. See, you had a lot of numbers, but no one had really ever checked on what they meant, or related them to strategy, or what they were costing in terms of resources.

Surprisingly, a great number of the international staff people were French, and so a lot of them stayed along and went to Brussels, which led to another series of interesting things. First, before I got involved, there was a Turk who was—there was a book about him, a novel. This was a Turk who, for ideological reasons, decided that information on NATO's capability should be given to the other side and vice versa. He didn't know enough about our intelligence. The other side would figure they didn't have that much about us, so he started passing things. I don't think he ever got paid or anything, but they found out about it, and he was trapped somehow or other and sent back to Turkey, where he disappeared in a hurry. Turks don't fool around.

I got involved in that, in checking out what damage might have been done by passing numbers. Of course, the conclusion you'd come to is that in an international organization it's almost impossible to prevent numbers from leaking out. Numbers from satellites are really meaningless. It's what your intentions are with respect to those numbers that's important. Also, there are the difficult things to judge, such as command capability, and the timing of using these things, as opposed to the actual things. Most of the things that would go over to the other side got into the numbers. So that was the kind of report I wrote.

Until a few years later, it was '68 or '69, one of the French who had come over there was in the area of classified duplication, and he had built up in his office a series of file cabinets, so that nobody could see him from the door and so on, and he'd be behind there. He was apparently taking pictures with a Minox camera or something equivalent—even had the measuring string and everything—of various documents and giving the different drops to what was reportedly a Rumanian. This is, again, skirting the edge of classification.

They became suspicious of him because he lived in a small area of France, not too far from Paris, where they made good paté. On the holidays and so on, he'd bring in a case of it and hand it out as gifts. And people liked it so much they started buying it from him. So every once in a while, when he'd go back to France, he'd bring some back and sell it. He got a little extra money that way. But he left his wife and family back in France. Then they found out that he had a Belgian girlfriend, and suddenly she blossomed into a nice apartment house, and she had a new car, and he had a new car. And somebody suspicious on the international staff started adding up what his income was and figured, "How in the hell?" They found out he paid for those other things.

So they started watching him and planted a camera somehow; that's how they caught him taking the pictures. So they grabbed him, and they had an idea of how long he'd been doing this. I don't know how they got that. They tried to get the French Government to do something about it, and they said, "Well, this didn't happen on French territory, and it had nothing to do with France. It was all NATO." As far as I know, the guy's still running around, at large, in France; they never did anything to him. Of course, he was canned.

The U.S., as usual, was extremely worried, so George Vest was the deputy chief of mission.* He's now the head of the State Department and Foreign Service. He's Foreign Service. He's a guy in the administration over there; he's a career person. He was the deputy chief of mission, and he said to me, "Why don't we check and see what kind of damage he caused and make a damage report. You're the only one who has a clearance."

I had clearances up to the ears by then, everything: nuclear, everything else. By this time, I could have gone into that room on the *Mount McKinley*. I used to go over to the U.S. military side, the mission to NATO, the U.S. military rep. I was one of the few that had the clearances. I would go over there and get all the military intelligence, and they'd make you read the book and sign something. I had all the special clearances. It took me years to get rid of that. If I ever were to be captured, I was supposed to be shot, and that sort of thing. Even when I was on the *Lake Champlain* for nuclear stockpiling. Anyhow, I'm all clear in that stuff now.

So I went through the list of all the possible things that were of interest to the United States that this Frenchman might have compromised and filled up a room of this size. It took me about three months. They said, "Well, do you want any help?"

I said, "Okay, who do you got?" They didn't have anybody. So they went through it in about three months. It came out the same way, that all these things were numerical-type things. He had been approached by the Rumanian, who bought some of his paté. He'd sort of heard about it, and then the Romanian started asking the Frenchman, "Hey, you know, we'd like to have the relations. [This is according to this

---

* George S. Vest served in Brussels from 1967 to 1969 as Deputy Chief of Missions of the U.S. Mission to the European Commission. In 1969 he became Deputy Chief of Missions of the U.S. Mission to NATO.

guy talking to the NATO people] Relations between Rumania and the West should improve, and so in order to do that, we'd like to know what we could sell you." And he got economic reports. It worked up into classified things of some magnitude, but nothing over secret, and nothing of intelligence situations. Certainly nothing of real war plans. Of course, that wasn't covered by this guy. That would all be out in SACEur, that sort of thing. So it was, again, a number-shuffling thing. I wrote about a five-page report on that. It was well received; nobody could argue with it, because nobody else had done it.

Now, when Nixon got in office in 1969, they went into a program called "Reduction of Cost in Europe"—red cost.* Also, they had a worldwide reduction of cost. One of the things they did was, in the first place Harlan Cleveland was going to be relieved by Robert Ellsworth.† Robert Ellsworth was delayed a little somewhat, because he had screwed up some sort of airline franchise deal, and instead of being a White House favorite was sent over into the Old Executive Office Building there and put in a corner. Then, the next thing you know, he was banished to be ambassador to NATO, which somehow the Europeans didn't like that. You shouldn't be sent to be ambassador as punishment. Henry Kissinger, of course, was really running things, even though Rogers was Secretary of State.‡ Other things happened like that too.

Anyhow, one day, after Ellsworth arrived and Cleveland was gone, I got called in, and the ambassador said, "Gee, I have sad news for you.

I said, "What's that, Mr. Ambassador?"

He said, "Your appointment as a foreign service officer is to be terminated."

I said, "Why? I have a minimum of five years with a possible continuation—a five-year agreement."

He said, "Well, that's what I got from the State Department."

So I went in to George Vest, who was a career guy, and I said, "What's going on?" He said he'd help me check into it, so he checked into it. Found out first that they'd have to give me a whole year more pay because of the agreement I had. Secondly, I guess the investigation into this loss hadn't been finished yet, and they had nobody else

---

* Richard M. Nixon was President of the United States from 20 January 1969 until his resignation from office on 9 August 1974.
† Robert F. Ellsworth served as U.S. ambassador to NATO from 1969 to 1971.
‡ William P. Rogers served as Secretary of State from 22 January 1969 to 3 September 1973.

around for that and other things with the proper clearance. So he got together with the ambassador, and they extended me until the year that I was supposed to have anyhow.

I wasn't really a political appointee in the absolute sense but close enough. I mean, I was on the list there as McNamara's representative. But that's a political thing, you know.

Paul Stillwell: What was life like in France for you and your family?

Captain Schwab: Oh, it was great. We always heard about the French being difficult and obnoxious, but I think that applies primarily to the people tourists run into. People don't have a high regard for—probably Washingtonians or New Yorkers or so on, if they're tourists. But if you live there and you get to know the locals where you live, they get very protective of you.

We had neighbors in our apartment in Paris who were rather elderly. Their name was Varinois; they're both dead now. I guess the wife, at that point, was around 75 and the husband around 80—very active, tall French people. We lived on the fifth floor, cinq etage, of this beautiful old apartment house. We rented it furnished. We didn't realize that most of the furnishings were antiques. If we'd had small kids, we'd have been worried. It was beautiful. We had a few things. We brought over an American refrigerator, which is essential, because the French refrigerators were about the size of a microwave. Aside from that, it was great, and everything was, you know, really antique, including the wiring.

The Varinoises were on the fifth floor, right opposite us. After we'd been there about a week, why, Madam Varinois came over one morning when I was working at NATO, and she said to my wife, "Do you speak any French?

My wife said, "A little." She'd had a year in college.

She said, "Well, that's fine. I speak English." She did. She had helped nurse Americans in World War I, out at Camp de Loge, which is, again, an American place. She said, "Well, I'll tell you what. Have you gone around to the shops here?"

My wife said, "Yes."

She said, "Well, if you're ready in an hour, I'll take you around and introduce you to all the shopkeepers." So she told my wife what to wear and everything. This was in July. She came over, well dressed, with a velvet hat. She said, "Now, when we get down to the street, and so on, you take my arm, because the younger woman always takes an older woman's arm." She took her around to all the shopkeepers and introduced her and said, "This is my new American neighbor. She speaks a little French, and you take good care of her, or you'll have to answer to me."

She'd been living there for 40 years or something. They'd watched the Americans march twice up the Avenue Champs-Elysées, and they said, "They saved us twice." Whenever there was an American holiday, where she thought we should put out a flag—we had a nice big balcony—she'd say, "Now, put your flag out." We had to put our flag out, and she'd go down over to avenue, and you could see she'd point it out to all her friends: "See, my American neighbors have their flag out." She was really great. The old geezer, Monsieur Varinois, had been a chemical engineer and had owned a big chemical factory. He had since retired and turned it over to his son. I think he understood English, but he didn't speak it, so we spoke French mostly.

The apartment was old, and they'd been living there long before there was an elevator installed, which was a narrow one. So when they first put those in those old buildings, they would rig them so they would go up, but once you got out, they would automatically return to the ground floor. You were supposed to walk down and save electricity. Of course, it cost as much, but that was the idea, and it was always waiting for somebody downstairs.

So in the morning, when I would walk to NATO, he would be coming out. He told me which stores you get the best baguette, and the best croissant, and the best anything else. Then he would go to a certain store in the morning to get his paper and his croissant for breakfast. You're always working on a fresh-food basis in Europe. You buy everything for the meal, not by the week or whatever, as we do here—frozen. So we'd usually see him come out of his door and my door at the same time. And he'd run down the stairs. This guy was 80 years old. I'd take the elevator, and he'd beat me down to the bottom. And we'd walk, God, like a house afire. He was great. We were chatting away, all the way.

But the funniest one was that when we would go on automobile trips. My son was always in college in the United States, except on rare occasions, but my two daughters were there all the time, he'd give us a route to follow. He didn't believe in going on the great big auto routes, like the throughways and toll roads. We had to go on the back roads, as far as he was concerned. We saw more of France on the back roads. Some of it was interesting.

When we went down to Barcelona once, he put us on a back road through France that went over the Pyrenees at a place called Bourg Madam, which is the customs station. When you're on the French side of the Pyrenees, it's not bad, because there's about a three-foot-high stone wall along the edge, see, and the roads are two-laned roads. They wind around the edge of the mountains. The minute you hit the Spanish side, there's no wall. You've got this drop-off that looks like a mile down. As you go around the corners, you can see your wheels kicking all the stones, but there are people coming the other way all the time.

For some reason, this was the preferred route by the Brits—I don't know why it was—instead of going along the shore road, which I guess is longer, on the Mediterranean side. That was the way we came back, I'll tell you. But going down there, when you looked over these mountains, which, I guess, were pretty new mountains, because they're bare. Beautiful colors in the stone. I had to keep my eyes from those things, because they were hypnotic. My wife and the daughters were huddled against the inside of the car, as if it would do any good.

There were some hazards on the road. The Brits drive on the left side and having the steering wheels on the right side. Here they were driving on the right side of the road. You looked up and you said, "This car has no driver." A lot of them were pulling small trailers, which they called caravans; but their engines were not equipped for hill climbing. You'd suddenly come around a corner, and there was someone stalled there.

That was hazardous, plus the fact there were lumber trucks on the road. These lumber trucks had a tractor up forward, as we have on our semis, but then they'd have these big trees—I don't know where they got the trees. The rear end would be like the rear end of a hook and ladder, but it was permanently fixed. They'd go around these things with part of the truck hanging over the corner, and the rear of every truck had—

besides the normal stop lights and so on, they have a red light and a green light mounted. If the red light's on, you're not supposed to pass, and if the green light's on, it's all right to pass, see. They also have horns on there that sound like a locomotive, so you hear one of those coming, you *know* he's coming. Before these people would come to a road, no matter which way they're going, where they think there might be somebody they can't see, they sound this horn. The thing reverberates; it's frightening. That was Monsieur Varinois. I don't know whether he was trying to punish Americans or what, but he certainly got us on these back roads. He was a great gent. They were great persons.

Paul Stillwell: Was there much social life connected with your job?

Captain Schwab: Oh, yes. Well, mostly, I'd say, in-house NATO. I'd say two-thirds of it was connected with the U.S. mission, that way. But all the diplomatic missions have a certain amount of representation funds that filter down from the ambassador. So every once in a while you were supposed to throw a reception for your contemporaries in the other missions. For our own mission we'd usually throw it at our apartment or something small, but they don't get any representation for that.

If we had something other than that, we'd throw it at the so-called Army-Navy Club or officers' club in Paris, which is a nice place. I think it had been an SS headquarters under the Germans.[*] It was a nice place, and they had good meals, and they had a room where you could have the big receptions. So we used to have all the people, and you get invited to them, in turn. They always threw very nice things. We found that if you were throwing one of these receptions, and you wanted to talk to Americans that you otherwise hadn't talked to very much, at the table you would have a good roast beef and a jumbo shrimp. So for the first 45 minutes or so, until they were gone, all the Europeans would be eating the roast beef and the jumbo shrimp, and you could talk to the Americans you wanted to talk to. It was very interesting.

It was great, and we got to see a lot of Paris, particularly Paris, probably more than we've seen of any American city we've lived in. Whenever we had the chance, usually on a weekend, we'd start from our house and go out another radial avenue to see

---

[*] Waffen SS was the Nazi Party's "Protective Squadron," which grew into a military force.

what happened to it. We'd find all sorts of interesting things. Of course, we hit every museum known to man. They're changing all the time, of course, just like they do here. They all charge money, too, as opposed to here. Then we toured the whole countryside. We did the Loire Valley at least a couple of times. We would rent this little apartment in a hotel down at Cannes for one month every year. There were all sorts of things; it was really an education.

My wife became super fluent in day-to-day French. She could talk about anybody, understand the television. Whereas I knew professional the professional language. I had six years of French in school, and I could read anything and understand the stuff, the lingo they used at NATO headquarters, but the day-to-day stuff was a little different.

Then we got to travel a lot in Germany and in Italy. Of course, I got over to England quite a few times. My wife was only over there once or twice, and she didn't like it because she didn't understand the language. [Laughter] We got to Berlin once towards the end, and Copenhagen, and then got to go across on a hydrofoil to Malmo, Sweden. That's where my wife's grandfather had been born.

We never got to Göteborg, where my wife's mother's family had been born. It was Betty's father's father who was born in Malmo. They were all Swedes, and all my ancestors were German. The two girls, while we still lived in Paris, with two other girls from the University of Maryland-Munich—the four of them bought a small Volkswagen bus and went all up to Sweden and Norway. The other two had Norwegian ancestors and ours had Swedish. It was a welcome-back-to-Scandinavia year when they went up there.

They wrote in advance and arranged with all the different towns for their youth hostels, things of that sort. They went up there, and en route they stopped in Copenhagen. They almost didn't get out of Copenhagen, because they were having so much fun there. But they finally got up to—I guess in a ferry—Sweden. Every town they went in, why, they were greeted like long-lost relatives. Girl scouts came out to greet them, things of that sort. It was apparently interesting. On their bus they'd painted the name "Willie" on the side, so every place they went they ran into people who recognized "Willie." They said the roads in Sweden were okay. In Norway apparently there were boulders all over the place. They went around the fjords; I never did any of that. That was a pretty good experience for them.

Paul Stillwell: What did your daughters do for education while you were in France?

Captain Schwab: Well, when we got over there, we signed the older one up for the University of Maryland in Munich, so she had that.* She was all signed up to go to college here in the United States, Mary Washington University down in Fredericksburg, Virginia. Anyhow, she decided to go over there instead, so she had two years at the University of Maryland in Munich. And then being good Lutherans—both the girls—we sent for a year down to Loyola University of Chicago in Rome, which was a Jesuit school. Not at the same time. So the older one started college as soon as we got over there, which was a little scary.

We didn't really understand it too much, but the previous year a whole planeload of students from the University of Maryland at Munich, flying back from Munich to Paris, I guess, had crashed and killed all of them. But we didn't know that at that moment, but when we sent the first daughter it was pouring rain. I guess Russ Dougherty was at the Evereux Air Force base. We went out there, and they had one plane for their baggage and one plane for the kids. Pouring. It might not have been Dougherty, but one of the Air Force officers said, "You don't have to worry, we're an all-weather Air Force." Then, when we got back, we found out about the previous crash, which was at Christmas vacation. So she did that, two years there, and then down to Rome.

The other daughter did the two years at Munich also, and then went to the University of Grenoble in '68 to study French.† We told both the girls they had to learn how to do something for the future. If nothing else, they could become teachers, if they didn't want to do anything else. So one of them opted to become an English teacher or qualify for that, and the other one, a French teacher. The one who opted to be an English teacher actually had tenure here as a high school teacher near Chicago. She went to Chicago because of a young man she met when she was in Rome. Ultimately that didn't

---

* Holly Elizabeth Schwab, born 15 December 1946. Holly died 27 June 2014.
† Trudi Sandgren Schwab, born 21 April 1948.

work out, so she came back to Chicago and had a job to sort of facilitate that. Well, she married somebody in Chicago, so she's there now.

Except for one year, the other daughter hasn't lived in the United States since 1964. She did all this, and then she went to Grenoble for a year for the Olympics. Also, she met a young German when she was at Grenoble, thinking he was French, I guess. But, anyhow, they eventually got married. The younger one got married in '71, and the older one in '72. One's in Chicago, and the other's in Munich. And they have a little boy in Europe, and two girls and a boy in Chicago.

Their education was supplemented by these neat tours that they do. The University of Maryland at Munich is unique. They send the kids to Israel and the Middle East—this was before the '67 war—and my wife even went along.* Not too many people went all through the Jerusalem-Jordan business, the Mandelbaum Gate stuff, and all that. So she got to see all that stuff in Lebanon and Beirut before it was war-torn and Cairo before all the mess started there. The only place my wife didn't get to was Turkey. She got every place else. If you're going to educate kids, that's a good way to do it. They're well knowledged.

My son missed out on all that; he probably still resents that. But he graduated from Tufts University in '65 and went on into the Navy and served his time. He became a commander in the Naval Reserve. His eyes were bad, so he went to the Navy Supply Corps. His destroyer was in Standing Force Atlantic for a while. Now he's in Washington. He was a senior economist for southerneastern Europe. Now he's for northern Latin America or something in the Export-Import Bank. He worked for Tim Stanley for a while at the International Economics Policy Association.

You find out, as you go on, that everybody gets related after a while; the intertwining of people is a continuing thing. One of the reasons my son is a supply officer was that he had been accepted, supposedly for the Navy, with the line to go into supply school, whatever that was. Then they changed the requirements; they increased the eye requirements. Well, he and two other young men were told that they were no

---

* The Six-Day War of June 1967 grew out of Egypt's action in closing the Gulf of Aqaba and moving troops into the Sinai Peninsula. Israel initiated the war on 5 June with air attacks on airbases in Syria, Jordan, and Egypt. In the days that followed Israeli forces completely defeated their Arab opponents and occupied the Golan Heights, West Bank of the Jordan River, the Sinai, and the east bank of the Suez Canal.

longer acceptable, but they had what looked to me to be a contract, practically, for X number of years.

So a classmate of mine, Rhythm Moore, George Moore, was by that time a vice admiral in the Naval Material Command.[*] So I called him up and said, "Hey, how about checking on this?" So he called up the Bureau of Supplies and Accounts, or whatever they called it, and they admitted they had made an error, so all three of them got in.[†] But, I mean, if you didn't know that, if you didn't have that kind of connection, why, I guess there are all sorts of justices and injustices occur from people. That's why the influence of a single person on things is tremendous, if you get the right person.

Paul Stillwell: Well, we're right near the end of the tape, so why don't we resume next time?[‡]

---

[*] Vice Admiral George E. Moore II, Supply Corps, USN, served from 1970 to 1973 as Vice Chief of Naval Material.
[†] In a 1966 reorganization the Bureau of Supplies and Accounts had become the Navy Supply Systems Command.
[‡] Sadly, there is no record of a tape for a fifth interview and no transcript.

Launched in 1969, the U.S. Naval Institute's award-winning oral history program is among the oldest in the country. Used in combination with documentary sources, oral histories offer a richer understanding of naval history through candid recollections and explanations rarely entered into contemporary records. In addition, they help depict the atmosphere of a particular event or era in a manner not available in official documents.

The nonprofit Naval Institute accomplishes its history projects through contributed funds and gratefully accepts tax-deductible gifts of all sizes for this purpose. This support allows the Institute to preserve the life experiences of today's service men and women so they may enlighten and inspire future generations.

For information about opportunities to underwrite Naval Institute oral history projects, please contact the Naval Institute Foundation at 291 Wood Road, Annapolis, Maryland 21402; by phone at (410) 295-1054; or by e-mail at foundation@usni.org.

Index to the Oral History of
Captain Ernest L. Schwab, U.S. Navy (Retired)

Acheson, Dean
In the mid-1950s the former Secretary of State delivered a guest lecture at the Fletcher School, 223-224

Air Force, U.S.
Connection in the early 1960s with the RAND Corporation, 273

Akers, Rear Admiral Frank, USN (USNA, 1922)
In the early 1950s served as Assistant Chief of Naval Operations for Undersea Warfare, 191

Alcohol
In the late 1930s-early 1940s junior officers in the battleship *Pennsylvania* (BB-38) received training in controlling alcohol consumption, 40
Ceremonial drinking by U.S. and Chinese naval officers in Taiwan in the mid-1950s, 204

Amphibious Warfare
Practice by the crew of the battleship *Pennsylvania* (BB-38) in the late 1930s-early 1940s, 56-57, 263
In 1962-63 the amphibious command ship *Mount McKinley* (AGC-7) was involved in training and other operations in the Atlantic and Mediterranean, 252-269

Antiair Warfare
Gunnery practice in the late 1930s-early 1940s on board the battleship *Pennsylvania* (BB-38), 45-48
East Coast air-defense exercise early in World War II, 78-79

Antisubmarine Warfare
Pre-World War II U.S. doctrine exaggerated the threat from depth charges, 71
Use of Army bombers for the mission in 1942, 76-77
Early in World War II Coast Guard ships were better than their Navy counterparts in antisubmarine warfare, 87
Japanese efforts against U.S. submarines in World War II, 83, 93, 106-108, 134-139, 141-142, 146
Interview by Representative Andrew May revealed that the Japanese were setting their depth charges too shallow, 83
Operations of SubDevGru 2 in the late 1950s-early 1960s, 172-187
Experimental development work on SOSUS in the late 1940s-early 1950s, 173, 190-201, 269-270
Tactical training in the late 1950s-early 1960s, 202, 244

The destroyer *Wedderburn* (DD-684) escorted aircraft carriers in the Seventh Fleet in the mid-1950s, 216-217

In the early 1960s, as flagship of Carrier Division 20, the *Lake Champlain* (CVS-39) was involved in ASW training and other operations in the Atlantic, 243-252

In the early 1960s the Defense Department and RAND Corporation were doing studies on NATO antisubmarine capabilities, 275-276, 279-280, 283

The Canadian Navy was effective in NATO ASW exercises in the mid-1960s, 286

Army, U.S.
Rangers landed on New Guinea in 1944, 126

Asserson, Captain William C. Jr., USN (USNA, 1926)
In the mid-1950s was professor of naval science for NROTC schools in the Boston area, 225-226

Athletics
U.S. warships fielded sports teams in the late 1930s, 65

Atkinson, Commander George Oliver Jr., USN (USNA, 1942)
Commanded the destroyer *Wedderburn* (DD-684) from 1956 to 1958, 209

Australia
Brisbane was the site of a rest camp for U.S. submariners between patrols in World War II, 115, 130

Rest camp at Surfers Paradise for the crew of the submarine *Darter* (SS-227) in early 1944, 129-130, 144

Rest periods for submariners at Fremantle/Perth during World War II, 144-145, 154-156

Schwab visited several cities while in transit during World War II, 145-146

Aviation Cadets
On board the battleship *Pennsylvania* (BB-38) in the late 1930s-early 1940s, 21, 58

Awards, Naval
To submarines and submariners for service in World War II, 141

Bagby, Lieutenant (junior grade) Oliver W. Jr., USN (USNA, 1938)
Attended Submarine School in 1941, 118-119

Bay of Pigs
In April 1961 the aircraft carrier *Lake Champlain* (CVS-39) had a potential, but not actual, role in the invasion of Cuba, 244

Beach, Captain Edward L., USN (USNA, 1939)
Stood second in the Naval Academy class of 1939, 10-11

Belgium
    In 1966-67 France withdrew from the NATO military organization, with the result that NATO headquarters moved from France to Belgium in October 1967, 284, 288-289

Bell Telephone Company
    In the late 1940s-early 1950s was involved in research and development efforts that led to SOSUS, 173, 191-192, 200

Benitez, Commander Rafael C., USN (USNA, 1939)
    In 1944 was executive officer of the submarine *Dace* (SS-247), 133
    Commanded the submarine *Cochino* (SS-345) at the time of her loss in 1949, 172-173, 177

Benson, Captain Roy S., USN (USNA, 1929)
    Made a training cruise on board a coal-burning ship in the late 1920s, 19
    Taught navigation at the Naval Academy in the late 1930s, 15, 28-29
    Commanded Submarine Development Group Two in 1949-50, 172-180, 190-192

Bergin, Commander Daniel E., USN (USNA, 1942)
    Commanded the destroyer *Kidd* (DD-661) in 1955-56, 201-202, 207, 209

Berlin, Germany
    In the late 1950s-early 1960s the political-military policy division of OpNav handled Berlin issues, 235

Bermuda
    Visited by the amphibious command ship *Mount McKinley* (AGC-7) in the early 1960s, 253, 259-262

Bloch, Admiral Claude C., USN (USNA, 1899)
    Served as Commander in Chief U.S. Fleet, 1938-40, 35, 49

Boston Naval Shipyard
    Repair work on the aircraft carrier *Lake Champlain* (CVS-39) in 1961, 247

Bowers, Lieutenant (junior grade) Richard H., USN (USNA, 1938)
    Served on board the submarine *Guardfish* (SS-217) in World War II, 101, 106

Bowman, Ensign Don C. Jr., USNR
    Served on board the submarine *Guardfish* (SS-217) in World War II, 101-102

Brisbane, Australia
    Site of a rest camp for U.S. submariners between patrols in World War II, 115

Brown, Lieutenant Commander Charles D., USN (USNA, 1938)
Wounded in action during World War II, 143

Brown, Major Wilburt S., USMC (USNA, 1924)
Commanded the Marine detachment on board the battleship *Pennsylvania* (BB-38) in the early 1940s, 55-56

Budgetary Considerations/Issues
For research and development work by the Bureau of Ships in the early 1950s, 191-192

***Bullhead*, USS (SS-332)**
Last U.S. submarine lost in World War II, on 6 August 1945, 154

Bureau of Ordnance, Washington, D.C.
Interaction with the Bureau of Ships in the early 1950s on the development of new weapons, 194-197

Bureau of Ships, Washington, D.C.
In the early 1950s the Underwater Sound Branch did research and development work in sonar, antisubmarine weapons, and electronics, 190-201
Interaction with the Bureau of Ordnance in the early 1950s, 194-197

Burch, Lieutenant Commander Charles A., USN (USNA, 1937)
Long tenure in the battleship *Pennsylvania* (BB-38) during World War II, 69

Burke, Admiral Arleigh A., USN (USNA, 1923)
Long-time advocate of postgraduate education for naval officers, 229-230
Served as Chief of Naval Operations, 1955-61, 230, 234-236, 239

Canadian Navy
A group of net tenders was in the Portsmouth Navy Yard early in World War II, 78-79
Effective in NATO ASW exercises in the mid-1960s, 286

Carrier Division 20
In the early 1960s was involved in ASW training and other operations in the Atlantic, 243-252

Carter, President James E., Jr. (USNA, 1947)
Concern with defense issues during his tenure in office in the late 1970s, 241, 282

Chamoun, President Camille
Served as head of Lebanon when the U.S. Marines landed in July 1958, 230-231, 237-238

China, People's Republic of
Posed a concern for the U.S. Navy in the mid-1950s, 203-205

Civil War
Schwab's great-grandfather was a member of the Union cavalry, 26

Claggett, Commander Bladen D., USN (USNA, 1935)
Served in the submarine *Guardfish* (SS-217) during World War II, 100-101
As best man for Schwab's wedding in April 1943, 119
Executive officer of the submarine *Pargo* (SS-264) in 1943, 120
Commanded the submarine *Dace* (SS-247) in 1943-44, 131-140, 148-149

Cleveland, The Hon. Harlan
Served as U.S. Ambassador to NATO in the late 1960s, 240-242

Clytie, USS (AS-26)
Long journey in 1945 from Australia to New London, 155

Coast Guard, U.S.
Early in World War II its ships were better than their Navy counterparts in antisubmarine warfare, 87

Coast Guard Academy, New London, Connecticut
Cadets made a training cruise to Europe in 1936, 14

Cochino, USS (SS-345)
Involved in ASW experimental work as part of Submarine Development Group Two in the late 1940s-early 1950s, 173-175, 185
Battery explosion, fire, and sinking in 1949, 175, 177, 188

Codebreaking
In World War II codebreaking revealed the locations for potential Japanese targets for U.S. submarines, 113, 151

Cold Weather Operations
North Atlantic deployment for the boats of Submarine Development Group Two in 1949, 173-179

Commercial Aircraft
Used in 1943 for transport of Navy personnel between duty stations, 115-116

Commercial Ships
In 1941 Schwab rode the liner *Matsonia* from Hawaii to California, 37
In World War II, Japanese merchant ships were targets for U.S. submarines, 113-114, 152-153
Operated in the vicinity of China in the mid-1950s, 205

In the summer of 1964 the Schwab family rode the liner *United States* to Europe, 279

Communications
Voice radio was new in the battleship *Pennsylvania* (BB-38) in the early 1940s, 257
Few outgoing radio messages from the submarine *Guardfish* (SS-217) while on patrol during World War II, 105
In World War II codebreaking revealed the locations for potential Japanese targets for U.S. submarines, 113, 151
Lag in message delivery to U.S. submarines in the Pacific in 1944, 131-132, 287
Short-range radio communications between submarines in the Pacific in 1944, 135
For the New London Submarine Base and ComSubLant in the post-World War II period, 157-160
Londonderry, Northern Ireland, had a U.S. naval communication station in the late 1940s-early 1950s, 178-179
Sophisticated capability on board the amphibious command ship *Mount McKinley* (AGC-7) in the early 1960s, 252-255, 258
Navy-Air Force problems communicating during the U.S. resupply of Israel in 1973, 287

Congress, U.S.
Application process for the Naval Academy in the early 1930s, 2, 6-9
Interview by Representative Andrew May revealed that the Japanese were setting their depth charges too shallow, 83

Cooke, Captain Charles M. Jr., USN (USNA, 1910)
Commanded the battleship *Pennsylvania* (BB-38) in 1941-42, 36, 70, 257, 264

Corsair, USS (SS-435)
Involved in ASW experimental work as part of Submarine Development Group Two in the late 1940s-early 1950s, 173-174, 187

Cromwell, Captain John P., USN (USNA, 1924)
As Commander Submarine Division 32, sacrificed his life to keep information about upcoming U.S. sub operations from the Japanese in November 1943, 112-113

Crowe, John H., USN (USNA, 1939)
As a midshipman made a training cruise in 1936, liberty in Sweden, 12-13

Cuba
In April 1961 the aircraft carrier *Lake Champlain* (CVS-39) had a potential, but not actual, role in the invasion of Cuba at the Bay of Pigs, 244
Role of the amphibious command ship *Mount McKinley* (AGC-7) and her embarked admiral during the October 1962 missile crisis, 254-255, 266-268

Cuban Missile Crisis
Role of the amphibious command ship *Mount McKinley* (AGC-7) and her embarked admiral during the October 1962 event, 254-255, 266-268

Curaçao
Island in the Caribbean Sea visited by the aircraft carrier *Lake Champlain* (CVS-39) in the early 1960s, 248

Cutts, Captain Elwin F., USN (USNA, 1908)
Commanded the battleship *Pennsylvania* (BB-38) from 1939 to 1941, 36, 39-40, 70, 264
From 1941 to 1944 commanded the Submarine School at New London, 39

Dace, USS (SS-247)
Operations during World War II, 112-113, 132-140
Role during the Battle of Leyte Gulf in October 1944, 132-140, 149

Damage Control
Readiness preparations on board the battleship *Pennsylvania* (BB-38) in the early 1940s, 43-44, 53

Darter, USS (SS-227)
Commissioned in September 1943, subsequent Atlantic operations, 115, 123
Operations in the Pacific during World War II, 112-113, 125-141, 145-146
Role during the Battle of Leyte Gulf, including going aground in October 1944, 132-141, 149, 287-288
Gambling on board in 1943-44, 124
Enlisted personnel during World War II, 125-126, 140-141, 265
Reunion of former crew members in the 1980s, 265

Davidson, Lieutenant John F., USN (USNA, 1929)
Served as the first commanding officer of the submarine *Mackerel* (SS-204) in 1941-42, 74, 82, 85

Defense Department
Webb-Lovett agreement in the early 1950s on sharing information with the State Department, 234-235
Handled Berlin issues in the late 1950s-early 1960s, 235
Work of OSD (International Security Affairs) in 1963-64 in doing capability studies as part of NATO strategy and planning, 271-278

De Gaulle, General Charles
Relationship with NATO in the late 1950s-early 1960s, 236
In 1966-67 withdrew France from the NATO military organization, with the result that NATO headquarters moved from France to Belgium in October 1967, 284

Denmark
> Was among the countries visited by the Schwab family as it explored Europe in the late 1960s, 296

Depth Charges
> Interview by Representative Andrew May revealed that the Japanese were setting their depth charges too shallow, 83
> Used against the submarine *Guardfish* (SS-217) in World War II, 141-142

Disciplinary Cases
> On board the destroyer *Wedderburn* (DD-684) in the mid-1950s, 215-216

Dominican Republic
> Visited by the amphibious command ship *Mount McKinley* (AGC-7) in the early 1960s, 262

Earle, Ralph II
> In 1968-69 was Principal Deputy Assistant Secretary of Defense (International Security Affairs), 276

East, Lieutenant (junior grade) Walter J., USN (USNA, 1935)
> Served on the CinCUS staff in 1941, 54

Eccles, Rear Admiral Henry E., USN (Ret.) (USNA, 1922)
> For many years taught logistics at the Naval War College, 165-166, 169

Eckert, Philip F., USN (USNA, 1940)
> Commanded the submarine *Halfbeak* (SS-352) in the early 1950s, 179-181, 184

Eisenhower, President Dwight D. (USMA, 1915)
> Role in international relations as President in the late 1950s-early 1960s, 237

Electric Boat Company, Groton, Connecticut
> Built the submarine *Mackerel* (SS-217), which was commissioned in 1941, 77
> Built the submarine *Guardfish* (SS-217), which was commissioned in 1942, 91

Eleuthera Island, British West Indies
> Site of early 1950s experiments that led to the development of SOSUS, 191, 200

Ellsworth, The Hon. Robert F.
> Served as U.S. Ambassador to NATO from 1969 to 1971, 291-292

English, Rear Admiral Robert H., USN (USNA, 1911)
> Served as Commander Submarine Force Pacific Fleet until killed in an airplane crash in January 1943, 83, 96-97

Enlisted Personnel
   On board the training ship *Wyoming* (AG-17) in 1936, 16-18, 20
   In the battleship *Pennsylvania* (BB-38) in the late 1930s-early 1940s, 20-21, 49-51, 59-60, 64
   In the crew of the submarine *Guardfish* (SS-217) during World War II, 104-106, 141-142
   In the crew of the submarine *Darter* (SS-227) during World War II, 125-126, 140-141, 265
   In the crew of submarine *Toro* (SS-422), 1949-51, 188-189
   In the crew of the destroyer *Wedderburn* (DD-684) in the mid-1950s, 202, 210-212, 215
   In the amphibious command ship *Mount McKinley* (AGC-7) in the early 1960s, 259-260, 263-265

Espionage
   In the 1960s French and Turkish officers assigned to the NATO staff passed on intelligence to potential enemies, 289-291

Fenno, Captain Commander Frank W. Jr., USN (USNA, 1925)
   Served in the late 1940s as commanding officer of the New London Submarine Base, 161

Fife, Rear Admiral James Jr., USN (USNA, 1918)
   While serving as ComSubLant in the late 1940s, there was a fire in his quarters at the New London Submarine Base, 161-162

Finletter, The Hon. Thomas K.
   Served as U.S. Ambassador to NATO in the early 1960s, 240-241, 273, 276-277

Fire Control
   In the battleship *Pennsylvania* (BB-38) in the late 1930s-early 1940s, 45-48

Fires
   One at the New London Submarine Base in the late 1940s was arson, 161-162
   The submarine *Cochino* (SS-345) suffered a battery explosion, fire, and sinking in 1949, 175, 177, 188

Fletcher School of Law and Diplomacy, Tufts University, Medford, Massachusetts
   Curriculum for naval officers' postgraduate education in international affairs, 1956-58, 219-230

***Florida*, USS (BB-30)**
   Furniture from the ship wound up on board the battleship *Pennsylvania* (BB-38) in the early 1930s, 43

Food

Shortages in Great Britain in the years shortly after World War II, 186-187

In 1951 the submarine *Toro* (SS-422) tested pre-packaged food during a North Atlantic deployment, 179-183

Excellent Kobe beef served to U.S. Navy men on liberty in Japan in the mid-1950s, 214-215

France

Midshipmen on liberty in the late 1930s visited Paris, 16

In the early and mid-1960s, Paris was the headquarters of NATO, 276-270, 283

In 1966-67 withdrew from the NATO military organization, with the result that NATO headquarters moved from France to Belgium in October 1967, 284, 288

In the 1960s a French NATO officer was passing information to the Rumanians, 289

Paris was a useful base as the Schwab family explored Europe in the late 1960s, 292-297

Frash, Second Lieutenant William M, USMC

Served in the battleship *Pennsylvania* (BB-38) in the late 1930s, 62

Fremantle/Perth, Australia

Site of rest periods for submariners during World War II, 144-145, 154-156

French Navy

Cooperation with a NATO ASW study in the mid-1960s, 283

Friedrick, Lieutenant Commander Ernest S., USN (USNA, 1937)

Commanded the submarine *Capitaine* (SS-336), 1945-48, 151

Furlong, Ensign Donald, USN (USNA, 1939)

Served in the battleship *Pennsylvania* (BB-38) after graduation from the Naval Academy, 38, 61-62

Gambling

On board the submarine *Darter* (SS-227) in 1943-44, 124

Gas Warfare

Preparations on board the battleship *Pennsylvania* (BB-38) in the late 1930s-early 1940s to defend against poison gas, 42-43

Gebhardt, Lieutenant Charles R., USN (USNA, 1938)

Served as first executive officer of the submarine *Darter* (SS-227), commissioned in 1943, 123

Germany

Schwab's ancestors originated in Germany, 26-28

In the late 1950s-early 1960s the political-military policy division of OpNav handled Berlin issues, 235
Concern about shifts in NATO nuclear weapons strategy in the early 1960s, 273
Was among the countries visited by the Schwab family as it explored Europe in the late 1960s, 296-298

Gimber, Commander Stephen H., USN (USNA, 1934)
Served in the early 1950s as head of the Underwater Sound Branch in the Bureau of Ships, 190

Göteborg, Sweden
Visited by the training ship *Wyoming* (AG-17) in 1936, 12-13

Great Britain
Boats of Submarine Development Group Two visited Portsmouth, England, in 1949 and 1951, 176-177, 180-181
The submarine *Toro* (SS-422) visited Rosyth, Scotland, in 1949, 186-187
Food shortages in the years shortly after World War II, 186-187
In 1958 dispatched troop carriers to Jordan, 231-232, 237-238

Greece
Visited by the amphibious command ship *Mount McKinley* (AGC-7) in the early 1960s, 252, 255-256, 263

Grouleff, Lieutenant Paul H., USN (USNA, 1932)
In early 1942 was acting commanding officer of the submarine *Marlin* (SS-205), 75-77

Groundings
The submarine *Darter* (SS-227) ran aground on Bombay Shoal in October 1944, 134-140

Guardfish, USS (SS-217)
Pre-commissioning period at Electric Boat Company, 88-92
World War II operations, 92-115
Gunnery against Japanese surface targets, 94
Through-the-periscope photos of sinking Japanese ships in World War II, 94-95
Enlisted crew members, 104-106, 141-142
Reliable Fairbanks Morse diesel engines, 111

Gudgeon, USS (SS-211)
World War II patrols under skipper William Shirley Stovall, 125

Gunnery-Naval
Practice by the battleship *Pennsylvania* (BB-38) in the late 1930s-early 1940s, 45-48, 55

Firing by the submarine *Guardfish* (SS-217) against Japanese surface targets in World War II, 94, 142

U.S. warships fired at the submarine *Darter* (SS-227) after she ran aground on Bombay Shoal in October 1944, 138

Firing by the submarine *Razorback* (SS-394) in World War II, 143

Habitability
On board the submarine *Marlin* (SS-205) during World War II, 87-88

Haig, Colonel Alexander M. Jr., USA (USMA, 1947)
Studied at Harvard in the 1950s, later was an assistant to Dr. Henry Kissinger, 225-226

***Halfbeak*, USS (SS-352)**
Involved in ASW experimental work as part of Submarine Development Group Two in the late 1940s-early 1950s, 179-182, 185
Tested food during a North Atlantic deployment in 1951, 179-182
Visited Portsmouth, England, in early 1951, 181-182

Halsey, Admiral William F. Jr., USN (USNA, 1904)
In 1944, when he was Commander South Pacific Force, he and his staff took a rest period in Australia, 129-130
Command decisions during the Battle of Leyte Gulf in October 1944, 287-288

Hardart, Lieutenant Evelyn, USNR
Served in communications at the New London Submarine Base in World War II and shortly after, 157-158

Harllee, Captain John, USN (USNA, 1934)
Commanded Destroyer Division 152 in 1955-56, 206-207, 211

Hart, Admiral Thomas C., USN (USNA, 1897)
At his behest the U.S. Navy built two small submarines before World War II, 74, 82

Harvard University, Cambridge, Massachusetts
In the mid-1950s Schwab took courses at Harvard as part of his post-grad work at the Fletcher School, 224-227

Hawaii
Site of liberty for Navy men, 1940-41, 37-41, 53
In 1941 Army and Navy personnel frequented prostitutes in Honolulu, 37-39
Submariners stayed at the Royal Hawaiian Hotel between patrols in World War II, 143-144

Hingson, Lieutenant James M., USN (USNA, 1939)
    Served in the battleship *Pennsylvania* (BB-38) after graduation from the Naval Academy and later in submarines, 40, 116-117

Hogaboom, First Lieutenant William F., USMC (USNA, 1939)
    As a Naval Academy midshipman in the late 1930s, 9
    Prisoner of war who died in the Philippines in 1944, 9, 158-160

Holloway, Admiral James L. Jr., USN (USNA, 1919)
    As CinCSpecComME was overall commander of the U.S. landings in Lebanon in July 1958, 231-232, 237-238

Holt, Lieutenant Commander Edward R. Jr., USN (USNA, 1939)
    Skipper of the *Bullhead* (SS-332), last U.S. submarine lost in World War II, August 1945, 154

Honolulu, Hawaii
    Site of liberty for Navy men, 1940-41, 37-41, 53
    In 1941 Army and Navy personnel frequented prostitutes, 37-39
    Submariners stayed at the Royal Hawaiian Hotel between patrols in World War II, 143-144

Intelligence
    In World War II codebreaking revealed the locations for potential Japanese targets for U.S. submarines, 113, 151
    In the 1960s French and Turkish officers assigned to the NATO staff passed on intelligence to potential enemies, 289-291

Ireland
    Londonderry had a U.S. naval communication station in the late 1940s-early 1950s, 178-179
    Visited in 1949 by the submarine *Toro* (SS-422), 186-187

Israel
    Did not interfere in 1958 when Britain sent troop carriers to Jordan, 232-233, 237-238
    Navy-Air Force problems communicating during the U.S. resupply of Israel in 1973, 287

Japan
    In 1940-41 a Japanese businessman in Hawaii invited junior U.S. naval officers for dinner, 52-53
    World War II U.S. submarine operations in the vicinity of the home islands, 93, 97-98, 107, 114
    The destroyers *Wedderburn* (DD-684) and *Kidd* (DD-661) visited the country in the mid-1950s, 203, 205-207, 213-214

Japanese Maritime Self-Defense Force
    In the mid-1950s Schwab met a self-defense force officer who had been a World War II submariner, 206

Japanese Navy
    Efforts against U.S. submarines in World War II, 83, 93, 106-108
    Lost cruisers to submarine attacks during the Battle of Leyte Gulf in October 1944, 133-134
    In the mid-1950s Schwab met a self-defense force officer who had been a World War II submariner, 206

Jarvis, Lieutenant Commander Benjamin C., USN (USNA, 1939)
    Served as executive officer of the submarine *Nautilus* SS-168) in 1944, 140

Johnson, Louis A.
    Budget-cutting while Secretary of Defense in 1949-50, 167

Jordan
    In 1958 Britain dispatched troop carriers to Jordan, 231-232, 237-238

Katzenbach, Edward L.
    Marine Reserve officer who taught at Harvard in the mid-1950s, 224-226

Kaufman, Lieutenant (junior grade) Robert Y., USN (USNA, 1946)
    Served on board the submarine *Toro* (SS-422) in the late 1940s-early 1950s, 177, 182, 185

Kennedy, President John F.
    Events in the spring of 1961 included the Bay of Pigs operation and a trip to Europe, 244-245
    Role during the Cuban Missile Crisis in 1962, 254-255, 266-268
    Assassination of in November 1963, 282

Kidd, Admiral Isaac C. Jr., USN (USNA, 1942)
    Interest in antisubmarine warfare while commanding the Atlantic Fleet in the 1970s, 249-250

***Kidd*, USS (DD-661)**
    Operations in the Pacific in the mid-1950s, 201-202, 207, 209

Kimmel, Admiral Husband E., USN (USNA, 1904)
    Served as Commander in Chief U.S. Fleet during part of 1941, 35, 49, 53-54

Kissinger, Dr. Henry A.
    Taught at Harvard in the 1950s, 225

In the late 1960s-early 1970s was national security advisor to President Richard Nixon, 291

Klakring, Lieutenant Commander Thomas Burton, USN (USNA, 1927)
Commanded the submarine *Guardfish* (SS-217) in 1942-43, 84-85, 88-89, 92-100, 102-103, 106-109, 141, 264
Commanded a submarine wolf pack late in World War II, 112

Klein, Burton H.
Eccentric RAND Corporation economist who was assigned to NATO headquarters in Paris in the mid-1960s, 273, 276-278

Kobe, Japan
Visited in the mid-1950s by U.S. Navy ship crews on liberty, 214-215

Kossler, Lieutenant Commander Herman J., USN (USNA, 1934)
In 1942-43 served as executive officer of the submarine *Guardfish* (SS-217), 99-100, 107, 141

Kotschevar, Lieutenant Commander Lendal Henry, Supply Corps, USNR
Supervised in 1951 as the submarine *Toro* (SS-422) tested pre-packaged food during a North Atlantic deployment, 179-183

Lake Champlain, USS (CV-39/CVS-39)
In the early 1960s served as flagship of Commander Carrier Division 20, 243-252
Recovered astronaut Alan Shepard after his space flight in 1961, 245
Hosted a visit from President Anastasio Somoza in 1961, 246
At the Boston Naval Shipyard in 1961, 247

Leahy, Admiral William D., USN (USNA, 1897)
As Chief of Naval Operations made the graduation speech at the Naval Academy in 1939, 35

Leave and Liberty
For midshipmen on training cruise to Europe in 1936, 12-13
In the Long Beach/Los Angeles, California, area in 1939-40, 60-63
In Honolulu, Hawaii, during the 1940s for Army and Navy personnel, 37-38, 41, 52-53, 143-144
Brisbane, Australia, was the site of a rest camp for U.S. submariners between patrols in World War II, 115, 130
In 1944 submariners and Admiral William F. Halsey took rest periods at Surfers Paradise, Australia, 129-130, 144
Rest periods for submariners at Fremantle/Perth, Australia, during World War II, 144-145, 154-156
The Schwabs made an enjoyable visit to New York City after a submarine food test in 1951, 183

In Japan in the mid-1950s, 206-207
Beach party in Greece in the early 1960s for the crew of the amphibious command ship *Mount McKinley* (AGC-7), 256

Lebanon
Landings by U.S. Marines in July 1958, 230-231, 237-238

Lee, Rear Admiral John M., USN (USNA, 1935)
In the early 1960s served as in the office of the Assistant Secretary of Defense (International Security Affairs), 271, 275

Leyte Gulf, Battle of
Role of the submarine *Darter* (SS-227), including sinking a Japanese cruiser and going aground, in October 1944, 131-141
Communication problems between the Third Fleet and Seventh Fleet during the battle, 287-288

Lindsay, Representative George W. (Democrat-New York)
Appointed Schwab to the Naval Academy in the early 1930s, 6-7

Linke, Commander Gerald D., USN (USN, 1921)
Served in the late 1930s-early 1950s as gunnery officer of the battleship *Pennsylvania* (BB-38), 40-41
In 1943 ran into former shipmates in New Caledonia, 117

Logistics
Emphasized in the curriculum at the Naval War College in the late 1940s, 164-170

Londonderry, Northern Ireland
Had a U.S. naval communication station in the late 1940s-early 1950s, 178-179
Visited in 1949 by the submarine *Toro* (SS-422), 186-187

Long Beach, California
Homeport of the battleship *Pennsylvania* (BB-38) in 1939-40, 34, 56-63

Lovett, Robert A.
Part of the Webb-Lovett agreement in the early 1950s on sharing information between the Defense and State departments, 234-235

Lynch, Commander Richard B. "Ozzie," USN (USNA, 1935)
Served on the staff of Commander Submarine Development Group Two in the late 1940s-early 1950s, 173, 192

***Mackerel*, USS (SS-204)**
Commissioning in 1941 and early operations in the Atlantic, 74
Served as a school ship in New London during World War II, 87

Marcy, Commander Lincoln, USN (USNA, 1939)
  Commanded the submarine *Corsair* (SS-345) in 1949-50, 173-174, 178, 187

Marine Corps, U.S.
  Detachment on board the battleship *Pennsylvania* (BB-38) in the late 1930s-early 1940s, 55-56
  First Lieutenant William F. Hogaboom was a prisoner of war who died in the Philippines in 1944, 9, 158-160
  Landings in Lebanon in July 1958, 230-231, 237-238
  Marines embarked in the amphibious command ship *Mount McKinley* (AGC-7) during the Cuban Missile Crisis in 1962, 267-268

Marlin, **USS (SS-205)**
  Commissioning in 1941 and early operations in the Atlantic, 74-79, 81-82, 86-87, 119-120
  Diesel engines, 75
  Served as a school ship in New London during World War II, 87
  Living conditions for the crew, 87-88

Marshall, Andrew W.
  Long-time director of the Defense Department's Office of Net Assessment served NATO headquarters in the mid-1960s, 276, 279-281

Martin, John Barlow
  Served 1962-64 as U.S. ambassador to the Dominican Republic, 262

Mason, Francis Van Wyck
  Historical novelist who in the early 1960s exchanged visits with Schwab in Bermuda, 261

Matsonia, **SS (Passenger Liner)**
  Ship in which Schwab rode from Hawaii to California in 1941, 37

McCain, Captain John S. Jr., USN (USNA, 1931)
  Commanded the submarine *O-8* (SS-69) in 1941-42, 72
  Served 1950-53 as Director of Undersea Research and Development in OpNav, 191, 193, 200, 269-270

McClintock, Commander David H., USN (USNA, 1935)
  Married Kirby Patterson, the daughter of an officer stationed at the Naval Academy, 148-149
  Commanded the submarine *Darter* (SS-227) in 1944, 130-140, 148, 264

McClintock, Robert
  U.S. ambassador to Lebanon during Marine landings in 1958, 231-232

McCrea, Vice Admiral John L., USN (USNA, 1915)
Served as executive officer of the battleship *Pennsylvania* (BB-38), 1938-40, 45, 70, 264

McNamara, Robert S.
Role in U.S. nuclear strategy in the early 1960s, 272-274

McNitt, Captain Robert W., USN (USNA, 1938)
Commanded the Atlantic Fleet Tactical Anti-Submarine Warfare School, 1959-61, 202, 244

Medical Problems
Broken nose for Schwab in the summer of 1936, 12-13
Heavy seas caused seasickness on board the training ship *Wyoming* (AG-17) in 1936, 17
Schwab got a broken tooth repaired on board the submarine tender *Clytie* (AS-26) in 1945, 156-157

Midway Island
Site of rest camp for submariners between patrols in World War II, 143

Miers, Commander Anthony C. C., Royal Navy
British naval officer who spent time on board the U.S. submarine *Darter* (SS-227) in 1944, 126-128

Military Academy, West Point, New York
Instructors in the late 1930s, 29
Use of the honor code in the late 1930s, 31

Moore, Vice Admiral George E. II, Supply Corps, USN (USNA, 1939)
Served on board the battleship *Pennsylvania* (BB-38) in 1941, 38, 65
Served 1970-73 as Vice Chief Naval Material, 299

Moore, Lieutenant Commander Raymond A., USN (USNA, 1938)
An injury in early 1945 kept him from becoming executive officer of the submarine *Capitaine* (SS-336), 151

Morton, Commander Dudley W., USN (USNA, 1930)
Commanded the submarine *Wahoo* (SS-238) in World War II, 85, 108-109

***Mount McKinley*, USS (AGC-7)**
In 1962-63 was involved in amphibious warfare training and other operations in the Atlantic, 252-269
Sophisticated communications capability in the early 1960s, 252-255, 258
Ship handling, 259
Enlisted crew in the early 1960s, 259-260, 263-265

Material condition in the early 1960s, 265-266

Movies
Provided recreation for the officers and crew of the submarine *Guardfish* (SS-217) in World War II, 103-104

Murray, Captain Stuart S., USN (USNA, 1919)
Interceded on behalf of two fellow submariners while in New Caledonia in 1943, 117

Nace, Rear Admiral Charles D., USN (USNA, 1939)
Friend of Schwab as a Naval Academy midshipman in the late 1930s, 10

Nautilus, **USS (SS-168)**
Fired her 6-inch guns at the grounded submarine *Darter* (SS-227) in 1944, 140

Naval Academy, Annapolis, Maryland
Application process for Schwab in the early 1930s, 2, 6-9
Plebe summer in 1935, 8-10
Summer cruises in 1936 and 1938, 11-19
Off-duty pursuits for midshipmen in the late 1930s, 22-23
Black personnel cleaned the rooms of upper-class midshipmen, 23-24
Midshipmen-written magazine *The Log* in the late 1930s, 24-25, 31
Academics in the late 1930s, 28-30
No formal honor code in the late 1930s, 31-32
Competition among classmates in the late 1930s, 32-33
Athletics in the late 1930s, 33

Naval On-Call Force Mediterranean
In the mid-1960s was established under the aegis of NATO, 284-285

Naval Reserve, U.S.
Reserve officers in the crew of the submarine *Guardfish* (SS-217) in World War II, 101-102

Naval War College, Newport, Rhode Island
In 1948-49 the senior course emphasized logistics and war-gaming, 164-172

Navigation
In early 1942 the submarine *Marlin* (SS-205) made it from the Virgin Islands to New London without a working compass, 76-77
Of the submarine *Guardfish* (SS-217) in World War II, 107
The submarine *Darter* (SS-227) ran aground on Bombay Shoal in October 1944, 134-141, 147
Quality of charts supplied to submarines in the Pacific in World War II, 140-141, 146-148

Netherlands Navy
    A Dutch submarine was in the East Indies in 1945, long after leaving the homeland, 154-155

New Caledonia
    Noumea was used as a base for U.S. Navy operations in World War II, 116

New London, Connecticut, Submarine Base
    Submarine School in 1941, 68-74, 80, 84-85, 91
    Homeport for the submarine *Marlin* (SS-205) in 1941-42, 74-77
    Site of Schwab's courtship and marriage in the early 1940s, 118-121
    Communications in the immediate post-World War II period, 157-160
    Homeport for the submarine *Toro* (SS-422), 1949-51, 189-190
    Housing for submarine skippers in the early 1950s, 184

News Media
    In 1943 *Life* magazine published a lengthy article on the wartime exploits of the submarine Guardfish (SS-217), 92, 94, 114-115
    On board the amphibious command ship *Mount McKinley* (AGC-7) during the Cuban Missile Crisis in 1962, 267

***New York*, USS (BB-34)**
    Midshipman training cruises to Europe in 1936 and 1938, 13-19
    Broken propeller shaft in 1938, 14-15

New York City
    Site of part of the Schwabs' honeymoon in April 1943, 121-122
    The Schwabs made an enjoyable visit to the city after a submarine food test in 1951, 183

Nicodemus, Commander Gordon K. Jr., USN
    Relieved Schwab of command of the submarine *Toro* (SS-422) in 1951 and bought his house, 184

North Atlantic Treaty Organization (NATO)
    In 1949 President Harry Truman passed out silver dollars to celebrate the founding of NATO, 223
    Handled Berlin issues in the late 1950s-early 1960s, 235
    Relations with France in the 1960s, 236
    Work of the Office of the Secretary of Defense (International Security Affairs) in 1963-64 in doing capability studies as part of NATO strategy and planning, 271-278
    Plans and studies at NATO headquarters in the mid and late 1960s, 240-243, 281-299
    In the mid-1960s the Standing Naval Force Atlantic and Naval On-Call Force Mediterranean were established under the aegis of NATO, 284-286

In the 1960s French and Turkish officers assigned to the NATO staff passed on intelligence to potential enemies, 289-291

Norway
Not alerted about the presence of U.S. submarines in Norwegian waters in the summer of 1949, 177-178
Was among the countries visited by the Schwab family as it explored Europe in the late 1960s, 296-297

Noumea, New Caledonia
Used as a base for U.S. Navy operations in World War II, 116

Nuclear Weapons
U.S. and NATO doctrine on weapons use changed in the early 1960s, 272-274, 281, 290

***O-8*, USS (SS-69)**
Used for training at Submarine School in 1941, 72

***O-9*, USS (SS-70)**
Lost with all hands in June 1941, 71-74

OpNav
Role of the political-military policy division organization from 1958 to 1960, 230-243

Ostroski, Ensign Allyn B., USN (USNA, 1939)
Served in the battleship *Pennsylvania* (BB-38) after graduation from the Naval Academy, 21, 61

Panama Canal
The United States sometimes slowed movement of Soviet bloc ships in the late 1950s-early 1960s, 235-236

Paris, France
Visited by midshipmen on liberty in the late 1930s, 16
In the early and mid-1960s, Paris was the headquarters of NATO, 276-289
Paris was a useful base as the Schwab family explored Europe in the late 1960s, 292-297

Parks, Captain Lewis S., USN (USNA (1925)
Shortly after World War II served as executive officer of the New London Submarine Base, 160

Passler, Lieutenant (junior grade) William T., USN
Served in the crew of the submarine *Darter* (SS-227), 1943-44, 124

Pay and Allowances
    Meager pay for Naval Academy midshipmen in the late 1930s, 23-24
    For ensigns on board the battleship *Pennsylvania* (BB-38) in the late 1930s-early 1940s, 55-56, 61
    Extra pay for submariners in the 1940s, 70

Pearl Harbor, Hawaii, Naval Base/Naval Station
    The battleship *Pennsylvania* (BB-38) was based there in 1940-41, 34, 37-39, 41-42, 51-54, 69-70
    Tests of security readiness at Pearl Harbor in 1940-41, 51-52

***Pennsylvania*, USS (BB-38)**
    Pacific operations in the late 1930s-early 1940s, 19-20, 45-48, 55, 65-70, 263
    Enlisted crewmen in the late 1930s-early 1940s, 20-21, 49-51, 59-60, 64
    Officers in the late 1930s-early 1940s, 20-22, 38-41, 45, 49-65
    Aviation cadets in the late 1930s-early 1940s, 21
    Officers still had old-fashioned formal uniforms in the late 1930s-early 1940s, 34
    Served as flagship if the U.S. Fleet in the in the late 1930s-early 1940s, 35, 41-42, 49, 53-54
    Gunnery in the late 1930s-early 1940s, 35
    Junior officers made social calls on their seniors, 39-40
    Readiness preparations after war started in Europe in 1939, 42-44
    Gunnery in the late 1930s-early 1940s, 45-48, 55
    In-port watch standing, 49-51
    Marine detachment in the late 1930s-early 1940s, 55-57
    Amphibious warfare practice by the crew in the late 1930s-early 1940s, 56-57
    SOC biplanes provided spotting and scouting, 57-58
    Ship's newspaper, *The Keystone*, in the late 1930s-early 1940s, 63-64
    Yard period in Bremerton, Washington, in late 1939, 67-68
    Communications capability in the early 1940s, 257

Philippine Islands
    Role of the submarine *Darter* (SS-227), including going aground during the Battle of Leyte Gulf, in October 1944, 131-141
    In 1945, near the end of World War II, the submarine *Capitaine* (SS-336) dropped off rescued Japanese mariners at Subic Bay, 153
    American prisoners of war held in the Philippines during World War II, 158-160

Photography
    Through-the-periscope photos of sinking Japanese ships taken from the submarine *Guardfish* (SS-217) in World War II, 94-95

Pirie, Vice Admiral Robert B., USN (USNA, 1926)
    Concern about threat to British planes flying to Jordan in 1958, 231-232, 237-238

Planning
    Work of the Office of the Secretary of Defense (International Security Affairs) in 1963-64 in doing capability studies as part of NATO strategy and planning, 271-278

Portsmouth, England
    Boats of Submarine Development Group Two visited in 1949 and 1951, 176-177, 180-182

Portsmouth Navy Yard, Kittery, Maine
    Built the small submarine *Marlin* (SS-205), which was commissioned in 1941, 77-78

Powell, Ensign Lucien C. Jr., USN (USNA, 1939)
    Played football at the Naval Academy and on board his first ship, the battleship *Pennsylvania* (BB-38), 65

Price, Lieutenant (junior grade) Walter H. Jr., USN (USNA, 1942)
    Served in the crew of the submarine *Darter* (SS-227), 1943-44, 123

Prisoners of War
    During World War II the Japanese tortured U.S. submariners, 112
    Americans held in the Philippines during World War II, 158-159
    In 1945 the submarine *Capitaine* (SS-336) rescued Japanese survivors in the Pacific, 152-153

Promotion of Naval Officers
    As soon as World War II started in December 1941, members of the Naval Academy class of 1939 received quick promotions to lieutenant (junior grade), 79
    In the late 1940s promotion exams were still used, 168

Propulsion Plants
    Diesel engines in the submarine *Marlin* (SS-205), commissioned in 1941, 75
    Reliable Fairbanks Morse diesel engines in the submarine *Guardfish* (SS-217) in World War II, 111
    Propulsion plant problems destroyer *Wedderburn* (DD-684) in the mid-1950s, 209-210

Prostitution
    Army and Navy personnel were often customers in Honolulu, Hawaii, in 1941, 37-39

***Queenfish*, USS (SS-393)**
    During World War II sank Japanese ships with U.S. prisoners on board, 159

Radar
    New in the battleship *Pennsylvania* (BB-38) in the early 1940s, 257
    Use of in the submarine *Guardfish* (SS-217) in World War II, 98, 106-107, 134-135
    Use of in the submarine *Darter* (SS-227) in World War II, 147

On board the submarine *Capitaine* (SS-336) in 1945-46, 151-152

Radio
Voice radio was new in the battleship *Pennsylvania* (BB-38) in the early 1940s, 257
Few outgoing messages from the submarine *Guardfish* (SS-217) while on patrol during World War II, 105
Lag in message delivery to U.S. submarines in the Pacific in 1944, 131-132
Short-range communications between submarines in the Pacific in 1944, 135
Sophisticated capability on board the amphibious command ship *Mount McKinley* (AGC-7) in the early 1960s, 252-255, 258

RAND Corporation
Role in the early 1960s in NATO planning and strategy, 271-277
Studies in the late 1970s, during the Carter administration, 282

Raw, Rear Admiral Sydney M., Royal Navy
Served as Flag Officer (Submarines) at Portsmouth, England, 1950-52, 181

Reedy, Rear Admiral James R., USN (USNA, 1933)
In the early 1960s commanded Carrier Division 20, 243, 245, 249, 251-252

Refueling at Sea
The destroyer *Wedderburn* (DD-684) refueled from oilers during Western Pacific deployments in the mid-1950s, 217-218

Research and Development
By the Bureau of Ships in the early 1950s, 190-201, 269-270

Richardson, Admiral James O., USN (USNA, 1902)
Served as Commander in Chief U.S. Fleet, 1940-41, 35, 41, 49, 53-54

Ricketts, Admiral Claude V., USN (USNA, 1929)
Prior to his death in 1964, he pushed for multi-national naval forces within NATO, 285

Rivero, Vice Admiral Horacio Jr., USN (USNA, 1931)
Served as Commander Amphibious Force Atlantic Fleet during the Cuban Missile Crisis of 1962, 254-255, 266-267
Ambassador to Spain, 1972-74, 266

Rohrback, Ensign Gilson H., USNR
Served on board the submarine *Guardfish* (SS-217) in World War II, 101-102

Roosevelt, President Theodore
Was a prolific author in addition to his other achievements, 226-227

Rosyth, Scotland
  The submarine *Toro* (SS-422) visited in 1949, 186

Rowen, Henry S.
  In the early 1960s served as Deputy Assistant Secretary of Defense (Planning and NSC), 271

Royal Navy
  Exploits of Commander Anthony C. C. Miers during submarine operations in World War II, 126-128
  Submariners in England, Scotland, and Ireland in 1949, 176-177, 186-187

Rubenstein, Al
  Worked in the underwater sound branch of the Bureau of Ships in the early 1950s, 240

Rudden, Rear Admiral Thomas J. Jr., USN (USNA, 1939)
  Friend of Schwab as a Naval Academy midshipman in the late 1930s, 10

Rumania
  In the 1960s received NATO intelligence from a French worker on the NATO staff, 290-291

Ryan, Midshipman Albert F. Jr., USN (USNA, 1933)
  In the early 1930s helped prepare Schwab for the Naval Academy, 1, 8, 27

SOC Seagull
  Provided spotting and scouting for the battleship *Pennsylvania* (BB-38) in the late 1930s-early 1940s, 57-58

Sailing
  Schwab and his wife had a misadventure while sailing in Bermuda in the early 1960s, 259-260

Sandgren, Commander Charles E., Supply Corps, USN
  While supply officer at the New London submarine base, his daughter married Schwab in April 1943, 119

San Francisco, California
  Site of a world's fair in 1939-40, 65-66

Scotland
  The submarine *Toro* (SS-422) visited Rosyth in 1949, 186-187

Seattle, Washington
  Visited by the battleship *Pennsylvania* (BB-38) in the summer of 1939, 66

Security
    Tests of readiness at Pearl Harbor in 1940-41
    Interview by Representative Andrew May revealed that the Japanese were setting their depth charges too shallow, 83

Schade, Commander Arnold F., USN (USNA, 1933)
    In the early 1950s served on the staff of CinCNELM in London, 181-182

Schreiter, Midshipman Ernest F., USN (USNA, 1939)
    At the Naval Academy in the late 1930s, 9, 11

Schwab, Commander Donald E., Supply Corps, USNR (Ret.)
    Born 1 March 1944 while his father was deployed, 122, 130, 163, 228
    Served in the 1960s on board the destroyer *Vesole* (DD-878), 286, 298-299

Schwab, Captain Ernest L., USN (Ret.) (USNA, 1939)
    Ancestors had a background in Germany and New York, 25-27
    Parents, 1, 5-6, 23, 27-28, 120-121
    Wife Betty, 83, 104, 118-122, 149, 163, 183, 218, 233, 253, 259-260, 278, 282, 292-293, 296
    Children, 122, 130, 163, 228, 282, 286, 292-294, 296-299
    Boyhood and education in New York City in the 1920s and 1930s, 1-9
    Application process for the Naval Academy in the early 1930s, 2, 6-9
    As a Naval Academy midshipman, 1935-39, 8-12, 22-35
    Served 1939-41 in the battleship *Pennsylvania* (BB-38), 19-22, 34-70, 257, 263-264
    In 1941 rode the liner *Matsonia* from Hawaii to California, 37-39
    Student at Submarine School, July-September 1941, 68-74, 80, 91-92
    Served 1941-42 in the submarine *Marlin* (SS-205), 74-79, 81-82, 86-88, 119-120
    Served 1942-43 in the submarine *Guardfish* (SS-217), 88-115, 264
    Marriage and honeymoon in April 1943 while between duty stations, 118-122
    Served as executive officer 1943-44 in the submarine *Darter* (SS-227), 123-151, 264
    Served as executive officer 1945 in the submarine *Capitaine* (SS-336), 151-155
    On the staff of Commander Submarine Division 301 for return to the United States, 1945, 155
    Served in various billets at the New London Submarine Base, 1946-48, 157
    Spent a year, 1948-49, as a student at the Naval War College, 164-172
    From 1949 to 1951 commanded the submarine *Toro* (SS-422), 172-190
    Served ashore from 1951 to 1954 in the Bureau of Ships, Washington, D.C., as head of the Underwater Sound Branch, 190-201, 269-270
    Commanded the destroyer *Wedderburn* (DD-684), 1954-56, 201-219
    Schwab did postgraduate work from 1956 to 1958 at the Fletcher School of Law and Diplomacy, Tufts University, Medford, Massachusetts, 219-230
    Served in OP-611, the political-military policy division of OpNav, 1958-60, 230-243
    In 1960-61 was chief of staff to Commander Carrier Division 20, 243-252
    In 1962-63 commanded the amphibious command ship *Mount McKinley* (AGC-7), 252-269

In 1963-64 served in the Office of the Secretary of Defense (International Security Affairs), 271-278, 282

From 1964 to 1970, first in uniform and then as a State Department civilian, served at NATO headquarters in Europe, 241-243, 279-299

Sculpin, USS (SS-191)
As Commander Submarine Division 32, Captain John Cromwell sacrificed his life in November 1943 to keep information about upcoming U.S. sub operations from the Japanese, 112-113

Sharp, Lieutenant George A., USN (USNA, 1929)
Put the submarine *Marlin* (SS-205) in commission as first skipper in 1941, 74-75, 88, 120

Sherry, Commander Harmon B., USN (USNA, 1937)
Served on the staff of Commander Submarine Development Group Two in the late 1940s-early 1950s, 173-174, 192, 200-201, 269-270

Ship Handling
On board the submarine *Toro* (SS-422) in the late 1940s-early 1950s, 176-177, 180-182, 189-190
On board the amphibious command ship *Mount McKinley* (AGC-7) in the early 1960s, 259

Shore Patrol
In Honolulu, Hawaii, in 1941 for Army and Navy personnel, 37-38

Sieglaff, Captain William Bernard, USN (USNA, 1931)
In the early 1950s commanded Submarine Development Group Two, 180-182, 190

Singapore
Visited by the destroyers *Wedderburn* (DD-684) and *Kidd* (DD-661) in the mid-1950s, 201, 212-213

Sixth Fleet, U.S.
Operations in the early 1960s, 252-253, 257-258

Skorupski, Ensign Walter J., USNR
Served in the crew of the submarine *Darter* (SS-227), 1943-44, 123-124, 136

Smith, Sidney P. Jr., USN (USNA, 1939)
Died on board the training ship *Wyoming* (AG-17) in 1936, 12

Somoza Debayle, General Anastasio (USMA, 1946)
Visited the aircraft carrier *Lake Champlain* (CVS-39) in 1961, 246

Sonar
   Experimental work in the late 1940s-early 1950s by the boats of Submarine Development Group Two, 173-185
   Experimental work in the 1950s by the Underwater Sound Branch of the Bureau of Ships, 193-201, 269-270

SOSUS (Sound Surveillance System)
   Experimental development work in the late 1940s-early 1950s, 173
   In the early 1950s the Underwater Sound Branch of the Bureau of Ships did research and development work that led to SOSUS and antisubmarine weapons, 190-201, 269-270

Soviet Union
   The United States sometimes slowed movement of Soviet bloc ships through the Panama Canal in the late 1950s-early 1960s, 235-236
   Nuclear weapons capability and planning in the 1960s, 272
   NATO studies showed weaknesses in the Soviet logistics and resupply system in the 1960s, 281-282

Spain
   U.S. Navy ships evacuated Americans in 1936, during the Spanish Civil War, 13-14
   Was among the countries visited by the Schwab family as it explored Europe in the late 1960s, 294-295

Spencer, Ensign John Curtis, USN (USNA, 1939)
   Served in the heavy cruiser *Houston* (CA-30) after graduation from the Naval Academy, 36

Spiers, Ronald I.
   Foreign Service Officer who participated in war games in the late 1950s-early 1960s, 240

Spruance, Admiral Raymond A., USN (USNA, 1907)
   President of the Naval War College, 1946-48, 170-171, 229

Spying
   In the 1960s French and Turkish officers assigned to the NATO staff passed on intelligence to potential enemies, 289-291

Standing Naval Force Atlantic
   Established under the aegis of NATO in the mid-1960s, 284-285

Stanley, Timothy W.
   Represented the Defense Department on policy issues in the late 1950s-early 1960s, 235-237

Stark, Admiral Harold R., USN (Ret.) (USNA, 1903)
In the mid-1950s wrote a letter to Schwab on the U.S. decision in 1941 to go to unrestricted submarine warfare, 222-223

State Department
Webb-Lovett agreement in the early 1950s on sharing information with the Defense Department, 234-235
Handled Berlin issues in the late 1950s-early 1960s, 235-237

Stovall, Lieutenant Commander William Shirley Jr., USN (USNA, 1929)
Commanded the submarine *Gudgeon* (SS-211) in 1942-43, 125
Commanded the submarine *Darter* (SS-227) in 1943-44, 123, 127-128, 130-132, 150, 264

Strategy
Work of the Office of the Secretary of Defense (International Security Affairs) in 1963-64 in doing capability studies as part of NATO strategy and planning, 271-278

Subic Bay, Philippine Islands
In 1945, near the end of World War II, the submarine *Capitaine* (SS-336) dropped off rescued Japanese mariners at Subic, 153

Submarine Development Group Two
Operations in the late 1950s-early 1960s out of New London, 172-190, 197

Submarine School, New London, Connecticut
Curriculum in 1941, 68-74, 80, 84-85, 91

Submarine Warfare
Training at Submarine School in 1941, 68-74, 80, 84-85, 90-92
Pre-World War II doctrine called for submarines as scouts, also intended to attack enemy warships, 71, 90-91
In World War II, the U.S. Navy did not generally publicize submarine losses, 82-84
World War II operations of the submarine *Guardfish* (SS-217), 92-115
Interview by Representative Andrew May revealed that the Japanese were setting their depth charges too shallow, 83
In the mid-1950s, while a student at the Fletcher School, Schwab wrote a paper on the U.S. decision in 1941 to begin unrestricted submarine warfare, 222-222

Swanson, Claude A.
Death in office in July 1939 while Secretary of the Navy, 66

Sweden
Visited by the training ship *Wyoming* (AG-17) in 1936, 12-13
Was among the countries visited by the Schwab family as it explored Europe in the late 1960s, 296

Syverson, Captain Douglas N., USN (USNA, 1939)
    Attended Submarine School in 1941, 80
    Commanded the submarine tender *Hunley* (AS-31) in 1962-63, 80-81

Tachen Islands
    Evacuation of Nationalist Chinese in February 1955 was the destroyer *Wedderburn* (DD-684) and other Seventh Fleet ships, 204-205

Tacoma, Washington
    The Tacoma Narrows Bridge collapsed in November 1940, 67

Tactics
    Approaches used by U.S. submarines in making torpedo attacks in World War II, 107-111, 114
    U.S. Navy tactical antisubmarine training in the late 1950s-early 1960s, 202

Taiwan
    Posed a concern for the U.S. Navy in the mid-1950s, 203-205

Taylor, General Maxwell D., USA (USMA, 1922)
    Effect on U.S. strategic thinking as Chairman of the Joint Chiefs in the early 1960s, 272

***Toro*, USS (SS-422)**
    Operations as part of Submarine Development Group Two, 1949-51, 172-185
    North Atlantic cruises in 1949 and 1951, 174-182
    Ship handling in the late 1940s, 176-177, 180-182, 189-190
    In 1951 tested pre-packaged food during a North Atlantic deployment, 179-183
    Enlisted crew members, 1949-51, 188-189
    One officer, a Naval Academy graduate, was disqualified from submarines, 189

Torpedoes
    Faulty depth and exploder mechanisms in U.S. torpedoes early in World War II, 71, 96-98, 111
    Long-range torpedo shot by the submarine *Guardfish* (SS-217) in World War II, 107-108
    Tests off Maine in late 1943, 123

Treitel, Lieutenant Colonel Paul S., USMC (USNA, 1940)
    While stationed in Japan in the mid-1950s, helped show American Navy men around for recreation, 213-214

Triebel, Captain Charles O., USN (USNA, 1929)
    As Commander Submarine Division Ten was on board the submarine tender *Clytie* for post-World War II trip from Australia to New London, 155-156

Truk Atoll, Caroline Islands
    Reconnaissance in the vicinity by the submarine *Darter* (SS-227) in 1944, 128-129

Truman, President Harry S.
    In 1949 handed out silver dollars to celebrate the founding of NATO, 223

Turkey
    In the 1960s a Turkish intelligence officer was passing information to the Soviets, 289

***Tusk*, USS (SS-426)**
    Involved in ASW experimental work as part of Submarine Development Group Two in the late 1940s-early 1950s, 173, 185
    Lost crewmen in 1949 while rescuing men from the submarine *Cochino* (SS-345), 175-178

Tuttle, Rear Admiral Magruder H., USN (USNA, 1932)
    In the early 1960s commanded Carrier Division 20, 243, 245, 248-249, 251

Tyler, Colonel James E., USA (USMA, 1940)
    Served in the Office of the Secretary of Defense (ISA) in the early 1960s, 242, 271, 275

Uniforms-Naval
    Officers still had old-fashioned formal uniforms in the late 1930s-early 1940s, 34
    In the early 1940s submariners wore more casual uniforms than officers in surface ships, 34

***United States*, SS (Passenger Liner)**
    In the summer of 1964 the Schwab family rode the liner from the United States to Europe, 279

Vest, George S.
    In the late 1960s served as Deputy Chief of Missions of the U.S. Mission to NATO, 290-291

War Games
    At the Naval War College in the late 1940s, 168-170
    State-Defense war games in the late 1950s-early 1960s, 240

Wayne, Commander John B., USN
    Did postgraduate work from 1956 to 1958 at the Fletcher School of Law and Diplomacy, Tufts University, Medford, Massachusetts, 219-221, 224

Weather
    Heavy seas caused seasickness in the training ship *Wyoming* (AG-17) in 1936, 17

The battleship *Pennsylvania* (BB-38) operated in fog in the late 1930s-early 1940s, 19-20

The amphibious command ship *Mount McKinley* (AGC-7) encountered rough seas in the Atlantic in late 1962, 254

Webb, James E.
Part of the Webb-Lovett agreement in the early 1950s on sharing information between the Defense and State departments, 234-235

***Wedderburn*, USS (DD-684)**
Operations in the Pacific, 1954-56, 201-210
Enlisted crew in the mid-1950s, 202, 210-212, 215-216
Correcting and maintaining the ship's material condition in the mid-1950s, 208-210, 219
Propulsion plant problems, 209-210
Morale enhancers for the crew, 210-212
Antisubmarine work with aircraft carriers while deployed to the Western Pacific, 216-217
Replenishment at sea in the mid-1950s, 217-218
Taking care of the wives of crew members in the mid-1950s, 218-219

Wilkinson, Captain Eugene P., USN
Served in the crew of the submarine *Darter* (SS-227), 1943-44, 123-124, 131, 134, 136-139, 157
Successful Navy career included command of nuclear-powered ships, 124-125

Wilson, Ensign John V., USN (USNA, 1939)
Served in the battleship *Pennsylvania* (BB-38) after graduation from the Naval Academy, 38, 61-62

Women in the Navy
WAVES served at the New London Submarine Base during World War II and shortly after, 157-160

Worthington, Commander Robert K., USN (USNA, 1938)
Commanded the submarine *Tusk* from 1949 to 1951, 173. 177

***Wyoming*, USS (AG-17)**
Midshipman training cruise to Europe in 1936, 11-19
Enlisted crewmen, 16-18, 20

Zumwalt, Admiral Elmo R. Jr., USN (USNA, 1943)
In the early 1960s served in the office of the Assistant Secretary of Defense (International Security Affairs), 271
As Chief of Naval Operations in the early 1970s eased the requirement for a major sea command in order to be considered for flag rank, 269

www.ingramcontent.com/pod-product-compliance
Lightning Source LLC
Chambersburg PA
CBHW080618170426
43209CB00007B/1460